Straight
STUFF

Straight
STUFF

THE REPORTERS,
THE WHITE HOUSE
AND THE TRUTH

James
Deakin

WILLIAM MORROW AND COMPANY, INC.
New York 1984

Library of Congress Cataloging in Publication Data

Deakin, James, 1929-
  Straight stuff.

  Includes index.
    1. United States—Politics and government—1945-
2. Press and politics—United States—History—20th century. 3. Deakin, James, 1929-   I. Title.
E743.D43 1984   353.03'5   83-19521
ISBN 0-688-02204-9

Printed in the United States of America

First Edition

1 2 3 4 5 6 7 8 9 10

BOOK DESIGN BY RICHARD ORIOLO

To Doris and David

ACKNOWLEDGMENTS

This publication was prepared under a grant from the Woodrow Wilson International Center for Scholars, Washington, D.C. The statements and views expressed herein are those of the author and are not necessarily those of the Wilson Center.

A grant from the John and Mary R. Markle Foundation of New York assisted me in completing the book. Again, the views are mine. I am grateful to both organizations for their encouragement.

For twenty-five years I worked with reporters who covered the White House. They made an immeasurable contribution to this book, and I regret that only a few of them can be mentioned: R. W. Apple, Marvin Arrowsmith, Dom Bonafede, David Broder, Lou Cannon, John Chancellor, Frank Cormier, Sid Davis, Anthony Day, Thomas DeFrank, Clifford Evans, Andrew Glass, Ralph Harris, Don Irwin, Ted Knap, Jerry Landay, Stuart Loory, James McCartney, Edward P. Morgan, James M. Naughton, Robert Pierpoint, John Pomfret, Dan Rather, Helen Thomas and Tom Wicker. And members of the Washington bureau of the *St. Louis Post-Dispatch*: Robert Adams, Gerald Boyd, Raymond P. Brandt, Marquis W. Childs, Richard Dudman, Helen-Marie Fruth, George H. Hall, Aloysia Hamalainen, James C. Millstone, Lawrence O'Rourke, Thomas W. Ottenad and William K. Wyant. I would also like to thank Howard Bray, Dennis Carey, Julius Duscha, Roderick French, Connie Gerrard, Walter W. Heller, Joseph Laitin, Bruce Lee, Robert Lescher, Ellen Reiter, Philip Robbins, Thomas B. Ross, Arthur M. Schlesinger, Jr., Elizabeth Terhune and Theodore H. White.

My deepest gratitude is to Doris Deakin.

CONTENTS

CONTENTS

Straight
STUFF

I

BIG STORY

On the morning of June 10, 1956, they got the old man out of bed. First he sat for a few moments on the edge, looking weary. Then two medical attendants helped him shuffle about fifteen feet to an armchair. This was standard procedure after surgery. The patient was to be ambulatory as soon as possible, to prevent circulatory and intestinal complications. He sat in the armchair for a while, practicing deep breathing; then he went back to bed. He was sixty-five years old, and he was tired.

His press secretary, James C. Hagerty, told the reporters that "to me, he looks very good and in good spirits." But two months after the operation, the president said he did not feel as well as he had a year before. He added, however, that he was confident he could carry on.[1] It was interesting that he mentioned the year before. He had had a heart attack then.

The next day, they got him up again. He walked about twenty feet this time, with a surgeon supporting him lightly by one elbow. The surgeon's name was Isidor S. Ravdin. Although Ravdin had been born in Evansville, Indiana, his name and appearance were European. The reporters looked at him and thought of Ravic, the refugee doctor in one of Erich Maria Remarque's brooding novels. Ravic drank Calvados in doomed cities and of course had a hopeless love affair.

Very romantic, but it didn't get into the newspapers. This was the era of objectivity. When reporters put their impressions into their news stories, editors took them out. It was journalism's fearful symmetry. What remained was that Ravdin was professor of surgery at the University of Pennsylvania. He was eminently respectable and respectably eminent.

He had been called in to assist a team of Army surgeons in an operation known as an ileo-transverse colostomy.

The operation took place at Walter Reed Army Medical Center in Washington. It began at 2:59 A.M. on June 9 and lasted for one hour and fifty-three minutes. The surgeons created a bypass around ten inches of the president's ileum—part of the small intestine. Major General Leonard D. Heaton, commanding officer at Walter Reed, said afterward that the diseased section of intestine had "the consistency of a hard rubber hose." Nothing could get through. The reporters sang a song with this refrain: "I'm not sick, I just can't go." That didn't get into the newspapers either.

It was an all-night session. The younger reporters were excited by the big story. The older ones, not so much. These around-the-clock writing jobs are one thing at twenty-five or thirty, another thing at fifty. The reporters stood on the lawn in front of the hospital, in a clear, cool night. With binoculars and even with the unaided eye, they had a pretty good view of the operating amphitheater on the third floor. They could see the indistinct figures of the six surgeons—Heaton, Ravdin and four others—and the nurses and technicians moving around the room. The reporters stood on a concrete fountain and climbed up on automobiles to get a better look. Journalism's detritus—coffee containers, cigarette butts, flashbulbs, empty film packs—littered the lawn. The flashbulbs, as brief as truth, illuminated the night.

Not only did they get him out of bed; they ran him again. It was the most cynical thing since the last most cynical thing. But with the other possible candidates, they could not be certain of victory.

So the big story was the health of Dwight David Eisenhower, the thirty-fourth president of the United States. On September 24, 1955, Eisenhower suffered a heart attack. On June 8, 1956, he was stricken with the ileitis for which he underwent surgery. On November 25, 1957, he had a stroke. The heart attack occurred two years and eight months into Eisenhower's first term. After much initial doubt, he decided to run again. The ileitis operation took place after he had announced that he would seek a second term, but before the election. After some more doubt—but not as much—he decided to stay in the race. The stroke occurred during his second term. He thought of resigning the presidency then, but decided not to.[2] Onward.

Eisenhower liked to say he was not a politician. He commented to his wartime aide Harry C. Butcher that he had an "abomination" of politics. After his first nomination, in 1952, he told at least three friends—lawyer-politician Herbert Brownell, Major General Wilton B. (Jerry) Persons and economist Gabriel Hauge—that the Republican party should begin developing younger prospects for the White House in 1956. He would be sixty-six years old when he completed his first term, Eisenhower pointed out, and "a second term would be virtually out of the question for me." He said later that his "determination to limit my political life to . . . four years . . . became so conscious an intent that . . . I planned to include such an announcement in my Inaugural Address."[3] He was talked out of that.

Nevertheless, he disclaimed any great enthusiasm for the presidency. After only a month in office, he told a press conference: "I never said I would like it. It is not a job that I suppose it is intended one should like. I merely say this: like everything else, there are compensations."[4]

During his convalescence from the heart attack, Eisenhower at first took it for granted that his illness ruled out a second term. The public, the news media and many Republican leaders assumed that he would not run again. A poll by the Newspaper Enterprise Association showed that 88 percent of the Washington press corps believed Ike would bow out in 1956. People began talking about alternatives—Vice-President Richard M. Nixon, Chief Justice Earl Warren, Secretary of State John Foster Dulles, Senate Republican leader William F. Knowland, former New York Governor Thomas E. Dewey and Harold E. Stassen of Minnesota. Nixon and Stassen took it seriously. They wanted to run. They kept at it for years.

Nixon was the leading contender. But Eisenhower had doubts about him. He had distrusted Nixon ever since the "Checkers speech" in the 1952 campaign.[5] Milton Eisenhower was probably his brother's closest adviser, and Milton did not like Nixon.[6] Some other members of the palace guard around Eisenhower also had reservations about Nixon's fitness to be president. In any event, if Nixon were the Republican nominee in 1956, the Eisenhower palace guard would be swept away. That would not do. So Nixon must wait, but only Ike could make him wait. Eisenhower was not without guile. He already had offered Nixon a post in the Cabinet if he would get off the ticket in 1956. Eisenhower wanted Robert B. Anderson, a Texas oilman, as his next running mate. He suggested that Nixon would do nicely as secretary of defense, but Nixon was having none of that.[7] He clung to the vice-presidency like a limpet. There was a constitutional reason for this.

So Eisenhower's palace guard had its work cut out for it. The president must be brought along slowly but surely. It had to be done nice and easy. The thing could not be pushed too hard or rushed, because if it was, Ike might decide not to run after all. The door had to be kept open for Eisenhower and quietly but firmly closed on the other Republican hopefuls. The man out front—the public spokesman who would have to keep the door open—was press secretary Hagerty. Gradually, and with great skill, Hagerty overcame the initial, almost unanimous belief that Eisenhower could not and would not run for reelection. The device he used was—the press.

The heart attack gave a rich new dimension to the word "foolhardy." On August 14, 1955, the president and his wife flew to Denver for a vacation. Ike and Mamie were fond of Denver; they had been married there in 1916 and over the years had occasionally vacationed there. This time, as before, they stayed at the home of Mamie's mother, Mrs. John S. Doud, at 570 Lafayette Street. A temporary presidential office and White House pressroom already were in place at Lowry Air Force Base near Denver—the previous year, Eisenhower had taken an eight-week Colorado vacation, and he had been there in 1953 as well.

On these Colorado trips, Ike did not spend too much time at his mother-in-law's house. As soon as he could, he went to Fraser, Colorado, a small, remote town high up in the Rockies. There he fished for trout and relaxed with old friends at Byers Peak Ranch, a little wickiup owned by Aksel Nielsen, a Denver investment banker. A small stream known as St. Louis Creek tumbled through the mountains. Standing in the icy water, Eisenhower went after the trout, twisting his torso back and forth for hours as he cast. The air was bracing but thin. The president was almost sixty-five years old. Uh, oh.

On September 23, he got word that a letter had come from Soviet Premier Nikolai A. Bulganin. It dealt with Eisenhower's "open-skies" proposal for aerial surveillance of the United States and Russia. Because Ike had initiated this proposal, he was anxious to read the letter.

The presidential motorcade raced away from the ranch like an Israeli rescue mission. Reaching speeds of eighty miles an hour, it dashed across the continental divide toward Denver, eighty-two miles away. In a pell-mell hour and forty-five minutes, Eisenhower was dropped 3,400 feet—from the ranch's 8,700-foot altitude to Denver's 5,280 feet. Uh, oh.

The president spent three hours in his office at Lowry Field, reading Bulganin's letter and doing some other work. Then he headed for the Cherry Hills Country Club. He played eighteen holes of golf. That felt good, so he played nine more—a total of twenty-seven holes of golf at a mile-high altitude. Uh, oh. For lunch, he ate a double hamburger with several big slices of onion. Uh, oh.

During the golf game, the president was informed that the secretary of state wanted to talk to him. Ike went to the clubhouse to take the call. But when he got there he was told that Dulles had gone somewhere and would call him back in an hour. Back to the golf course, irritated, and then back to the clubhouse an hour later. This time something was wrong with the long-distance circuit. Back to the golf course, fuming, and then back to the clubhouse again when the circuit was okay. This time, he talked to Dulles.

It is a terrible thing to come between a golfer and his golf. Ike wrote later that "my disposition deteriorated rapidly" as he went to and from the clubhouse. That was an understatement; he was furious.

The president ate his hamburger and onions. He resumed his golf game. He was again informed that the secretary of state wanted to talk to him. Back to the clubhouse for the fourth time, incensed. This time it was a mistake. Someone in Washington or Denver, not knowing that Ike and Dulles had finished their conversation, had placed the call again. The Eisenhower temper reached an inspiring level. Uh, oh.

The president finished his twenty-seven holes, went to his mother-in-law's home, ate dinner, played some billiards with his friend George Allen and went to bed. At about 1:30 in the morning—*mirabile dictu*—he woke up with pains in his chest. He always said afterward that it was those damn telephone calls.[8]

The press corps that accompanied Ike to Denver for his vacation that year consisted of twenty-two persons. There were seven newspaper reporters, three wire service reporters, two newsmagazine reporters, two television reporters, three wire service photographers, four television cameramen and one newsreel cameraman.

They were not expecting to cover one of those end-of-the-world stories. There was a foreign ministers' meeting coming up in Geneva and there was the open-skies plan, but no one thought either of those would get anywhere. There were no big crises at home or abroad. Things were spread out better in those days.

So the journalists settled in at the Brown Palace in downtown Denver, one of the last hotels in America where shoes would be shined if left outside the room at night. Each morning at ten and each afternoon at four, assistant press secretary Murray Snyder held a briefing in the pressroom at Lowry Air Force Base. Hagerty, after flying out to Denver with Ike in August, had gone back to Washington for, of all things, a vacation. Eisenhower himself was at the Nielsen ranch much of the time. When he did come to Denver, he showed up in his office at Lowry at 7:30 or 8 in the morning, did a little work, no heavy lifting, and was on the golf course by late morning or early afternoon. Snyder, a tall, rather shy man who had been a reporter for the *New York Herald Tribune*, seldom had anything important to announce.

It was a piece of cake. The stories were short, short, short. The reporters took their ease at the Navarre restaurant across the street from the Brown Palace, where the martinis were generous, and at the Studio Bar and the Belmont. They went sight-seeing or shopping. They played poker or Scrabble—no one knew why a Scrabble craze swept the pressroom that year. And they slept more than usual. You do that when you can. But most of the journalists turned down an invitation to attend a University of Colorado football game in Pueblo on the afternoon of Saturday, September 24. For this instinct, they were later very grateful.

At the Columbia Broadcasting System, the instincts were not so keen. Things were so slow in Denver that CBS pulled reporter Charles (Chuck) von Fremd off the Eisenhower assignment to do something else. When the big story broke, CBS had only a soundman in Denver. The soundman, Andrew Willoner, covered the heart attack until the network could rush out some heavies. No one knew the difference.

Not only did the reporters not anticipate a big story, they had no way of knowing that they would be parties to a deception of the American people. When they found out, they were not greatly surprised. Reporters are accustomed to being misinformed so as to mislead the public; it is one of journalism's most frequent occupational hazards. This time it happened this way:

In response to one or more telephone calls from Mamie Eisenhower, the White House physician arrived at the Doud home shortly after three o'clock in the morning. He quickly diagnosed a coronary thrombosis. Because he did not want to alarm Mrs. Eisenhower, who had a slight heart condition herself, he did not tell Mamie that her husband had suffered a heart attack. Except for the other doctors he called in, he did not tell anyone.

The physician's name was Howard McC. Snyder. He was a major general in the Army, an old cavalryman, an old friend of the Eisenhower family, a gentleman of the old school. He listened to Ike's heart with a stethoscope, took his pulse and blood pressure, administered morphine and made arrangements to transfer the president to Fitzsimons Army Hospital later in the day. For the rest of the night, Snyder kept a vigil at the bedside of the stricken leader.

Shortly before 7 A.M., Snyder called the president's personal secretary, Ann C. Whitman. He told her Eisenhower had a digestive upset and would not be in his office that day. An understatement.

The White House staff at Lowry did a call-out to reporters at the Brown Palace, summoning them to the pressroom. There, at 8 A.M., Murray Snyder (the assistant press secretary and the White House physician were not related) announced that Eisenhower had "suffered a digestive upset in the night."

The bulletins clattered over the wires of the Associated Press, United Press and International News Service. The president had an upset stomach.

Snyder held additional briefings at 9:30 A.M. and 12:15 P.M. Each time, the word was the same: a digestive upset. At the 12:15 briefing, Snyder told reporters: "I just talked with Gen. Snyder and he tells me the president is resting. He said that this indigestion is not serious and he says that it is the same type of indigestion that many people have had. It is not serious."

Snyder added: "This is the kind of 24-hour stuff many people have. . . . As far as I know, the [president's] appointments Monday will be kept and he will be in the office. . . . The fact that Gen. Snyder will not remain in constant attendance is a good indication that it is not considered serious."

Some of the reporters were suspicious—Earl Mazo of the *Herald Tribune* kept saying it might be something much more serious—but they accepted the word according to Doc Snyder. So, for a good part of that day, Americans who read a newspaper or listened to a radio or TV newscast were in Rick's position. Rick says he has come to Casablanca for the waters. He is told there are no waters in Casablanca. "I was misinformed," says Rick.

The public's misapprehension ended shortly before 2:30 P.M. After another telephone call from the White House doctor, Murray Snyder came back into the pressroom. He announced that the president had suffered a heart attack.

Later, Dr. Snyder gave his reasons. In a letter to Jerry Persons of the White House staff, the doctor said: "It was difficult for me to assume the responsibility of refraining from making public immediately the diagnosis of coronary thrombosis." Nevertheless, he said he decided to delay the announcement "because I wished the president to benefit from the rest and quiet induced by the sedation incident to combating the initial manifestations. This decision also spared him, his wife and mother-in-law emotional upset upon too precipitate announcement of such serious import. . . . This action, I believe, limited the heart damage to a minimum and enabled us to confirm the diagnosis by cardiogram and make an unhurried transference from home to hospital."[9]

A big story is almost always more than a big story. It is an object lesson in differing perceptions. All human beings perceive things differently, and the differences are never more striking than when the news media and the government look at the same event.

Dr. Snyder's view: The English language might have sued him for malpractice, but even so, the doctor's overriding purpose and concern were clear. He wanted to keep his patient quiet as long as possible, to give the healing process a chance to begin. He wanted the president insulated from the tension and anxiety that might have filtered through to him if the heart attack had become known immediately. Later, the chief medical consultant on the president's case, Dr. Paul Dudley White, said he had seen heart attack patients seriously affected by the worried faces of relatives and friends.

The reporters' view: The newsmen at Lowry did not seriously challenge the secrecy of the first few hours. They understood Dr. Snyder's reasons. They were distinctly unhappy about misinforming the public, and they did do some probing into the cover story and the delay, but it was just a light workout. Snyder's actions in the early morning hours were not questioned strenuously.

But when the reporters began to sort things out, the customary journalistic doubts arose as to where judgment and discretion had left off and secrecy had commenced. The press fastened on the fact that a stretcher had not been used to carry Eisenhower down from his second-floor bedroom at the Doud house. Instead, he had walked downstairs, assisted by the doctors. Nor had he been taken to the hospital in an ambulance. It was all done very quietly—a car was backed up the driveway; the president came out of a side entrance, got in the car and was driven to Fitzsimons hospital.

The reporters wondered whether medical judgment dictated that no stretcher or ambulance would be used, or whether secrecy had taken over by this time. It was 2:30 in the afternoon when Ike was taken to the hospital—broad daylight. The neighbors on Lafayette Street might have grown curious if the president of the United States had been carried out of the house on a stretcher and put into an ambulance.

Or a stray reporter might have spotted an ambulance parked outside the house. Marvin Arrowsmith of the Associated Press recalls that his normal route from the Brown Palace to Lowry Air Force Base took him past the Doud house. He was on his way to Lowry just before Eisenhower was taken to the hospital. Arrowsmith certainly would have noticed an ambulance if there had been one in front of the house; as it was, he believes he missed seeing the president's car pull away by only a matter of minutes.[10]

The government's view: There was no attempt at secrecy. There never is. Hagerty, after he returned to Denver, said the doctors simply decided it would be easier for Eisenhower to walk down the stairs, "rather than put him on a litter or a stretcher and carry him down . . . and then try to get him into the car." It did not involve any dangerous exertion, Hagerty said. "It was done without the expenditure . . . of physical effort on the president's part."

It was only a small coverup. Dr. Snyder had made the first diagnosis of coronary thrombosis shortly after three in the morning. An electrocardiograph was brought to the Doud house, and a cardiogram was taken at one o'clock in the afternoon, after Eisenhower woke up. It confirmed the heart attack. Ike was taken to the hospital shortly before 2:30, at which time the announcement was made at Lowry. So the heart attack was concealed for a little less than twelve hours.

Wasn't it better to do it that way, rather than having an ambulance and a stretcher and rumors spreading like wildfire through the neighborhood and thence throughout the city of Denver and God knows how fast and how far and how distorted? And what might it have meant to the president's condition if the press had been told earlier and Eisenhower had been carried out on a stretcher, through a howling, pushing, shoving mob of reporters and photographers? That was the nub of the thing. The way they did it was safer. And it was more *orderly*.

And when all was said and done, so what? What difference did it make? It was such a small thing. Why did the reporters make a fuss about it? Why do they always make a fuss about things? The truth was withheld for a few necessary hours, but then it was made known. Why did they quibble?

The reporters' view: Their argument was frail and tremulous. All they had, to answer prudence and authority, was an instinct. By itself, this instinct did not prove anything. The reporters could not rely on it absolutely. They seldom can. Often, in weariness or disillusion, or lacking time, they ignore their inner promptings. They accept the more confident voice of officialdom. Sometimes they follow their instinct and are mistaken.

But the instinct was there. It is always there. Even in this instance, with safety, prudence, order and, if you will, common decency arrayed against it, the instinct had to be followed. So some of the reporters at Lowry, not all of them by any means, and not very vigorously, followed it.

And what *was* this precious, goddamned instinct? It was an instinct against secrecy. Reporters are born with an instinct against secrecy. Even then, even in those simpler times, the reporters were suspicious of secrecy, suspicious of the mere appearance of secrecy. It was not a conviction that anyone had actually done anything wrong in holding up the news of Eisenhower's heart attack. It was a conviction that secrecy in any form, large or small, was a bad thing that led to bad things. It must be challenged, even in marginal episodes. It must not be permitted to go unremarked. Reporters believe things should be made known. They are against concealment, except in extraordinary circumstances—and when extraordinary circumstances are claimed, they are usually dubious about *that*. They *will* question. They *will* quibble. It is their nature.

Some journalists would argue that theoretically at least—that is, from the standpoint of the ultimate health of democracy—it would have been better to have a noisy crowd outside 570 Lafayette Street than to have the president's heart attack concealed from the American people a moment longer than was absolutely necessary. Then they would question how long was absolutely necessary.

When it comes to these recurring conflicts and tradeoffs, however, journalistic opinion is divided. The news media have not devised any universal formula defining their priorities and responsibilities. Sometimes they go along with secrecy; sometimes they do not. Douglass Cater, a former reporter and a student of the press, has said there must be "a sense of realization among reporters, and more particularly among editors, that the decision to publish news affecting national security should be based on a higher standard than . . . 'news judgment.'"[11] The president's health was certainly a matter of national security. But Chapter Six will show that most of the time, national security is impossible to define. There is simply no agreement on the "higher standard." So columnist Tom Wicker, also a student of the press, says "the true freedom of the press is to decide for itself what to publish and when to publish it."[12] The key phrase is "*true* freedom."

The news media as a whole decline, modestly, to be apodictic on the subject of their own behavior. The First Amendment says the government cannot make the decision. The courts have ruled now one way, now another. So there is no formula that encompasses every situation. Each conflict between secrecy and candor, between privacy and publicity, is fought out *ad hoc*. Each is played by ear. Discordantly.

In general, reporters are more tolerant of chaos than are presidents, Supreme Court justices or moral movements. Confusion and controversy are the occupational materials of the journalist. His temperament accepts them; he grows accustomed to them; he has a vested interest in them. Trouble is his business; he goes in harm's way.

In addition, there is the controversial matter of professionalism. Journalists define their professionalism as the pursuit of facts and explanations. Not just the government's version of the facts, and not just the government's explanations. *Many* facts and *many* explanations. The result is constant conflict between the news media and the government, because the government wishes *its* facts and *its* interpretations to prevail. Several versions doubtlessly are more confusing and more chaotic than one version. This regrettable pluralism is known as democracy.

Last, and most heretical, journalists are not always convinced that prudence, safety and order are infallible guides. They have seen too many mistakes committed and then concealed, too many crimes perpetrated, too much injustice prolonged, too much progress thwarted in the name of that sacred trinity: prudence, safety, order. Government is order. Journalism is disorder. Life imitates journalism.

All these tensions—the difference in perception between the news media and the government, the chronic dispute over secrecy, the multiplicity of facts and explanations, the question of what can and cannot be justified in the name of prudence, safety or order—underlay the brief confrontation over the ambulance that was not summoned and the stretcher that was not used. To understand those few moments in the pressroom at Lowry—why the government said what it said and why the reporters said what they said—is to understand an entire mechanism. The same tensions, the same unresolved conflicts, make themselves felt at every presidential press conference, every briefing by the White House press secretary, every face-off between journalists and officials. They underlie the entire relationship between the news media and the government. As a matter of fact, they *are* the relationship.

Then something interesting happened. It happened because Hagerty had been a reporter. He knew how reporters felt about secrecy. The clue to Hagerty's success was that he knew how to turn that bit of professional knowledge to his own advantage—or, rather, to the advantage of Dwight Eisenhower.

Hagerty could not prevent a few questions about the delayed announcement. But thereafter he swamped the reporters with information. He opened the bag for them. He told them so much that they had no way of knowing whether he was telling them everything. They could not discriminate; there was no time to find out whether any nuggets were missing from the avalanche. Hagerty overwhelmed the reporters. He answered their questions on the spot or got the answers quickly. He gave them information they wanted. He gave them information they should not have wanted but did want. He gave them information they did not want at all. He loved 'em to death.

Hagerty issued medical bulletins three or four times each day. He told the reporters what the president had for breakfast, lunch and dinner. He told them how many calories Ike was getting. He went into excruciating detail about some vegetable soup that Eisenhower's valet, Sergeant John Moaney, had made for him. ("First you get the beef and beef bones and put them in a pot and stew and simmer them all day long. Then you let that sort of jell overnight and you take the fat off that forms at the top. . . . The second day you put in the vegetables and chop them up, and then you go through the same process again. . . . Simmer off and on the whole day. . . .")

Hagerty not only told the reporters what Eisenhower ate, he told them what Ike wanted and could not have. Coffee, especially. He told them the color of the president's pajamas and described the decor of his hospital suite. He told them who visited the president and how long they stayed. He told them when the president slept and how long he slept and how he felt when he woke up. ("He awoke refreshed and cheerful.") He told them when Eisenhower was in an oxygen tent and when he was not, and which doctors and nurses were in attendance at what times. He described the birthday gifts that Ike's grandchildren gave him: playing cards and bubble gum from three-year-old Susan, stationery and bubble gum from six-year-old Anne, a book and bubble gum from seven-year-old David. The book was *The Mackenzie Raid*, by Colonel Red Reeder, one of Ike's favorite authors. It was "a story of Texans on the border about 1873," and it cost twenty-five cents. Ike read the book, but at the 10:30 A.M. briefing of October 5, 1955, Hagerty announced that the president had not chewed the bubble gum. No sparrow's fall escaped the press secretary.

Each book that Ike asked for was duly reported to the press, and so were the musical selections he was listening to:

Hagerty: " . . . The first one is 'Moods in Music' . . . 'Music for Listening' . . . and the orchestra is the Melachrino Strings. . . . All of these records are long-play and they have anywhere from eight to ten pieces on them. The first record has the following pieces, if you want them . . ."

Reporter: "Sure do."

Reporter: "Fire away."

Hagerty: "'Clair de Lune' by Debussy."

Reporter: "How long is this list, Jim?"

Hagerty: "Somebody said they want it. I copied it down, and by golly, I'm going to read it. . . . 'Serenade' by Drigo. Then the rest—I did not get the composers: 'Greensleeves,' 'Festival,' 'Dream of Olwen' . . . I see some of you fellows don't like music at all."

Reporter: "Can you whistle that?"

Hagerty: "Sure, sure. 'Waltz in C Sharp Minor,' 'Song of My Love,' 'Flirtation Waltz,' 'Mattinata' . . ."

Reporter: "I'm going to skip this."

Hagerty: "'Amourese' . . ."

Reporter: " . . . music for oxygen tent."

Reporter: "None of this is vocal?"

Hagerty: "The lack of knowledge of some of you fellows!"

Reporter: "Just have them mimeographed."

Hagerty: "I'm not going to. I wrote them down and I am going to read them. . . . The president also asked for some symphonic recordings, particularly Brahms and Bach, and we are in the process of taping those. . . . He also called for some . . . what they call reading records . . . that carry a story—mystery, Westerns or Shakespeare. Somebody reads them out."[13]

Hagerty was extremely fond of classical music. So was Jack Romagna, the White House stenographer, who had to transcribe these cultural exchanges. The reporters were a sore trial to them.

Robert J. Donovan of the *New York Herald Tribune* was given extensive access to the inner workings of the Eisenhower administration for his book *Eisenhower: The Inside Story*. When Eisenhower was stricken with the heart attack, Donovan wrote, Hagerty and Murray Snyder made an immediate decision not to withhold any details of the illness. Donovan related this conversation between the assistant press secretary in Denver and Hagerty in Washington:

Snyder: "Jim, I intend to play this straight and give the fellows [the reporters] everything as fast as we can get it."

Hagerty: "Right. Give it to them absolutely straight. I'll catch a plane out as soon as I can."[14]

Nothing appeals more to a reporter than the impression that he is being told everything. Nothing so disarms him. His natural suspicions are lulled. And even if the suspicions of the newsmen at Lowry were not entirely silenced, Hagerty kept them so busy that they had no time to listen to their inner voices.

On that first day—September 24—Snyder held twelve briefings, the first one at 8 A.M. to announce the "digestive upset," the last at 10:20 P.M. Hagerty got to Denver around midnight that night, went immediately to the hospital, talked to the doctors and then headed for the pressroom. His first briefing—the thirteenth of that day or the first of the next day, depending on the individual state of grogginess—was held at 1:12 in the morning. The change in tone was dramatic; the reporters liked Murray Snyder and thought well of him, but he was not varsity. With Hagerty came brisk, unsentimental efficiency and the first freshets of information that quickly swelled to a mighty flood.

The postmidnight briefing ended in the middle of the night, but the press secretary was at the hospital at 6:30 in the morning and back in the pressroom at 8 A.M. for another inundation. He held five briefings that day, the last one at 9:20 P.M. The modern presidency is an endurance contest. By that definition, the modern presidency began on September 24, 1955, in a pressroom in the administration building at Lowry Air Force Base, Denver, Colorado. There is no historical marker.

A pattern was quickly established; even chaos has a routine. The day began at 7 A.M. with a medical bulletin describing the president's night— how long he slept, how well he slept, how he felt when he woke up. This was followed by a longer briefing in late morning, another briefing in midafternoon and a final session at about 9 P.M. A four-briefing day is nothing to laugh about, and Hagerty kept it up for seven weeks.

The reporters wrote day leads, night leads, inserts, add-at-ends, overnights, new leads on the overnights, sidebars, features, wrapups, interpretives, analyses, political situationers and medical backgrounders. They asked each other how to spell "occlusion" and "prothrombin." The initial contingent of 22 reporters, photographers and cameramen quickly grew to more than 100. The typewriters and telephones were never silent. In the seven weeks that Ike was in Fitzsimons hospital, the reporters filed 2,250,000 words to newspapers, wire services and magazines.[15] An imperial performance—it was more than twice the total number of words in the English language. There were days when every reporter felt he had accounted for the entire output himself.

Sleep? Sleep was for the masses. My own experience was reasonably typical. Arriving in Denver after the heart attack, I went fifty-seven hours without sleep; some sinister force made me keep count. In the first phase of the crisis, the reporters slept on Army cots in the hallway of the bachelor officers' quarters. They named this corridor Pig Alley in tribute to the quality of the accommodations. The journalists slept fitfully. Their nervous, hag-ridden slumbers were interrupted frequently by functionaries who appeared in the corridor and shouted, *"Press!"* to summon them for another briefing or bulletin. There went the neighborhood.

William H. Y. Knighton, Jr., had been covering the White House for the *Baltimore Sun* for many years. He was a big man with a very deep, very resonant voice. In Pig Alley, he talked in his sleep. He rewrote his stories or shouted for a Western Union man to come get his copy: *"Western!"* or *"President Eisenhower is . . . mumble, mumble, snore."* The first time one of these detonations shattered my dreams, I levitated straight up from my cot. The most welcome visitor each morning was a White House physician who showed up in the pressroom to dispense "jolly pills." These were Dexamyl. They were good for several new leads.

At the outset, Hagerty got a break. A noted heart specialist, Dr. Paul Dudley White, had been called in to head the team of physicians treating the president. Dr. White was an elderly New Englander who believed in exercise and practiced what he preached; in his late seventies, he walked up thirteen flights of stairs at the National Press Club to make a speech to an audience of awe-struck journalists.

Dr. White was a dominant and authoritative figure in cardiology. His verdict on Eisenhower's condition and his prognosis for the future would be crucial. Dr. White examined Ike on September 25 and held a press conference the next day. He said the chances for a complete recovery were "reasonably good." And he said that if the president made a complete recovery, he would be physically able to run for a second term. The door opened. Now all Hagerty had to do was keep it open.

Dr. White's first press conference was notable in another respect. He reported that the president had had a normal bowel movement. This was considered very significant. The theory was that if Ike could go, he must be alive. Nevertheless, there was a lot of soul-searching before this development was printed. The 1950's were prerevolutionary. Bodily functions had not been invented. At the Associated Press, Marvin Arrowsmith remembers, the bowel movement produced a crisis.[16] But Dr. White had announced it—as a matter of fact, he had emphasized it. So it must be important. With a mixture of trepidation and dismay, editors put the bowel movement on the front pages of family newspapers across the nation.

Irreverence is the small fire at which reporters warm themselves. A journalist in Boston saw the story in his own newspaper and was reminded of Emerson's lines commemorating the battle of Concord. The reporter composed the following quatrain:

> O'er this rude pan that arched the bed,
> His ass to autumn's breeze unfurled,
> Our embattled prexy sat,
> And fired the shit heard round the world.

In the first week after the heart attack, Eisenhower began signing documents. Hagerty then announced these presidential "decisions," but he did not overplay his hand. He made it as impressive as he could, but he did not present these as decisions over which Eisenhower had labored and sweated for hours, lying there on his bed of pain poring over reports and memoranda and then making up his mind. The reporters knew that all the work had been done in Washington. They knew that Eisenhower got only a few words of explanation or at most a one-page summary to read before signing. Except on issues of great importance, this was the way he operated when he was well.

It was one of those I-know-that-you-know-but-what-are-you-going-to-do-about-it? propositions. Hagerty knew that the reporters knew what was going on up there on the eighth floor of Fitzsimons Army Hospital. They knew it was strictly perfunctory. But Hagerty also understood several other things of great advantage. He knew it did not make any difference what the reporters knew. He knew they had no choice but to write that the president was making decisions. And he knew that even if they knew it was mostly a put-up job, a charade, little flavor of this would get into their stories.

The reporters had scant success in their efforts to infiltrate the eighth floor. The doctors, nurses and other medical personnel were not talking. And—above all—this was the era of journalistic objectivity. As practiced by the wire services and by most of the nation's newspaper editors in those days, objectivity meant that major governmental news consisted largely of what the government said it was.

Eisenhower was extremely popular. His policies were soothing. Most newspaper publishers were Republicans. Their editors were salaried employees. It was a rare editor who would grant his reporters much license to commit lese majesty. The reporters knew this. They tried sporadically, but they could not demonstrate a full-scale alternative to the official line. And they knew that if they somehow succeeded in doing this, they would find it virtually impossible to get it into print. So they did not try too hard. Hagerty knew this, too. It was what you call an atmosphere, a climate.

So the stories out of Denver carried the portentous news that Eisenhower was making decisions—in other words, that he was functioning as president. There might be a hint or two farther down in the story that things were other than they seemed. There might be a couple of sentences or a paragraph pointing out that Ike spent only a few minutes on these "decisions." There would be as much truth as the reporters could pry out of Hagerty. It was not a lot of truth. It was just a little table scrap of truth, a leftover from the great, copious banquet of exaggeration.

And yet, Hagerty was not lying. He was not like Nixon two decades later. He did not defy reality. He just played with it. There was a kernel of truth in Hagerty's version. Eisenhower at least took a look at the stuff. He could have overruled the staff consensus if he had wanted to, although what basis he would have had for disagreeing is hard to say. Lying there on his bed of pain, as it were.

So it was one part truth and nine parts exaggeration. And whether it wanted to or not, the press supplied a goodly part of the exaggeration. The decision itself got the lead paragraph—and the headline. The story left an overall impression, as Hagerty knew it would. Headlines and overall impressions were what he was going for. The caveat was buried in the corpus of the story, as he knew it would be, to be unearthed only by the most diligent reader. Those are not plentiful. The reporters might *know* what was actually going on—common sense would tell them, as much as anything, as well as their awareness of Ike's methods—but they could not *demonstrate* it. And if they could not demonstrate it, they could not write it.

They had to write it this way: "President Eisenhower was described today as keeping in close touch with the flood disaster in New England, and was considering possible relief measures."[17]

They could not write it this way: "In an essentially phony announcement designed to portray a bedridden chief executive as fully in charge of the government, the White House claimed today that President Eisenhower was keeping in close touch with a flood disaster in New England that he could not possibly know very much about." The press, Tom Wicker wrote later, had wrapped itself in the paper chains of objectivity. [18]

Day after day, Hagerty announced Eisenhower's activities. He was reviewing a draft of his next State of the Union message. He issued a statement on the Big Four foreign ministers' meeting in Geneva. He approved a program to alleviate unemployment and another one to speed up the administration of justice. The reporters duly reported all this. They knew they were reporting gross exaggerations, but they could not prove it.

Hagerty shuttled between Denver and Washington. Each time he returned to Denver, his briefcase was full of decisions for Ike to approve, statements to be announced, press releases to be released.

In the third week of Eisenhower's recovery, the government came to Denver. Bringing its briefcases, of course. The vice-president was first; it was said that he and the president discussed the foreign ministers' meeting. The secretary of state was next. It was said that, working together, Ike and Dulles drafted a short letter to Premier Bulganin on disarmament. But Dulles had his briefcase with him. Could the draft have been therein? Through it all, there ran an undercurrent of briefcase.

In the fourth and fifth weeks, the rest of the briefcases arrived at the hospital. Each spread its treasures before the president. In those two weeks, Eisenhower conferred with every member of his Cabinet except Secretary of Commerce Sinclair Weeks. The commerce secretary felt this keenly. His staff spent days trying to explain it. His briefcase was inconsolable.

The news stories that resulted from these visits were much of a sameness. The unifying point was that all of them could have been written in Washington. With the Cabinet member or even an underling as the source, and no mention of the president. But that was precisely what Hagerty did not want. He did not care all that much what else was in the story, as long as the president was. So he shepherded each Cabinet member over to the pressroom at Lowry, there his tale to unfold.

A typical lead was "Secretary of Defense Charles E. Wilson predicted today after a conference with President Eisenhower that defense spending in the next fiscal year might run slightly higher than the predicted 34.5 billion dollars. . . ." [19] Up a billion, down a billion—it did not matter, as long as that "after a conference with President Eisenhower" was in the lead.

By the time Eisenhower left Denver, after seven weeks of convalescence, the impression had taken hold that the heart attack had not impaired his ability to serve as president of the United States. Columnists and pundits who had written seven weeks before that Ike could not and would not run again now said he might very well stand for reelection. This was Hagerty's accomplishment. The door that had seemed so nearly closed was wide open again.

Hagerty's press-agentry had had the desired impact on the press and the public. Eisenhower, however, remained to be convinced. What brought him around was five weeks of nasty winter weather in Gettysburg, Pennsylvania. Specifically, the icy temperatures froze the golf courses.

The president had gone to his farm near Gettysburg to continue his convalescence. Reporters who covered both Denver and Gettysburg, including myself, were puzzled by the contrast in his moods. Each time we had seen him in Denver—when he was brought out on a sundeck in a wheelchair or received photographers and a "pool" reporter in his bedroom—he was wreathed in smiles and cheerfulness. He was obviously happy to have survived a heart attack.

But in Gettysburg, Eisenhower moved morosely between the farm and his office in the Gettysburg post office (Postmaster L. E. Oyler, a Democrat, had yielded his first-floor suite to the president). Hagerty, perhaps reflecting Ike's mood, was notably surly. One morning, as the reporters shivered outside the post office in weather that would have ended the Civil War a lot sooner, I called out a question. Hagerty strode over and snarled: "Why are you such a goddamned Boy Scout?" His hangovers were fearsome. At night, if the press secretary was being overserved, Merriman Smith of United Press would remove some vital part from the engine of Hagerty's car, in an effort to ground him. It did not always work. Then the reporters would have to chase around the countryside to locate the Free World's spokesman.

Later, Robert J. Donovan talked to some of the president's closest friends and wrote: "For Eisenhower, Gettysburg came close to being five weeks of torment. In Denver, he had escaped the depression that often follows a coronary thrombosis. At Gettysburg, it struck. His morale slumped. His spirits were low. He fretted over government affairs. On top of this, the weather turned bad and he was confined as he had never been in his life except in the hospital. Sometimes he would not go out at all, and when he did, the putting green on the farm as likely as not was frozen stiff. . . . Indoors he was tense and nervous and stalked about the house with a golf club for a cane."[20]

Donovan wrote that the president's intimates believed that "in the gloomy November and December days at Gettysburg, Mrs. Eisenhower [came] to the conclusion that her husband was not ready for retirement."[21] Eisenhower was an American male; he had the itch he could not scratch.

On February 29, 1956, Eisenhower announced that he would run for a second term. That seemed to take care of that. Nixon would have to wait. Then, just as Hagerty was thinking he had finished his part of the job, he had to do it all over again.

On the night of June 7, Eisenhower attended the annual dinner of the White House Photographers' Association. Sticking to the diet prescribed after the heart attack, he had some consommé, a filet mignon without any sauce or garnishment, a baked potato without butter, and peas. He passed up the cake and ice cream, drank caffeine-free coffee and took only a ceremonial sip of wine. After the dinner, he returned to the White House and went to bed.

At about 12:45 A.M., he woke up with a pain in his abdomen. He vomited several times. Mrs. Eisenhower called Dr. Snyder. The doctor decided it was a digestive upset. He told Mamie to give Ike some milk of magnesia.

The president took the milk of magnesia. It did not help. Mrs. Eisenhower called Dr. Snyder again. This time, the doctor made a house call, arriving about 2 A.M. He discovered that Eisenhower's abdomen was distended. His bowel sounds were faint and after a while could not be heard at all. X rays showed later that the intestine was almost completely blocked. Major General Leonard Heaton, one of the surgeons who performed the operation, said afterward that if the intestinal obstruction had not been relieved, it could have led to gangrene of the bowel. At 2 A.M., in other words, Dr. Snyder discovered that the president was seriously ill. The doctor diagnosed an attack of ileitis—an inflammation of the lower part of the small intestine.

But when Hagerty gave reporters the first news of the illness, at 8:50 in the morning, his statement was as follows: "The president has an upset stomach and headache this morning. We have postponed his schedule today. Dr. Snyder has been with him since early this morning. There is nothing wrong with his heart." The last three sentences of this statement were true.

At 10:30 A.M., Hagerty saw the reporters again. He emphasized that Eisenhower was not sick. "This is just a stomach upset," he said. "Anybody can get a stomach upset." Hagerty did not seem to be under any strain. He was in and out of the White House's west lobby several times during the morning, and each time he greeted the reporters affably. The customary banter and small jokes were exchanged. Either Hagerty was in Rick's position—misinformed—or he was a fine actor, which no one ever doubted.

Then, at 12:25 P.M., Hagerty called the reporters into his office and read quite a different statement: "The president has an attack of ileitis. . . . As a precautionary measure, he is being taken to Walter Reed Hospital this afternoon." The coverup had lasted about ten and a half hours.

Hagerty worked even faster this time. On June 11, two days after the operation, he announced that Eisenhower had transacted ten minutes of official business. On June 12, he revealed that the president had sent a foreign aid message to the Senate, had conferred for fifteen minutes with White House chief of staff Sherman Adams and two other staff members, had signed an executive order, an official letter and a new international wheat agreement and had walked eighty feet in his hospital room, supported by Dr. Ravdin. All this by a sixty-five-year-old man who had had major surgery three days before and a heart attack less than nine months before that. The election was four and a half months away.

The next day, Eisenhower signed twenty-seven bills, documents and letters, dictated for five minutes to his personal secretary, Ann Whitman, talked to Adams for twenty-five minutes and conferred with the chancellor of West Germany, Konrad Adenauer, for a half hour. The chancellor was a press agent's dream. After seeing Ike, he told the reporters:

"I was very happy to . . . have seen him in such excellent shape. . . . I have asked the doctor to explain this miracle, and he has told me that it is a healthy organism which offers the best foundation to overcome any obstacle of this kind. I must say that I would not have thought it possible that a person, so few days after an operation, could look that way, could talk that way and could participate so vividly in the discussions." [22] It was the age of miracles.

Eisenhower spent five weeks recuperating from the ileitis operation, much of the time at his Gettysburg farm again. He left Gettysburg on July 15 with the permission of his doctors to be reelected.

On January 21, 1957, he was sworn in for a second term. Ten months later, on November 25, he had a stroke. This time, everything went to hell entirely. Hagerty was in Paris. He rushed back, but for a time associate press secretary Anne Wheaton had to handle the crisis. Mrs. Wheaton was a former official of the Republican National Committee who had been brought over to the White House. She probably regretted it.

Eisenhower was now sixty-seven years old. On the afternoon of November 25, sometime between three and four o'clock, he was in his office, getting ready to sign some papers. Suddenly he felt dizzy. He tried to pick up a document but could not do it. He looked at the piece of paper. The words, he said later, "seemed literally to run off the top of the page."

He tried to get up from his chair and almost fell down. He rang for his secretary. When Mrs. Whitman came in, Ike tried to tell her something was wrong. All that came out was an incoherent jumble. Eisenhower wrote later that "it was impossible for me to express any coherent thought whatsoever."[23] The president could not talk.

Dr. Snyder ordered Eisenhower to bed. At 6:20 that evening, Mrs. Wheaton informed the reporters that the president had developed a chill. Just a chill. She said it was not considered serious. Not serious.

There was a longer coverup this time. Dr. Snyder, it was revealed later, had realized almost immediately that Eisenhower had suffered a cerebral occlusion—the closing of an artery in the brain, due to a clot or a spasm. But it was not until 3 P.M. the next day, November 26, that Mrs. Wheaton announced the true nature of the illness. Twenty-four hours went by before the nation learned that the president had had a stroke.

During those twenty-four hours, wild confusion prevailed. There was a riot of rumors as long black limousines drew up to the White House, disgorging grim-faced officials who would not answer questions. It was obvious that a crisis was at hand, but the reporters did not know what it was and could not find out. The milling-around area was jammed with journalists in more than their customary state of frustration.

(The milling-around area is any area where reporters are confined while they wait to be told something. When newsmen enter an auditorium or hotel where an important event is to take place, a senior correspondent sometimes demands to be taken immediately to the milling-around area. That is what is going to happen anyway, so it saves time. There is nothing worse than milling around waiting to be taken to the milling-around area.)

These things bring out the worst in people. The scene in the lobby of the West Wing—the White House's milling-around area in those days—resembled the fall of the Bastille. Patience wore thin, which is *its* customary state. The deadlines for most editions of afternoon newspapers had come and gone. Editors of morning newspapers were inquiring of their reporters what in God's name was going on.

At 3 P.M., Mrs. Wheaton summoned the press into Hagerty's office. She handed out a bulletin. It said the president had suffered "an occlusion of a small branch of the middle cerebral artery on the left side. It cannot be determined at this time whether the condition . . . is one of a small clot or a vascular spasm. All findings indicate no brain hemorrhage." The bulletin added that Eisenhower had "no abnormal signs or symptoms other than a mild aphasia [difficulty in speaking]." That was all it said about the exact nature of the president's illness.

Pandemonium ensued. The reporters had no difficulty speaking. They bombarded Anne Wheaton with questions. Was it a stroke? How serious was it? What was the outlook for recovery? What other symptoms were there? Was the president incapacitated? If he was, would it be necessary to turn over the reins to Vice-President Nixon? When would the doctors be available for questioning? Was Eisenhower in bed or could he walk around? Did the doctors know what had caused it? What was the treatment? How long would it be before he could resume normal activities? What was meant by difficulty in speaking? Just a problem with some words, or had he been stricken mute? And above all, again and again, *was it a stroke?*

The reporters knew what the word "cerebral" meant. It pertained to the brain. They also knew what an occlusion was—the heart attack had taught them that. It meant a blockage or stoppage. There was something wrong with the brain of the president of the United States. But what exactly was it? The reporters were not doctors. They were reasonably sure it was a stroke but they could not be *absolutely* sure. It might be something short of a stroke or related to a stroke. They wanted the White House to spell it out. They wanted an authority to quote. They could not call it a stroke solely on the basis of their own lay knowledge. It was too important.

But Mrs. Wheaton would not go beyond the terse wording of the medical bulletin. The doctors had given her a piece of paper, and that was that. The angry mob surged around the Bastille, hurling questions, shouting, imploring. Was it a stroke? She would not say. Well, was it something else then? She would not say. She read them the bulletin again and again. An occlusion of a small branch of the middle cerebral artery on the left side. Well, didn't that mean it was a stroke? She would not say.

By now, the frustration level had broken all previous records. However, when reporters are balked in one direction, they try another. They could not get Mrs. Wheaton to define the word "cerebral." So they grasped at another straw: "occlusion." That was the word that had been used at the time of the heart attack. Well, for God's sake, maybe it was something to do with Ike's heart again. Or some combination of heart *and* brain. Something new to medical knowledge. It was certainly new to journalistic knowledge. The reporters closed in on Mrs. Wheaton again. Did "occlusion" mean it was some kind of heart attack?

Kierkegaard wrote that life could only be understood in the past but must be lived in the present. So in retrospect, this was all very silly. But not at the moment. Human beings—reporters, government officials, ordinary citizens—live in the moment. Washington is a momentary city. And at that moment, the reporters were desperate. They needed—they absolutely had to have—a general description of Ike's illness in terms that the public could understand.

And even at the moment, the reporters were not as dim-witted as they sounded. At least, most of them were not. Not only do reporters try different directions when they are being stonewalled, they have other stratagems as well. Sometimes they feign ignorance. Robert Pierpoint, when he was covering the White House for CBS, was famous for this technique. Sublime innocence throbbed in Pierpoint's voice as he told a press secretary: "I'm not sure I understand . . ." or "I'm confused . . ." Like hell he was. He was working. At other times, the reporters will try to get a briefing official so flustered or so angry that the truth is blurted out in sheer fury. Most of the reporters knew perfectly well that the word "cerebral" ruled out a heart attack. But perhaps they could get Mrs. Wheaton so confused that she would tell them more than what was on that sheet of paper from the doctors. The reporters could not get anything, so they had to try everything. They asked her whether it was a heart attack.

At this point, things took a turn for the worse. When the Bastille fell, it fell in both directions. Mrs. Wheaton had been hounded beyond endurance. She had been assailed with questions that came so thick and fast that she could hardly refuse to answer one before another was asked. So when she was asked whether it was some form of heart attack, her defenses crumbled.

She replied: "This is a form of heart attack, as I understand the medical language." That did it.

By this time, the journalists were confusing each other, which is not unheard of. Another reporter inquired how it could be a heart attack when the bulletin used the word "cerebral." Mrs. Wheaton was groggy but still game.

She replied: "As I understand it, 'cerebral' does have the connotation of something to do with the head."

The age-old question: head or heart? The reporters now had it both ways from the official spokesman for the American government. They broke for the telephones to dictate their own bulletins. But what would they say? Reporters are not fond of these deadline moments of truth, when they must go with unanswered questions and inadequate knowledge. Facing the phones, they communed silently with the god of journalists and found no comfort. But they communed only briefly, for there was no time. There never is enough time.

United Press solved the problem with awesome simplicity. Its initial bulletin said the president of the United States had suffered "a heart attack of the brain."

* * *

It is a sloppy world. Some of the confusion was cleared up a few moments later, when Mrs. Wheaton, after a telephone call to Dr. Snyder, announced that "there is no heart involved." But the most important question never really was answered. The White House never did officially acknowledge that Eisenhower had had a stroke. The reason, according to Snyder, was that the doctors could not be sure.

The president's physician insisted that "no doctor could tell you it's a stroke. . . . We would not describe it as a slight stroke because we do not know whether it is a small clot [a stroke] or a vascular spasm."[24] But Dr. David D. Rutstein, a prominent heart specialist, said cerebral occlusions were "almost always due to a clot," and Dr. Irving Wright, another leading heart authority, said flatly that Eisenhower had suffered "a small stroke."[25] After a while, it just sort of became generally accepted that Ike had had a stroke, but it was never tied up neatly and definitively. The election was over.

This time, however, the reporters were more persistent about the delay in announcing the stroke or the vascular spasm or whatever it was. For several days, they probed for the reasons. Mrs. Wheaton confirmed that Dr. Snyder had diagnosed a cerebral occlusion almost immediately— that is, sometime between 3 and 4 P.M. on November 25. Why, then, had the acting press secretary announced at 6:20 P.M. that the president had a chill?

"That is what I was told," Mrs. Wheaton replied. "I issued the [chill] statement on the advice of the doctor."

Why had twenty-four hours elapsed before it was announced that Eisenhower had suffered a cerebral occlusion? Mrs. Wheaton said Dr. Snyder "wanted to have the full facts of the case before making it known to the American people." She added that the White House chief of staff, Sherman Adams, had been aware of the "chill" statement.

Adams was unquestionably the best-informed and most powerful member of Eisenhower's White House staff. In his memoirs, he wrote: "The reporters . . . were baying . . . for a statement, and Anne Wheaton . . . was trying to pacify them without a definitive medical report to give them."[26]

But what "full facts" were being awaited? It was known to be a cerebral occlusion on the afternoon of November 25. Adams himself wrote that "there were obvious signs of a cerebral occlusion" that afternoon, although he said "the extent of the damage was unknown."[27] It was still a cerebral occlusion on the afternoon of November 26, when it was announced. Some additional medical data may have been obtained in those twenty-four hours, but the diagnosis did not change. That left questions: Why the delay in announcing it? Why not announce that the president had suffered a cerebral occlusion whose full effects were not yet known? Of course, confusion would have arisen if it had been stated that the full effects were not yet known. But confusion arose anyway. Meanwhile, the American people were misled about the condition of the chief executive. They were told he had a chill.

In his book, Adams gave an explanation. The doctors, he wrote, "could not tell us how seriously the shock . . . had affected the president's nervous system, or whether it might be only the first in a series of more damaging strokes." And then the decision: "We decided to wait and see for a day or two."[28] That left other questions: Why the cover story? Why was it described as a chill?

Adams's account of the Eisenhower administration was not published until 1961—four years after the stroke. During the crisis itself, the reporters were not given even this much explanation. They were given only Dr. Snyder's explanation. They tried to get more. They did not succeed.

Then Hagerty got back from Paris. By this time, he had had plenty of practice. On November 28, he announced that Eisenhower had conferred with Nixon and Adams for fifteen minutes and had signed twelve documents. He told the reporters that the president was sitting up in an easy chair and joking about his "slight difficulty" in saying certain words. Eisenhower was back in his office a week after the seizure. He presided at a Cabinet meeting on December 2 and met with congressional leaders on December 3.

And that was that. Hagerty was back on the job, and Eisenhower's popularity was great. The newspapers pointed out that the White House had concealed the actual nature of the president's illness for twenty-four hours. But they did not make a federal case out of it. Nor was there a national outcry over it. The whole thing just faded away. The stroke coverup was like the heart attack coverup and the ileitis coverup. They were just *little* coverups. Who cared? It could never happen again.

II

PRESIDENTS

round the south lawn with Lyndon. Around the track with Lyndon. Around the bend with Lyndon. A straggle of reporters, trying to keep up with the president as he takes a walk around the White House grounds. The Ellipse and the Washington Monument in the background, Lyndon Baines Johnson in the foreground. That is as it should be—The Order of Things According to Lyndon. He is the President of the Free World, played center stage under a spotlight that never dims, to applause that never stops, if he can help it.

He is half-loony now, maybe more—who can tell? The reporters know there is something wrong, but how to define it? He is functioning, after all. He is even rational—in Lyndon's terms. And consider an additional factor: He has always been a megalomaniac. Joseph Alsop delights Georgetown when Johnson becomes president: "Of course he's a monster, but he's *our* monster." Georgetown delights easily, but it is true: This is an excessive personality, grossly excessive. However, if he has always been like this, then perhaps there is nothing to worry about. He is really all right, down deep. Isn't he? It is just Lyndon As Usual. Isn't it?

Seeking reassurance, I talk to Clifford Case, a senator from New Jersey, a careful, prudent man. I tell him how the president is behaving. The lies—ceaseless, constant lying about everything, lies about important and unimportant things, nothing too large or too small to be lied about; obvious, transparent lies, easily exposed, as if he actually wants to be caught lying. The boasting—wild, inane braggadocio, far beyond the standard huffing and puffing of the parvenu. The gigantic vanity that says the scar from his gallbladder operation is of consuming interest to the nation. The exhibitionism that causes him to have bowel movements and enemas in front of mixed audiences in his bathroom or bedroom. The insecurity that compels him to belittle everyone else—John F. Kennedy, he tells reporters, was a pale, sick man with "rickety little legs." The frantic, senseless traveling—no funeral, for instance, is too remote to attend. A memorial service for a departed Australian prime minister becomes a madcap dash around the world—26,959 miles in four and a half days, Honolulu, Pago Pago by moonlight, Canberra, Melbourne, Darwin, sundown over the Java Sea, Thailand, South Vietnam, Pakistan, Rome—conferring along the way with seventeen leaders secular and one spiritual (he drops in on the pope in a helicopter, and the reporters recall George S. Kaufman's line; it shows you, they say, what God could do if he had money.) And above all—the incessant talking, the interminable nervous monologues, tirades, harangues. Talk, talk, talk. The president cannot stop talking.

Clifford Case has known Lyndon Johnson for years. "He has always been like this," the senator says. "It is just his style." Nothing new.

But Vietnam is new. Vietnam is tearing the country apart. There are demonstrations, sit-ins, riots, casualty lists, bloody newscasts, burning villages, endless arguments, endless anguish. The students chant: "Hey, hey, LBJ, how many kids did you kill today?" The president can visit foreign lands but not American cities; the Secret Service says it cannot guarantee his safety except at military installations. The opponents of the war say it is the power of the imperial presidency running wild, but Johnson complains to the reporters that he has no power at all—just the power of nuclear weapons "and I can't use that." So he bombs and bombs and bombs, and lies and lies and lies, and tries to have a war on the cheap and a war in secret—and nothing works. The contradictions are tearing him apart.

Sometimes the reporters are called into the president's office or the Cabinet Room. The president wants to talk at them. He wants to tell them everything is going well. He says he is sending more troops to Vietnam.

July 13, 1967. The Oval Office. In an armchair: Johnson. On a sofa, three wise men: General William C. Westmoreland, the U.S. commander in Vietnam; General Earle G. Wheeler, Chairman of the Joint Chiefs of Staff; and Robert S. McNamara, the secretary of defense. Westmoreland has asked for 100,000 to 140,000 additional American troops. Johnson is going to give him 35,000 to 50,000, although he refuses to tell the reporters how many.

Johnson: "The answer is, yes, we have reached a meeting of the minds. The troops that General Westmoreland needs and requests, as we feel it necessary, will be supplied. General Westmoreland feels that is acceptable, General Wheeler thinks that is acceptable, and Secretary McNamara thinks that is acceptable. It is acceptable to me, and we hope it is acceptable to you [the reporters]. Is that not true, General Westmoreland?"

Westmoreland: "I agree, Mr. President."

Johnson: "General Wheeler?"

Wheeler: "That is correct, Mr. President."

Johnson: "Secretary McNamara?"

McNamara: "Yes, sir."

Johnson: "Mr. Spivak [Alvin Spivak of United Press International]?"

Spivak: "Yes, sir."[1]

These scenes are interesting. The Vietnam strategists—Johnson, McNamara, Secretary of State Dean Rusk—are exhausted men. The reporters file into the Cabinet Room after a meeting between the president and his advisers. They see a collection of burned-out cases. Men in late middle age, slumped in their chairs, rubbing sleepless eyes under which are dark purple pouches. These men are worn out. How good is their judgment?

Rusk has taken to questioning the loyalty of the press. At a background session in February 1968, the reporters question him persistently about the contradictions.

The secretary of state and other senior officials have been saying that the Tet offensive was a major setback for the Communists. The offensive, they point out, did not trigger a popular uprising against the South Vietnamese government. The Viet Cong failed to hold some of the thirty-six provincial capitals that they attacked. The South Vietnamese army performed well. Oh.

But middle-level American officials are saying privately that the offensive demonstrated that almost all of South Vietnam's cities and villages remain vulnerable to the Communists; the pacification program, intended to make them secure, has failed. These officials tell reporters that the offensive achieved surprise because the people of South Vietnam were afraid or unwilling to come forward with information about a massive Viet Cong infiltration into the cities in preparation for the Tet attacks. Someone has not won the hearts and minds.

And the greatest contradiction of all: With a half-million American troops in Vietnam, with all the sophisticated weapons, all the body counts of dead Viet Cong, all the Communist supply lines and bridges destroyed over and over again, all the villages pacified over and over again, how is it that at this late date the Communists were able to mount an offensive of the magnitude of Tet?

At this point, Rusk invokes patriotism. When the gap in perceptions between the press and the government becomes very wide, patriotism is rushed into the breach. Vietnam is not a minor confrontation over the twenty-four-hour coverup of a presidential stroke; the ultimate weapon must be used. The reporters (although not all the newspapers and networks they work for, by any means) have become convinced that the government is attempting a profound deception of its own people.

At the background briefing, Secretary Rusk states the government's perception. He tells the reporters: "There gets to be a point where the question is, whose side are you on? None of your papers or your broadcasting apparatuses are worth a damn unless the United States succeeds. They are trivial compared to that question. So I don't know why, to win a Pulitzer Prize, people have to go probing for the things that one can bitch about when there are 2,000 stories on the same day about things that are more constructive in character."[2]

And at about this time, Lyndon Johnson goes for a walk on the south lawn.

A cry is heard: "He's out." There being only one "he" in Washington, the press corps rushes to the south lawn and falls in behind the president. The reporters never know whether these occasions are business or pleasure. They follow a rule of thumb: Ask him a question. If he answers, it is a press conference. On this day, Johnson answers a question, and a press conference takes place. Twenty or thirty reporters are loping along behind a big, untidy-looking man, trying to hear what he is saying, trying to take notes on the move.

Most of the questions are about Vietnam. For three years, the reporters have been bludgeoning Lyndon Johnson with questions about Vietnam. For three years, they have persecuted him. And not just the reporters. The students, the professors, the doves in Congress, the prime minister of Sweden, the South Vietnamese Army that will not fight and the Vietnamese guerrillas who will not stop fighting, the North Vietnamese politicians who will not negotiate on American terms and the South Vietnamese politicians who will not negotiate on any terms—Lyndon Johnson is a man of towering ambition who is watching his ambitions being torn to shreds by people and forces he does not understand and cannot control.

I ask him a question. It is about Vietnam. The president stops and turns around. He is a bear at bay, the hounds bedeviling him. He puts his heavy, scowling face close to mine. And then he says furiously: "Why do you always sell your country short?"

July 11, 1961, a little after six in the evening. Ideal weather. My wife and I arrive at the Washington Navy Yard. One hundred and thirty-four guests are assembling, the women in evening dresses, the men in summer dinner jackets. They go aboard a flotilla: the presidential yacht, known at that time as the *Honey Fitz* in honor of John F. Kennedy's grandfather; a yacht used by the secretary of the Navy; and several smaller boats.

The boats cast off. It is a floating cocktail party down the Potomac River. Accordian players serenade the guests; Navy stewards serve drinks and mounds of shrimp on large platters. My wife has a long conversation with the finance minister of Pakistan. She tells him she is delighted to meet a finance minister because she has always had trouble adding and subtracting. The minister says his country is so poor that all he has to know is how to divide its scarce resources. It is a festive cruise, with much brilliant conversation of this sort.

A few miles down the river, the boats tie up at a pier. The guests disembark and walk up a rustic path illuminated by flaring torches. Stationed along the path are marines in full dress, rigidly presenting arms. The path leads to Mount Vernon.

The home of the nation's first president overlooks the Potomac. On the lawn facing the river, a thirty- by fifty-foot yellow and green barkcloth pavilion has been set up. The floor of the tent is covered with green carpeting. Hurricane-type electric lights have been installed on the center poles in fixtures entwined with luxuriant garlands of calendulas and begonias. The tent was loaned by Mr. and Mrs. Paul Mellon of Upperville, Virginia. Display experts from Tiffany's and Bonwit Teller in New York have designed the decorations and lighting for tonight's party, assisted by the Mellons' head gardener.

Seated at tables of eight persons, the guests dine on Avocado and Crabmeat Mimosa, Poulet Chasseur, Couronne de Riz Clamart, Framboises à la Crème Chantilly, Petits Fours Sec, demitasse and liqueurs. With the avocado and crabmeat, Haut-Brion 1958 is served; with the sautéed chicken and rice, Moët et Chandon Imperial Brut 1955. The cutlery is gold, the plates gold-trimmed. The food has been prepared by the White House's French chef, René Verdon, and transported to Mount Vernon in Army trucks.

During dinner, the Air Force's Strolling Strings serenade the guests. The violinists play *ensemble*, then split into small groups around the tent, continuing to play in perfect unison. The champagne flows and flows. The guests discuss the crises of the day—Berlin, Laos, the Congo. They examine the slow pace of the administration's legislative program. They examine the hostess's strapless white evening gown. A young woman argues with a midwestern senator about Vietnam; the next day, the senator sends her a dozen roses and a gallant note, but he does not change his views on the war. Another young woman asks a companion what she is supposed to do when the president of the United States puts his hand on her leg. Columnist Doris Fleeson amuses herself by flipping the medals of her dinner partner, General Curtis LeMay, Chief of Staff of the Air Force. LeMay, a heavy-jowled man, stares straight ahead. He appears unperturbed by Miss Fleeson's many witty comments as she toys with his decorations. Both are smoking cigars.

After dinner, a fife and drum corps, in Revolutionary War uniforms, presents a ceremonial parade. Then, sitting on George Washington's lawn overlooking the Potomac, in the starry night, the guests drink more champagne and listen to the National Symphony Orchestra play Mozart, Debussy, Morton Gould and George Gershwin.

A nice party. The guest of honor at this state dinner was the president of Pakistan, Mohammed Ayub Khan. The host and hostess were John F. Kennedy and his wife, Jacqueline.

There was an incident early in the evening. The Kennedys and Ayub Khan and his daughter were greeting the guests in a receiving line. When my turn came, I shook hands with Kennedy and we exchanged the customary word or two. Kennedy then introduced me to Ayub Khan. The leader of Pakistan gave me a very perfunctory handshake, a Sandhurst stare and no words at all. I received the distinct impression that journalists were not the aristocracy of Pakistan. This Raja Sahib seemed to be wondering why a mere scribbler had been invited to a state dinner.

Oh, well. I moved on to shake hands with Ayub Khan's daughter. Next to her was Jackie Kennedy, the vision in the white strapless gown. It would be a pleasure to exchange the customary word or two with her, because on occasions such as this, Mrs. Kennedy was a very high class production.

But Kennedy had observed the snub. You could almost see the wheels turn. It is possible that he did not want my feelings hurt, although Kennedy knew that, in order to do their work, reporters learn to ignore slights and rebuffs. They become, in J. D. Salinger's stupendous simile, as sensitive as a toilet seat. So it is more likely that JFK was thinking of Ayub Khan. To Kennedy, it was probably much more important that the Great Khan not get the idea that any rabble had been invited to the party.

However, Kennedy was a quick-witted man. His contrivance covered both egos. He reached out, snatched me away from Jackie and plunked me down in front of Ayub Khan again. He made sure that he had Ayub's full attention and then said firmly: "Mr. Deakin is a distinguished correspondent for one of our most distinguished newspapers."

Johnson on the south lawn. Kennedy at Mount Vernon. One of these presidents knew how to handle the press.

The relationship between the president of the United States and the nation's news media is a subject of endless fascination. It exerts an irresistible attraction for presidents, members of the White House staff, reporters, editors and broadcasters, politicians, bureaucrats, political scientists, historians and an increasing number of ordinary citizens. For a long time, it was a local cottage industry in Washington, of no great interest to the rest of the country. Now it is a vast national enterprise whose tentacles spread into every village and shire.

How is the president getting along with the news media? Are they treating him well or badly? Is he a master of communications or an ineffective performer on the tube? Is he accessible to reporters and candid with them? Or is he secretive, misleading the press and throwing a cloak of national security over the administration's precious bodily fluids? Why doesn't he have more press conferences? Why have his press conferences become such increasingly meaningless spectacles? Why does he manipulate the press so brazenly to achieve his purposes? Why doesn't he use the press more effectively to achieve his purposes? Why is the press so subservient to the president? Why is the press so hostile to the president? The relationship between the president and the news media is a long-running soap. Drama. Suspense. Conflict. And a large, rapt audience.

Most presidents occasionally comment in public, and much more often in private, about the news coverage they are receiving. They usually find it deficient. The news reports do not please them. And so it has been, between the president and the press, since the founding of the Republic.

A Cabinet meeting of 1793, as recorded by the secretary of state, Thomas Jefferson: "The president was much inflamed, got into one of those passions when he cannot command himself, ran on much on the personal abuse which had been bestowed on him, defied any man on earth to produce one single act of his since he had been in the government which was not done on the purest motives . . . that *by God* he had rather be in his grave than in his present situation. That he had rather be on his farm than to be made *emperor of the world* and yet they were charging him with wanting to be king. That that *rascal Freneau* [Philip Freneau, editor of the *National Gazette*] sent him three of his papers every day, as if he thought he would become the distributor . . .

that he could see in this nothing but an impudent design to insult him. He ended in this high tone. . . ." George Washington was reading more and enjoying it less.[3]

In a letter of 1792, Washington wrote that he would "be happy to see a cessation of the abuses of public officers, and of those attacks upon almost every measure of government with which some of the gazettes are so strongly impregnated; and which cannot fail, if persevered in with the malignancy [with which] they now teem, of rending the Union asunder." And in 1793, he wrote that "we have some infamous papers, calculated for disturbing if not absolutely intended to disturb the peace of the community."[4]

One hundred and eighty-seven years later—the Union having survived—President Jimmy Carter expressed similar concern about the community's peace. At a "town meeting" in Philadelphia on May 9, 1980, Carter complained about the "burning desire on the part of the American press to put forward new ideas and to explain controversy and to report debate and to emphasize disagreement and to let us know about transient disappointments and temporary aggravation. . . . So in the process of hearing about these things in the evening as you watch the network news or reading about them in the newspapers, listening to them on the radio all day long, we get the impression in this country that all there is to it is the debate or the argument or the temporary inconvenience or transient disappointment. What we tend to forget is the blessing [of living] in the United States of America, because God has blessed us far more than we recognize. . . ."[5]

The news media continued to prey on Carter's mind after he left office. In March 1981, he went to Princeton University to consult with scholars about the preparation of his memoirs. While there, he talked with a group of students. One of them, Steve Yelenoski, said Carter complained that "the American press to some extent [had] hampered his ability to act" in the presidency. So *that* was the reason. Yelenoski quoted Carter as saying that the media "deliberately distorted information and didn't check out all the facts."[6]

Between George Washington and Jimmy Carter, thirty-six other men served as president of the United States. Each conducted the office according to his ability, intellect, personality, temperament and predispositions, his educational, cultural, family and economic background, the circumstances under which he became president, his political skills, the events that took place during his presidency and his capacity to react and adjust to them, the political and economic conditions and social values of his time, the state of human knowledge at that moment and the inability of humankind to predict the future. And each president had trouble with the press. Why?

The relationship between the president and the press is the *Jarndyce* v. *Jarndyce* of relationships: an endless dispute. There is no single, comprehensive explanation for the chronic stresses and strains between the government and the news media. Instead, there is an interminable list of reasons. Heading the list is a basic phenomenon that has many implications:

The government wishes its point of view to prevail. In any situation, it wants its version of the facts and its explanation of those facts to be accepted by as much of the public as possible. Unanimity is best. The government believes its programs and policies are the correct courses for the nation, and it desires them to be seen as such. The reason for the government's attitude is simple. Unless its versions of events and the justifications it offers for its actions are acceptable to a large number of citizens, it cannot govern effectively.

That was the fate of Lyndon Johnson in Vietnam, Richard Nixon in Watergate, Gerald Ford in the Nixon pardon and Jimmy Carter in the energy and Iranian crises. The news media were a major factor in all these events, but there were many other important factors: casualty lists and massacres in Vietnam, crimes and lies in Watergate, public indignation in the pardon episode, public frustration and anger in the energy and Iranian situations. The news media communicated the details of these events to the public. They communicated the government's version of the events. They communicated additional information their reporters had uncovered. And they communicated the alternative explanations and proposals and criticisms brought forward by individuals and groups that were opposed to the government's actions.

The journalist reports the government's version of events and describes the policies with which it proposes to deal with problems. If only it could be left at that. The government's view would prevail. We could all go to the seashore. But the journalist then asserts his professionalism. He insists on seeking out and reporting views that differ from the official view. He informs the public of other facts, other explanations, other proposed courses of action. These dispute the official version. They disagree with it. They criticize it.

At length, the public decides to agree with the government—or with the other side. And here is a terrible problem of semantics. It is clear what is meant by agreeing with the government. But what is meant by agreeing with the other side? Does it mean agreeing with the *journalists*? Have they persuaded the public to agree with *their* point of view? Have they beguiled it, these wily propagandists, with slanted stories and biased accounts? Or does it mean that the public has come to agree with other facts, other explanations, other proposals that are merely *relayed* by journalists?

Is it a power struggle between the government and the press? Or is it a power struggle between the government and the alternatives to the official view, with the press as a conduit for *both*? There is a world of difference, a chasm, between these two concepts.

It is not possible to dissuade those who believe deeply. To the believers, the contemporary news media are not merely a powerful force, which no one denies. They are more than that. They are a recognizable power *bloc*, with well-defined attitudes and objectives. They are dominated and impelled by a liberal philosophy. They are antagonistic to conservative causes and governments. They are sympathetic to liberal causes and governments. They scorn many of the values and institutions of the American society. And to promote their political and social goals, they present information (news) selectively. They emphasize certain things and omit or minimize others. They slant. They distort.

Dissuasion being impossible, nothing remains but perspective. At this moment, the believers define the most influential media as implacably liberal. But not long ago, many persons believed with equal conviction that the most influential media were implacably conservative. They were intensely hostile to the liberal New Deal programs of Franklin D. Roosevelt.

Another perspective: The alternatives—the other facts, other explanations, other proposals—would exist even if there were no news media. Someone would be certain to call them to the attention of the public, using whatever device could be contrived. Someone who disagreed with the government's position. Some group that fervently espoused a cause or passionately desired a course of action not favored by the government. The word would get out somehow. The journalist can claim a professionalism based on the pursuit of many facts and many explanations precisely because there *are* so many. But they seldom originate with him. The journalist is the midwife, not the parent.

Of course the midwife is selective. Of course the news media give more prominence to some events and issues than to others. But the issues and events are *there*, regardless of the media. That old friend, the hypothetical question: Suppose the Constitution were suddenly suspended and the media were forbidden to print or broadcast anything at all about some deeply felt issues: for instance, environmental protection, women's rights or the nuclear arms race. Not one word about them. No news stories, no editorials, no op-ed arguing, no television coverage, no advertisements, nothing.

There is no doubt that this would profoundly reduce public awareness and discussion of these issues. A total media blackout would be a terrible blow to those on both sides of these issues. But would the issues go away? Would all interest in them simply cease? Would there be no further effort to pass laws for or against them in Congress or the state legislatures? No further drives for constitutional amendments? No public demonstrations at nuclear plants? No membership campaigns or financial appeals?

To argue that the medium is the message is to describe *part* of reality, which is all anyone can do. It could be called the *contemporary* reality: The media greatly influence the message. They often shape and mold it. More than any other factor, they determine whether it is widely heard or must struggle for attention. But an older reality persists also. It could be called the *human* reality. If human emotions and beliefs and energies are committed to a message, the message will be *there*. The world, not the media, sees to that. Human beings see to that. In their restlessness and dissatisfaction, their aspirations, their changing conditions, their ambition and ego, their idealism or prejudice, their poverty or avarice. Everyone wants the fall of *his* tree to be noticed by Dan Rather. But *all* the trees fall whether Dan Rather sees them or not. McLuhan was partly right, but Bishop Berkeley was wholly wrong. The issues exist, independent of the observer.

As a matter of fact, the news media originate not too many issues but too few. There should be more investigative and explanatory journalism. There should be more examination of error, more exposure of misdeeds and corruption and injustice, more in-depth analysis of problems, more exploration of the reasons for things, more discussion of alternatives, more criticism, more comment. The news media *should* create a certain type of issue. It is the issue that otherwise would not be created—either because there is so much ignorance or because concealment is of so much benefit to some. There are many such issues.

When the media emphasize some events or explanations over others, it is most often the result of a news judgment that some things are more important than others. Frequently it is due to limited space or limited time. Sometimes it is lack of knowledge or simply a mistake—the fallibility of people who govern is fully matched by the fallibility of people who report and edit news. And sometimes it is bias. Now, journalistic bias is a monster of so frightful mien, as to be hated needs but to be seen. So it will be examined in the next chapter.

A final perspective: The government and other institutions resent the reporting of alternatives. Unquestionably it makes their job harder. Unquestionably it is sometimes inaccurate, incomplete or unfair. But the final perspective is a question: What would happen if there were *no* reporting of alternatives? What would happen if the news media reported only the official or organizational view? There would then be one widely known set of facts in any situation, and one only. There would be one dominant explanation and policy. Very tidy. Those who deem this desirable consider themselves orderly persons. They set great store by orderliness. Actually, they are gamblers. Recklessness is in their souls. They are wagering that the truth will be *their* truth. They are betting it will not be someone else's truth, something not nearly as compatible. They are taking a chance that it will be a truth with which they will agree and under which they will prosper. It will be genial. Under no circumstances will it become oppressive, authoritarian or corrupt. Lots of luck.

There are many other reasons for the endless conflict between the government and the news media:

- The government has great difficulty in obtaining enough information to enable it to make wise decisions and formulate effective policies. Disraeli once said no British government ever made a decision with more than 25 percent of the information it needed to make a good decision. The percentage may be a little higher these days; billions of dollars are devoted to the effort. But the memoirs of modern officials continue to be anguished; it is always so damned difficult to find out what is going on. Then, operating with incomplete information itself, the government frustrates and angers the press by giving it only part of that.
- Since its information is always incomplete, the government wishes to withhold public comment or specific action until it obtains more. But the news media impatiently demand immediate comment or instant action. To these entreaties, the White House press secretary or the departmental spokesman makes hallowed reply: "When we have something to announce, we will announce it." The spokesman has reasons. He has no idea what is going on. Or his information is fragmentary. Often, his superiors have instructed him to say nothing. Their information may be similarly deficient—or they may be covering up. They know either too little or too much. Lastly, the spokesman may have been told to remain silent because a policy is indeed being prepared but is not yet ready. None of this makes any difference. The reporters clamor at him.

● Why do they clamor? One reason is that journalism is an intensely competitive enterprise. Another is that governments wish to remain silent while they are reaching their decisions, but the media wish to report the decision-making process *while it is under way.* Of all the causes of discord between the press and the government, none is more irritating to both sides than this one. And none produces a greater difference in perceptions.

The government's view: The government is with John Donne, slightly paraphrased: For God's sake, hold your tongue and let me think. When an official policy is being formulated, the usual practice is to consider many possible courses of action. The government wishes to examine many alternatives, in order to avoid overlooking any. Some of these options are discarded during the decision-making process. They are judged unwise or ineffective, perhaps too expensive, perhaps too extreme. One option might alarm this country's allies. Another might produce a political backlash at home. So they are rejected, and a policy is fashioned from one or several of the remaining possibilities.

The policymakers consider it unfair and unwise when the options under consideration leak out before a decision has been reached. When this happens, the government in effect is held accountable for things it probably is not going to do. In all likelihood, it will encounter plenty of heat for the policy it *does* adopt. So it resents being blamed for possibilities that were considered along the way but rejected. What is the point of a public fracas over things that are not going to happen? There are enough fights anyway.

Of course, government officials themselves often leak this or that option to the news media. It may be a trial balloon to test public response to a certain course of action. Or it may be a maneuver by an individual official. He hopes to pressure his superiors into adopting the policy he favors. Or he is using the media in an effort to overcome the opposition of other departments or agencies. Sometimes he is simply bursting with the pride of authorship. These leaks appear in the media with great frequency. They are an indispensable technique of government; their role will be discussed in Chapter Six. They are also an inevitable consequence of human nature.

Nevertheless, the principle remains. The government argues that it should be held responsible only for what it actually does, not for what it only talks about doing. It is saying it should not have to make policy in the Super Bowl. With the coach announcing to the fans all the plays he is considering on each down. And the fans haggling over the options before the play is run. Delay of game.

The reporters' view: The journalists are with Lyndon Johnson, a remarkable irony. When he was Senate Democratic leader in the 1950's, Johnson told the White House that Congress wanted to "be in on the takeoffs as well as the crash landings." Similarly, the reporters insist there must be some public discussion of the options *during* the decision-making process. They argue that the American people have a right to know at least something about the alternatives being considered by the government. It being their government and all. The ultimate decision will affect the public, for good or ill. The people will pay, in lives, money, economic well-being or hardship, or in some other way. They will have to carry the can. So the final decision cannot be presented to them as a *fait accompli*, with no public debate over other possible courses of action. Democracy is invoked.

The journalists argue, moreover, that the broader the discussion, the less likelihood that mistakes will be made. The American people, it is often said, might have risen in alarm and forbidden the use of U.S. combat forces in Vietnam if they had learned of Lyndon Johnson's plans in time. The operative words are "might have." There is no way of knowing whether the public would have put a stop to it. But the point is that the nation did not know the combat option was being considered. During the 1964 presidential campaign, Johnson had repeatedly promised that "American boys" would not be sent to "fight a war that Asian boys should fight." The public was in Rick's position as to Johnson. Misinformed. And when he sent the troops in and authorized them to engage in combat, the decision was kept entirely secret. Of course, the presence of American combat forces in Vietnam quickly became known. But it was a *fait accompli*. There was little or no public debate *before* the decision. Except for Johnson's inner circle, no one knew there was anything to debate. The American philosopher Ralph Barton Perry, arguing against unrestricted elective courses at Harvard, said: "Students do not know what it is that they do not know." That is true of everyone. The journalists, therefore, argue that the public cannot make informed choices unless it knows what alternatives are being considered. If the government will not tell the people, the journalists will try to. The operative word is "try."

It is interesting to note that Congress takes the same position. The legislators endlessly seek information about the policy alternatives being considered by the president and his advisors. The White House spends as much time in resisting these supplications as it does in stonewalling the reporters. Everyone is to hold his tongue.

● In the hope that its viewpoint will prevail, the government seeks maximum publicity for many (although not all) of its activities. The journalists, exercising their news judgment, insist on picking and choosing what they will emphasize or neglect. To be a reporter, editor or television news executive, in Washington or any other city, is to listen to endless complaints. Why was this important story overlooked? Why was that significant development or important argument ignored? Why were those vital facts omitted? Journalists are convivial folk; they enjoy cocktail parties and buffet suppers. But the wine and cheese are admixed with dread. What is to be done? A spirited defense? A point-by-point rebuttal? An explanation of space or time limitations? A mention of deadline tyranny? A lame rejoinder that the desk must have taken it out? A promise to look into the situation? A pledge to do better next time? A muttered reminder that all human institutions are imperfect? Another drink? There is no universal answer that silences all criticisms. This is especially true when the criticisms are valid.

● After publicity there is the question of accuracy. The government wants its performance to be reported accurately. Everyone does. Everyone, however, does not agree on what is accurate. This is because everyone does not agree on what is true. The accuracy issue quickly becomes epistemological. The journalist's approximation of truth will be discussed in the next chapter. All that needs to be said here is that the government is frustrated and angry when it believes the media have reported its activities inaccurately, incompletely or prejudicially. Now and then it asserts furiously that a journalist has managed to do all three in the same story. This is known as the hat trick.

● While seeking maximum publicity for many of its activities, the government wishes to conduct others in secret. The press desires to penetrate the secrecy. Sometimes the secrecy cloaks the decision-making process; the media's answer to that has been stated. However, the government's best-known and most widely used justification for secrecy is an elusive concept known as national security. The journalists sometimes accept the national security argument, but they often reject it. They have seen an immense amount of hypocrisy, contradiction and political opportunism in national security as it is actually practiced. The chronic dispute over national security will be examined in Chapter Six.

● The government wishes to manipulate the news media to its own advantage. Another name for this ubiquitous practice is news management. A mammoth expenditure of time, manpower and money is devoted to manipulating the media. Two articles in the *Wall*

Street Journal in May 1977 cited an estimate that the government was then employing 19,000 publicity agents, at a cost of $400 million annually. When the government's motion picture, radio and publications activities were added, the total was at least $1 billion annually.[7] The apparatus and techniques used by the White House to originate, present and manage news will be described in this book. However, space does not permit an examination of the even larger news operations at the Defense Department and many other federal agencies.

The news media do not wish to be exploited by the government. However, their vigilance is not eternal. They can be had. Moreover, journalists are inescapably manipulated by the government in the ordinary process of gathering and reporting news. There is no avoiding it, as the actress said to the bishop. When someone tells something to another person, knowing the second person will tell it to someone else, then the first person is using (manipulating) the second person. He has a reason for imparting the information. He hopes to accomplish something through the second person. The president, the press secretary, the government official, Deep Throat —all of them know that the journalist fully intends to tell other people what he has been told. The so-called symbiotic relationship, another name for the basic news process, involves constant manipulation.

The journalist is acutely aware that he is being used. That is one reason he goes beyond the basic news process whenever possible. He attempts to dig below the surface of the official line. He reports alternatives to the official version when he can. He seeks other facts, other explanations. He is trying to preserve his professionalism. Otherwise, it is the night the old integrity went down.

• The news media challenge the president and the other officers of government to explain, defend and justify their actions. Every presidential press conference, every government briefing, every formal encounter between reporters and officials involves first the basic news-gathering process. The reporters are seeking news, facts, information. But another process also is under way. The journalists are trying to compel the government to explain what it is doing, to give reasons for it and to justify it.

The government, of course, does this continually, without being asked. Every presidential speech, every announcement, every briefing is an explanation and justification of something. However, things are omitted. Wishing its view to prevail, the government explains and justifies selectively. Usually *very* selectively. The reporters try to fill in the gaps. They ask for comment on all the harsh and unflattering things that people are saying about the government's position. They inquire about the terrible consequences that are being predicted or have actually occurred as the result of a policy. How does the government justify these misfortunes? And the reporters want to know why the government did what it did. What considerations went into a decision? What were the causes and motives? Why were some alternatives chosen over others? Whose view prevailed? Whose was rejected? And why? Always why. The reporters want to know the *why* of everything. Ha, what are your answers to all these things? Then the fight starts.

- The government, except on rare, heartening occasions, does not wish its mistakes brought to public attention. The news media bring the government's mistakes to public attention.
- The government, composed as it is of human beings, does not like to be criticized. The news media criticize the government.
- The government and the media then disagree over whether a mistake was actually a mistake. They further disagree over whether a criticism was valid. They disagree. They disagree. They disagree.

So the causes of conflict are endless. There is no satisfactory way to summarize them. But one phrase comes close: conflicting purposes. The government and the press simply have conflicting purposes. The purposes are not only different; they actually conflict. And because their purposes are so dissimilar, their perceptions differ. The government and the press see things in very different ways.

None of these problems can be solved. None of the conflicts can be ended. The fundamental differences between the government and the press are beyond the wit of man to reconcile.

But this is not a bad thing. It is a good thing. The differences should not be reconciled. The government should continue on its course and the media on theirs, as imperfect and unsatisfactory as these courses often are. Certainly there could be improvements. The government could be less secretive and manipulative, if it chose to be. This would benefit the nation, not harm it. The news media could be less superficial, less hasty and less sensational, if they chose to be. This also would benefit the nation, as the nation is superficial enough already. But the basic conflicts should not be removed. The government and the press should function at arm's length. If they do not stay apart, if their purposes are forced into an artificial and unnatural agreement, the nation *is* harmed.

When it is realized that the basic conflicts are irreconcilable, there are two possible outcomes:

1. There can be an accommodation, a *modus vivendi* based on at least a modicum of understanding. John and Mary Bickerson settle down to coexist in acrimony, suspicion and uneasy tolerance. They cannot abide each other, but each comprehends that the other has a place in the grand democratic experiment. The Republican editor William Allen White wrote of Franklin Roosevelt: "We who hate your gaudy guts salute you." That was an accommodation.

2. Or there can be a siege. When the siege mentality takes over at the White House, not even a scant understanding is possible. The president and his subordinates come to believe that the news media are remorselessly bent on their destruction. The White House is a beleaguered entrenchment, and the enemy is the press. A list of enemies is drawn up, with vengeance sworn. And the paranoia spreads outward until not just the media but almost everyone is out to get them. Walter Cronkite has turned against the war, but there is more than that. The people of New Hampshire have cast 28,791 votes for a *poet*. The justices of the Supreme Court have struck down our claim of secrecy. A base ingratitude, considering that we appointed four of them. Congress is surly. The Gallup poll is gloomy. All is indubitably lost.

Each president deals with the press in his own way. The machinery is essentially the same in every administration. Each president uses the standard equipment, but each uses it according to the dictates of his personality.

On the mechanical level, for instance, no modern president would think of operating without a press secretary. For a short time after he was elected in 1968, Richard Nixon did not have one; Ronald Ziegler was called "press assistant." The reporters speculated that Nixon either was showing his disdain for journalists or that Ziegler was considered too young. It turned out that Nixon was looking elsewhere. Mike Wallace had been approached for the job. That would have been something to see. But Wallace turned it down, and Ziegler soon got the title.

So every president has a press secretary. But that is only a serviceable generalization. There is a great deal of latitude. There are many variations and nuances.

Eisenhower held press conferences regularly; he was very dutiful about it. Other than that, however, he left relations with the news media in the hands of his press secretary. He did this because he had great faith in Jim Hagerty and because it saved a lot of work. That was important.

Kennedy was basically his own press secretary. This was partly because he liked reporters and was not afraid of them. But mostly it was because he *wanted* to handle his own press relations. He believed he could do it better than anyone else. This self-confidence communicated itself to the press.

Johnson tried it both ways and succeeded at neither. Sometimes he was his own press secretary, and sometimes he left it to An Unfortunate. He tried everything. He tried being as friendly as all get-out. Then he tried being aloof, like Charles de Gaulle, but funny, he did not look like De Gaulle. He tried blandishment ("You stick with me," he would tell a reporter, "and I'll make you a big man"). He appealed to the better angels of journalism's nature ("I know you don't like your corn pone president") or to the Ultimate Pragmatism ("Remember, I'm the only president you've got"). Nothing worked. Johnson thought there was some secret to it. If he just tried harder, he could solve the mystery and make those smart, mean, ungrateful news bastards like him, and do what he wanted them to do. He was convinced Kennedy had known this secret and many other secrets of charisma while he, Lyndon Johnson, did not. For which he admired and hated Kennedy. Johnson could not live with what he had.

Nixon left press relations essentially to his press secretary. But it was not a matter of faith in the expertise of Ron Ziegler. Nixon was nutty but not stupid. It was simply because he loathed and feared reporters. Absolutely despised them. Wished to avoid contact with them. On presidential trips, most of the press travels on a separate plane, but a small "pool" of reporters accompanies the president on Air Force One. The pool is confined to a small area in the rear of the plane. Once Nixon came into the rear area when the reporters were not there. Pointing to the empty press seats, he commented to a group of Air Force stewards and Secret Service agents: "It sure smells better back here, doesn't it?" The word got around.[8]

Statistics are not a reliable guide to the role of a presidential press secretary. Eisenhower was in office eight years and had only one press secretary, Hagerty. Nixon was in office five and a half years and had one press secretary, Ziegler. Carter was in office four years and had one press secretary, Jody Powell. But while Hagerty and Powell had a substantial amount of power and influence, Ziegler had very little, until the final days. This, as it turned out, saved his skin. However, the fact that Hagerty and Powell had a lot of clout did not mean they were similar in other respects. Hagerty knew a great deal about journalism. Powell knew very little.

Kennedy was president for not quite three years and had one press secretary, Pierre Salinger. Johnson was president for five years and had five press secretaries—Salinger, George Reedy, Bill Moyers, Robert Fleming and George Christian. Six if Joe Laitin is counted, and he should be. Things were never simple with Johnson; once he had two press secretaries at the same time. Ford served two and a half years and had two press secretaries, but one of them was done in by his principles. After only a month on the job, Jerry ter Horst resigned when Ford pardoned Nixon. Ter Horst was succeeded by Ron Nessen, who told reporters he was "a Ron but not a Ziegler." Peter Lisagor of the *Chicago Daily News* immediately commented that "two Rons don't make a right." Lisagor apparently knew something.

Some press secretaries have been good at the technical side of their job. Some have been policymakers. Others have not been notably proficient in either role. Hagerty—by all measurements the best press secretary in history—was a superb technician. But he also dominated the Eisenhower administration's press policy and operated in some other policy areas as well.

Salinger understood the technical, journalistic aspects of the job but was not greatly interested in them. He had a voice in press policy, but on other important issues he was not in Kennedy's innermost circle of advisers. Kennedy was informed on October 15, 1962 that aerial photographs had revealed Soviet missiles in Cuba, but Salinger was not told about them until October 21, seven days later.[9] Salinger was an intelligent, witty, somewhat cynical man. He conducted day-to-day press relations with a sort of sloppy verve. On the big stuff, however, he was strictly an adjunct to Kennedy.

Lyndon Johnson so arranged things that it was difficult for any member of his staff to do a good job. After Kennedy was assassinated, Salinger stayed on for a while at LBJ's urging. Then he departed for California to pursue a political career, and Reedy became press secretary. One day, Johnson told a group of reporters, including myself, that Salinger had called him from California about a problem facing the administration. Johnson said Salinger had an idea for coping with the problem. The president was impressed. "An honest-to-God idea," said LBJ. "That's the kind of people Kennedy had. They had ideas." Then, his voice dripping with scorn, he added: "And who have I got? *George Reedy.*" When, later on, George Christian became press secretary, Johnson warned him to be wary in dealing with the White House reporters. "Remember," he said, "those people are smarter than you are."[10] He was a wonder at building morale.

Struggling along under these ringing endorsements, Johnson's press secretaries did the best they could. When Reedy was left alone to do his job—which was not often—he could be impressive. His briefing on a national railroad strike was a memorable performance. Thoroughly conversant with the subject, Reedy guided the reporters patiently and skillfully through the issues and complexities of the strike. His finest hour—but there were not many of them, as most of Reedy's weary days were spent being one of Johnson's punching bags.

Moyers, who succeeded Reedy, had little interest in the technical side of the job—announcements, briefings, arranging coverage of events, travel schedules and the like. He preferred the role of policymaker. What Moyers liked to do was to sit down with one or two reporters in his office and talk about the president's options and alternatives in a given situation.

Robert Fleming, then chief of ABC's Washington bureau, had an interesting experience. One day in 1966, Johnson persuaded him to join the White House staff. At a press conference, Johnson announced that Fleming would have the title of deputy press secretary but actually would be "my press secretary." The president emphasized this. He said Fleming "will be doing a good deal of the press secretary's work. As far as I am concerned, I will want to call him my press secretary. . . ." It seemed Fleming would be the press secretary.

Things are not what they seem. In a few masterly words, doublespeak destroyed Bob Fleming. A reporter asked whether Moyers would still have the title of press secretary. Johnson replied: "Special assistant to the president. It has always been that. You can call him press secretary, though, if it gives you any thrill. . . . I don't object to what you call him." Johnson told the reporters they could go right on getting information from Moyers: "If you can't get to me, you can get to Bill. If you can't get to him, you can get to Fleming. . . . I have no objection to your getting to anyone you want to if they know what I am thinking."[11] But Fleming would be "my press secretary." Now we are two.

The reporters considered the situation. They knew Johnson and Moyers were very close, almost a tyrant-and-son relationship. They figured Fleming would have a tough time developing *any* relationship with Johnson, short of evisceration. They knew Moyers was familiar with top-level policy matters, was willing to talk about them and was articulate, although they were not always sure whether he was talking about Johnson's policy or Moyers's policy. Johnson, who had the soul of a KGB agent, knew all about the little sessions in Moyers's office. He was saying, in effect, that they could continue. They did. And after a while, Fleming just faded away. It is cold in Washington.

The last ones in from the cold were George Christian, a technician, and Joseph Laitin, a survivor. Christian was phlegmatically competent and competently phlegmatic. He was Lyndon Johnson's last press secretary, and he held the job for two years, an achievement. Laitin never had the title of press secretary; the highest he got was "acting." Nevertheless, he was a press spokesman and friend to mankind in several administrations.

Nixon's press secretary, Ron Ziegler, was a protégé of Harry Robbins (Bob) Haldeman, a California advertising man who prepared for national destiny by hustling Sani-Flush and Black Flag bug killer. An endless supply of Ron Zieglers is available in Washington. They are the capital's cannon fodder—generation after generation of young men stamped monotonously from the Great American Machine, with eager dentition and Orphan Annie eyes that reflect no light. They were born not yesterday but this morning. On one occasion, Ziegler was asked to comment on an action by the Group of Ten, the name given to the leading industrial nations. An internal struggle took place there on the press secretary's podium. It was obvious Ziegler was not familiar with the Group of Ten. It was like Nixon and the Italian lira. However, Ziegler wished to contrive an answer that would sidestep his ignorance. "Well," he said finally, "we're not wedded to any particular number."

Ford's press secretary, Ron Nessen, and Carter's spokesman, Jody Powell, as well as the strange, the very manipulative press relations of Ronald Reagan, will be discussed in a later chapter on these presidents.

In addition to the press secretary and the extensive news and publicity operation that he directs, the White House has a large array of other machinery for dealing with the news media. Every president since Nixon has had a separate "communications" or "media liaison" office. The purpose of this office is not to deal with the Washington press corps but to bypass it. The message is to be conveyed directly to newspaper editors, news directors of television and radio stations and other opinion-makers across the nation. It is not to be defiled by the presumed bias, the greater knowledge and the dangerous expertise of the Washington reporters. There are, moreover, presidential speechwriters and editors to prepare the message, presidential photographers to capture imperishably every moment of imperialism, and various senior White House staff members, political consultants and presidential polltakers who meet frequently with journalists.

The White House, of course, uses all the ancient and modern techniques of press and public relations. In the Atari Age, the foremost of these is the televised presidential speech. Nothing equals the big TV speech to the nation as the prime method of presidential communication. In addition, the president occasionally has interviews with TV anchormen, prominent columnists, individual reporters or small groups of journalists. There are briefings of all kinds by White House officials and other government sources. These take place constantly, under a variety of conditions and rules. There are trial balloons, manufactured news, surprise announcements and, now and then, planted questions. And there is that most venerable of techniques: the leak.

But next to the televised speech, the machinery that is best known to the American people is the presidential press conference. It is one of the most familiar and most controversial devices. Countless books and academic dissertations have been written about it. Political scientists and journalists dissect it in endless panel discussions and articles. Complaining letters are written to newspapers about it. The presidential press conference has been—and is being—studied to death. It is receiving the same anguished attention that is devoted to whales and California condors—and for the same reason. The presidential press conference is an endangered species.

It is dying young. The presidential news conference is not an ancient institution. Until late in the nineteenth century, presidents handled their press relations on a very individual basis. And usually a very restricted basis. They dealt directly with influential newspaper editors, who were too important to be ignored, or with a few individual reporters whom they knew and trusted. That does happen. They fed these favorites an occasional story—when they dealt with them at all. Usually, the president's secretary was the link with the press. Important announcements were handed out by the secretary or disclosed in a letter to a prominent politician, who then made the news public. Cabinet members and congressmen close to the White House were other sources of presidential news.[12]

Grover Cleveland apparently was the first chief executive who met occasionally with groups of reporters rather than individuals. His relations with the press were described as "dignified."[13] That was Cleveland all right. Theodore Roosevelt brought the reporters into the White House and gave them a room of their own (see Chapter Seven). Roosevelt was acutely aware of publicity's sweet uses. He cultivated some individual reporters assiduously, but he did not hold full-scale press conferences. That honor apparently goes to William Howard Taft, who tried to see the reporters once a week although he did not always make it. Woodrow Wilson, Warren Harding, Calvin Coolidge and Herbert Hoover held press conferences, but they were not the press conferences we know and love. The president could not be quoted directly unless he gave express permission. This he did very seldom. Instead, the reporters had to write that "The president is considering . . ." or "The president is understood to believe . . ." Or they had to attribute his remarks to "a White House spokesman" or "a source close to the White House."[14] It was a portentous day when those "White House sources" were invented. They have endured. Woodrow Wilson was one of the most insistent practitioners of presidential anonymity at press conferences. Hypocrisy also endures; one of Wilson's famous Fourteen Points called for open diplomacy.

Under Harding, Coolidge and Hoover, the reporters had to submit their questions in writing, before the press conference.[15] The president then answered those he wanted to answer and ignored the rest. A story, possibly apocryphal, tells of repeated, unsuccessful efforts to get an answer from Coolidge on some important issue. Finally, the journalists agreed that all of them would submit the same question at the next press conference. Most of them did so. Without a word, Coolidge discarded each question on the vital issue. Then he came to one from a reporter who had not gone along. There is always a reporter who will not go along. "I am asked about the condition of the children of Puerto Rico," said Coolidge. "The condition of the children of Puerto Rico is as follows . . ."

Thus, Franklin Roosevelt was not the first president to hold press conferences. But Roosevelt is the dominant figure in the history of the institution. Its apogee was reached with him, and its decline began after him. FDR loved his encounter sessions with the reporters. He relished them. He used them mightily to his advantage. And when he was gone, a slow and then a rapid deterioration commenced.

Roosevelt was in office for just over twelve years. In that time, he held 998 press conferences. In peacetime, he held two a week. He was scrupulous about it. When the war came, the average dropped to one a week, but the total for the twelve years nevertheless averaged out at six press conferences a month.

Compared to today's press conferences, the transcripts of FDR's sessions make remarkable reading. With only a few days between each one, there were fewer developments for the reporters to ask about. This meant that issues and events could be explored in greater detail— and they were. The questions for the most part were far more specific than they are today. The Roosevelt press conferences went into problems and issues comprehensively. The reporters delved deeply into FDR's programs and often sought his views on legislation on an amendment-by-amendment basis. There were a great many more follow-up questions seeking amplification of previous answers. Things were examined to a degree that would be almost inconceivable at one of the modern East Room extravaganzas.

The reasons for this? It was partly Roosevelt's temperament. It was partly the fact that the times were simpler. But it was mostly a matter of frequency. Only so much could happen between Tuesday and Friday. There wasn't so much to cover. An interesting side impression from reading those old transcripts: Both the president and the reporters come across as better informed than they are today.

Harry Truman was in office almost eight years. He held 322 press conferences. That was 3.4 a month. Today's press corps would be ecstatic if the situation could be restored to Truman's average. But the frequency curve had started downward.

Dwight Eisenhower held 193 press conferences in his eight years as president. This was an average of about two a month. Between Roosevelt and Eisenhower, in other words, the frequency of presidential press conferences decreased by two thirds. The two-a-month pattern held more or less steady under the next two presidents. John F. Kennedy was in office three years and held sixty-four news conferences. This was almost two a month. Lyndon Johnson held 135 press conferences in his five years as president, an average of two a month.

The next big dropoff took place under Richard Nixon. Let's not always see the same hands. In his five and a half years as president, Nixon held thirty-nine press conferences. This was an average of one-half news conference a month, which is not possible except arithmetically. For purposes of comparison with other presidents, it means that Nixon held a press conference approximately every two months. That is a long time between questions.

Jerry Ford improved on Nixon's average but only slightly. He was in office thirty months and held twenty-four press conferences. That was not quite one a month. Jimmy Carter, when he took office, promised to hold two news conferences a month. He did not make it. He held 59 in his four years as president, an average of 1.2 a month. As of September 28, 1982, as this book was nearing completion, Ronald Reagan had been in office twenty months. He had held thirteen press conferences. That was an average of 0.6 a month. So the situation was back to Nixon. The presidential press conference is more than a familiar piece of machinery; it is an essential part of the news process. But it is dying. Why?

On March 8, 1933, Franklin D. Roosevelt held his first presidential press conference. He began by noting that he had met frequently with reporters when he was governor of New York. Then he said: "My hope is that these [presidential news] conferences are going to be merely enlarged editions of the . . . very delightful family conferences I have been holding in Albany for the last four years." The choice of adjective was revealing: "delightful."

On February 8, 1977, Jimmy Carter held *his* first presidential press conference. He began with the promise to meet with reporters twice a month. Then he said: "I look forward to those confrontations with the press to kind of balance out the nice and pleasant things that come to me as president." The choice of noun was revealing: "confrontations."

Roosevelt and Kennedy were the only modern presidents who showed any sign of enjoying their press conferences. Carter and the others did not. FDR viewed his meetings with the reporters as one way of conducting the public's business. Not the only way, certainly, but one. Information about the government's actions was to be conveyed to the public through the reporters. Explanations and reasons were to be given. Not completely, but *something*. Of course, the press conference was also a device for manipulating the news media to the president's advantage. The reporters would be handmaidens in helping his view prevail. But *both* elements were there. Some manipulation took place. Some public business was carried on.

And it was a two-way proposition. The reporters' questions would give Roosevelt an indication of the public's mood. Today's chief executives have resident polltakers to do this for them. That aspect of the press conference is no longer important to them. Nevertheless, a two-way element remains. The press conference is one of the few devices for two-way *communication* between the president and the public. The reporters assume the role of surrogates for the public. On its behalf, they question the president. This infuriates those persons who consider journalists unrepresentative of the values and verities of American life, as defined by those persons. A certain number of people, their minds continuing to function, derive information and insights from watching the nation's leader respond to questions, challenges and criticisms. How he handles himself tells them something. Still others are simply amused or entertained by the spectacle. The presidential press conference strongly resembles the other institutions created by humans. It is not perfect. But, as imperfect as it is, the press conference is two-way communication. There isn't much of that around. Write me a letter. Raise hell.

For most contemporary presidents, however, the press conference has become simply an unpleasant chore. It is to occur as infrequently as possible. When it can be avoided no longer, it is to be got through somehow. It is a confrontation with a group of noisy, tricky, rather dreadful people intent on embarrassment and entrapment. The idea of doing any of the public's business in this forum? No, no, impossible. The journalists and their news organizations are too superficial. They are interested only in the sensational, not the substantive. That was Carter's view.

But there had been aggressive reporters at Roosevelt's press conferences. Reporters pushing and probing and trying to lay traps. What made Roosevelt believe the public's business could be carried out in this way? What made Carter think it could not?

The conventional answer is television. And certainly television has made a giant difference. Millions of people watch a televised presidential news conference. The president's evasions, mistakes, ignorances or weaknesses are seen. His anger or irritation is seen. If he is tense or has something to hide, that is seen or at least sensed. If he falters under pressure, that is seen. His personality is seen. And seen in a way that written words in a newspaper or magazine can never convey. By more people than any newspaper or magazine could ever reach. The consequences of a poor performance on television can be immense. Especially for an ambitious person.

But if the president is skillful and adroit, that is also seen. If he has a good grasp of the issues and problems, that is seen. If he has an attractive personality, that is seen. If the reporters, in his hands, appear foolish, superficial, sensation-minded or unfair, a gaggle of geese or a rabble of rantipoles, that is seen. It is a matter of wonderment that presidents do not hold more press conferences; they almost always show to better advantage than the journalists. And if the president has a sense of humor and is not afraid to let it flash and dart, that is seen best of all. This was Kennedy's great asset; it would have been Roosevelt's if there had been television in his time. A tense and overly serious Jimmy Carter may have lost the 1980 election in one brief moment on the tube. Ronald Reagan glanced in his direction, smiled that easy, practiced actor's smile and said: "There you go again." Two ambitious men. Two driven men seeking the presidency. But one came across as driven and the other did not.

So something deeper has been there right along. Television has magnified it. Television has made it much more difficult to handle. But this *thing,* this terrible thing, has always been there: *The driven man feels he has so much to lose.* It is this anxiety, not television per se, that determines the relationship between presidents and reporters. All journalists—on the tube and in print—are a threat to a president in direct proportion to how driven he is and how much he feels he has to lose.

The president's senior advisers define the relationship in the same way. They know their man. They know the depth of his ambition and the extent to which he can tolerate obstructions to it. They know how he reacts to pressure and criticism—on television or in print. They know whether he has a sense of humor. He usually does not.

So it is not surprising that the man who permitted the first television coverage of presidential press conferences proceeded very slowly and cautiously. There is a general impression that TV coverage of presidential news conferences began early in 1953, when Dwight Eisenhower became president. Ike's press secretary, Jim Hagerty, simply let the cameras in and lo, the brave new world. But it was not like that at all.

Two years went by before Hagerty permitted TV coverage of a press conference. The decision was preceded by months of negotiations between the press secretary and the networks. Veteran Washington correspondents for newspapers viewed the prospect gloomily. One wrote that "such an innovation would greatly change the character of the president's meetings with the press."[16] Sometimes they get it right.

Finally, on January 19, 1955, a presidential press conference was televised for the first time. But it was not live coverage. The nation did not see the news conference as it was actually taking place. It was filmed for later broadcast. Virtually all of Eisenhower's televised press sessions were filmed and then shown later. This gave Hagerty time in which to edit out material that he did not want the public to see.

There was only one live telecast of an Eisenhower press conference in his first term, and it was not in Washington at all. It took place at the Republican national convention in San Francisco, on August 22, 1956. As late as January 1959, however, Ike's Washington press conferences were still being filmed, although Hagerty gradually eased up on the editing as he and Eisenhower grew more accustomed to the innovation.[17] But for all practical purposes, live TV coverage of presidential press conferences began with Kennedy. He was not afraid of fluffs.

The briefing. This familiar piece of machinery, unlike the presidential press conference, is thriving. There will always be a briefing. Even the so-called Doomsday Plane that the president might use in the event of a nuclear war has a briefing room. On one occasion in the Carter administration, some reporters were permitted to go inside this plane. It is formally designated as the National Emergency Airborne Command Post. The acronym for this is NEACP, so the plane is known in military circles as Kneecap. That should fool the Russians.

One of the rooms on Kneecap's main deck is a briefing room. At the front of this room are two screens on which maps or slides could be shown. Nearby is a lectern, with a microphone, for the briefing officer. He would be briefing the president and other senior officials, not reporters, but a briefing is a briefing. It will not be permitted to end the world without a briefing.[18]

There are dozens of briefings in Washington every day. They are held constantly. The best known is the daily briefing by the White House press secretary. The press officers of the State and Defense departments also hold regular briefings for the reporters assigned to those two important sources of news. The press spokesmen for the other Cabinet departments and government agencies brief reporters frequently. When this book says the government seeks maximum publicity for many of its activities, this book means exactly that. In addition, the leaders of both parties in Congress hold briefings, and so do individual senators and representatives. Moreover, there are hundreds, nay thousands, of individuals, groups and organizations that hold briefings. Washington is Briefing City.

What *is* a briefing? It is simply a meeting at which a government official, political figure or private organization presents some news or information to a group of reporters. It may be the announcement of a new government program or policy. It may be a briefing by a group that is opposed to a government program or policy. It may be the presentation of a new government report on some subject, or a study by some private organization such as the Brookings Institution, Common Cause, the American Enterprise Institute or a Ralph Nader group. It may be the monthly statistics on unemployment, inflation, retail sales or housing construction. The president's activities, the secretary of state's meeting with a foreign dignitary, a report on a trip by a Cabinet member or a congressman, the AFL-CIO's latest plan to create jobs or some mayors or governors who have come to Washington for a usually unhappy meeting with federal officials and want to tell the reporters about it. You can tell a reporter about anything. Feel free. The list of subjects on which briefings are held is endless, inasmuch as everyone has an announcement, a proposal, a plan, a report, a study, a criticism or a desire for attention.

The desire for attention. It is a common affliction. Washington is a city of epidemic ambition. It would require an encyclopedia to deal adequately with the ambego—ambition and ego—of the nation's capital. When one of the big egos briefs the press, things get livelier. The reporters are amused. Snickers are heard.

The desire for attention works in strange ways. In 1957, a man named James T. Pyle was head of the Civil Aeronautics Administration. One day, Pyle suddenly fired or transferred six of the agency's seven press officers. He told them they had failed to make the CAA "as glamorous as the FBI." The poor chaps had done their best, but who could compete with J. Edgar Hoover? When I talked to him, Pyle told me: "Our contribution to the nation is just as glamorous as the FBI's, and look at the publicity they get." Pyle said he was not interested in personal publicity. But he added that it was "a useful gimmick" to have his name in the newspapers as a symbol of the CAA. He said he was "willing to sacrifice myself to get the story across." Then he got down to cases. It was his mother. She lived in Far Hills, New Jersey, and she was complaining that she had not seen a word about the CAA in the newspapers for eight months. One of the press officers, Charles E. Planck, was offered that classic governmental alternative: Resign or accept a transfer to Anchorage, Alaska. He was only eleven months away from retirement, so he went to Anchorage. Another, Raymond W. Nathan, was offered Kansas City. He resigned. Sacrifices are required of all.[19]

What happens at a briefing? Usually a press release is given to the reporters. It announces whatever the department, agency or private group wants to announce, and gives details. If the briefing has been called to publicize a report of some sort, copies of the report usually are handed out also. The person or persons conducting the briefing then discuss the announcement or report. When they finish, the reporters ask questions. They seek to clarify points about which they are not certain. They want this or that aspect amplified. They inquire about the background circumstances that prompted the new policy or led to the study. They ask about the political, social or economic factors and the implications for the future. They always want to know what is *going* to happen. No one can tell them, although many try.

There is another category of briefing. This one is simply a get-together between a group of reporters and a government official, politician or other newsworthy person. This person makes himself available to talk about this or that and to answer questions. Often, this type of briefing is initiated by an official for his own purposes. He wants to "background" the reporters on an issue or say something without having his name attached to it. Frequently, however, reporters themselves invite a news source to meet with them. Over the years, groups of journalists have organized regular or semiregular sessions of this sort, and the practice is now fairly widespread. The Sperling Breakfast is one of the best-known examples. It was started in 1966 by Godfrey (Budge) Sperling, Jr., of the *Christian Science Monitor*. Periodically,

Sperling assembles about twenty journalists for ham, eggs and interrogation of presidents, former presidents, presidential candidates,
Cabinet members, White House aides, legislators, political strategists
or Jane Fonda. The questioning is mainly on the standard reportorial
level. Which means that information is sought, and sought with considerable persistence. Senator Charles Percy of Illinois has called it
"the toughest workout in town." But real blood on the floor is rare.
Budge, a gentleman to the core except when offered barbequed spareribs, creates a reasonably polite atmosphere. Even he, however, has
his moments. He once ruined a morning for Senator Jake Garn of
Utah, an ardent ally of Ronald Reagan. "Does Reagan really know
what he's talking about?" Sperling asked. [20]

What is the difference between a press conference and a briefing?
There is no essential difference. Both involve the basic news process:
receiving information, asking questions and then reporting the news.
However, there are nuances. One is based on the prominence of the
person giving the information. Another concerns the ground rules
under which the information is given. The ground rules are a pain in
the ass.

If the session involves a high-ranking official or other well-known
person, and if the information is on the record, it is usually called a
press conference. But most briefings by the White House press secretary and other government press officers are on the record, too. Yet
they are called briefings, not press conferences. There are several reasons for this: The White House and major government departments
hold briefings every day, or at least regularly; the news announced is
usually routine or only moderately important; and press officers are
not especially prominent. There is a hierarchy; "press conference"
sounds more important than "briefing." It is like the captain's barge. It
don't go a bit faster, but it makes the old bastard feel large.

On the other hand, high-ranking officials also hold briefings, lots of
them. When they are called briefings, rather than press conferences, it
is sometimes simply because the official wants to call it a briefing. But
more often it is because his answers are not on the record. They are on
a background or deep background basis. Occasionally, they are off the
record. You have to pay attention when I get into this complicated
stuff.

Some of the ground rules under which the news process operates go
all the way back to Woodrow Wilson. As noted earlier, Wilson insisted
that his statements to reporters must be attributed to "an official
spokesman" or "a high authority." [21] From these misty origins, a set of
rules has evolved that now governs press conferences, briefings and

individual interviews between a reporter and an official (known as one-on-one interviews).

"On the record" means that all statements made by an official can be attributed to him *by name*. His words can be put in direct quotes. He stands behind what he says. This is strongly preferred by the reporters.

"Background" means that the statements must be attributed to "a government official," "an administration official," "a White House source" or some other concealment. Direct quotes can be used, but who is being quoted? Ah, that is a secret. The background procedure is used extensively. Government officials insist that they must have this anonymity if they are to talk frankly to journalists about sensitive matters.

How much additional candor results from background sessions? It varies. There is no doubt that it sometimes produces important information that otherwise would be withheld. But the familiarity-contempt sequence is well known. Background has become a great comfort and convenience for the government. So it is abused. It often cloaks an official who is furnishing information of staggering ordinariness.

During Henry Kissinger's shuttle diplomacy in the Middle East, the background rule became a joke. Kissinger briefed and briefed the reporters who accompanied him. He said each of these many briefings must be attributed to "a senior U.S. official." Kissinger knew very well that this did not fool Israel or the Arab nations. They did not think it was William Jennings Bryan who was holding those briefings. But Kissinger argued that when his statements were masked in this way, they would not require a formal response from either side that might harden its negotiating position.

The problem was that, while expedient, it was dishonest. The reporters traveling with Kissinger grew restive. Richard Valeriani of NBC News, one of the regulars on the trips, wrote later that some of the journalists "felt it was misleading and a little too tricky, since virtually everybody except their readers knew who the 'senior official' was."[22] Their readers. That is, the American public. So, Valeriani wrote, the reporters "became bolder and bolder in their efforts to unmask the 'senior official' to their readers."[23] Little references crept into their stories and broadcasts. The senior official who spoke with a German accent. The senior official who always traveled with Henry Kissinger. In a radio broadcast, Bob Schieffer of CBS described a senior official "who often shows up in various parts of the world where Henry Kissinger happens to be visiting. . . . No one knows his name [but he] knows a lot about U.S. foreign policy. . . ."[24] The reporters put up with a lot of "background" manipulation. They know there are sometimes legitimate reasons for it. But there occasionally comes a point at which they decide the public is being deceived too egregiously. The government is less sensitive. It customarily takes the position that the public exists to be deceived. It is good for them. Builds character.

"Deep background." This variation came into use during World War II. The reporters wanted to know at least something about wartime strategy and operations. Tremendous battles were being fought in Europe and the Pacific and elsewhere. Thousands of Americans were being killed. The journalists wanted to be able to tell the nation something about the reasons for these costly battles—their objectives, their justification. Government officials were willing to discuss these things to some extent, but serious risks obviously were involved. The military chiefs, in particular, could not afford the slightest chance that their plans would become known in advance. So a compromise was devised by Ernest K. Lindley of *Newsweek*. It is still referred to occasionally as the Lindley Rule. But it is commonly known as deep background. It is still used fairly frequently.

Under this rule, the reporter cannot attribute information to anyone. Nor can direct quotes be used. The journalist must report the material strictly on his own authority. He must write it this way: "It is understood that . . ." or "It is said that . . ." Occasionally, he grows daring and uses "reliable sources," but that comes close to a violation. Strictly interpreted, "deep background" means that the reporter cannot give any indication whatever that the information came from an official source, and he must paraphrase what the official said. He then hopes someone will believe the stuff.

"Off the record." The journalists, of course, like this rule least of all. There actually have been occasions when reporters have walked out of interviews or briefings when an official announced that he was going to speak only on an off-the-record basis. They were protesting a rule that dictates that the information cannot be printed or broadcast at all. The official is going to give the reporters some information for their "guidance" or their general knowledge. He is very altruistic. He wishes them to be better-informed citizens. But the material cannot be publicized in any way. For a journalist, this is an occupational contradiction.

However, there are nuances again. Let us now praise famous nuances. Without them, much less would be known. The nuance is that off-the-record information seldom stays off the record very long.

Strictly speaking, the reporter who accepts off-the-record information cannot even tell it to his bureau chief, editor or producer or to other reporters who were not at the briefing. Especially not to them. He is like that German sergeant on television a few years ago. He knows nothing, *nothing*. But this is not realistic. The material almost always leaks out somehow. Journalists who were not at an off-the-record briefing are not bound by the rule. If they can get the information somehow, they are free to use it. Not wishing to be scooped, the reporter who *was* at the briefing infiltrates the information into his stories bit by bit, over a period of time. A short period of time.

A more frequent tactic is on-the-spot negotiation. When an official announces that he is going off the record, the reporters usually try to talk him out of it. If that fails, they interrupt the flow with pleas to be allowed to attribute this or that piece of information. "Oh, come on now," they say. "*That* doesn't have to be off the record, does it? Let us put that on background." The situation can get immensely confusing. No one can remember what can be used and what cannot. The reporters' notebooks are filled with brackets and scrawls designating certain things as off the record, other things as printable. The grand jury can figure it out later.

The government knows all this. An experienced official may label something off the record in order to conceal his identity even more deeply than background or deep background. Or he may do it to emphasize the importance of the material, or to delay its publication for a few days. But he seldom does it in the belief that it actually is going to *stay* secret. Not if he has been in Washington more than twenty-four hours. If he *really* wants to keep something secret, he tells no one, *no one*.

The only way to understand the confusion is to realize that the government sets the ground rules, for its own purposes. It says to the reporter, in effect, take the information on a background (nonattribution) basis or we will give it to some other reporter who will. That is the competitive rub. Most Washington journalists accept the ground rules. As a matter of fact, most of them have long since become accustomed to the arrangement and are quite comfortable with it, as long as they get their piece of the action. A few resent the procedure deeply, but one and all feel there is little they can do about it. They could unite in protest. They could cry: Enough of this nonsense. Give us the news on the record, with a name and face attached to it, or we won't show up at your damn briefings. But they are almost never willing to do this.

Why not? Because they need the news. Their newspapers, wire services and networks assigned them to Washington to get the news. The home office may understand the problem, but it does not wish to be scooped by an opposition reporter who went along with the ground rules. The office will give you a ticket to see the chaplain—but first, get the news. It is interesting to speculate on the stalemate that would result if the Washington press corps boycotted all briefings until the government agreed that everything would be on the record. The government would suffer a grievous loss of publicity. The media would suffer a grievous loss of news. Eyeball to eyeball. Who would blink first? The smart money would be on a media blink.

Lyndon Johnson defined the ground rules as Humpty-Dumpty defined words: "When I use a word, it means just what I choose it to mean." Many persons do this, and are then surprised when they get low marks on college examinations. Johnson once asked a reporter for *Life* magazine: "Why didn't you use that story I gave you a few days ago?" The reporter replied: "But Mr. President, you told me that was off the record." Said Johnson, with some exasperation: "I *know* that, but why didn't you use it?"[25]

I regret to disclose that the same thing happened to me. Once Johnson flew to Atlanta to attend a funeral. I was the newspaper pooler on Air Force One. This meant I would write a pool report for the journalists traveling on the press plane, relaying any news that was disclosed on Air Force One. During the flight, Johnson gave the poolers a medium-size story, nothing earthshaking. Then he swore us to secrecy. It was totally off the record. He was extremely insistent: "Nothing in the pool report, you hear? Not a word."

On the press bus into Atlanta, Bill Lawrence of ABC questioned me about the flight. Lawrence was a tough, experienced veteran. He was suspicious of the pool report. It was entirely too short for a flight with Lyndon Johnson. Lawrence smelled a rat, and when Lawrence smelled a rat, he was Gordon Liddy. He gave me a very hard time: "You mean you were on that plane with Lyndon Johnson for an hour and a half and you never *saw* him? He never *talked* to you?"

However, the machinery being slow that day, I did not fink. I said nothing. I wrote nothing. I should have. Never mind honor; get to the typewriter. A few days later, I picked up the morning papers. There was the story. It was attributed to White House sources. Inquiry disclosed what Johnson had done. He had waited a day or so, and then when the story did not appear, he simply called in another group of reporters and gave it to them.

Johnson was very fond of summoning the pool reporters to his compartment on Air Force One and giving them what he regarded as a briefing. This consisted of talking at them for hours. When he became president, he had the executive compartment enlarged. Behind his big, kidney-shaped desk, there was a large chair. The Secret Service agents called it The Throne. Now, this was an unusual chair. At the touch of a button, the chair went up or down. Before the reporters came in, Johnson elevated himself. The reporters sat on a rather low couch facing the desk. The press looked up at the president. The president looked down on the press. He never understood the consequences. The consequences were human.

On these imperial occasions, I was reminded of a scene in a Charlie Chaplin movie, *The Great Dictator*. Chaplin, as dictator Adenoid Hynkel, is conferring with Jack Oakie, who portrays dictator Benzini Napaloni. For some reason, they are in barber chairs. Each wants to be higher than the other. They keep raising their chairs until they reach the ceiling. Life imitates art.

Joe Laitin, a government spokesman in several administrations, recalls the ultimate ground-rule story. A press officer was being hammered hard for information about an important development. He was under stern instructions from his superiors to say nothing. The reporters were equally determined that he would say something. They questioned him persistently. Finally he burst out: "No comment! And that's off the record!"[26]

All government briefings have three purposes. They convey information, they convey image and they convey selectivity. The quality of government spokespersons varies from administration to administration. Many are able and responsible people who do their job conscientiously. They are not colorful personalities, being *apparatchiki*, but they sometimes make a sincere effort to give out facts and explain complex matters. However, they always operate under limits. These restrictions are imposed by their superiors. Being political, these superiors are as much concerned with image and selectivity as with substance.

I. F. Stone, one of the most valuable journalists ever to work in Washington, once said: "Every government is run by liars, and nothing they say should be believed."[27] While sympathizing with his outrage, let us rephrase it: Every government is run by people who seek to wield and retain power. To do this, they must convince the public of certain things: that their policies are correct. That their facts and explanations should be accepted. That they are in control of events and situations. That sounds nicer. And it comes out at the same place.

Therefore, most briefings are a complicated, subtle mixture of substance and image. The information is the substance. The image is that of a government whose policies are coping effectively with problems, achieving results and maintaining control. If there are conflicts between substance and image, they are easily resolved. Information is presented selectively. Things are left out. Things are denied.

The reporters want the information. They try to get as much of it as possible. They believe it will be of interest and value to the public. They resist the image-making to whatever extent they can. They have two main defenses against this news management: the exercise of news judgment and the expansion of the news process. The government may *say* something is important, but the journalists reserve the right to agree or disagree. Their news judgment may put the story on the front page or on page 72, just above the truss ads. It may lead the evening TV news or be downplayed or ignored. And, as mentioned earlier in this chapter, the journalists expand the basic news process to report alternative explanations, proposals and criticisms that challenge or dispute the government's version.

Nevertheless, even after doing this, the journalists are of the world, worldly. They know they are being used to convey images. That is the price of the information. So they cooperate, willy-nilly, in an image-making process. It is symbiosis. It is manipulation. It is communication. It is propaganda. Take your choice. All choices are correct.

Taking all this into account, it is easy to define an ideal briefing officer from the reporters' point of view. He would convey maximum information and minimum image. He would reveal the information his superiors authorized him to reveal—and argue that more should be revealed. He would exercise as much leeway as he could get away with. Then he would exceed his authority if his common sense or his concept of public service told him that his instructions were arbitrary, unnecessary, unjustified or undemocratic. We pass over outright illegality. Further, the ideal briefer would explain things as fully as he could. And he would not exaggerate. Above all, he would not exaggerate. He would understate. He would deal in facts. He would make no grandiose claims as to progress, achievement or control. He would leave the image-making to the power-seekers. He would get into a lot of trouble.

The image part would be the hardest. The White House press secretary considers image-making a fundamental aspect of his job. So do most of the senior members of the president's staff. Political scientists Michael Grossman and Martha Kumar, after a two-year study in the 1970's, concluded that at least 30 percent and more likely 60 to 85 percent of the White House staff is engaged directly in putting a high gloss on the president's image.[28] Cabinet members, agency directors and their press officers likewise give imagery a high priority. As a result, an ideal briefer nowadays is hard to find.

And yet the thing gets done somehow. It gets done mainly because it *has* to get done. Consider the alternatives and you will keep on trucking. Democracy could survive without the posturing. And how it could. But it could not survive without the information. So it gets both.

There are many briefings that simply convey information. It is often very valuable information, enabling the reporters to write more complete, better-informed stories. At the other end of the spectrum, a briefing may consist almost entirely of swagger. A classic example was Ron Nessen's rodomontade after the Vladivostok meeting between Jerry Ford and Leonid Brezhnev in 1974. Ford and Brezhnev had reached agreement on a missile and bomber ceiling. Henry Kissinger warned press secretary Nessen not to overplay it—"I think the president should be modest," he said.[29] Kissinger knew the agreement had been years in the making and Ford was simply the last-minute beneficiary. It is also possible that he did not want Ford to get all the credit. Nevertheless, it was good advice. Big-power agreements can come unstuck, and exaggeration can backfire. But Nessen had image-making on his mind and vodka in his bloodstream. Bursting into the pool compartment on Air Force One, he informed the reporters that "Richard Nixon could not achieve this in five years [but] President Ford achieved it in three months."[30] Nessen's understated technique was widely remarked.

The most frequent combination lies between the extremes. It is possible to convey information and image simultaneously. A balance can be maintained that is more or less tolerable. Ve haf vays, as a very skillful briefer used to say. It is possible because the reporters accept image-making as the price of information. If they are getting the goods, they grumble less and write fewer stories about White House puffery. And vice versa.

That was Kissinger's secret. There is no doubt that many reporters were beguiled by the Herr Doktor. Their stories lacked perspective. They did not know what Kissinger was doing when he was not holding briefings. But in his glory days as the White House's super briefer, Kissinger was giving them *information*. His command of the material of foreign policy was awesome. His briefings on the nuclear arms negotiations, in particular, were unmatched in depth and in grasp of detail. The journalists had never encountered strategic arms briefings of this caliber— and they never have since.

Thus, it is a balancing act. The reporters must constantly evaluate the information they are given. They must try to separate the substance from the posturing and the deception. This is no more difficult than Riemannian geometry, which deals with the fourth dimension. There are few blacks and whites. It is mostly grays. The Ford-Brezhnev agreement, for all Nessen's bombast, was important and newsworthy. How much was substance and how much was swagger? But the journalists cannot even begin the sorting-out process unless they have information.

When it comes to officials who conduct briefings, the reporters are like the Supreme Court justice and pornography: They know a good one when they see one. Kissinger, John F. Kennedy, Jim Hagerty, Bill Moyers, Joe Laitin and Robert McCloskey (the State Department's chief press officer from 1963 to 1973) were among the few who were adept at this delicate art. Lyndon Johnson never figured it out. And neither did:

- Ronald Reagan's first secretary of state, Alexander Haig, who invaded the White House briefing room—horse, foot and dragoons—to proclaim that he was "in control here" after Reagan was shot. During the Watergate crisis, the reporters had discovered that whatever nature had in mind for Haig, it was not briefings. He was asked whether he or someone else had ordered a particular action. It was not an end-of-Western-civilization affair. Just an ordinary question that could have been answered with a simple yes or no. But Haig drew himself up rigidly, threw out his chest and shouted at the top of his voice: *"Guilty!"* The reporters wondered how many times *he* had seen *Patton*.
- Jimmy Carter's national security assistant, Zbigniew Brzezinski, whose briefings were lectures, complete with maps and a pointer and a laborious joke to warm up the class. Worst of all, they were freshmen lectures. Brzezinski's briefing before Carter's 1978 foreign trip was almost as long as the trip itself. The reporters, many of whom had been covering foreign policy for years, listened raptly as Brzezinski disclosed that the British empire was no more. Fancy that. As a result of the downfall of empire, Brzezinski said, many nations were now free of British domination and were asserting themselves. Imagine. Furthermore, Brzezinski revealed, a population explosion was changing the international picture. Rip out page 1—I've got a story that'll blow the lid off this town. Brzezinski then gave the increase in the world's population every fifty years since 1750. He did not miss a single fifty-year interval. The sound of notebooks slamming shut could be heard all over the room. However, the briefer then got down to the significance of it all. What

would it mean for Carter's trip? What specific situations and problems would he encounter? That was what the reporters were there to find out. The notebooks flipped open. "The broad policy implications of those changes are, first, that the reaction of the West to the politically-awakening world has to be largely on the level of creative innovation," Brzezinski said. There was more of this. Much more. And every single word of this staggering ordinariness was on background. Brzezinski could not be identified as the source. Another international crisis averted.

No briefings are more important for the White House's image-makers than those that take place on Air Force One. A presidential trip displays the chief executive at his most glorious. He descends from the skies in a magnificent jet airplane, accompanied by the boast of heraldry, the pomp of power and members of Congress seeking reelection. If it is a domestic trip, he is greeted by local dignitaries and clamorous crowds. On a foreign venture, he is welcomed by honor guards, booming cannon and famous statesmen. Occasionally there is a mishap. In June 1974, seeking to escape Watergate, Richard Nixon made a foreign trip. When he arrived in Amman, the capital of Jordan, the military band at the airport was playing "The Washington Post March." But most presidential trips are a different march: the "Grand March" from *Aïda*. Dramatic, colorful, richly sonorous, ripely overblown. It is image-making time. So the press pool on Air Force One is briefed and briefed.

Sometimes the president does the briefing himself. More often, it is a Cabinet member, the president's press secretary, some other White House staffer or a political strategist. On a domestic trip, the briefer may discuss the political situation in the state or region being visited, the results of the latest poll, or the impact of a presidential program on the area. On an overseas trip, the secretary of state or national security assistant furnishes background information on U.S. relations with the nations on the president's itinerary, the subjects to be discussed or the status of negotiations on various issues.

The pool reporters take notes, ask questions and then write a pool report for their colleagues on the press plane. Good, solid, useful stuff most of the time. But image-making all the time. The president's accomplishments on the trip are extolled and extolled.

On Air Force One, the pool reporters are confined to the rear of the plane. Four of them—always the AP and UPI reporters and usually the newspaper and television poolers—sit in four seats that face each other, with a table in the middle. It is a cramped situation, with very little leg room. If there are other poolers, they sit in nearby seats. The reporters are not permitted to go into other compartments of the plane unless invited to do so by someone in authority.

So there they sit. Cramped and captive, but pampered. On the table is a dish of candy, chewing gum and cigarettes, frequently replenished. There are individual stereo headsets with six channels—usually two for pop music, two for country, one for specialty numbers and one for classical. Air Force stewards serve drinks and food. A typical dinner on Air Force One: tossed green salad, broiled filet mignon, baked stuffed potato, green beans amandine, rolls and butter, German chocolate cake, choice of beverage. Real men don't eat quiche.

There are printed menus. There are also Air Force One drinking glasses, cigarettes, matches, napkins and place cards. Imprinted on them are the presidential seal and the words "Air Force One" or "Aboard the Presidential Aircraft" or "Welcome Aboard Air Force One." These imperial souvenirs cost the taxpayers dearly, especially since the stewards report much pilferage by the prominent passengers on the president's airplane. Even the reporters sometimes snitch a few mementos, to assist them in writing books.

So there they sit, eating, drinking, talking and listening to the old stereo. Just like home. But after a while, someone decides it is time to brief the pool. Why, here comes the national security assistant. What do you suppose he wants?

Or perhaps it is someone even more important. Richard Nixon's encounters with the pool reporters were rare. They were unusual. They were mystifying. In July 1969, Nixon was flying across the Pacific on his way to Vietnam. Suddenly he appeared at the rear of the plane. The reporters had not asked to talk to the president, so they assumed he had something he wanted to say about the trip. Or about some other important matter. At the least, they assumed, he was making himself available for questions. So they asked him a question about Vietnam.

"You know," Nixon replied, "the [Washington] Senators and my friend Ted Williams [the Senators' manager at that time] have gone into a little slump. What they ought to do is make some trades."

That took care of Vietnam. So the reporters decided to try him on the nation's economy. He answered with lengthy additional comments about baseball.

So they tried the Russian space program. He replied by saying that Christian Adolph Jurgensen, then the quarterback for the Washington Redskins, was getting a little old. In consequence, the president said, Sonny was having trouble with his passing. Then Nixon turned around and walked back to his compartment.

It made an interesting pool report.

III

RELATIONS

I hear new news every day [said the melancholy Burton] . . . those ordinary rumors of war, plagues, fires, inundations, thefts, murders, massacres, meteors, comets, spectrums, prodigies, apparitions, of towns taken, cities besieged in France, Germany, Turkey, Persia, Poland, etc., daily musters and preparations, and such like, which these tempestuous times afford, battles fought, so many men slain, monomachies, shipwrecks, piracies and seafights, peace, leagues, stratagems, and fresh alarums. A vast confusion of vows, wishes, actions, edicts, petitions, lawsuits, pleas, laws, proclamations, complaints, grievances are daily brought to our ears. . . . Now come tidings of weddings, maskings, mummeries, entertainments, jubilees, embassies, tilts and tournaments, trophies, triumphs, revels, sports, plays: then again, as in a new-shifted scene, treasons, cheating tricks, robberies, enormous villainies of all kinds, funerals, burials, deaths of princes, new discoveries, expeditions: now comical, then tragical matters. Today we hear of new lords and officers created, tomorrow of some great men deposed, and then again of fresh honors conferred; one is let loose, another imprisoned; one purchaseth, another breaketh; he thrives, his neighbor turns bankrupt; now plenty, then again dearth and famine; one runs, another rides, wrangles, laughs, weeps, etc. Thus I daily hear . . . both public and private news . . . the gallantry and misery of the world—jollity, pride, perplexities and cares, simplicity and villainy, subtlety, knavery, candor and integrity, mutually mixed and offering themselves. . . .[1]

That was the news in 1621. The reporter was Robert Burton. He was an Englishman and an observer of the human condition. That tended to make him mournful. He described himself as "a mere spectator of other men's fortunes and adventures, which methinks are diversely presented unto me. . . ."[2]

They don't make monomachies like they used to. Otherwise, nothing has changed. The news remains as Burton defined it: a vast diversity. The journalists bring a tremendous variety of information to the public. They report on government and politics at the international, national, regional, state and community levels. Summit conferences, presidential campaigns, economic problems macro, micro and impossible, legislation of broad scope—and local ordinances. The journalists cover wars, revolutions, terrorists, massacres and disasters. They cover crimes and criminals and trials. They report on poverty and deprivation and affluence and avarice. They tell of the abuse of children, the delinquency of juveniles and the ignorance of adults. They cover endless disputes over an endless number of things: the fate of the environment, the exploitation of women, the victimization of minorities, the bilking of consumers, the mistreatment of the aged, infirm and handicapped, the ethics of abortion, the morality of this and the evil of that. As a result, much of the news reported by the journalists is either intensely controversial or highly unpleasant

The late Philip L. Graham, publisher of the *Washington Post*, called journalism the first rough draft of history.[3] But Edward Gibbon, one of the greatest of historians, had already described the final draft. Human history, Gibbon decided, was "little more than the register of the crimes, follies and misfortunes of mankind."[4] So the news, since it is destined to be history, is doomed to be bad, bad, bad.

But the journalists also bring news of human achievement and enjoyment. Humanity continues to be intellectually curious and culturally creative even while it is bashing and smashing itself. So the reporters tell of science, medicine and education. They tell of research and discoveries and advancement of knowledge in physics, chemistry, archeology, anthropology, space exploration and a host of other fields. They cover the theater, music, books, dance, painting, sculpture, design and the other arts. They furnish news of sports, movies and a multitude of other recreations and entertainments. They bring news of crimes, follies and misfortunes, but they bring news of accomplishments and worthwhile things as well. Human progress may be real or illusory. Either way, the journalists report it. Gibbon was just tired.

This book deals with only one aspect of the diversity: the dealings between journalists and the government officials and politicians whom they cover. These dealings are shaped and determined by two fundamental relationships: the symbiotic relationship and the critical relationship. In the view of some persons, there is another: the adversary relationship.

1. The symbiotic relationship. This also can be called the cooperative or basic news-gathering relationship. In symbiosis, two organisms that are very different form an association that is beneficial to each. That fits the press and the government. Presidents, members of Congress and other politicians, and even unelected bureaucrats, find it greatly to their advantage to have their views and programs receive the widest possible publicity. Also their real or claimed accomplishments. Journalists, on the other hand, depend on government officials and politicians for news, information and the official explanation of events. The government must have its publicity, and the press must have its sources of news, come what may. These implacable needs exert a continuing pressure on both sides that holds the relationship together. Like Mr. and Mrs. Jack Sprat, linked inseparably down the corridors of time by metabolic necessity.

As a result, the ordinary, day-to-day process of news-giving and news-receiving involves a considerable degree of cooperation. At the White House and elsewhere in government, announcements are made, press releases are distributed, coverage of events is arranged and the rest of the daily news routine is conducted in relative amity.

Two political scientists, Michael B. Grossman and Martha J. Kumar, were admitted to the Eleusinian mysteries of the White House pressroom in the mid-1970's. They spent two years observing the dealings between reporters and White House officials on an almost daily basis. Considering the impact of Vietnam and Watergate on the press-government relationship, they reached a somewhat surprising conclusion: There is at least as much cooperation as conflict.

"In contrast to the view that they are adversaries," Grossman and Kumar wrote, ". . . the White House and the news media are involved in a continuing relationship rooted in permanent factors that affect both sides no matter who is president or who is doing the reporting. Continuing forces shape both sides more than specific incidents, however traumatic, or the impact of particular personalities, however unusual. *What's more, the co-operative elements in this relationship are at least as strong as those that are antagonistic,* for a fundamental reason: presidents and news people depend on each other in their efforts to do the job for which they are responsible [emphasis added]."[5] The traumatic incidents, of course, were Vietnam and Watergate, and the unusual personalities were Lyndon Johnson's and Richard Nixon's. But Grossman and Kumar were observing the symbiotic relationship at work. They came away convinced that it had survived such tribulations because each side got so much out of it.

Because it essentially involves only the basic news process, the symbiotic relationship is not usually a matter of great controversy. People will argue about anything, but generally speaking, the symbiotic relationship is much less disputatious than the next two relationships.

2. The adversary relationship. Some people are convinced that this term sums up the *real* relationship between the news media and the government. Never mind the day-to-day cooperation; that just applies to the routine stuff. What the media are *really* out to do is to get the president. That is, if he is a conservative president.

"Adversary relationship" is a dry and legalistic term, as befits the clash of institutions. It came into vogue during the Nixon administration, which was big on law, lawyers and law-breaking. No one knows who first applied the term to the media's attitude toward the government, or when. However, Nixon used it at the first meeting of his Cabinet (see Chapter Nine), and the rest of the boys picked it up.

It meant that the news media were unrelentingly hostile toward conservative administrations, and especially that of Richard Nixon. The media, dominated by a liberal elite, were implacably bent on discrediting Nixon and all his works. On the other hand, the journalists displayed a loving partiality for liberal administrations and liberal programs. Nixon has departed from the scene, more or less, but the adversary concept remains entrenched in the minds of some as the true description of the media-government relationship.

The description is faulty on two counts: accuracy and reality. Other than that, it is a world-beater. It is inaccurate because it is a legal term incorrectly applied to journalism. A prosecutor, in an adversary posture toward a defendant, operates with a legal arsenal that is not available to a reporter—and properly not. Journalists cannot subpoena evidence. They have no legal power to compel people to talk to them. They have no power to put people under oath and require them to tell the truth or face a charge of perjury. It is not a crime to lie to a reporter, which is the main reason so many lies turn up in the news. If the news media uncover indications of wrongdoing, the wrongdoer suffers no legal punishment unless law enforcement agencies proceed against him. He may suffer social opprobrium, and it may be very harsh. He may indeed undergo a "trial" in the media, but the only penalty is public scorn. He does not pay a fine or go to jail unless a jury and judge decide he should. The press can expose and alert and cause all kinds of embarrassment, but it cannot convict in any legal sense. This delicate distinction should be kept in mind when the power of the news media is examined. Presumably it has been noted by the many malefactors who have escaped with only a bad press.

The adversary relationship also has survived its many encounters with reality. In presidential campaigns, for instance, the Republican candidate almost always enjoys a lopsided lead over the Democratic nominee in editorial endorsements. In 1968, every newspaper proprietor in the nation had every reason to know exactly what kind of person Richard Nixon was. The evidence had been there for years (see Chapter Nine). Of course, it could be ignored. That is a great convenience. So a survey by *Editor and Publisher* magazine midway through the campaign showed that Nixon had been endorsed by 499 daily newspapers, while Democratic candidate Hubert Humphrey had been endorsed by 93. In the middle of the 1980 campaign, Ronald Reagan had been endorsed by 221 dailies and Jimmy Carter by 59.[6]

But that is old stuff. Newspapers do not determine the outcome of presidential elections anymore. It is television. With its winks and sneers and lifted eyebrows, its carefully edited film footage, and its cleverly slanted "commentaries" by Ivy League liberals, directed at an audience of millions whose intellects are presumed to be despicable. The adversary relationship would be lost without its television. Absolutely indispensable to the theory.

But another team of political scientists—Michael J. Robinson and Margaret A. Sheehan of Catholic University in Washington—studied the news coverage of the 1980 presidential campaign by the most influential and controversial television network, CBS. They also examined the campaign reporting of a major wire service, UPI. When the study began, Robinson said, the researchers anticipated that the news coverage would be "highly subjective." Instead, they found "much less subjectivity than we expected, and *virtually no partisan bias* [emphasis added]."[7] What a dirty trick. It turned out to be professionalism.

It is important to try to look at the American news media *as a whole*. Unfortunately, few citizens have the time, the resources or the inclination to do this. It is easy to find fault with an individual newspaper story or TV newscast. An important fact or point of view may be omitted, or the reader or viewer may simply disagree with the reporter's approach, his attitude or his conclusions. However, the news media are engaged in a continuous game of catch-up ball. If an individual story was incomplete—which could make it seem biased, since important elements may have been left out—very often there will be another story a day or so later. This one will try to give a more complete picture. It broadens the original "spot news" story, adds background, fills in omissions. These are often called news analysis or interpretive stories, and they are. But they are also catch-ups from an earlier story. First-rate newspapers do this frequently. Television news does some of it and should do more.

That is why the Robinson-Sheehan study was important. It examined the performance of CBS and UPI over an entire political campaign. An equally important study was conducted by political writer Walter Karp. It dealt with news coverage by the three major TV networks over the entire first year of the Reagan administration. Karp's conclusion: The network news programs, *viewed as a whole over a substantial period of time*, covered almost the entire spectrum of American political opinion. At one time or another, they reflected the views of the far right, the near right, the old right, the new right and all the little rights. They also reflected the middle of the road, the neoconservative liberals (the Democratic "hawks with a heart") and the traditional liberals. The only opinion that Karp found consistently frozen out of TV news? The *far left*. At last, an adversary relationship.

Karp found that the networks differed sharply in their political outlook. But they were not always predictable. Their reactions to the news often did not conform to popular impressions. Upon examination, the stereotypes suffered the common fate of stereotypes:

- CBS, supposedly the liberal network, went into a "Cold War lather" when the Communist regime suppressed the Solidarity movement in Poland. CBS's reporting, Karp said, "seemed determined to further the cause of American intervention" in Poland. CBS's broadcasts sounded like that old Republican free-the-captive-nations-of-Eastern-Europe rhetoric.
- NBC, in contrast, "treated the Polish news with notable calm and detachment." That was strange, Karp noted, because NBC's *Nightly News* has long had an image of "old-fashioned Republicanism." However, it tended to be midwestern isolationist Republicanism, not eastern internationalist Republicanism. On the other hand, Karp said, "NBC's report on the Marxist regime in Nicaragua was so hostile [that] it verged on the inflammatory."
- ABC was initially "calm [and] detached" about the Polish crisis, and it remained cool and analytical about some aspects of the situation. But it soon joined CBS in viewing the crackdown on Solidarity "as if it somehow menaced America." Karp concluded that ABC was the "least consistent" of the networks in its politics, but "on the whole . . . it has cast its lot with Reagan and the Republican right."
- On the other hand, ABC was intensely skeptical of Reagan's "Libyan menace story," Karp found. So was NBC, which sharply rebuked the White House for leaking reports that Colonel Qaddafi's hit squads were

about to blow away America's leaders. However, Karp pointed out, the "liberal" network, CBS, accepted the Libyan story without question. There is a journalistic cliché: The reporters call 'em as they see 'em. The temptation to use clichés must be resisted.

- CBS was predictably probing and critical in its coverage of Reagan's economic policies. At last, some consistency. NBC played down the recession as late as December 1981, but in the following month it began an extended and penetrating critique of Reagonomics. Said Karp: "It became clear after watching NBC News for several weeks that its old-fashioned Republicanism was deeply offended" by Reagan's economic program. But, he added, "ABC most certainly was not."

The viewing public, in other words, can find most of the American political spectrum on its television screen—if TV is evaluated *as a whole*. The conclusion? The world of TV news according to Karp? "The network news shows," he wrote, "represent, with considerable fidelity, the active political forces in this country."[8]

3. The critical relationship. The right wing has simply renamed this fine old relationship. It has renamed it pejoratively. It calls it an adversary relationship. But the traditional term, "critical relationship," remains the most accurate description of the dealings between the news media and the government. The press is the permanent, resident *critic* of government. A critic, not an adversary. When they do their job well—which is not always the case by any means—the news media draw attention to the mistakes, shortcomings, abuses and corruptions of those in power. And they do this impartially, regardless of which party and which individuals are in office.

Impartiality, of course, is the crucial word. Nixon's central argument was that the media were out to get him because he was Nixon and because he was a Republican. He had done things for which the liberal establishment media could never forgive him. His chief offense was that he had brought down that establishment arbiter elegantiarum, Alger Hiss. But as the years passed, Nixon's theory wore a bit thin. In 1948, when Whittaker Chambers denounced Hiss as a Communist spy, Carl Bernstein was four years old and Bob Woodward was five. They had no personal knowledge of the Hiss case. But later, as young reporters investigating the Watergate burglary, they knew a good crime story when they saw one.

But ignore Nixon's personality, if possible. What about the rest of his theory? That the media were against him because he was a Republican? Had he been a Democrat, would all have been well? Under this hypothesis, the news media should have swooned in ecstasy over John F. Kennedy, Lyndon Johnson and Jimmy Carter. The first was a Democrat who advocated moderately liberal programs. The second was a Democrat who put through very liberal programs. The third, although not as liberal, was certainly a Democrat. If American journalism is in thrall to a liberal bias, Kennedy, Johnson and Carter should have got a free ride. But the news media criticized all three of these presidents vigorously and persistently. It is salutary to recall these things, as many persons were not even born this morning but this afternoon.

The press criticized the slow pace of Kennedy's legislative program, his delay in proposing a civil rights bill, the failure of the Bay of Pigs invasion, the appointment of one brother as attorney general and the nepotic flavor of another serving as senator from Massachusetts. It took the president to task for his inability to make a dent in the peasant imperviousness of Nikita Khrushchev at the Vienna summit conference. It raised merry hell with him over the "news management" and "censorship" issues (see Chapter Six), and it muttered about the growing American involvement in Vietnam. For those who look back in irony, there was even much talk in the news media about Kennedy's "lack of leadership." Irony is hard on journalistic reputations. Discussing the *New York Times*, Kennedy remarked to aide Ted Sorensen: "I'm convinced that they keep in stock a canned editorial on our 'lack of leadership' and run it every few weeks with little change."9 The publisher of the *Dallas News*, E. M. (Ted) Dealey, told Kennedy to his face: "We need a man on horseback to lead this nation, and many people in Texas and the Southwest think you are riding Caroline's bicycle."10 Mr. Nixon, meet Mr. Dealey.

Lyndon Johnson gave the nation the most liberal legislative program since the New Deal. The war on poverty, the Civil Rights Act of 1964, Medicare, federal aid to education—a torrent of liberal blueprints poured from the White House until Vietnam overwhelmed Johnson's ambitions. Under the Nixon theory, the "liberal" Washington press corps should have sworn Johnson its undying fealty. Instead, the journalists took long, hard looks at his pathological lying and deception, his highly dubious finances (they never proved anything, but Lord, how they tried) and the grossness of his personal behavior. And *some* individual journalists and *some* news organizations read the fiery words of Vietnam early and correctly. They foresaw the terrible reckoning against Johnson and the war. *Mene, mene, tekel, upharsin*. God hath numbered thy kingdom, and finished it. Thou art weighed in the balances, and art found wanting. But not all of the journalists and not all of the news organizations translated the letters of fire early or correctly. In the news media, as in the nation itself, there are few Daniels and many Belshazzars.

The general impression these days is that the news media were united

in vigorous opposition to Johnson's Vietnam policy almost from the beginning. There is a further impression that this contributed massively to
his downfall. This was true in one sense and not in another. It was true in
the television sense, since TV brought the war to the American people
with a visual immediacy and vividness that no government and no nation
had ever experienced. It was also true that a small group of American
journalists in Vietnam persevered in exposing the duplicity of U.S. and
South Vietnamese official statements and statistics. (The role of the news
media in Vietnam will be discussed more extensively in Chapter Eight.)
But in another sense, it was not true—at least not until late in the game.
The reaction of the news media *as a whole* was not as quick or as monolithic as many people now believe it was. Some of the nation's best-
known reporters and most influential columnists and news organizations
stayed with Johnson on the war for a long time. They did not play follow-
the-leader behind the eastern establishment. And if they had, whom
would they have followed? The *New York Times* broke with Johnson on
the Vietnam issue in February 1965.[11] But the *Washington Post* supported his Vietnam policy editorially until the fall of 1968, almost four
years later.[12] Johnson is said to have commented that the *Post*'s editor at
that time, J. Russell Wiggins, was worth two American divisions.[13]

Nevertheless, there was the credibility gap at the beginning, and there
was Vietnam at the end, and there was much in between. Throughout
his five years in office, this liberal Democrat with his liberal social and
economic programs was subjected to intense and sustained criticism by
the ostensibly liberal news media. Mr. Nixon, meet Mr. Johnson.

The media's criticism of Jimmy Carter was almost equally intense and
sustained. Double-digit price increases. Rising interest rates and slump-
ing production. General stagflation and universal malaise. Carter's slowness in formulating an energy policy. His inability to work with Congress.
His indecisiveness and ineffectuality in office. The Bert Lance affair.
Ham and the bars, Billy and the beer. And the two towering events,
supreme in their shock and devastating in their impact on the Carter
presidency: the seizure of the American hostages in Iran, and the failure
of the rescue mission. Carter could not free the hostages. Seldom in
history has a president suffered greater embarrassment.

In the Iranian crisis, the television networks beat Jimmy Carter to a
pulp. Night after night, ABC carried a special program entitled *America
Held Hostage*. Night after night, Walter Cronkite closed CBS's evening
news by reminding the nation how long the hostages had been captive.
The TV films and interviews were endless: films of howling Iranians
demonstrating in front of the U.S. embassy, films of people running
through the streets and burning American flags; interviews with Abol-

hassan Bani-Sadr and Sadegh Ghotbzadeh and other Iranian officials, interviews with experts on the Middle East and seventh-century Islam and the Soviet role and the Saudi reaction and the Libyan menace, interview after interview with the families of the hostages. NBC interviewed hostage William Gallegos, a Marine corporal, and then gave an Iranian militant identified only as "Mary" five minutes in which she attacked the United States and the deposed shah. Mike Wallace of CBS interviewed the ayatollah Khomeini for an hour. The end of the world will not get that much time on TV, for various reasons.

Television's coverage of the Iranian crisis was sharply criticized. Carter's press secretary, Jody Powell, called the Gallegos interview "cruel and cynical" (Gallegos told the NBC audience that "everybody's okay," which presumably was a cruel message for the families of the hostages).[14] Speaker of the House Thomas P. (Tip) O'Neill, Jr., accused NBC of falling "into the trap of Iranian propaganda."[15] Representative Robert Bauman of Maryland, an influential Republican at the time, said the Mary interview deserved "the Benedict Arnold Award for broadcast journalism."[16] State Department officials fretted over the damaging effects of "television diplomacy." *Their* diplomacy was not accomplishing much in Iran.

The reactions of the journalists themselves were less unanimous. Reporter Ford Rowan resigned from NBC on the ground that his network had permitted itself to be used as an instrument for Iranian propaganda. He said NBC should have presented a spokesman for the American view at the same time that it broadcast the Mary interview. Television, of course, had presented the American view again and again, from the president on down. Apparently Rowan assumed the TV audience could not remember this.

On the other hand, NBC reporter George Lewis said: "We knew that some people would accuse us of spreading propaganda for Iran or . . . not being pro-American, but we are not here to be pro-American. We are here to tell people what is happening [in Iran]."[17] It was Vietnam again. There had been a famous press conference in Saigon. Admiral Harry D. Felt, the American commander in the Pacific, had some words for Malcolm Browne of the Associated Press. "So you're Browne," said the admiral. "Why don't you get on the team?"[18] The government always wants the reporters on the team. But if the journalists are on the team, who will report the game?

It is instructive to recall that Carter brought much of the saturation TV coverage on himself. Not to mention the public outcry. He began with some of the most egregious mistakes ever committed by an American president. He admitted the shah of Iran to the United States for medical treatment that could have been obtained elsewhere. At the same time, he accepted the assurances of one of the world's most unstable and unreliable governments that if he admitted the shah, the U.S. embassy personnel in Tehran would be safe. So he did not pull the Americans out.

Then, when the hostages were seized, the president reacted with a series of strong statements and emergency actions. He warned the government of Iran repeatedly that there would be "grave consequences" if the Americans were harmed.[19] He froze Iranian assets in U.S. banks. He suspended Iranian oil imports into the United States. He ordered most Iranian diplomats to leave the country. He ordered the deportation of Iranian students who were in the United States illegally. He tried to get America's allies to take joint economic action against Iran. He asked the United Nations Security Council to impose economic sanctions. He reinforced the U.S. naval contingent in the Indian Ocean, to put more warships as close to Iran as possible. He announced that he would not leave Washington for speaking appearances or campaign trips until the crisis was resolved.

It was instructive but not comforting. Because what else could Carter have done? If he had done less, if he had tried to downplay the crisis, it is a safe bet that the American people would have screamed for his head. What, abandon the hostages to their fate? Do nothing? Carter was in enough trouble over the indecisiveness issue already. It had been only a short time since a president had faced impeachment; the taste of it was still there. Carter *had* to react strongly. Moreover, he probably had other things in mind as well. In the early stages of the crisis, he probably assumed it would help him politically. The public would rally round. Presidents do not have the luxury of single motives. They are jugglers of motives. Some of the motives are worthy. Some are pragmatic. Some are base. But all of them must be juggled all the time. None can be dropped.

So for a variety of reasons, Carter had to treat Iran as a major crisis. But when the president of the United States defines something as a major crisis, when he warns of grave consequences and cancels his out-of-town appearances and moves military forces into position, the news media treat it as a major crisis, too. Like Carter, what else could they have done? How else could they have handled it? Play it down? Give it the second or third spot on the evening news? Put it on page 2? Considering what the president was saying and doing, how would the nation have reacted to *that*? These days, some political scientists argue that the news media set the national agenda. It is said that they decide which issues the public will think about and talk about. But the agenda-setting in Iran took place in this order: the ayatollah first, the president second and the media third.

The Iranian crisis was a human event. It was an event set in motion by the human dissatisfactions and aspirations discussed in Chapter Two. The Iranians rid themselves of a dictator they detested. They raged against a nation that had supported that dictator. They committed violence against that nation. They installed a theocracy. They did many things, fair and foul, for many reasons, fair and foul.

And the crisis was also a media event. The Iranians sought to publicize and justify their actions. They did this by trying to manipulate the news media, not just the American media but media throughout the world. It was a human event and a media event, simultaneously. Some persons believe it is easy to differentiate between these two. It is not. The American colonists were not troubled by the distinctions that torment modern thinkers. They knew the two were inseparable. The American Revolution was the human event. It was very violent. The Declaration of Independence, with its appeal to world opinion, was the media event. It was very manipulative.

Were the news media manipulated by the Iranians? Certainly. The news-gathering process almost always involves manipulation, as the previous chapter pointed out. It is the price. Then, having got the news, did the media overplay it? The answer to this is discovered by every president or politician who makes grandiose promises, issues strong statements or takes urgent actions. Jimmy Carter discovered it in Iran. The answer is: It is easier to turn the news media on than it is to turn them off. And the media are a competitive, profit-making, free-enterprise industry.

As time went on, Carter found that the crisis was no longer working to his political advantage. Fifty-two hostages were still being held. The rescue mission failed, with the loss of eight American lives. A *New York Times*–CBS poll showed that only 39 percent of the public approved of Carter's handling of the hostage problem.[20] The 1980 election was drawing near, and as the politicians say, the hostage issue had begun to cut against the president. The situation not having improved, it was time to play down the situation. All governments do this. They learn it in school. So on April 30, 1980, Carter told a group of community leaders that the Iranian crisis had become "manageable enough . . . for me to leave the White House for a limited travel schedule, including some campaigning. . . ." The Iranian statements were fewer and fainter. No more warships moved.

But the networks declined to join Carter in playing down the situation. Havoc had been cried. Havoc was playing well. Havoc was paying better. ABC had discovered that its *America Held Hostage* program was attracting large audiences. To the joy and wonder of the boardroom, it was occasionally outdrawing the evening sitcoms and the Johnny Carson show.[21] When something outdraws Johnny, you keep it going. The

Nielsen ratings were telling the networks that the Iranian crisis was very good for business. They responded with a frenzy of competitive coverage. They were spending $1 million *a day* on it.[22]

Was it legitimate news, or was it overkill? Was the public demanding all available information about the hostages, or was it merely responding to media hype? The journalists and political scientists argued about which came first. Both demand and overplay were obviously there. But neither came first. Profits came first. Carter could not call off the money, could he?

But, to regain the thread, the "liberal" media were doing all this damage to a *Democratic* president. Something was wrong. Under the adversary theory, the media were supposed to behave with such ferocity only toward conservatives. But first Kennedy, then Johnson and now Carter . . . apparently the theory needed revising. However, many persons were loath to accept the critical relationship as the most accurate description: the press as the permanent, resident *critic* of government, regardless of which party is in power. They wished to retain that word "adversary." It was such a *vivid* word. So descriptive. So evocative of animus and bias and conflict and all the things people relish. Moreover, it is hard to discard a theory. Check your local listings for the Flat Earth Society.

So they broadened the theory. The journalists were not just hostile to conservative governments. They were hostile to *all* governments. The news media had become so habituated to criticism, so steeped in antagonism, so besotted with power that they were making it impossible for *anyone* to govern the United States. No president would get a fair chance; the moment he assumed office, the media would set about the task of destroying him. Automatically. Mindlessly.

This revision fit in neatly with other developments. For some time, political analysts had been writing about the "voodoo" phenomenon at the state and local levels. The voters, it was said, began sticking pins in governors and mayors as soon as they were elected. The terrible problems of the old industrial states and the dowager cities could not be solved, so the public angrily turned out governors and mayors after one term and tried someone else. Now the same thing seemed to be happening on the national level. Nationally, the problems were even worse; it appeared that no president could survive them. Not since Dwight Eisenhower had a chief executive served two full terms. One had been assassinated, another had decided not to seek reelection in the midst of an unpopular war, another had resigned and two had been defeated.

What was responsible for this instability? The rational remnant among the population recognized that the problems were horrendous; the sheer weight of events, in other words, was the chief cause. It was helped along by a truly impressive accumulation of errors, ignorances, prejudices and greeds. And two of the presidents, of course, had had grave defects of character. But some people found a more convenient culprit: the news media. Journalists had played a major role in bringing down two presidents. And, as Moriarty remarked to Holmes, they had seriously inconvenienced several others. That obviously was power, a great deal of power. If they were wielding that much power, they must be damned dangerous. After Vietnam and Watergate, a reaction against the news media was inevitable.

The government-wrecking idea was not new. There was George Washington, morosely convinced in Chapter Two that the "gazettes" would rend the Union asunder. There was Stanley Baldwin, a British prime minister in the 1930's. Baldwin, during a hot fight with some newspapers, defined journalists erotically. They were, he said, persons who exercise "power without responsibility—the prerogative of the harlot throughout the ages." Those prime ministers knew their harlots.

But new or not, it was a grave charge. The revised adversary concept was much more serious in its implications than the original version. The news media, grown reckless with power, were making it impossible for the nation to be governed. Scary. But, like so many things that are made up to frighten us, untrue. Some reasons:

1. The adversary concept is merely a more sophisticated version of the old blame-the-messenger-who-brings-the-bad-news. This is one of the most venerable cop-outs of all, but anything can be renovated. Lear, demented with grief, believes ungrateful children are responsible for Edgar's madness. The old king cries: "What! Have his daughters brought him to this pass?" The news media often resemble Goneril and Regan: petty, proud, mistaken. Nevertheless, for all their faults, they did not bring us to this pass. There would be bad news, including the troubles of governments, even if there were no courier to bring it. Compare bad news—human events—to those unwelcome envelopes that arrive at the first of the month. You could blame the mail carrier for delivering the bills. Convenient, but irrational. *You* ran up the bills. Presumably the mail carrier blames *his* mail carrier. The beat goes on.

2. Although it is often overlooked these days, the founding fathers did not intend to make it easy to govern the United States. They intended just the opposite. They divided the power among three branches of government. They then invited each branch to restrain, inhibit and generally make things difficult for the others. Nay, not invited. They *mandated* it. Then, for good measure, the founders loosed the press to bedevil all three branches. They had sound reasons for doing all this, and the reasons remain sound. It was not to be too easy to govern the United States lest

the United States be governed *too well*. Because then it almost certainly would be governed autocratically. The founders did not want this. They had had experience of it. We should not want things to be too *easy*. *Fructus esse idem diuturnus ac praecox nequit*. What is enjoyed too soon is not enjoyed long. It is necessary to *work* at governance.

So, for reasons ancient and modern, the critical concept is the most accurate description of the relationship between the news media and the government. Not adversary. Not wrecker. Critic.

Why don't the news media tell the *truth*? The question is asked by conservatives. The question is asked by liberals. It is asked by presidents, politicians, generals, admirals, businessmen, scientists, doctors, educators, students and ordinary citizens. Why do the journalists write or broadcast news stories that are biased or slanted? Why are other stories or broadcasts incomplete or ill informed? Why aren't the reporters simply *honest*? Why don't they tell things the way they *really are*? On the other hand, why aren't they *objective*?

In 1968, a phenomenon was observed. Thousands of industrial workers voted for Robert F. Kennedy in the presidential primaries and then, a few months later, turned around and voted for George C. Wallace in the general election. No two politicians were more different in outlook than Kennedy and Wallace. Many of the blue-collar workers said they knew this. Nevertheless, they said, they supported these two opposites because each seemed to be telling the truth as he saw it. The voters said they felt they were getting the straight stuff, and they were grateful.

There is much evidence that the American people deeply thirst for truth. They want their politicians, newspapers, television networks and Howard Cosell to tell it like it is. However, the public wishes to do with truth as everyone wants to do with cake. The truth is desired, but each person defines the truth. A politician will be punished if he defies a prejudice or challenges a belief or imperils an economic interest. So the politician seeks the perfection of Alben Barkley.

The almost-forgotten Barkley was a senator from Kentucky and then Harry Truman's vice-president. In his day, strong emotions were aroused by the Fair Employment Practices Committee, an early civil rights measure. It was one of those no-win propositions that politicians dread; to support or to oppose the FEPC would lose votes. During a Barkley speech, a heckler shouted: "How do you stand on FEPC?" Barkley shouted back: "I'm all right on that."

The public, culpable but nonetheless frustrated, turns to the news media. What is the result? Do the journalists present the straight stuff?

Once I organized a meeting between a group of students and Bob

Woodward of the *Washington Post*'s Watergate investigative team. One of the students asked Woodward to define his goal as a journalist. He replied: "Truth."[23]

God help us. There must be something *easier*. Truth, like beauty, is in the eye of the beholder. One person's self-obvious and deeply believed truth is another person's damned lie. It is impossible to state a truth that will convince everyone, every last person. There is no unanimity on the truth of anything. Only occasionally, usually under the duress of grave emergency, is there as much as a working majority. A problem of the utmost obduracy confronts the journalist at every moment: the belief of each human being that he is right. Those holding a different view, therefore, are wrong. "I beseech you in the bowels of Christ," said Cromwell, "think it possible you may be mistaken." Well, they would not think any such thing. To tell the truth, truth is unattainable. Compromise averts anarchy, but it does not eliminate belief.

"There is no absolute knowledge," wrote the mathematician and philosopher of science Jacob Bronowski. "All information is imperfect. . . . That is the human condition."[24] Since there is no absolute truth, journalists cannot deal in it. What actually happens in the news process is that other standards are substituted: accuracy, completeness and fairness. The reporter tries to make his story as accurate and as complete as possible, and he endeavors to be fair by presenting the various sides of an issue.

These standards are journalism's approximation of truth. They are the reporter's steps to the Olympus of truth. What with one thing and another, he never gets there. He is frequently inaccurate. He is never complete. He is often unfair. However, if he approximates the approximation, which is as close as he ever gets, he gains something almost as precious as Olympus: credibility. His account of events will be believed, more or less, and his explanation of the reasons for events will be given at least a hearing. This is why people read David Broder, for instance, with a reasonably open mind; it is because Broder himself has a reasonably open mind. And it is why they do not read Evans and Novak in quite the same way.

But if completeness is one approximation of truth, only a few newspapers take even a few faltering steps toward Olympus. On a national average, about two thirds of an American newspaper is occupied by advertisements. Only about a third is devoted to "news." Moreover, the "news" includes the comic strips, the sports pages, the "personality" or "people" columns, the recipes for brandied spareribs, the advice to the lovelorn and the rest of the entertainments that are offered to attract and retain readers. The amount of space that is left for actual news—news of the world, the nation and the community—is pitifully small. There are about 1,750 daily newspapers in the United States (in 1916, the peak year, there were 2,461). It is possible to count on the fingers of one hand the quality newspapers—those that devote sufficient space and news-gathering resources to give their readers reasonably comprehensive accounts and some explanation of the events and issues that affect their lives.

Incompleteness is one of journalism's cardinal faults. For an example of how it works out in actual practice, consider a White House announcement on an important subject. Both the print and electronic media will be examined in this example.

The president has decided to propose a new program. It deals with a complicated subject. He is going to send a message to Congress, requesting the necessary legislation. The news process begins when the reporters are given copies of the message. It is five to twenty single-spaced, legal-size pages. It contains a great deal of information: the background or history of the problem that the new program is designed to solve, the details of the program itself, the objectives it seeks to achieve and usually its projected cost.

In most cases, the reporters are then given a White House "fact sheet" on the new program. The fact sheet describes the problem and explains the proposal in even greater detail. White House fact sheets are customarily twenty or twenty-five single-spaced, legal-size pages. There have been some that were 50 or even 100 pages long. That is when you call the office and ask whether there is a specialist who wants to handle the story.

After the reporters have had a little time—never enough—to skim through this mass of material, the press secretary ushers in a group of government officials to give a briefing on the message. The officials describe the president's proposals in great, redundant detail. The reporters then ask questions. The briefing usually lasts a half hour and often an hour or more. A lot of ground is covered.

The reporters emerge from the briefing. They are clutching huge wads of paper—scores or even hundreds of pages. Their notebooks are full of information from the briefing. Their heads are congested with facts, figures and quotes. The material is complicated and abstruse. It must now be conveyed to television viewers, radio listeners and newspaper readers. A funnel has a large opening into which much can be poured, and a small end from which little emerges. We have now reached the small end.

The TV reporter heads for the White House lawn to do a "standup" for the evening news. A typical TV standup or radio spot is a minute or a minute and fifteen seconds long. That is 100 to 120 words. Occasionally, a voluptuous 150 words can be wrangled from New York. The president is proposing something of substantial importance to the nation. The TV reporter has 100 to 120 words with which to describe it. In 1976, shortly after leaving his White House assignment, Dan Rather of CBS said: "There is no way that I . . . can come out there [for] a minute and 15 seconds and give the viewer even the essence, never mind the details or the substance [of a story]."[25] The TV and radio reporters are at the bottom of the information ladder. The most pervasive news media—the conduits from which more Americans get news than any other—are the least complete. This is known as an irony.

Next, the wire services. Their importance is great, being equaled only by their anonymity. Their stories go to thousands of newspapers, radio stations, financial institutions and a variety of other clients, not just in the United States but around the world. And to the TV networks in New York, which rely heavily on the wires in deciding what to cover. How many words an AP or UPI or Reuters reporter has for each story depends on the importance of the story. It is not possible to be specific, but there is an overall average that is indicative of the completeness problem. The average story on the AP's "A wire"—the main news wire—is about 400 words long.[26] Lincoln did it in 266 words, an inspiration to all wire service reporters. And at that, he backed into the lead. With an average of 400 words, then, the wire service reporter is a step above the TV or radio reporter on the information ladder.

Finally, the "specials"—the reporters who work for an individual newspaper or a chain of papers. Here, again, it is impossible to be specific; the length of a story will depend on its importance. However, on the type of story being considered here, most newspaper reporters will have 600 to 700 words—about a column of newsprint. If their paper is not greatly interested in national news, they may have only half or two thirds of a column. At the upper end of the scale, a reporter for a large newspaper may have 1,000 or even 1,200 words with which to tell the story. This is the top of the information ladder, but it is nowhere near Olympus. A thousand words will tell more and explain more than a TV standup, but for complicated stories it will still be far from adequate. And the vast majority of national and international stories are complicated. Ignorance, therefore, is not bliss. It is relative.

These have been generalizations about completeness. They did not take into account television's efforts to supplement the evening news with special, in-depth programs on major issues. They did not take into account the fact that the wire services will let important stories run long. They omitted the handful of quality newspapers that are available to conscientious citizens. They did not take into account the analytical, explanatory and investigative articles with which good newspapers follow up the spot news or delve deeply into significant issues. Or the newsmagazines.

Or the small journals of comment and opinion in which some of America's best reporting is often found. The completeness problem has been treated broadly and on the basis of averages. Fortunately, there are exceptions. In human affairs, it is remarkable how often the exceptions are the salvation.

But even when the print and electronic media try to be more complete, there is a persistence of problems. And of these, the greatest is time. The reporter's efforts at completeness are obstructed by time, in its various guises. Assigned to do a think piece or a situationer on a major issue, the journalist quickly discovers that every problem stretches backward in time. It has become unpleasantly clear, for instance, that the energy problem goes back at least to the interstate highway program of the 1950's, when the automobile and oil lobbies drove mass-transit systems from the scene. The Arab-Israeli crisis goes back at least to the Balfour Declaration of 1917, the Soviet-American crisis to a venerable folly known as the Cordon Sanitaire—or to Peter the Great.

As a result, the reporter usually discovers that someone—a congressional committee, a federal agency or a private group—has been studying the problem for years. One of the Laws of Applied Journalism states: If a Senate committee hasn't studied it, a House committee has. The journalist's desk vanishes under a vast accumulation of information. He has at hand the work of commissions, committees, boards, study groups, research organizations and special-interest pleaders. The research spreads ever outward. Each study invokes previous studies. There is no end to it—but for the reporter there has to be an end to it. The editor knocks upon his door with the insistence of an unpaid madam.

The luxury of tracing each problem back to the Industrial Revolution, the doctrines of John Calvin or the Pliocene drought is denied the working journalist. Sooner or later—usually sooner—he has to cut things off and start writing. He has not read everything. His truth is incomplete.

Even more discouraging, he has not talked to everyone. This is time in the guise most familiar to the journalist. As he turns to his typewriter or to his video display terminal—an incomprehensible new device that does not work just before deadline—he is beset by a daily pang of conscience. He has talked to some people, but there are undoubtedly many others who know something about the subject. The conscientious reporter—there are such creatures—leaves the office each night with the nagging knowledge that there was not enough time to talk to enough people. There is information that did not get into his story. Its absence makes the story incomplete. It may even—angels and ministers of grace defend us—make it wrong. Arriving home, he calls for strong drink.

From the relativity of truth and the incompleteness of its approximation, it is a short, reluctant journey to that monster of frightful mien: journalistic bias. When a reporter states something in a story, those who agree with the statement—those who believe it to be true—nod their heads and say: "Yes, that's it. He has put his finger on it." Everyone has had this experience a few times in life. But those who do not agree with the statement—those who do not believe it to be true—scowl in anger and say . . . well, they say many things. The story is slanted. It is not objective. Epithets are heard. The favorite is: The reporter is biased. He has not reported the facts dispassionately and neutrally. He has injected his personal feelings into them, causing distortion. He has not imparted information free of personal judgment. The wretch. But . . .

"There is no way of exchanging information that does not demand an act of judgment," wrote Bronowski.[27] I say to you the electron is a wave. I am imparting information, but it includes a judgment I have made: that the electron is a wave. You reply that the electron is a particle. The information you are imparting contains a judgment that the electron is a particle. Information has been conveyed, but we disagree over the judgments. Human beings are made of electrons and other indeterminacies. So it works the same way with us.

Except for the barest facts—12 persons have been killed in a hotel fire, 12 million persons are unemployed—virtually every news story and news broadcast contain judgments that some persons agree with and some do not. The reporter, after checking, after talking to people, reports their view that the hotel was a firetrap. The families of the victims agree; the owners and insurers do not. The reporter, after checking, after talking to people, reports the view that the president's policies have caused the unemployment. The president says his policies did no such thing.

Does this mean that journalistic bias is simply anything that someone disagrees with? In that case, it is not bias; it is just disagreement. Or is actual bias demonstrable? Can it be shown to exist *as* bias? The answer is that it is *frequently* disagreement and *sometimes* bias. But when bias is examined, its components turn out to be complicated. One of them, the relativity of truth, has been discussed. The others have to do with facts, explanations, conclusions and, to beat it to death, incompleteness.

The journalist defines his professionalism as the pursuit of facts and explanations. If there is a preeminent reason for the endless controversy over media bias, it is this unhappy insistence. Because facts are uncomfortable things. They embarrass officials and institutions and organizations. They nag at ordinary people. They disturb the status quo. They challenge accepted practices. They affront complacency. It is hard to relax with a fact. It was a long day. Things were miserable at the office.

The children were impossible. The hell with it. That damned Mike Wallace is just biased.

Then, as if all this were not bad enough, facts demand explanations. They do not make sense without explanations. There was a hotel fire—but *why*? There is unemployment—but *why*? But explanations are even more uncomfortable and more challenging than facts. And they are more controversial. I agree; you disagree. Finally, facts lead to conclusions. What else is there to do with them? The journalists, when they are doing their job properly, insist on going where the facts lead. And the facts point to conclusions, which are the most controversial of all. The situation is now intolerable.

There is a simple request that can be made, and it is made all the time. The journalists are asked *to stop the process at the first stage.* They are asked to report the bare facts and nothing more. Disagreement will be reduced. Comfort will be enhanced. But this the journalists refuse to do. They say they will not be a bulletin board. They say the whole thing would be meaningless without explanations and conclusions. They are correct. Even when their explanations and conclusions are incomplete or downright wrong, their argument is correct.

And the journalists have an ace up their sleeve. They know, in their rough and unscientific way, the human species. They know human beings have chronically contradictory desires. They want order and certainty and comfort. But they also want to know, sooner or later, the why of things.

The news media interfere with humanity's deep desire for tidiness and certainty. No, no, they say, you cannot have the world as you want it—you must have it as it is. In some persons, this produces battle fatigue, with symptoms. They harken to ignorant and opportunistic leaders to whom it has been revealed that Lincoln was wrong: The dogmas of the quiet past *are* adequate to the stormy present. They enlist under the agitated banners of moral absolutism. They scurry here and there, seeking certainties from charlatans. Some peoples in history *have* achieved certainty. They were then clear as to what they must do. The Germans come to mind. But the Americans, groaning under the yoke of freedom, have only the chaos offered by the news media. It is tiring.

The journalists present a portrait of the world that is confused, untidy and dangerous. Charles Dickens had a quiet childhood in Kent. But when he was ten years old, his father's financial difficulties forced the family to move to cheap and squalid lodgings in London. The boy Dickens journeyed alone and fearfully to the metropolis in a smelly coach on a sad, rainy day. Later he reflected that "life was sloppier than I had expected to find it." There are some who can cope with the sloppiness.

These indomitables will always want to know the why of things. A few weeks at the seashore and they can contemplate Mike Wallace with renewed fortitude.

It is the argument of this book that facts, explanations and conclusions in and of themselves do not prove journalistic bias. Nonetheless, bias does occur. The most serious form involves the *selection* of explanations. When a journalist has assembled as much information as possible, he presents the explanation that he believes comes closest to the truth. Then, with stoic calm, he awaits the storm. It is his right and his *responsibility* to emphasize the news development that he considers most important, and the explanation that he considers best supported by the facts. From among competing views, he has selected the one he considers most valid. But there *are* competing views. They have a legitimate right to be reported. If the journalist ignores them, if he does not acknowledge that they exist, if he deliberately excludes them from his story or broadcast, then that *is* bias. As General Haig would say: *"Guilty!"*

Recall the journalistic approximation of truth: accuracy, completeness, fairness. It is the latter two that are crucial in determining whether bias has been committed. The journalist has the right to give priority to one explanation or conclusion. The facts, to him, have pointed preponderantly in that direction. Moreover, it is not possible to get every voice in the Tower of Babel into the first paragraph. But the reporter does not have the right to exclude other views.

Of course, it happens. Entire organizations are devoted to convincing the American people that it happens constantly. But it does not occur as often as these true believers say it does. The Michael Robinson–Margaret Sheehan study of CBS and UPI showed that. The Walter Karp study of the networks showed that. The media criticism of Kennedy, Johnson and Carter showed it. And most news stories show it.

A news story usually follows a pattern. The first paragraph, known as the lead, makes a statement. It is essentially one statement, one view. But if it involves a controversial matter about which there is or will be disagreement, the body of the story almost always contains paragraphs reporting opposing views, rebuttals, denials. There are key words to watch for: "However, a White House spokesman defended the president's proposal, saying . . ." Or "Meanwhile, on Capitol Hill, critics contended . . ." Or "But the mayor, responding to the charges, asserted that . . ." Those "howevers" and "meanwhiles" and "on the other hands" are the fortifications against bias. My wife, a writer and former journalist, calls them the "but" paragraphs. When reading one of my stories, she would say: "Here comes the 'but' paragraph." She caught them every time.

However, the average newspaper reader seldom notices this back-and-forth of charge and answer, statement and rebuttal. He is so accustomed to it that he is not aware that a professionalism is at work. A professionalism of fairness to all sides. Experienced reporters do this automatically; they have been trained to do it. Here are two random examples from the *Washington Post* of February 2, 1983. Emphasis has been added to underscore the words that introduced the opposing views and sought to avoid bias.

The first story was written by Helen Dewar, who covers Congress for the *Post*. The lead paragraph was: "House Democrats, brushing aside Reagan administration claims that its economic recovery plan will generate millions of jobs, announced yesterday that they will push for quick enactment of an 'emergency' program that could include money for jobs, medical insurance for the jobless, food and shelter and protection from home and farm foreclosures."

Then the second paragraph: "The Democratic plan was sketched by House Speaker Thomas P. (Tip) O'Neill Jr. (D-Mass.) *even as* President Reagan's three top economic advisers told the House Appropriations Committee that economic recovery outlined in the president's budget was the best way to get Americans back to work."

So. First the lead, with the news development: an announcement by House Democrats. Then the second paragraph, *with the opposing view*. It could be argued, and undoubtedly will be, that the appearance of Reagan's economic advisers before the appropriations committee should have led the story, with the Democratic announcement second. The headline would then have been based on the administration testimony instead of the Democratic plan (the administration got the subhead, or "deck"). But the choice of lead was a matter of news judgment, not a case of slanted reporting. The Democratic plan was a new development. The administration had testified many times on behalf of its economic program, and those previous appearances had been covered. The American people cannot miraculously be enabled to remember everything they read in newspapers or see on TV newscasts. A pity. Some of them choose not to remember. Also a pity.

The remainder of Dewar's story ran seventeen paragraphs. Six of them gave the Democratic point of view. They quoted various Democratic leaders on the benefits that would accrue from their proposals. But five other paragraphs reported the administration's point of view. Various administration spokesmen described the benefits that the president's economic program would bring about. In the third "graf," for instance, budget director David A. Stockman was quoted as saying the administration expected 4.6 million new jobs to open up in two years or less, if its budget was approved. In the fourth graf, Secretary of the Treasury Donald T. Regan was quoted as saying: "The worst [of the recession] is now over." Regan said also that the president's new budget was "a reasonable approach . . . that should be credible to the financial markets, the Congress and the American people."

The other six paragraphs of the story were neutral. They described the details and background of the controversy. The final score: Democrats, 7 grafs (with 1 for newness); Republicans, 6 grafs; neutrals, 6 grafs; bias, 0.

The second story was by George C. Wilson, the *Post's* veteran Pentagon correspondent. The lead was: "Members of both parties on the Senate Armed Services Committee called on Defense Secretary Caspar W. Weinberger yesterday to suggest cuts in President Reagan's $238.6 billion defense budget, and Sen. John W. Warner (R-Va.) floated as one possibility reducing the active-duty military force by 5 to 7 percent."

The second graf quoted another Republican senator, Dan Quayle of Indiana, as warning Weinberger that Congress was going to cut the military budget anyway and it would be better if the Defense Department came up with its own list of reductions. Then the third graf: "*But* Weinberger said, as he has repeatedly, 'We simply cannot reduce defense spending any further without endangering the security of the United States.'" The fourth graf quoted him further on the imprudence of slowing down military spending.

The remainder of the paragraph count: 8 grafs for Weinberger and Senator John G. Tower of Texas, who supported Weinberger; 4 grafs for senators who wanted to cut military spending; 1 neutral graf; and 2 that could only be called standoffs. In these, the senators and Weinberger argued in the same paragraph.

However, there is one area of journalism in which bias is almost always present: investigative journalism. This is fortunate, because without bias there would be few investigative stories. There are two types of article that rescue the news media from being merely the government's bulletin board: the explanatory story and the investigative story. One tries to give the reasons for things—the *why* of events and issues. The other uncovers crimes, injustices or mistakes that have been concealed.

Most of the governmental news in the American news media is furnished by . . . the government. A 1973 study by Leon V. Sigal showed that 58.2 percent of the news in the *New York Times* and the *Washington Post* came from press conferences, press releases and other official sources. Another 25.8 percent came from interviews and other activities that in many cases served official purposes.[28] The score thus was: government 84, victims 16. Lou Cannon of the *Washington Post* wrote that "this means that the two newspapers usually considered most skeptical, independent and critical of government wound up printing pretty much what the executive branch of government gave out."[29] Tom Wicker of the New York Times has said that the reliance on official sources for news is "the gravest professional and intellectual weakness of American journalism."[30] (It is possible to think of others. Superficiality is a candidate.) And Bill Moyers, who has worked for both government and the news media, has said: "Most of the news on television is, unfortunately, whatever the government says is news."[31]

So explanation and investigation are journalism's glories. The reporter working on an investigative story usually starts with a rumor, a tip or some preliminary information that something is wrong. He then begins a dogged routine: endless interviews and telephone calls, endless reading of documents. Often the facts simply do not demonstrate any wrongdoing. They may be there, but he cannot get them. Or they are just not there. Reporters and editors retire with memories of investigations that did not pan out. But if the facts exist and the reporter gets them, then the nation learns:

From reporter Morton Mintz that a drug called thalidomide, given to pregnant women, was causing terrible defects in babies. From reporter Seymour Hersh that American soldiers had massacred Vietnamese civilians at My Lai. From reporters Bob Woodward and Carl Bernstein that . . . but Watergate does not need to be rehashed. From reporter Jean Heller that a "research" project had been under way for more than forty years in the area around Tuskegee, Alabama. It had begun in the 1920's and was still going on when Heller wrote her first story about it for the Associated Press, in June 1972. Hundreds of black males suffering from syphilis were located by the U.S. Public Health Service. They were told only that they had "bad blood." They were not treated for syphilis. In due course, they died. Their bodies were then examined to determine whether syphilis affected blacks differently than whites.[32] Jean Heller, Morty Mintz and Sy Hersh did not win Pulitzer Prizes for their stories. Nor did Woodward and Bernstein win for Watergate (although the Washington Post did). Those prizes need to be looked at.

A reporter working on an investigative story is impelled by ego, of course. He is ambitious, he knows he has a big one going, and he hopes for recognition. However, there is another motive: bias. The journalist is biased in favor of revealing facts. Only the genuinely deranged disagree with this principle. And the reporter has still another bias: He hopes to bring about improvement. He seeks the correction of a bad situation. But a bad situation cannot be corrected unless it is first known. The reporter is following Thomas Hardy's advice: "If a way to the better there be, it exacts a full look at the worst." There is an old journalistic saying: Scratch a reporter and you will find a reformer. Many journalists have a strong streak of reformer in them.

At one time or another, this type of bias brings the news media into conflict with just about everybody. It turns out that reform, like truth, is in the eye of the beholder. People disagree strongly over what reform *is*. The media inform the public that conditions in a local facility—a nursing home, a hospital, a jail—are very bad and urgently need improvement. Not so, cry the local officials; the reporters are biased. The media inform the public that a local corporation is polluting a river or a local utility is overcharging its customers and these things should be stopped. Not so, cry the corporate officers; the stories are slanted. The media inform the public that a national policy has failed and should be changed. Not so, cries the White House; the media are prejudiced, the policy is fundamentally sound and there is light at the end of the tunnel. Always there is light at the end of the tunnel.

Thus, there is bias. Some is deliberate, when opposing views or conclusions are intentionally omitted. Some has a reform motive. And some is inadvertent. This is the most common form, so medical science is baffled. Bias may simply be due to a mistake or to carelessness. It may be the result of faulty news judgment or deadline pressure. Most frequently of all, it occurs because newspaper stories and television newscasts are violently truncated. The limitations of space and time mean that important facts or opposing views are left out. This causes oversimplification that is easily mistaken for bias. There is increasing specialization among reporters, but that is little protection. If a reporter is conscientious, he cringes and writhes inwardly when he visualizes a story he has written being read by someone who really *knows* something about the subject. No matter how many people he has talked to, he knows he cannot possibly treat a complicated matter adequately in a few hundred words. Sins of omission vastly exceed sins of commission in journalism. That is true of all human behavior. In the news media, the sin of omission is incompleteness.

Incompleteness has an energetic partner: superficiality. Much of the American news media is superficial. The human condition is reported sketchily, by fits and starts but with unflagging attention to Brooke Shields. Many important things are not reported adequately—especially complicated things. However, symmetry is preserved. They are also not explained adequately. Only a few newspapers and an occasional television special give even a hint of what the philosopher Alfred North Whitehead called *connexity* in human affairs. When connexity is described, when it is realized that issues are interwoven, that problems are all tangled together, that a thing in the present was caused by other things in the past and will cause other things in the future—then explanation begins. Understanding begins. *Comprehension* begins.

But journalism deals with *now*. And *now* is overwhelming in quantity. The reporters, the news tickers, telephones and satellites bring incessant news of *now*. The A wire operates twenty-four hours a day, transmitting news of *now*.

However, journalism cannot be absolved simply because there is so much *now* to handle. The news media have assigned themselves four tasks: to report the news, to explain the news, to investigate and, in some cases, to advocate. Since these are self-appointed roles, it is fair to ask how well they perform them. The answer is: Considering their financial resources, most of the media do not perform nearly as well as they *could*. And considering their pervasiveness—the number of people they reach and influence—not nearly as well as they *should*. They have the money. They have the impact. They have the responsibility. They should do more.

The television networks are very wealthy. They are accredited members of the Fortune 500. When they are litigated against, the amounts sought are in the millions. Most of the nation's large newspapers are profitable enterprises. Some are mammoth news conglomerates. They own other newspapers, newsmagazines, news syndicates, book-publishing companies, paper mills and stands of timber that are not long for this world. Almost all newspapers in large and medium-size cities own television and radio stations. A local TV station is a device for the manufacture of Swiss francs and Krugerrands. The elderly afternoon newspapers in the old cities may soon be as dead as Marley, but otherwise, my God how the money rolls in.

What do they do with it? Various things. If they can, they buy more TV stations. They acquire more and more newspapers to form larger and larger chains. They achieve short-term maximization of profits, a new term meaning greed. But except for the handful of quality newspapers, not much of it is spent on news, and even less on explanation. On a national average, as noted earlier, only about one third of an American newspaper is not devoted to advertising. Look not at the *New York Times* but at an ordinary newspaper in an ordinary city, and see how much actual *news* there is after page 3 or page 5. The television anchormen fit the news into a half hour that actually turns out to be twenty-one and a half minutes. Print or electronic, there is not much left for connexity. This works to the government's advantage and the public's disadvantage.

The anchormen. And the other high-paid, high-visibility television journalists. The household names. The celebrity journalists, as famous among the public as . . . my blushes, Watson. I was about to say, as Brooke Shields. What about journalism in the hands of celebrity journalists? Does connexity stand a chance against a $1-million salary and a twenty-one-minute newscast? Money talks, but it does not explain. Is television destroying the news process? Cronkite fears it may be, and he may be right. He knows the territory. But a close look shows that it depends on the individual TV journalist. It will continue to depend mostly on the individual.

When he was president, Richard Nixon spent considerable time at his home in California. On one of his vacation trips, Dan Rather and I took our children to Disneyland. In the Nixon era, this was coals to Newcastle. Rather was not as well known then as he is now, but he was on the way. We rode around in one of those mini-buses. A middle-aged woman stared fixedly at Rather throughout the tour. She kept saying: "I know you, I know you. I can't quite place you, but I know you." Rather grew uncomfortable; he was not yet accustomed to The Stare. I said: "Keep working at it, lady. It will come to you." However, it did not come to her. I tried to think of someone on television who looked as unlike Dan Rather as possible. Brinkley, that was it. Those sleepy eyes. That lopsided smile. Not Rather at all. As we got off the mini-bus, I informed the woman in tones of utmost confidentiality: "Madam, you have been riding with David Brinkley." She was greatly relieved. "Oh, yes," she said, "I *knew* I knew him."

Rather's career is illustrative. After many adventures, he found himself in competition for the top spot. The national jaw was agape with suspense as CBS tried to decide whether Rather or Roger Mudd would succeed Walter Cronkite. The national eye was riveted on the announcement. The national envy speculated on Rather's salary when he emerged the winner. Of course, it was at least $1 million a year. Everybody gets a million. But the crucial question was: Had Dan Rather broken the $1-million barrier? Was it, as *Time* magazine reported, $8 million spread over five years—$1.6 million a year? Thirty thousand dollars a week?[33]

The defeated candidate, Roger Mudd, said: "The management of CBS and CBS News has made its decision on Walter Cronkite's successor according to its current values and standards. From the beginning, I have regarded myself as a news reporter, not as a newsmaker or a celebrity."[34]

But ABC's Barbara Walters—twenty thousand dollars a week—observed: "Star quality was important with [Edward R.] Murrow, with Huntley and Brinkley and with Walter. Dan has star quality, too, and he is a good newsman."[35] First things first.

In 1979, Jimmy Carter visited Saudi Arabia, where they know all about money. The president and his entourage were guests at a banquet in one of King Khalid's palaces. In a nearby room, the American reporters accompanying Carter had dinner with lesser Saudi moguls. One of the sheiks asked Judy Woodruff of NBC whether it was true that Barbara Walters earned $1 million a week. No, no, said Woodruff, it's $1 million a *year*. Oh, said the Saudi, only a *year*. He lost interest.[36]

Carter's trip also took him to India. During the flight, some of the reporters on the press plane played a game to pass the time. Some of these games are a little macabre. This one consisted of imagining how the headlines would read if the press plane crashed, killing all the prominent journalists aboard. Knowing that ABC's star was on the trip, my contribution was BARBARA WALTERS, OTHERS PERISH.

Unfortunately, Walters was nearby. She overheard her name and saw the smiles, without hearing the joke itself. When we arrived at the hotel in New Delhi, she was waiting for me. A small woman, with a set expression on her face. Grim, actually. I tried to explain. A joke, you know? Really rather flattering when you think about it. She remained grim. Her reply was "I try not to be more paranoid than I have to." Were people after Barbara's job? Did others covet that million bucks? Will Lois Lane marry Superman?

After Rather got the nod as Cronkite's successor, the *Columbia Journalism Review* asked Uncle Walter whether he thought any journalist was worth "eight million dollars over five years." Cronkite replied: "Compared to a rock-and-roll singer? Yes. Compared to a teacher? No."[37]

As he neared the end of his career as America's uncle figure, Cronkite grew increasingly concerned about the effect of celebrity journalism on the news process. The old anchorman had started from a base in print journalism. He had worked for United Press in places like Kansas City, El Paso and Houston. For perspective, there is absolutely nothing like raising children on a wire service salary. Cronkite could handle fame when it arrived, because he was older and because he had known the flip side. Fame was better. Nevertheless, he worried about the TV journalists. They were not sweating out an apprenticeship on the *Cedar Rapids Gazette* or in the AP bureau in Sacramento. This was not just a matter of hazing cub reporters. It was a question of whether TV's neophytes were learning the *news process* and becoming dedicated to it. Or whether they were learning to be celebrities.

So Cronkite worried about the six-figure salaries being paid to very young people. Could they cope with this acceleration? Wouldn't it be better to work up to it gradually? That is called the good old days. Of course, it was broader than that. Cronkite was worrying not just about TV journalists but about instant gratification generally. *Fructus esse . . .*

He worried, too, about their notoriety. Their ambitions, their switches from network to network and from assignment to assignment, their arguments with New York, their social lives, love affairs, marriages, babies—all these were *news*. The other news media—newspapers and magazines—were covering the TV journalists as celebrities. But what, then, is TV journalism? There is a great temptation to answer that it is entertainment, and let it go at that. But this is not possible. There are three reasons. First, because some TV journalists are trying to make the news process work. Second, because a vast number of Americans rely completely or almost completely on TV for news. And lastly, because the number of first-rate newspapers is so small, and confined to so few cities, that if the news process cannot be made to work on TV, *there will be no news process.*

Still Cronkite worried. There was something else. The kids could not write. There was no irascible, unreasonable city editor in their memories. No old fart slashing away with a copy pencil and demanding that a plural noun be assigned a plural verb. These things is going out of style. Yes, but a 120-word standup? What did that have to do with writing? The answer was that if they had not learned to write, they had not learned the news process. The conveying of information requires a clear, serviceable prose. The computer aren't able to do it.

And most of all, Cronkite worried about motivation. Were the young ones going into TV news to be journalists or to be celebrities? And if the latter, what would happen to news and explanation? The Old Avuncular summed up his concerns in an interview in the *Columbia Journalism Review* and then in the Washington Journalism Center's annual Frank E. Gannett Lecture.

"There is a great body of people coming out of so-called 'communications schools' who really don't seem to me to be qualified to be practicing journalists . . ." Cronkite said in the *Columbia* interview. "They've learned the techniques of broadcasting. But I have a great concern about their motivation. I'm afraid that they're being lured into thinking of this as a glamorous business—and perhaps by the money. They really want more to be personalities, stars if you will, than journalists. I don't think they've got that gut drive which is required for all good journalists . . . [that] feeling that [the] truth needs to be known. . . . So I wonder about these people. I wonder what reporting in the next generation is going to be like. I think we could solve this problem overnight if we got back to requiring print experience before going into television."[38]

Then in the Gannett Lecture: "There are, certainly, some very bright, talented and dedicated people coming along in our profession, but we have some right to be concerned that too large a proportion . . . are more committed to being instant successes—stars—in show business than in being journalists. Their ambitions are fed in some degree . . . by the excesses in our business, not the least of which are the hiring practices at too many local [TV] stations that put the highest premium not on reporting but on the ability to giggle. It seems to me as I travel about the country that all it takes today to be an anchorperson is to be under 25, fair of face and figure, dulcet of tone and well-coiffed. And that is just for the men! . . ."[39]

The younger generation, of course, has been going to hell since ancient Sumeria. Clay tablets to that effect have been unearthed. They date from about 3000 B.C. But Cronkite's anxieties could not be dismissed generationally. Television news *is* a star system, like the rest of TV. The question is whether the stars can operate a news process. Interesting thing about human beings: Except for some physical, mental and cosmological limitations, they can do almost anything they *want to* do. It will take them a long time to figure out how to live forever. It will probably take them as long to understand themselves. They may never know God. And, possibly due to certain omissions in the evolution of the frontal lobes, they may blow themselves up. But it is not beyond their capacity to report and explain news on television. They can do that—if they *want to.*

In 1976, at a low point in his career, Dan Rather had spoken of the limitations of TV news: no essence, no details, no substance. Four years later, when he was selected to be CBS's anchorman, his tone was different. He told Tom Shales of the *Washington Post:* "I don't like the focus on the money, but I understand the realities of it. The whole star system is . . . part of the new reality."[40] Since you got money, sang Bessie Smith, it done change your mind.

But had it? Rather, now a star, was nevertheless determined to remain a journalist. He had a meager twenty-one and a half minutes each night in which to cover a vast and unruly world. But one evening in December 1981, he turned over five minutes and twenty-six seconds of this priceless time to Bill Moyers for a report on the Alaska pipeline.

This project would cost an estimated $37 billion. Moyers described legislation pending in Congress that would compel natural gas consumers to pay for the pipeline before it was built. The consumers would pay higher rates now. When they were older, they would get the gas. A list of campaign contributions by the chairman of the pipeline company was given. It was a long list. The program also quoted a Republican member of Congress, Representative Tom Corcoran of Illinois. He said the legislation was "potentially the greatest consumer ripoff in the history of the United States."

Moyers said later that Rather, as managing editor of the *CBS Evening*

News, made the decision to go ahead with the pipeline story. "I told Dan about it, and he said, 'Do it,'" Moyers said. "I said, 'It's going to be long [and] it's going to be tough,' and he said, 'Do it, for God's sake.'"[41] That was not celebrity journalism. That was journalism.

There is a saying about swallows and summers. However, the pipeline story was not an isolated instance. The TV networks, especially CBS, have made some efforts to redress the inadequacy of their prime-time news programs.

The most favored device is the special or documentary or "white paper." This is usually an hour-long treatment of a single subject, although *60 Minutes* normally deals with several topics. *Sixty Minutes* is the best known of these supplements. It has occasionally led the Nielsen audience ratings and is often cited as evidence of television's increasing maturity and its willingness to examine complicated or controversial issues.

And there is other evidence that some celebrity journalists have remained journalists. CBS's *People Like Us* (which dealt with unemployment), *The Uncounted Enemy: A Vietnam Deception* and *Central America in Revolt* were serious journalism. The reporters on these and other specials described and explained important and greatly disputed issues. They informed those persons with open minds and angered those with closed, which is what serious journalism is all about. NBC has offered strong specials on the Reagan presidency. ABC's *Nightline* is often superior news work. On public television, *The MacNeil-Lehrer Report* is nonpareil.

The addition of Moyers to the *CBS Evening News* was one of the most hopeful signs that television, against all the odds, may be able to preserve the news process. His role can be appreciated only when it is realized that most owners of local TV stations (the affiliates) are wealthy and conservative. They want the hairdo and giggle that Cronkite talked about. However, that is *all* they want. But Moyers tries to explain things. He tries to squeeze in some connexity. Moyers and Rather are *journalists.* Lastly, they and some other TV journalists are persons of conscience. Now and then, consciences are brought to bear when television presents the news. How long will the affiliates let that go on?

Journalism, like all human endeavors, must confront Wordsworth's challenge: "High instincts, before which our mortal nature did tremble like a guilty thing surprised." Only a few newspapers meet this challenge with reasonable consistency. Others fulfill it sporadically, but they seldom sustain the effort very long. The majority of the nation's newspapers have matured as most institutions mature—into a comfortable mediocrity that seeks to give as little offense as possible.

Now it is the turn of television news. It is not necessary to invoke only

Murrow, Sevareid and Fred Friendly as role models. There are journalists working in television and radio today whose professionalism equals the best in the print media. They have the qualities essential for serious journalism. They are intelligent, intellectually curious and intellectually receptive. Above all, they understand the news process and try to make it work, despite the limitations of their medium: John Chancellor, Sid Davis, Fred Graham, Phil Jones, Bernard and Marvin Kalb, Herb Kaplow, Ted Koppel, Jerry Landay, James Lehrer, Irving R. Levine, Stuart Loory, Robert MacNeil, Edward P. Morgan, Bruce Morton, Bill Moyers, Roger Mudd, Edwin Newman, Robert Pierpoint, Dan Rather, Bob Schieffer, Barry Serafin, Carl Stern, Richard Valeriani, Mike Wallace, James Wooten and others.

But what about the new generation? What is it to be, young men and women of television news? Professionalism? It is not impossible; it can be done. Or is the money too good? The fame too sweet?

IV

ON THE ROAD

At the Hotel Splendide-Plastique, all is in readiness. The hotel staff and the advance team from Washington have put together a marvel of tidy usefulness. The room is equipped with rows of long tables covered with serviceable white cloths. Some hotels favor green table coverings, which give the pressroom a passing resemblance to a pool hall, but at the Splendide-Plastique the motif is virginal whiteness.

Arranged at intervals on each table are neat little stacks of working materials: notebooks, pads of inexpensive typing paper, sharpened pencils. These have been provided by international communications companies that will transmit the reporters' stories to a waiting world. The notebooks bear the insignia of the companies—ITT, RCA or Western Union International—and sometimes an identification of the event: "Tokyo Summit 1979" or "President Carter's European Trip." The reporters take the notebooks home to their kids, who draw pictures in them.

At the entrance to the pressroom, there is a reception desk where the journalists will pick up their room assignments. At the far end of the room, a lectern from which the president's press secretary will cast his pearls. The hotel's emblem is prominently displayed on the lectern. This ensures that the name and fame of the Splendide-Plastique will be carried to distant lands by television and photographs. If the president comes to the pressroom to cast some pearls of his own, the hotel's name will be hastily covered with the presidential seal. A replica of the seal is carried on all presidential trips for this purpose. Publicity is the lifeblood.

Along one wall is a row of Telex machines. The operators are lounging beside their instruments, waiting to send the stories that the reporters will write about the summit conference, the presidential visit or the campaign stop. If the event is taking place in the United States, there will only be a certain amount of conflict between man and machine. There will be garbles in transmission, and the words that are jumbled or omitted invariably will be crucial to the sense of the story. Or a journalistic triumph intended for the *Chicago Tribune* will somehow wind up at the *Fort Worth Star-Telegram*. However, these are familiar fardels that can be borne. But if the event is overseas, the language curtain will descend. The American reporter and the foreign Telex operator will engage in an epic struggle. *Regardez* the protagonists in this contest. On one side are sweet reason and noble patience. On the other are nationalistic perversity and pigheaded stupidity.

That is what the bar is for. After losing the contest, the reporter will take his sorrows to it. The Splendide-Plastique has installed a bar in the pressroom, *naturellement*, and with that, the preparations are complete. Everything is ready. Everything is neat and tidy and well organized. The pressroom awaits the press. Like a maiden in a Gothic novel. Clean. Chaste. Demure. The pressroom is about to discover what maidens discover.

Several buses draw up outside the hotel. The group that disembarks is not the Executives' Club. It is not the annual sales meeting or the bargain tour of Romantic Rio. The motley nomads of the press have arrived.

They are an assortment. They come in all sizes, shapes and lifestyles. It is often said that reporting is a game for young persons, what with the hours, the travel, the tension, the roar of the crowd and the grease of the food. So it was not surprising that a 1977–1978 study indicated that 83.6 percent of the Washington press corps was between the ages of twenty and forty-nine. The thirties were the largest age group, accounting for 37.8 percent. The forties were next, at 25 percent, and then the twenties, with 20.8 percent.[1] But a substantial number of journalists are still grinding it out in their fifties and sixties, and a few in their seventies and even eighties. These durables climb stiffly off the press bus. They are grumbling that today undoubtedly will be worse than yesterday. Their motto is: Once a newspaperman, always a fathead.

Statistics measure whatever they measure. But they do not measure variety and individuality. There are tall reporters, short reporters, thin reporters and fat reporters. There are reporters with sculpted blow-dry haircuts that cost fifty dollars; these will adorn the evening news. And there are reporters whose hair appears not to have been cut since their sophomore year. There are reporters from the *Detroit News* and from *Dagens Nyheter* of Stockholm. From ABC and *Asahi Shimbun* of Tokyo. From the *Los Angeles Times*, the *London Daily Telegraph* and *Le Monde* of Paris. From the *Boston Globe* and the *Toronto Globe and Mail*. From

Chicago and Calcutta, Miami and Melbourne. From German television—*mein Gott*, there are a lot of people from German television.

The press corps is dressed every which way. There are journalists in Brooks Brothers and journalists in leather jackets. There are tweedy types from the *New York Times* and seedy types from obscure, impoverished news organizations. Most of the older hands are in rumpled suits or vintage sport coats that will never make a fashion list but will get them through four continents in three days. Some of the younger generation travels semipreppie: sweaters, cords, no tie. Others are in jeans or chinos and some sort of jacket, any sort. Of course, the bureau chiefs always go formal.

The television cameramen and the photographers must be able to move quickly, and they are burdened with equipment. So they dress very informally. They are object lessons in the number of combinations that can be created to go with cowboy boots.

Richard Nixon used to relax by walking on the beach fully attired—coat and tie, conventional shoes, the works. That was one difference between Richard Nixon and a reporter. The press wears what it pleases, achieving a utilitarian scruffiness. There is no dress code. When a rumor ran through the White House pressroom that the Reagan administration might impose one, the journalists reacted with the fury of a creationist reading a book. If Helen Thomas of United Press International ever is compelled to give up her raincoat, it will be the end of American journalism as we have known it. It has historic significance, that one.

Disembarking from the buses in front of the Splendide-Plastique, the press is encumbered. The reporters carry typewriters, tape recorders, briefcases and, in some instances, portable video display terminals. These are coming into increasing use as the latest blessing from technology. The portable versions of the VDT weigh between fifteen and thirty pounds. The reporter writes his story on the VDT, and the little wonder then transmits it directly into a computer in the home office. The computer then loses the story.

The reporters are further burdened with vast amounts of paper, which they carry in large, untidy bundles or cram into their typewriters or briefcases. This stuff just comes in; nothing can be done about it. To begin with, there is a detailed, minute-by-minute schedule of the president's activities that the White House gives to reporters at the outset of a trip. This schedule is known as the bible. On international trips, moreover, the White House hands out a thick notebook that discusses in excruciating detail each foreign nation that the president will visit. The bible is indispensable and is not to be discarded. It will be discussed in more detail later in this chapter. Some reporters get rid of the bulky country-by-country notebook early in the game. Others find it useful as background information for their stories; they hang on to it grimly, although the Special Theory of Journalistic Relativity states that everything weighs more in the next time zone.

The reporters also are loaded down with press releases, announcements, transcripts, newspapers and newspaper clippings, magazines and other reference material. They bring some of this with them and acquire more—much more—as the trip proceeds. The high-speed copying machine aboard the press plane operates ceaselessly, grinding out great masses of paper. As the plane is airborne after each stop, young women from the White House press office move down the aisle distributing the stenographic transcript of the president's speech in the last city, the prepared text of his speech in the next city, the transcript of the press secretary's briefing in Brussels, the agriculture secretary's background briefing in Baton Rouge or the national security assistant's deep backgrounder in Buenos Aires. It may be an announcement that the president will make in Nashville, information on the aircraft carrier he will inspect at Newport News or the world leader he will meet in New Delhi, a press release on the new program he will unveil in Toledo or the conference he will attend in Tokyo, a last-minute addition to the bible for the unscheduled stop in Pittsburgh or a statement clarifying that unfortunate misunderstanding in Paris. The press groans. The press writes the story. Then the press stores the stuff away somewhere. It may be needed for a Sunday interpretive.

In 1973 or 1974, after traveling many thousands of miles with Richard Nixon, two reporters made up a little chant. It consisted of six words repeated over and over: "On the bus, off the bus; on the bus, off the bus." The idea was to see in how many lugubrious ways these six words could be sung. It sounded best in a Yiddish accent—a sort of media *Vay iz mir.* The authors—Jerry Landay, then with ABC News, and I—considered that the chant expressed the innermost meaning of contemporary journalism.

So the reporters get off the bus and straggle into the Hotel Splendide-Plastique. They are weary, rumpled, sweaty, thirsty or on deadline. They need a drink, a shower, a bed and peace of mind. But what they absolutely must have is a pressroom and a telephone.

The first problem is finding the pressroom. If the hotel is used frequently for presidential speeches or to house politicians and journalists during political conventions or summit meetings—a so-called headquarters hotel—the reporters will know where the pressroom is. At the Waldorf-Astoria, up a couple of flights to the Terrace Court. At the George V in Paris, down one flight to a very large room. It is not hard to find. A bar will be in place. A French waiter will sell you a drink and correct your pronunciation. At hotels where the location of the pressroom is not known, the lobby becomes the milling-around area. There is a brief, desperate moment during which wasted lives are reviewed and stern resolutions sworn as to other lines of work. Then someone spots a handwritten sign or a hotel functionary pointing The Way.

The press bursts into the pressroom. The press invades, swarms into and assaults and batters the pressroom. The Mongol hordes led by Genghis Khan were as nothing. The virgin pressroom meets its fate. The bridegroom is not neat.

The pristine tables, so chaste, so white, vanish under a monumental clutter of typewriters, video display terminals, tape recorders, microphones, cassettes, tape spools, cameras, camera cases, television mini-cameras, tripods, extension cords, light meters, film packs, briefcases, attaché cases, flight bags, raincoats, jackets, newspapers, magazines, notebooks, crisp new press releases, dirty old press releases, transcripts, schedules, photocopies of stories, carbon copies of stories, clippings of stories and a vast amount of other impedimenta. Everything is unloaded in the pressroom. It is piled higgledy-piggledy on the tables, with the overflow in untidy heaps along the walls. Instant mess.

The reporters scramble to secure work spaces before the tables are covered with electronic and photographic gear. They mark their territory with a few scrawled words on a scrap of paper: Frank Cormier or Jim Gerstenzang of AP, Helen Thomas of UPI, Ralph Harris of Reuters, Don Irwin of the *Los Angeles Times,* Jim McCartney of Knight-Ridder, Tom DeFrank of *Newsweek,* Andy Glass of the Cox newspapers, Ted Knap of Scripps-Howard. In selecting a work space, two considerations are paramount: It should be close enough to a telephone so the phone can be claimed as belonging to that work space, and it should be as brightly lit as possible. The telephone company has installed several phones on each table, but there are never enough. The ideal work space is directly under a light and in close proximity to a telephone. The quick thinking necessary to evaluate these factors and swiftly select a good work space is typical of the split-second decisions required in journalism.

Like the creation of the universe, there is a great deal of noise in those first few minutes in the pressroom. Chiefly it is the noise of several dozen reporters urgently using telephones. There are many differences between reporters for newspapers, magazines, television networks and radio stations—differences in news coverage, techniques, deadlines and other things—but the telephone is the great unifier.

A reporter is a person in chronic need of a telephone. When he is on the road, the need becomes acute. Cut off from his home office during long airplane flights or bus rides, the reporter's first thought when he reaches a pressroom is to call in. He wants the editor to know where he is. He wants to know what is on the editor's mind, what he wants done and whether there are any problems. He has basic insecurities in these areas.

Even more important, the reporter wants to know what has been happening in the world in the last several hours. It will often be necessary for him to include in his story developments that have taken place elsewhere. Otherwise the story may be incomplete or outdated. When this happens, it offends the journalist's self-esteem, which is considerable. And the story may not be used, which is worse.

Every reporter dreads the day he writes a story from, say, Grand Junction, Colorado, to the effect that the president, while visiting Grand Junction, has just announced a new effort to settle a major labor dispute. Back in Washington, however, the secretary of labor has just announced that the dispute has been resolved. Reporters live in mortal fear that they will be overtaken by events.

Another reason for the telephonitis is simply that reporters are people who want to know what is going on. They crave information, and when they are on the road it is harder for them to keep up with the news. Lastly, the traveling reporter is nagged by the suspicion that the office may forget about him. Absence does not make an editor's heart grow fonder. Nothing does. The reporter knows that his editors handle many stories every day. Some of them, heaven forfend, may be as important as the story he is covering. The editors may be busy and distracted. They may lose sight of their man in the field, especially if he is on a long, slogging assignment that has not yet produced much. It can even happen on a presidential trip.

In 1962, John F. Kennedy visited Mexico. It was a state visit, with honor guards, salutes, anthems, the diplomatic corps in medals, a performance of the famous Ballet Folklorico and much high-speed motorcading around Mexico City. Kennedy was young, dashing and charismatic. Moreover, Jackie accompanied him; the Mexicans greeted *her* like the fair white goddess of the Aztecs. Immense crowds turned out; the estimate was 2 million people. In the main airport building, a large, thick observation window shattered under the pressure of human bodies. It made a helluva noise. The motorcade into Mexico City was surrealistic, by Dali out of Dante. Huge surging masses of people, hundreds of Mexican motorcycle cops racing along the route, swerving ferociously at the crowds to push them back, engines roaring, people scattering, then the motorcycles spinning around in clouds of dust and zooming back into the motorcade. A ballet *homicidico*.

Being young and impressionable, I thought it was the greatest story since sliced bread. The eyes of the world, including St. Louis, Missouri, must surely be centered on the Kennedy trip. The pressroom in Mexico

City was in the Hotel Maria Isabel. As soon as the press bus got there, I called St. Louis. The call was taken by a grizzled old news editor, a veteran of many stories. "Hello," I said, "this is Deakin." The connection was excellent. I could hear him just fine. "Where are you?" he said.

In the pressroom at the Splendide-Plastique, the noise is increasing. Typewriters and Telex machines begin to clatter. Some reporters give their stories to a Telex operator to transmit; others dictate them to a machine in the home office. This is interesting to listen to. The punctuation must be treated as words: "President Carter comma beginning a six hyphen nation trip to Europe comma the Middle East and India comma . . ."

Other reporters have nothing to write about at the moment. Some of them belly up to the bar. It must be, as Harry Truman used to say, five o'clock somewhere. Some head for their rooms. They can take a shower if they do not mind wearing the same sweaty shirt afterward; the luggage will not be delivered for hours.

Then there is the question of dinner. The reporters begin trying to track down an official for the purpose of eating, drinking and picking of brains. They discovered a long time ago that the White House staff, Cabinet members and other important news sources tend to be more accessible on the road than they are in Washington. So there is a considerable amount of wining and dining of news sources in the most costly restaurants the expense account will sustain, and a lot of late-hour drinking in hotel bars. These social contacts may be pleasant and convivial, or they may be tense and argumentative. It depends on the president's relations with the news media at that moment, the disposition of the official and many other factors that make the intercourse between journalists and public officials so adventuresome.

In the fall of 1973, Richard Nixon was at his home in San Clemente, California, brooding about Watergate. The press corps was housed, as usual, in the Surf and Sand Hotel in Laguna Beach. One evening, four reporters—R. W. (Johnny) Apple of the *New York Times*; Bernard Kalb of CBS; Pat Sloyan, then in the Hearst newspapers' Washington bureau and now with *Newsday*; and I—wandered into the bar on the top floor of the Surf and Sand for a drink before dinner. In the bar, we encountered two members of the White House staff—Richard Moore and Ken W. Clawson. A dinner invitation was extended. After an interval, the six of us crowded into Apple's car and set out for an Italian restaurant up the coast.

The interval may have been too long for Clawson. During the drive, he began to discourse upon the strangeness of life. Just think, he said, if we were in Washington I would never dream of having dinner with a bunch of reporters. No, indeed. Wouldn't think of it. The atmosphere in the car grew strained. We wondered what kind of evening it was going to be. But Apple drove on. Nothing daunted Johnny Apple.

It was a strange attitude for Clawson to take, because he had been a reporter himself. Before going to work for the Nixon administration as deputy director of communications, he had been assistant national editor and then a national reporter for the *Washington Post*. However, he was a very ambitious man. He had wanted to be the *Post's* assistant managing editor for national news, but that job went to someone else. So when Charles W. Colson (the man who wanted to fire-bomb the Brookings Institution, the man who boasted he would walk over his own grandmother to get what he wanted, the man who . . . but what the hell, everyone remembers sweet old Chuck Colson) and then Fred Malek and then Bob Haldeman (two more of America's sweethearts) urged him to join the White House staff, Clawson said yes.

The transfer of loyalties, as they say, was complete. One of Clawson's first White House projects was a statement denouncing *New York Times* columnist Anthony Lewis for an error in a story from North Vietnam. For this, he received an autographed photo of presidential speechwriter Patrick J. Buchanan. The photograph, which Clawson displayed prominently on his office wall, was inscribed: "To the man who gunned Tony Lewis." Then Clawson helped organize a complaint to NBC about Cassie Mackin's campaign reporting. He boasted to friends that he was responsible for the fact that Mackin was temporarily moved to a lesser assignment. Then Marilyn Berger, a diplomatic reporter for the *Post*, told of an evening when Clawson came to her apartment, drank Scotch and bragged that he had written the "Canuck letter." This was an anonymous letter that said Senator Edmund Muskie of Maine had uttered a racial slur against French Canadians. Berger said Clawson told her: "I wrote the fucking letter." When this got out, Clawson said Berger had misunderstood him. What he actually had said, Clawson insisted, was "I *wish* I had written that." It was on his mind. Then during the Watergate hearings, when former White House counsel John Dean was testifying about the coverup, Clawson tried hard to peddle some lubricity to reporters about the sex life of Dean's wife, Maureen. When one reporter demurred, Clawson said: "You've got to use it. Charlie [Colson] is going to kill me if I don't see this thing in print."[2]

Arriving at the restaurant, we ordered dinner and another round of drinks. While we were waiting for the food, Clawson began to talk again. He dwelt at length on one of his favorite topics—the letter he had written to the *New York Times* about the mistake in Tony Lewis's story. "I killed him," said Clawson. "I destroyed him. I bored him a new asshole." Then he switched to Apple. He said he had more journalistic experience than Apple. He said he had written more page-1 stories for the *Post* than Apple had for the *Times*. Then he switched to me. "I haven't seen many of your stories," he said. "But if I ever catch you doing the kind of thing Tony Lewis did, I'll do the same thing to you that I did to him. I'll kill you. I'll bore you a new asshole." It was getting boring.

Just as the food arrived, Clawson abruptly got up and left the table. The four reporters and Dick Moore, an older, white-haired man who was a guru to the White House staff, ate dinner and talked of this and that. After a while, we began to wonder where Clawson was. He had not come back. His veal parmigiana was getting cold. We figured him for a long visit to the men's room.

We finished dinner. We talked some more. We dragged it out. No Clawson. Finally we paid the bill and went in search of the deputy director of communications. He was not in the men's room. Thinking he might have wandered into the ladies' loo by mistake, we asked a waitress to check. He was not there. Nor was he in the kitchen or anywhere else in the restaurant.

There was a motel next door to the restaurant. It is not uncommon to check into a motel to sleep one off, so we went next door and inquired. No Clawson. By now we were thoroughly puzzled. We stood in front of the restaurant, trying to decide what to do. I had an idea. I went around to the rear of the restaurant; perhaps he had gone there to be sick and had passed out. It was the first time I had ever poked around a bunch of garbage cans looking for a member of the White House staff. No Clawson.

It was a long way to Laguna Beach. How would Clawson get back? Finally we decided to drive slowly up the highway and look for him. Maybe he had decided he could not stand the American news media anymore and was hoofing it home. We got into the car. There was Clawson, stretched out on the back seat. He was sleeping like a baby.

There is activity in the pressroom at the Splendide-Plastique: telephone calls, earlier stories being finished, reporters reading newspapers, reporters standing around talking. But in another sense there is nothing going on. Because the briefing has not been held. Until there is a briefing, the reporters are really only marking time. They may be working on a feature or an interpretive, or checking with a source. But they have no *news* to report. They are as the eager youths and diaphanous maidens on that Grecian urn, frozen in a tableau of expectancy:

When is the briefing? How long till the briefing? When the hell is he going to brief? When is the press secretary going to come to the pressroom to tell the reporters what the president has done, is doing and plans to do? When is he going to make himself available for questioning? On the road, the pressroom is the reporters' workplace, social club, reading room and milling-around area, but above all it is the place where they ask their questions, the place where they try to find out what is going on. The emphasis is on "try."

A pressroom has a rise and fall of sound. The arrival of the reporters, the preliminary sorting-out of rooms and work space, the dumping of gear all over the place—all these are the prelude. Anticipatory strings, the other voices unheard but waiting—the opening bars of the Beethoven Ninth or the Mozart C minor. A tremolo leading to a fortissimo. The briefing is the fortissimo.

And after the briefing, there is a long and vigorous tutti. Almost all the reporters are working now. They are working hard, and they are working fast. They are looking hastily through their notes, searching for that quote that will be just right for the second paragraph. They are asking each other quick questions: "What's the British unemployment rate?" "Have you got a copy of the pool report?" "How much did the House vote for defense?" The reporters are sawing away at their typewriters and VDT's. They are dictating urgently into telephones or hurrying across the room to give their stories to a Telex operator. It is deadline time. If you are a media groupie or a curious hotel guest attracted by the show, this is not the moment to venture into the pressroom and inquire which one is Dan Rather. Some codger will snarl at you. The press is working. The news is being reported.

And then it begins to die away. One by one, the typewriters fall silent. The reporters drift out of the pressroom. The photographers and cameramen pack up their gear. The Telex machines clatter a while longer, catching up with the backlog of copy, but eventually they are silent, too. As at Esterház, the musicians extinguish their candles and tiptoe from the room.

Later in the evening, after dinner, there is a reprise. A few reporters return to the pressroom to write overnight stories for afternoon newspapers of the next day. When the overnights are done, the pressroom is truly quiet. It is very late now. Nothing remains but a great jumbled confusion of empty coffee cups, overflowing ashtrays, crumpled wads of typing paper, discarded press releases, empty film packs, abandoned newspapers. The sweepers and cleaners of the Splendide-Plastique enter the pressroom to clear away the mess. "Come, children, let us shut up the box and the puppets, for our play is played out."

For the reporters, photographers, cameramen and technicians, a presidential trip begins at Andrews Air Force Base, often early in the morning. There is adventure and romance when Holmes wakes his sidekick in the predawn darkness and whispers urgently: "Quick, Watson, the game is afoot." But the hushed wonder of a 5 A.M. check-in at Andrews escapes the journalists. They have struggled out of bed at three or four in the morning for a long, long drive to the base. Most of them come by way of the beltway that encircles the Washington area. If they live in the District of Columbia, they may use a road known as Suitland Parkway. The parkway dead-ends near Andrews. The beltway, of course, has no end, but if it did it would be at Andrews.

Arriving at the Andrews passenger terminal and base operations building, the journalists straggle into a small room that has been set aside for them. It is the first of many milling-around areas. At five or six in the morning, with the president's departure several hours away and no news to report, there is nothing much to do at Andrews but drink coffee and stare groggily at each other.

That being unprofitable, the press goes outside and forms a line. A member of the White House's transportation staff checks off names against a list of those making the trip. It is not a very tight arrangement, but the transportation officer knows all the regulars, and there is a sort of recognition factor in the press corps itself. Veteran reporters cannot remember an instance in which an interloper succeeded in getting on the press plane, or even tried to. The hours are lousy.

As the transportation officer checks off names, a Secret Service agent assigned to travel on the press plane hands out small identification tags. The reporters and photographers hang these "trip passes" around their necks and try not to lose them. The trip pass is the only press identification that the Secret Service readily accepts on a presidential trip, and sometimes it even works with the local cops. The journalists are not encouraged to display their regular White House credentials when traveling; very few local police officers recognize a White House press pass, since to an untrained eye it appears to have been issued by the Pennsylvania Railroad. Nevertheless, some reporters wear all their identification—trip pass, White House pass, a new pass for political campaigns and all the other credentials that are handed out along the way by foreign governments, local authorities and sponsors of events. They operate on the assumption that if one pass will not get you in, another may. These optimists end up looking like a package about to be mailed.

With their names checked off, the journalists get on blue Air Force buses and are driven across the tarmac to the press plane. It is the first of many bus rides. Military buses are unusual in that they are designed with square wheels.

Judging from the occasional comments of people who come to an airport to see the president, some Americans have the idea that the government pays for the press plane. Some of them even believe the journalists are government employees. Their notion of the First Amendment is hazy. They see an airplane arrive shortly before Air Force One, and they see a lot of people get off. These nomads obviously are connected with the presidential trip in some way. The citizens conclude that their taxes are paying for the plane and perhaps for the nomads, too. (The press plane always takes off *after* Air Force One and lands *before* it does. This gruesome procedure ensures that if the president's plane crashes during takeoff or landing, the national media will be there to cover it).

However, the suspicions of the taxpayers are unfounded. The government does not employ the reporters and photographers. It does not pay for the press plane. The White House's transportation office handles the chartering of the plane, as a convenience for the press and, of course, to encourage maximum coverage. But the cost is borne by the news organizations that decide to cover the trip. The expense is prorated; if a TV network has ten or fifteen people on a trip, it pays ten or fifteen shares of the cost.

Journalistic interest in the imperial presidency is so great that it is often necessary to have two press planes, to accommodate the crowd. Occasionally, three are required. By long custom, one plane is allocated to the reporters. The other is for the photographers, cameramen and technicians. The reporters call this one the zoo plane. Snobbery is everywhere. The cameramen travel with a lot of equipment. Because it will be needed the moment the plane lands, it cannot be stored in the baggage compartment. The minicams, in particular, are so bulky that they are often given seats of their own. On commercial flights, the TV networks sometimes have to pay for seats for the minicams, but on White House flights they travel free. If there are many people and a great deal of equipment on a trip, the transportation office simply charters a third press plane. The minicams sit side by side, blinking their lights and talking in a strange tongue about the old days on Krypton.

It is expensive to cover the president when he travels. The cost includes:

● Plane fares, at rates ranging from coach to first class, or more. For a long time, first-class fares or higher were the rule. But these days, competition among the airlines sometimes means that they submit charter bids to the transportation office at coach rates. The food is abundant and there is no limit on drinks, but the seats are not always first class in width. A press corps fatty is a pitiful figure unless he has managed to grab a first-class seat. On long, overseas trips, the entire press plane usually is configured first class. But on shorter trips, there is the customary small first-class compartment and the rest of the seats are the familiar traveler's delight. Somehow the first-class area is almost always occupied by senior reporters of dignity and girth. Experience is the key. They have learned little tricks by which they arrange things beforehand with the transportation office.

- Waiting time for the plane. If the president spends only a short time in a city, the press plane remains at the airport. The cost of this waiting is included in the cost of the trip. If the president stays somewhere for a substantial period of time—a vacation for instance—the chartered press plane or planes resume regular service. In that case, there is another charter for the return flight to Washington. Often, however, the president takes side trips during a vacation. This can mean a lot of waiting time if the press plane stays at the airport for the side trips, or it can mean several charters.

- The cost of many other forms of transportation: the press buses that accompany the presidential motorcade into town and, when possible, from event to event, and finally and exhaustedly back to the airport; the pool cars; an occasional train ride when nostalgia overcomes the chief executive; sometimes even a steamboat trip. And, of course, the helicopters. The news media pay for their seats on the Army and Marine helicopters that grind and roar the presidential entourage from place to place. Oh, God, the helicopters. Reporters retire deaf.

- The cost of renting pressrooms, and the cost of installing telephones and Telex machines in the pressrooms. A pressroom is set up at virtually every stop on a presidential trip; the known world is littered with the debris of pressrooms. The cost is often very high. On a trip by President Reagan in December 1982, a Beverly Hills hotel set a charge of $2,200 for a room to serve as the pressroom and one other room for equipment storage—for thirty-six hours. The price was still being negotiated as this book was being written.

All these costs—press planes, press buses, helicopters, pressrooms and the rest—are rolled together in one big total and prorated among the news organizations covering a presidential trip. In addition, the individual journalists pay for their hotel rooms, meals, drinks, laundry, tips and miscellaneous expenses. They also pay for the long-distance calls or Telex time to talk to their offices and send their stories. That is, their news organizations pay for all these things. Drinks are always miscellaneous.

Now and then there are unexpected travel costs. During Jimmy Carter's trip to India in 1978, an elephant showed up one morning at the Ashoka Hotel in New Delhi, where the press corps was staying. There was a mahout on the elephant. A mahout is a man who drives an elephant. This mahout was selling elephant rides.

Dale Leibach and Connie Gerrard of the White House staff were the first to venture aboard. They did well. John Chancellor of NBC was next. Chancellor is a man of many talents. He rode the elephant with regal ease, humming Mozart's "Turkish Rondo" in the hope of speeding up the beast. Other reporters decided that an elephant ride was just the thing that had been missing from their drab lives. Soon everyone was riding the elephant. Even Jody Powell, the president's press secretary, rode the elephant. There were many jokes about this. It was said that Powell, when asked a difficult question, had a memory like an . . . what's the name of that animal? Things like that.

The mahout was a capitalist. He had a keen sense of economic opportunity. He charged Gerrard and Leibach 10 rupees each—about $1.25. By the time the last reporters boarded the elephant, the price had risen to five bucks a head.

It is beyond the scope of this book to describe the growth of the imperial presidency. There are the alliances, treaties and executive agreements that commit the United States to defend about a fourth of the nations of the world. There are the bilateral assistance agreements under which vast amounts of military equipment are supplied to scores of other countries. There is the immolatory lunacy known as the nuclear arms race. There were the assassination plots, government overthrowals and other imperial misadventures that culminated in Vietnam. There is the attitude of the government and the news media that the United States must respond to almost everything that happens on this planet. And there is the government's enormous publicity and propaganda apparatus, atop which sits the president, being created daily in his own image.

No one can fix an exact date for the beginning of the regal presidency; like Topsy, it just growed. The wealth and power of the United States increased, the American chief executive became the cynosure of national and international attention, and the imperial trappings simply followed.

The news media and the government collaborated in magnifying the presidency. As Jerry Ford discovered later, the press decided that nothing about the chief executive was too trivial to be reported. An early incident pointed the way to a superficial future. It occurred in 1959, when Eisenhower was conferring in London with Prime Minister Harold Macmillan. A reporter asked a question of staggering insignificance. Eisenhower's press secretary, Jim Hagerty, should have disdained to answer. But Hagerty would answer anything that kept the spotlight riveted on Ike. He even described this particular piece of information as—you are not going to believe this—"hard news":

Hagerty: "I have one bit of hard news. Mr. Berding [Andrew Berding, the State Department spokesman on the trip] was asked this morning if the president was sleeping in a four-poster bed, and the answer is yes, and also if he had ever slept before in a four-poster bed, and the answer is also yes."

This time, the British led a revolution. Hugh Pilcher of the *London Daily Herald* roared: "Mr Hagerty, are any of us to take these briefings seriously? Are we going to hear anything about the great international issues, or are we going to hear simply what they ate? . . . Now, a straight answer for once."[3] The American reporters applauded. Why did they applaud? They had started the whole puerile business.

A young journalist named Art Buchwald was working for the Paris edition of the *Herald Tribune*. He attended some of Hagerty's briefings in London. The four-poster bed and other imperialisms prompted Buchwald to write a famous parody:

"Q. Jim, whose idea was it for the president to go to sleep?
"A. It was the president's idea.
"Q. Did the president speak to anyone before retiring?
"A. He spoke to the Secretary of State.
"Q. What did he say to the Secretary of State?
"A. He said, 'Goodnight, Foster.'
"Q. And what did the Secretary say to the president?
"A. He said, 'Goodnight, Mr. President.'"[4]

Buchwald's Law remains a cornerstone of the press-government relationship: To get a banal answer, ask a banal question. But Buchwald never developed the corollary: Ask a serious question and get no answer at all.

The imperial presidency will not go away. There isn't much anyone can do about it. It can only destroy itself, which does not bear thinking about. Jimmy Carter, when he took office, attempted a symbolic and to some extent an actual reduction of the imperial colossus. But Carter's trip to Europe, the Middle East and India less than a year later, when he was still in a nonimperial mood, nevertheless involved an entourage of 300 persons, 4 jet airplanes, 2 special trains, helicopters, limousines, 6 tons of television equipment and immense amounts of White House communications and press office gear.[5] When Carter attended the economic summit meeting in Tokyo in 1979, it took 12 limousines to transport the American delegation to the Akasaka Palace for the opening session. The other dignitaries also required limousines—a procession of 124 long, black gas-guzzlers was drawn up outside the palace. To keep their air conditioning going, their motors ran throughout the two-hour-and-forty-five-minute meeting.[6] At that time, the Western world was experiencing one of its periodic energy crunches; in the United States there were long lines at gasoline stations. Imperialism is made of stern stuff.

When the president travels to foreign lands, he is accompanied by an "official party"—usually the secretary of state and often other Cabinet members; high-ranking State Department officials; the U.S. ambassadors to the countries that will be visited; the national security assistant and other senior White House staff members; and other advisers. But the official party of fifteen or twenty persons is only imperialism's visible surface.

The president's state is kingly. Thousands at his bidding speed and post o'er land and ocean without rest. He is accompanied also by personnel from the White House press office, the White House Communications Agency (known as WACA), the White House transportation office and other White House and State Department staffers, as well as military aides, protocol officers, Secret Service agents, physicians, nurses, medics, valets, maids, hairdressers, interpreters, customs officials, pilots, navigators, stewards, stewardesses and special baggage handlers. There are, in addition, hordes of reporters, columnists, TV producers, photographers, cameramen, soundmen, lighting technicians, film editors, unit managers, engineers and communications company representatives. Advance men have gone ahead to plan the president's schedule on a minute-by-minute basis and to arrange hotel accommodations and press facilities. The Secret Service has checked the kitchens that will prepare the president's food, the bedrooms where he will sleep, the public places where he will appear. The host countries have mobilized thousands of policemen, detectives and antiterrorist squads; the cost of a summit meeting these days is upward of $10 million. Presidential limousines have been flown from Washington, courier planes are waiting to carry people and documents back and forth, Navy ships are patrolling the ocean routes over which Air Force One will fly, the Joint Chiefs of Staff and U.S. military installations have been alerted to be alert, and everyone has liaised with everyone else until everyone is red in the face. Lincoln had two secretaries.

The gargantuan logistics of presidential travel gave rise to a story that may or may not be true. Before Richard Nixon's first trip to the Soviet Union, the story goes, a White House advance man was talking to a Russian official.

"First, we'll need three hundred rooms in the Intourist Hotel," the American said.

"No problem," said the Russian.

"Then we'll need twenty Telex machines," said the American.

"No problem," said the Russian.

"And we'll need forty long-distance lines," said the American.

"No problem," replied the Russian, "because it's all impossible."

One of the little-known measurements of imperialism is the bible. This, however, is a secular humanist bible. The reporters are given this detailed schedule of the president's trip shortly before departure. The bible always has been a lengthy document, but in recent years it has often reached proportions that overwhelmed the White House's copying machines. It is hard to overwhelm a White House copying machine. Sometimes the entire bible is handed out at the beginning of a trip, but other bibles are so long that they have to be distributed piecemeal, on a day-to-day basis. The next day's schedule becomes known the night before. This adds a certain spice.

The bible for Eisenhower's trip to Latin America, a classic of the genre, was thirty-five pages long. It apparently was drawn up by the man who writes instructions for assembling children's bicycles on Christmas Eve. One section of this bible illustrated the meticulousness with which the Free World conducts its affairs. The segment covered a period of a few minutes during a state dinner in Buenos Aires:

> 9:10 p.m. The president, accompanied by Ambassador and Mrs. Beaulac, arrives at the principal entrance to the Plaza Hotel (Point A). He is met at the door by the chief of protocol, Ambassador Luti. Ambassador Luti escorts the president through the lobby, up the stairs at Point B (18 steps) to Point C, where he meets President Frondizi, Mrs. Frondizi, Foreign Minister Taboada, Mrs. Taboada and Secretary Herter.
>
> 9:12 p.m. The two presidents with Mrs. Frondizi and Ambassador and Mrs. Beaulac proceed up eight steps on the left to Point D while Secretary Herter, Foreign Minister Taboada and Mrs. Taboada turn right and walk directly to their seats at Point E. At Point D the two presidents converse briefly (Col. Walters is at President Eisenhower's side) and then (with President Frondizi offering his arm to Mrs. Beaulac and President Eisenhower to Mrs. Frondizi and with President Frondizi going first) go down eight steps at Point F to the banquet hall floor where all the guests are standing by their seats. The members of the party walk to Point E where they sit down. . . .

Got that? The reporters puzzled over it for quite a while. Some were of the opinion that it was in Swahili. Nonsense, said others, it's a new code. This means war. Things never did get sorted out. Where was Luti after Point C? If Eisenhower and Frondizi went up eight steps to Point D, why did they go down eight steps at Point F? Where were Boardwalk and Park Place?

The Reagan administration is showing a spirit of retrenchment. The bible for Reagan's trip to the Ottawa summit meeting in 1981 was only ten pages long. However, it was accompanied by seven pages of pool assignments and other information. Moreover, it was only a preliminary bible. There were admonitions such as this one: "Press Note: During the dinner meeting of the heads of state and government, their schedule for Monday, July 20 will be finalized. The following information is, therefore, tentative." That meant the bible would grow and grow. Until it was finalized.

The man who writes the bicycle instructions is still on the job. Points A through F have disappeared, but they have been replaced by throws, risers and cutaways: "Camera Positions: The camera throw for the arrival of Air Force One is approximately 150 feet. The Air Force One pool will exit via the rear stairs and will be escorted under the left wing for cut-away coverage, after which it will disband. The throw for the president's arrival at Montebello is between 150 and 250 feet and will be 50 feet when the president is escorted by Prime Minister Trudeau to the Château. There will NOT be a riser for the official group photograph. . . ." What? No riser?

Sometimes there are supplements to the bible. When Carter went to South America and Africa in 1978, the reporters were given a two-page "health advisory" prepared by the White House medical office. Judging from this document, the president and the hundreds of people traveling with him were heading into unimaginable dangers. In all four countries on the itinerary, it warned, water and food were "possible sources of contamination." The advisory said only well-cooked foods should be eaten— no salads, no milk. It listed a large number of diseases that could strike at any moment, among them amoebic dysentary, gastroenteritis, hepatitis, rabies and schistosomiasis, whatever that is.

In Brasília, the capital of Brazil, "all animals should be avoided," the advisory said. In Rio de Janeiro, "theft is a great problem, especially on the beach and in the streets. Carry little of value with you." Those doctors don't miss anything. And in Lagos, Nigeria, "fresh water is contaminated. Beaches are unsafe due to the severe undertow. The sun is extremely hot and there is great danger of sunburn, even on overcast days."

By this time, the press had the nervous wobblies. But still to come was the deadly mamba. In Monrovia, the capital of Liberia, "poisonous snakes, particularly the mamba, are prevalent," the advisory warned. "Avoid the shoreline and areas of thick vegetation. Report all bites immediately." Sometimes I think the drums will drive me mad.

It turned out that the real peril was electricity. Arriving at the hotel in Caracas, Venezuela, hot, dusty and tired, the press corps discovered there was no power. There were no lights or running water in the rooms. The

Telex machines were not operating. The beer was warm. After an hour or so, the electricity came on. Then it went off again. Then on, then off. And still to come, up ahead somewhere, was the deadly mamba.

As scholars never tire of pointing out, the imperial presidency is partly the creation of the imperial media. The press contingent that accompanies the chief executive when he travels has reached proconsular proportions. Caesar, in his *Commentaries on the Gallic War,* described the proposed migration of the Helvetians—the inhabitants of the Alpine regions. He listed the immense amount of impedimenta—goods, chattels, wagons—that would be involved. When the president and the press travel, it is the migration of the Helvetians.

On a major campaign swing or a foreign trip, the press corps will number 150 to 200 persons or more. As a result, many of the president's activities have to be covered by pools of reporters, photographers and television personnel, selected on a rotating basis. In a modern bible, there often is more about the pools than there is about the president. The scrambled comings and goings of the pools have a Marxian quality. Groucho, not Karl. Here is a half day in the life of Ronald Reagan and his poolers:

> 6 a.m. Frenette House pool assembles at the U.S. Press Center and departs en route Frenette House.
> 7:30 a.m. Frenette House pool arrives Frenette House.
> 8 a.m. The president has breakfast with Prime Minister Suzuki. Press coverage to be determined.
> 9:30 a.m. Press pool number six assembles at the U.S. Press Center and departs en route Montebello.
> 11:10 a.m. Press pool number six arrives Montebello Media Center and proceeds to press area.
> 11:30 a.m. Press pool number seven assembles at the U.S. Press Center and departs en route the National Media Center.
> 11:45 a.m. Press pool number seven arrives National Media Center and departs en route Government House.
> 12 noon. Press pool number seven arrives Government House and is escorted to Marine One landing area.
> 12 noon. Press pool number eight assembles at the U.S. Press Center and departs en route National Media Center.
> 12:15 p.m. Press pool number eight arrives National Media Center and departs en route Government House.
> 12:30 p.m. Press pool number eight arrives Government House and is escorted to press area.

12:30 p.m. The president departs Château Montebello en route Government House, via Marine One. . . .

It is nice to meet up with the president again after all this time.

All this complicated dashing around the landscape had a simple purpose. The press pools were being positioned in advance at the places the president would be. During the morning, Reagan was going to leave Frenette House and go to the Château Montebello and then Government House for various meetings and events. Press pool number six was going to cover him at the château. Press pools seven and eight were both going to be at Government House but to cover two different events—a reception given by Prime Minister Pierre Trudeau and a luncheon given by the governor-general of Canada.

It would have been impossible for buses filled with the entire press corps to keep up with Reagan's limousines and helicopters (Marine One is a presidential helicopter). The buses would have arrived long after the president. The reporters would have missed whatever was said or done outside the château and Government House, if anything. The "photo opportunities" would have been lost. Most important of all, it takes time for TV crews to set up their equipment.

So most of the coverage is done by pools. The reporters who have not drawn a pool stay in the pressroom and cover the event from TV. Ain't modern life wonderful? They do not like it, but there is nothing they can do about it. However, they often see more on the tube than they would if they were in the madding crowd. Some things on the schedule are marked "open coverage," meaning that anyone can be there, but as the imperial media grow and grow, open coverage dwindles. It is a logistical nightmare and has to be reserved for only a few major events.

The modern press bible is designed primarily for television. Network news executives have to know how many camera crews will be required and where they will have to be positioned and how much time will be available for transporting and editing videotape. The bible tells them how many media events there will be and when and where they will take place. The press corps as a whole may not get the bible until the last moment, but the TV news executives usually know its highlights well in advance. The schedule for a presidential trip has increasingly become a shooting script for a television program.

The duty of a pool reporter is to cover an event for the other reporters and write a pool report for them. The pooler does his report before filing anything to his own newspaper, magazine or network, so that everyone has the news simultaneously. The wire services—the Associated Press and United Press International—are represented on all pools and are exempted from writing pool reports, although in a pinch they will do so.

A pool report is simply an account of what happened. But since only the facts in it are going to be used and the pool report is not going to appear in print as written, little comments creep in. They are mostly of a sarcastic nature. They reflect the irreverence and disillusionment of men and women whose work puts them in constant contact with the nation's chief politician. The shifts and expedients, dodges and twists, personality defects and intellectual shortcomings of *any* politician, if observed too closely for too long, produce an overwhelming inclination to jump off a bridge. In a president, these imperfections are writ large. But the reporters are straitened by the paper chains of objectivity; very little of a president's real *flavor* gets into their stories. The pool report is their escape valve. Instant catharsis.

The humor is often predictable. If the president (or any candidate) discards the prepared version of a speech and wings it, the pool report is almost certain to refer to him as a textual deviant. Or a president—a Democrat, let us say—is rebuffed when he seeks to kiss a frightened baby. The pooler is likely to comment that the infant was probably a Republican. Or the president has been working the crowd at an airport— shaking hands and greeting people. "Having healed the sick," the pool report begins, "the chief executive reboarded Air Force One . . ." A variation says the president "cured six cases of scrofula in Sioux Falls." If the president—Lyndon Johnson in this case—tries to pattern himself after Franklin D. Roosevelt, the pool report on a White House event concludes: "His cigarette holder at a jaunty angle, the president wheeled himself slowly from the room." God knows how old these are, but each new generation of reporters rediscovers the eternal verities.

Sometimes true heights are reached. Pye Chamberlayne of UPI Audio was the author of this commentary during the 1980 presidential contest: "'I don't think this campaign can reach a much lower level of nastiness,' Reagan press secretary Lyn Nofziger said today, adding that President Carter has not yet recovered from his case of venereal disease." On one of Carter's overseas trips, the pool on Air Force One was briefed and briefed and briefed by officials anxious to draw attention to the president's diplomatic triumphs. Each briefing necessitated another pool report. Curtis Wilkie of the *Boston Globe*, the newspaper pooler, began the last of the interminable series as follows: "I tried, oh Lord I tried, lodge brothers and sisters, but I could not prevent another pool report."

Old pool reports fade away. Their authors are forgotten. It is a pity. On a long-ago Eisenhower trip, a pool reporter discovered that the motorcade had got so far ahead that he could hardly see it. "Looking into the distance," he wrote, "I could see a man standing in an open car with his hands raised above his head. I think it was a stick-up."

The enemy is fatigue. On presidential campaigns and foreign trips, the working days are measured in double-digit hours and thousands of miles. A 2,500-mile day is routine, a 3,000-mile day is a piece of cake, a 5,000-mile day is not uncommon. The reporters are flying, riding buses, covering speeches and writing stories eighteen hours a day, twenty hours a day, who's counting? Terminal exhaustion sets in early.

In 1960, John F. Kennedy and Richard M. Nixon staged an endurance contest and called it a presidential campaign. Kennedy was forty-three years old; Nixon was forty-seven. Both were determined to present a vigorous contrast to the incumbent, Dwight Eisenhower, who was seventy and ailing. They went at it like whirling dervishes.

Nixon was operating at a disadvantage: He had promised to campaign in every state. This meant he spent precious time sewing up small states while Kennedy concentrated on the heavily-populated states with lots of electoral votes. Early in the campaign, in Greensboro, North Carolina, Nixon banged his left knee on a car door. The bruise became infected and he was hospitalized from August 29 to September 9. This would have given him a perfect excuse to forget about the every-state pledge, but he kept his promise.

The campaign was a ball-buster. September 13 was a typical Nixon day. It began in San Francisco with a press conference at 7:30 A.M. and then a speech. The candidate then flew to Portland, Oregon, motorcaded to Vancouver, Washington, for a noon speech, went back to Portland for two more speeches and then flew to Boise, Idaho. The last speech of the day was in Boise at 10 P.M. It was not unusual for Kennedy to make fifteen to twenty speeches a day. His record was set on October 25, in Illinois, when he made twenty-four speeches. The reporters called it "a day that will live in infamy."

As the campaign neared its end, Nixon had not visited Alaska. There it was—three whole electoral votes. So in the final forty hours, Nixon flew from Los Angeles to Anchorage, a distance of about 2,500 miles. Then he flew from Anchorage to Detroit—3,100 miles across Canada's vast western provinces. In Detroit, he held a telethon, answering called-in questions for four hours. Then he flew to Chicago, where he appeared on a windup television program with Eisenhower and the Republican vice-presidential candidate, an easygoing man named Henry Cabot Lodge. Then Nixon flew back to Los Angeles. The total distance traveled in those forty hours was more than 8,000 miles—about a third of the way around the world. In that time, the reporters never saw the inside of a hotel, never changed a shirt, never did anything but fly and write.

After three hours' sleep, the candidate got up and went to East Whittier, California, to vote. He arrived at 7:30 in the morning at the polling place, a rumpus room in the home of Mr. and Mrs. Roger McNey. I was one of the pool reporters. As Nixon and his wife left the McNey house, I happened to fall in step beside Mrs. Nixon. I was wiped out. I could not think of anything to say. What finally came out was inane. "How do you feel, Mrs. Nixon?" I asked.

For a moment, Pat Nixon's smile vanished. The smile that had stayed on her face through 64,000 miles of campaigning (this was the Nixon staff's estimate—heaven help us, 30,000 miles a month). The smile that had held fast through countless rallies at airports, shopping centers and auditoriums. Through an infinity of "Nixonettes" wearing white dresses and chanting: "We want Nixon, we want Nixon, we want Nixon, to be our prez-ee-dent." Through endless hands to be shaken and bouquets to be held in her lap while her husband made speeches. Through all the frantic days and restless nights and hasty meals (in Secaucus, New Jersey, Nixon stopped for lunch during a motorcade. I shared a booth with the candidate and his wife at a roadside restaurant and discovered that Nixon had no small talk, no casual conversation at all; stolidly and silently he worked his way through a cheeseburger and a pineapple malt). Through all the cities and towns and farmlands and mountains and painted deserts, that smile had remained frozen on Pat Nixon's face. And then, at last, the trumpets trailed in the dust and the big parade came to an end. And Pat Nixon's smile suddenly disappeared. And she snapped a bitter, brief reply:

"How *should* I feel?"

The exhaustion shows up in many ways. The literature is replete with reporters who missed baggage calls and wake-up calls and bus and plane departures. Reporters have strong drink taken, in an effort to unwind after a twenty-hour day, and in consequence have failed to write their stories. Folklore tells of a reporter who had been overserved. Five colleagues learned of it, separately. Each came to his assistance. "Liked all five stories," the editor wired back. "Number three was best."

One morning, Robert Semple of the *New York Times* struggled out of bed for an early baggage call. Almost all baggage calls on political campaigns and presidential trips are very early. It takes a long time to transport the mountain of luggage from the hotel to the airport and stow it on the press plane. "Bags in the lobby at 5 a.m." is the bible's daily, dismaying instruction. Some reporters believe there is an infallible way to spot a political loser: his campaign schedule has baggage calls at a civilized hour. However, this one was a very early call, and the day before had been hell on wheels. Groggily, Semple began to pack. As tired as he was, he nevertheless was thorough. He had only one pair of shoes with him. He packed them.

A classic exhaustion story concerned a reporter who drove halfway across the state of Iowa during the night to join the vice-presidential campaign of George Bush. With no sleep, the reporter then put in a long, long day of speeches and travel. In his hotel room in Des Moines that night, he called his office to talk to his editor. "Just a minute," the operator said. She put him on hold. The reporter settled back on the bed to wait. Six hours later he woke up. He was still on hold.

The exhaustion must be overcome. The tedium must be relieved. Day after day, mile after weary mile, the reporters listen to the candidate deliver his set speech at an infinity of shopping malls and an eternity of rallies. The standard speech is new to the folks in Cedar Rapids or Miami Beach, but the reporters have heard it scores of times. John F. Kennedy, in the 1960 campaign, addressed many college audiences. On almost every campus, he quoted Otto von Bismarck. It seems the Iron Chancellor had said that one third of Germany's students drank themselves insensible every night. Another third spent their time fighting duels. But the last third—ah, the last third would rule Germany. Bismarck probably said this only once, but Kennedy said it repeatedly. In the same campaign, Richard Nixon told his audiences a sad story about his impoverished childhood. One of his brothers wanted a pony, but there was no money for ponies. Nixon told this story so many times that the reporters came to know exactly when he was leading up to it. Just before he got to his brother's deprivation, a low but audible chorus would be heard. It was the reporters. They were singing, "Pony Boy, Pony Boy."

The "basic speech" used by almost every presidential candidate has led to misunderstandings. Timothy Crouse, in his book on the 1972 Nixon-McGovern campaign, criticized "pack journalism." He accused the reporters of being reluctant to lead their stories with some element that differed from the wire service leads. "They wanted to avoid 'call-backs'— phone calls from their editors asking why they had deviated from the A.P. or U.P.I.," Crouse wrote.[7] The result, he said, was a bland journalistic uniformity. A herd mentality in which everyone went along with the wires.

This missed the point. By the time a presidential campaign is a few weeks old, the national journalists traveling with a candidate have reported his basic speech many times. They have covered his major positions again and again. The basic speech is original and wondrous to the local newspapers—and besides, the honor of the thing! The candidate is visiting their hometown! They cover it like the dew covers Dixie. But the basic speech is *not* new to editors of large newspapers whose reporters have been covering the campaign right along, or to news executives of wire services and TV networks. So the national reporters are looking for something *new* at each campaign stop. They recognize instantly a new proposal by the candidate, a change in his position, an inconsistency with something he has said before, a reply to criticism, a denunciation of his opponent, a resort to demagoguery or anything else that adds a fresh dimension to the campaign. The wire service reporters lead with it. So do the rest of the national reporters—and for the same reason. It is new. *That* is pack journalism.

To combat the monotony, a considerable amount of poker is played on the press plane. The wives and children of the journalists do not make political trips, but when the president takes a vacation, the reporters and cameramen are permitted to bring their families. The journalists never have to ask where their children are. They are watching the poker game. Hour after hour, the kiddies observe the big bread pile up. They gain the impression that their fathers are wealthy and undoubtedly will be able to send them to Harvard. Achieving, at last, an elite. It does no good to point out that press plane poker is like life itself: no rich without poor.

Games with names also help relieve the tedium. During the 1960 campaign, Nixon made a speech on the grounds of the Florida state capital at Tallahassee. A man named Hoskins was running for a state office on the Republican ticket. His supporters were displaying signs promoting his candidacy. Art Buchwald had recently returned from Paris and was covering the Nixon campaign. He wished to refamiliarize himself with the curious folkways of his native land. The Nixon campaign qualified.

No one knows why certain things strike reporters as funny. But Buchwald and Charles (Chuck) Roberts of *Newsweek* decided that Hoskins would amuse their colleagues. Night had fallen. The boys were slumped in the bus, waiting for Nixon to finish. Buchwald and Roberts organized the Hoskins forces. Suddenly a mad parade of Hoskins signs encircled the press bus, marching round and round. Led by Buchwald and Roberts, the procession urged the reporters to support Hoskins, to write about Hoskins, to thrust Hoskins onto the national scene. Hoskins was the answer to the country's problems. Win with Hoskins.

For sometime thereafter, the reporters made up slogans about Hoskins and wrote jocular stories about Hoskins. The climax occurred on the press plane late one night. The plane was on its way from Misery to Affliction. The reporters were tired and were trying to sleep. But Buchwald, in a rear seat, was thinking about a famous episode a decade before in which Secretary of State Dean Acheson had said he would not turn his back on Alger Hiss when Hiss was accused of espionage. Nixon had made the Acheson statement a major political issue. The reporters awoke to see Buchwald striding dramatically up the aisle. At the front of the plane, he spun around, spread his arms wide and cried: "And just remember one thing: *Hoskins never turned his back on Alger Hiss!*"

Sometimes the reporters play a game in which they roll an orange or a tennis ball up and down the aisle of the press plane. During the 1980 campaign, Nancy Reagan did this each time the plane took off, for good luck. But the press corps has been doing it for years; damned if I know why. Some reporters decorate the press plane with photographs of presidents or other political figures. Sardonic comments are written on these photos. The radio reporters provide one of the most reliable amusements. They save tapes of speeches in which prominent politicians engage in a life-and-death struggle with the English language, and lose. These tapes are played repeatedly. A longtime favorite was a speech by Hubert Humphrey at the Bedford-Stuyvesant housing project in New York. Humphrey simply could not pronounce Bedford-Stuyvesant. He tried again and again. Finally he burst out desperately: "What the hell *is* the name of this place?" Another classic was Jerry Ford's effort to say "fly swatter." At the end of a long day of campaigning by train in Illinois, Ford tried to tell a crowd that Jimmy Carter "speaks loudly but carries a fly swatter." It had been a *very* long day. Refreshments had been served. Ford could not say "fly swatter." He fumbled it so many times that the crowd began to laugh. Ford began to laugh. Everyone was laughing. The closest he got was "fly spotter." Some reporters thought the best version was "shy flotter." Others preferred "sply shotter."

Some reporters write songs. More accurately, parodies of songs. The reasons for this are not known. They just have the urge. The parodies are intensely topical. They are you-had-to-be-there songs. Therefore, background information is required to make them intelligible years later.

In 1961, for example, President Kennedy appointed G. Mennen Williams to be assistant secretary of state for African affairs. Williams, who had been governor of Michigan, was known as Soapy because his family manufactured shaving lotion and other toiletries. At that time, the new African nation of Zaire (formerly the Belgian Congo) was coming into existence, under the presidency of Joseph Kasavubu. A civil war was under way; the Congo was a dangerous place. So the reporters sang a song to Williams. It began:

> *Far across the ocean blue,*
> *Kasavubu waits for you.*
> *Bye, bye, Soapy.*

Also in the early 1960's, an election was held in Canada. Prime Minister John Diefenbaker, a Conservative, was pitted against Lester B. (Mike) Pearson, the Liberal leader. A major issue in the campaign was Diefenbaker's plan to sell wheat from Canada's western provinces to the People's Republic of China. The American reporters covering the campaign wrote several songs. One was entitled "The Daring Young Dief on the Flying Trapeze." It contained these lines:

> *Oh, he floats through the provinces*
> *With the greatest of ease,*
> *Selling stale wheat to the Commie Chinese . . .*

Diefenbaker did not speak French very well, a political handicap in Quebec. So another stanza went:

> *He zips through Quebec*
> *With magnificent ease,*
> *Mangling his vowels and spitting his P's.*
> *The natives all love it,*
> *They think it's Chinese—*
> *Diefy is running again.*

Perhaps the merriest of the journalistic troubadors was Laurence Burd of the *Chicago Tribune.* Eisenhower once listed Burd as one of his friends in the press corps. They did play golf together now and then, but Ike presumably never heard the songs Burd wrote about him. His finest effort was entitled "We're Ike's Millionaires." Journalistic songs, like pool reports, do not survive long. But if the voters persist in electing presidents with very wealthy friends, Larry Burd's masterpiece may remain relevant:

> *We're Ike's millionaires,*
> *We're Wall Street's bulls and bears,*
> *And we've got*
> *Our pockets full of dough.*
> *Our bank accounts aren't light,*
> *And that seems to count with Dwight,*
> *Cause we've got*
> *Our pockets full of dough.*
> *We're Triple A in Dun and Bradstreet,*
> *We've got fleets of Cadillacs,*
> *And we calculate we're worth our weight*
> *In income tax.*
> *Ike's our cup of tea,*
> *He's our pal in luxury,*
> *Cause we've got*
> *Our pockets full of dough.*
> *We've got oil and cola stocks,*
> *We didn't buy them in odd lots,*
> *Cause we've got*
> *Our pockets full of dough.*
> *We make the stock exchange our hangout,*
> *But when Ike wants us near,*

Shine or rain, we hop a plane,
And answer, 'Here!'
Ike's our president,
Down to our last red cent,
Cause we've got
Our pockets full of dough. [8]

The reporters never tired of singing Larry Burd's songs. The maestro himself led the singing, slapping his hand on his knee to keep the beat, his eyes squeezed shut in creative ecstasy. It was a great comfort on a press bus at two in the morning. Refreshments again were served.

Equally comforting were the contrivances of James M. Naughton, then of the *New York Times*. Without doubt, Jim Naughton was one of the greatest tedium-breakers and mischief-makers in American journalism. Naughton of the *Times*. The reporter who brought the sheep into the Peoria Hilton. And charged the beast to his expense account, under the heading "share of ewe rental." The reporter who wore a chicken costume at a presidential press conference. And charged *that* to his expense account likewise. The reporter who sent the beloved planetary message to the editors in New York and then left for Philadelphia. An able reporter, slight and wiry and with a choirboy's smile. But behind that seraphic innocence was sinful humor.

The sheep was first. In 1976, Jerry Ford and Jimmy Carter were campaigning for the presidency, amid mounting indifference. In Illinois one day, Ford spoke interminably about agriculture. Arriving at the Peoria Hilton many long hours later, Naughton had agriculture on his mind. It occurred to him that *Newsweek*'s White House reporter, Thomas M. De-Frank, was a graduate of Texas A & M. That had something to do with agriculture. Naughton decided DeFrank might welcome a reminder of his college career.

A conspiracy was quickly organized. Naughton enlisted some other journalists. They talked to a White House advance man who was familiar with the local scene. The advance man located a farmer who was willing to rent a sheep for a few hours. The fee was twenty-five dollars. Cheap at twice the price. In order to get DeFrank out of his hotel room for a while, Naughton brought Ford's press secretary, Ron Nessen, into the plot. Nessen lured DeFrank into the bar by promising him a hot item for *Newsweek*'s "Periscope" column. You always wondered where those came from. Ford himself was kept informed of the conspiracy at every step. As a matter of fact, he was invited to join it. The president regretfully declined.

The conspirators gathered at the motor entrance to the hotel to wait for the sheep. Attracted by the milling around, a man and woman joined the group. They were either staying at the hotel or had been drinking in the bar; no one ever knew which. After a while, a pickup truck arrived, but the sheep was not in the back where the reporters expected it to be. Instead, it was up front with the farmer. John Mashek, then the White House reporter for *U.S. News and World Report,* opened the passenger door. He was looking at the sheep's rear end. Mashek knew little about agriculture. "Do you have a leash?" he asked the farmer.

The journalists were inexpert but determined. They maneuvered the sheep into an elevator and up to DeFrank's room. The man and woman who had strayed into the situation came along with them. Once inside the room, the group of about a dozen reporters, photographers and laity tried to find concealment. Some hid in the closet, but it was not large enough for all. So the rest, including the unknown man and woman, crowded into the shower. "Do you do this all the time?" the woman asked. Naughton was nonchalant. "Oh, every other night or so," he replied. There was giggling and hilarity behind the shower curtain. The sheep wandered around the room, bleating disconsolately and leaving little tokens of its nervousness.

DeFrank, when he got back to his room, handled the situation professionally. He said it made his ulcer act up. Naughton immediately sent Ford a shower report, describing the episode in detail. The next morning, the president encountered DeFrank. "I understand you had a visitor last night," Ford said sweetly. Naughton put a five-dollar item on his expense account, for his share of the sheep rental. He wondered whether New York would know what a ewe was. "It went right through," he said.

This story has no moral, this story has no end, sang Frankie immediately after plugging Johnny. This story only goes to show that you had better not mess around with Tom DeFrank. He quietly vowed vengeance. It was not long in coming.

The campaign continued. In October, Ford addressed a rally in San Diego. While the crowd waited for him to arrive, it was entertained by various celebrities. These included Zsa Zsa Gabor and a local radio personality dressed in a chicken costume. Naughton took one look at the costume and said: "I've got to have that." Specifically, he wanted the chicken head. Nessen overheard the remark and took Naughton backstage to meet the chicken man. Naughton tried to buy the head. No way, said the chicken man. However, after some further discussion, the chicken man said he had a spare head. He would sell it for one hundred dollars. "Done," said Naughton, and gave him a check. Money was no object.

The next day was another of those endurance contests that substitute for rational discourse in American politics. Hour after hour, the president and the press careened up and down the West Coast. When they finally arrived in Portland, Oregon, the Free World's leader and the national press were a collection of basket cases. Every tortured fiber cried out for sleep. But the bible said sleep was not to be in Portland but in Pittsburgh. That meant a flight of almost 3,000 miles in the middle of the night. By this time, Naughton recalls, "I was getting surly."[9]

Everyone was getting surly. But all right, said the reporters, if that's the way it has to be, at least let's get on the goddamn plane and go. However, there was a delay. Press secretary Nessen was not happy with the news coverage that Ford had received that day. One more effort must be made to capture the West Coast. So Nessen decided the president would hold a press conference at the Portland airport before departing for Pittsburgh. This would be primarily for the local and regional media; the deadlines back east had long since passed.

Ford arrived at the airport and the press conference began. Local reporters, alert and eager, crowded to the front to ask questions. The national press drooped wearily on the fringes. At this point, Naughton recalled later, "an impulse overtook me." He slipped aboard the press plane, put on the chicken head and rejoined his colleagues at the rear of the news conference. Ford's chief of staff, Richard Cheney (now a congressman from Wyoming), spotted the chicken head. Cheney knew the *New York Times* was underneath those feathers. He urged Naughton to ask the president a question. This is known as the needle.

"Suddenly it occurred to me that I might have made a tactical error," Naughton said later. Certain qualms came to him. They had to do with A. M. (Abe) Rosenthal, managing editor of the *Times*. Rosenthal can be excitable. "I thought to myself," said Naughton, "is Abe going to understand this?"[10]

However, all might still have been well. The chicken head was at the rear of the crowd of reporters. It was not especially noticeable. No photographs had been taken. Naughton began a discreet withdrawal toward the press plane.

And then Tom DeFrank got his revenge. DeFrank sized up the situation rapidly. There was a television camera behind Ford. It was pointed at the reporters. If the chicken head could be elevated above the crowd . . .

DeFrank motioned to a couple of colleagues. There was no need for words; journalists are quick-witted. DeFrank and the others blindsided that chicken head. They grabbed Naughton and hoisted him aloft. They held him high. They bounced him around. The chicken head gyrated madly in full view of the TV camera—and into national prominence. The morning TV shows ate it up. The front pages of newspapers likewise. Consider the situation: the *New York Times*. At a presidential press conference. In chicken drag.

At this point, Naughton got very lucky. A short time before, managing editor Rosenthal had decided it was time to get the feel of the campaign. He had spent a few days with the press contingent covering Jimmy Carter. He had seen at first hand the boredom and frustration of the reporters as they covered a tedious and mediocre campaign. He had observed their fatigue. He had heard the jokes and songs with which the traveling press attempts to lighten its exhaustion. An article of faith with many editors is that their Washington correspondents ought to be brought back to the home office from time to time, to find out what the "real America" is like. Somehow it does not occur to them to find out what the real reporting is like. However, Rosenthal had spent some time on the bus. He was disposed to be tolerant.

That was Naughton's first break. Then, sometime later, he encountered the *Time*'s publisher, Arthur Ochs (Punch) Sulzberger. Naughton told Sulzberger he was going to put the chicken head on his expense account. "Sure, go ahead," said the publisher. Naughton filed an expense account with a hundred-dollar item: "Chicken for the president—authorized by Mr. Sulzberger." Back came a letter from an editor in New York. He was very dubious about the hundred dollars. However, there was that Sulzberger authorization. The editor suggested that the *Times* pay half. As Naughton was weighing this offer, another letter arrived. This one was from the chicken man in San Diego. He said he had had so much fun reading about the episode that he could not bring himself to charge for the head. He returned Naughton's check.

The head now belonged to Naughton, gratis. But he did not feel right about keeping it. So it is now in the Gerald R. Ford Museum in Grand Rapids, Michigan.

Memory is the curse of the writing class. DeFrank could not forget the sheep. Those sad, reproachful eyes. That mess in his hotel room. So he consulted with Cheney, the White House chief of staff. The result was the Great Ford Interview Scam.

A few days after the 1976 election, Cheney called Naughton. He said the defeated president was going to Camp David for the weekend, without telling anyone. Cheney offered Naughton an exclusive interview with Ford. He said Ford had "a lot of things he wants to get off his chest." If the *New York Times* wanted the interview, Cheney said, Naughton should show up at Camp David at 9 A.M. the following Saturday. Did the *Times* want an exclusive interview with the president of the United States, lame duck though he was? Why, yes, it did.

Naughton stayed up until two in the morning, preparing questions for the interview. The *Times*'s veteran Washington photographer, George Tames, was in Georgia with the president-elect. Tames was summoned back in a hurry to take photos during the interview. Everything was kept very hush-hush. The *Times* was about to get a biggie.

At the appointed hour, Naughton and Tames were at Camp David. They approached the Marine guard at the gate. They told him who they were. They said they were there to interview the president. The Marine guard said, "Huh?"

Right there at the entrance to the famous presidential retreat, in the autumn splendor of the Catoctin mountains, James M. Naughton of the *New York Times* felt a pang. He smelled a sheep. He found a telephone and called Cheney at the White House. By arrangement, DeFrank was in Cheney's office. They were waiting for that call. Cheney put DeFrank on the line. The *Newsweek* reporter does not remember exactly what he said. Presumably he was Churchillian—In Victory: Magnanimity. But he remembers what Naughton said: "Nice work, nice work. I've been had."[11]

But Naughton also was Churchillian—In Defeat: Defiance. During the transition period from Ford to Carter, there was a farewell party for Cheney. The central attraction on the buffet table was a large cake. It looked delicious. The guests eagerly awaited the cutting and eating of the cake. But first there were two and a half hours of speeches and conviviality. During that entire time, Jim Naughton crouched inside the cake. It was uncomfortable. But what was discomfort compared to the last laugh?

Finally, Cheney prepared to cut the cake. His farewell to the power and prestige of the White House. His big moment. As he lifted the knife, the cake burst apart. It exploded. Out sprang James M. Naughton of the *New York Times*.

At length, Jim Naughton wearied of reporting, with its frequent costume changes and rich desserts. He switched to the *Philadelphia Inquirer*, where he became associate managing editor. As the time grew near for his departure from the *Times*, Naughton cast about for a suitable farewell. Not just anything would do, not for Naughton.

After much thought, he decided on a final gesture to the *Times*'s bureaucracy in New York. It is a large bureaucracy, with many editors. The reporters sometimes find it burdensome. In this anxious, conformist era, some Washington journalists have become good, safe team players. Others, perhaps a vanishing breed, cling to individualism. For them, it is often onerous to deal with the huge aggregations of editors, subeditors, producers, assistant producers, computer specialists and other functionaries that comprise a modern news organization. They feel about these bureaucracies as Lord Palmerston felt about delegations: "A noun of multitude, signifying many but not much."

Naughton knew what would appeal to the *Times*'s bureaucracy. So on his last day, he scheduled a story dealing with new scientific discoveries about the planet Uranus.

Ever since the days of Carr Van Anda, a long-ago, legendary managing editor who sponsored polar expeditions and other scientific ventures, the *New York Times* has had a strong interest in science. Therefore, the editors in New York eagerly awaited Naughton's story. And that meant a lot of editors. Naughton recalls that his message scheduling the Uranus story went to about ten different desks.

The day wore on. No story arrived from Naughton. There were consultations among the editors. Where was the story? Then, at the last possible moment, as he walked out of the Washington bureau on his way to Philadelphia, Naughton sent another message to each and every one of those desks. It said: "Please scratch Uranus."

V

IKE AND JIM

ames Campbell Hagerty was born in Plattsburg, New York, on
May 9, 1909. He was Irish, he was tough, he was intelligent, he
drank and smoked, he had ulcers and he was the best presidential
press secretary who ever lived.

His father, James A. Hagerty, was a greatly respected political reporter
for the *New York Times*. The son displayed the same tendencies; after
graduating from Columbia University he was a *Times* reporter from 1934
to 1942. Then he became press secretary to Governor Thomas E. Dewey
of New York. After Dwight Eisenhower won the Republican presidential
nomination in 1952, he asked Dewey to recommend someone to be his
press secretary. Let me give you mine, said Dewey; he's the best there is.

Eisenhower considered Hagerty a public relations genius. That was the
key to their relationship. It was the area in which Hagerty excelled and in
which he was of the greatest value to Eisenhower, and Ike knew it.

But the general also had a high regard for Hagerty's political acumen,
although with Ike that was true of anyone who knew there were two
parties. In the 1952 campaign, the elder Hagerty, still batting it out for
the *Times*, predicted that the Republicans would come down from upstate New York with 700,000 votes to offset the Democratic bulge in New
York City. The son disagreed; he said upstate would give Eisenhower at
least 1 million votes. It turned out to be more than 1.2 million. Ike
carried New York, and in his eyes Hagerty was ever after a political expert.[1]

So greatly did Eisenhower rely on his press secretary that when Ike
suffered a heart attack in 1955, he said: "Tell Jim to take over and make
the decisions—and handle the story."[2] There was a general impression
that Hagerty ran the American government for several days after the presi-

dent was stricken. Hagerty himself never agreed with this interpretation. He told reporters, including myself, that Ike simply meant he should handle the press coverage of the heart attack and otherwise carry out his duties as press secretary.

But Eisenhower's instructions were fairly clear. He said Hagerty should "take over and make the decisions." Ike knew that White House chief of staff Sherman Adams was in Europe, inspecting NATO installations. He knew that Hagerty, who was in Washington when the heart attack occurred, could get to Denver substantially sooner than Adams.

Robert J. Donovan, a reporter with access to the inner circles of the Eisenhower administration, took note of Hagerty's disclaimer that he had been given a broad grant of authority. But Donovan wrote: "The fact remains . . . that as the senior White House official on the scene for several days and as the president's only authorized spokesman, he [Hagerty] was in a position of authority far greater than is customarily exercised by the press secretary. Indeed, it is difficult to think of anyone whose authority in those first couple of days exceeded that of Hagerty, a very sure-footed official with a large capacity and a readiness to make decisions."[3]

Immediately west of the White House, across a closed-off street, is a gigantic structure known as the Old Executive Office Building. There was a time when this monumental pile housed three entire departments of the American government—the State, War and Navy Departments. Nowadays, it contains the Office of Management and Budget and other overflow presidential staff that cannot be accommodated in the White House itself.

On the fourth floor of the Old EOB is an ornate room called the Indian Treaty Room, although no treaties with Indian tribes or nations were ever signed there. Eisenhower held his press conferences in the Indian Treaty Room. For eight years, the reporters were witnesses to one of the closest relationships that any president ever had with his press secretary. It would be stretching the point only slightly to say that in the Indian Treaty Room, Eisenhower and Hagerty held *their* press conferences.

The president stood behind a desk with a double microphone on it. Hagerty sat a few feet behind him, watching and listening intently as the boss fielded questions. The press secretary's suits were usually a little rumpled. His dark hair was brushed straight back; a long and slightly drooping upper lip gave him a passing resemblance to Humphrey Bogart; his accent was Sidewalks of New York.

At the press conferences, the president turned repeatedly to his press secretary for information about the government, the political situation and the issues confronting the White House. Little things like that. Sometimes Eisenhower would check with Hagerty before answering a question. Or he would answer a question and then tell the reporters that Hagerty would amplify the answer later, which often meant translating Ike's syntax and explaining what he had meant. Or, frequently, Hagerty would move swiftly to Eisenhower's side and whisper to him *during* the answer. Then the answer would change:

Question (James B. Reston, *New York Times*): "Mr. President, have you considered asking Prime Minister Bulganin to publish your letter [on a possible summit meeting]?"

Eisenhower: "I think it says in the letter—I think if you will read the letter, if you did—."

Reston: "I did, sir."

Eisenhower: "All right. It said, 'I hope that this letter will have the same publicity in Russia that we gave yours,' as I recall. Now maybe in one draft that might have gone out, but that is the way I remember it. (Confers with Hagerty). Sorry, I have apparently made a goof. Isn't that in the letter?"

Hagerty: "No, sir."

It was a familiar sight: Eisenhower, his shoulders hunched slightly, his head bent forward, a portrait of puzzlement, as Hagerty whispered to him while the reporters waited for the rest of the answer. Then the executive nod, regaining control, and here came the revised version.

Question (Mrs. May Craig, *Portland* [Maine] *Press-Herald*): "Mr. President, the simultaneous translation of the Khrushchev TV appearance was very sketchy. Did our embassy in Moscow . . . take a tape or a transcript for our use, or on what are you depending for the text?"

Eisenhower: "Nothing except what the rest of you have seen on the— in the—have we got—(confers with Hagerty). Mr. Hagerty says we have it. I haven't seen it. All I have seen is what you saw on the television."

Almost all presidents are briefed by their press secretaries *before* they hold a press conference. There is a run-through of the questions that are likely to be asked. Answers—or evasions—are prepared. The president decides in advance what he wants to say or not say. But with Ike, the process continued *during* the press conference. No president before or since Eisenhower consulted so frequently with his press secretary during actual press conferences. Most of them never did.

The stenographic transcripts of Eisenhower's press conferences are sprinkled with the phrases "Confers with Mr. Hagerty" or "Mr. Hagerty conferred with the president." (The White House stenographer at that time was the quiet, cultured Jack Romagna. At the end of a day of Ike's sentence structure, Romagna went home and played the piano. He played Bach beautifully. Bach is very precise.)

Hagerty often had to remind Eisenhower what the government was doing that day:

Question (William H. Lawrence, *New York Times*): "You have not then given your approval in principle to this other idea that the money might go to the Secretary and be allocated by function?"

Eisenhower: " . . . Now, there is this about it: You will recall, I believe in my State of the Union message or maybe it was in my military message of more recent date, I did say that I thought the Secretary ought to have research and development funds appropriated to him . . . (confers with Hagerty). My Good Man Friday here reminds me of something, that I am sending not only a letter to the Congress today, but with it will be the exact terminology of the provisions in the bill that we propose. . . ."

Question (Robert Clark, International News Service): "Some Democrats have complained that they have not been adequately consulted on Indochina. . . ."

Eisenhower: ". . . Since the first of the year—I have looked up the record only recently—there have been numerous consultations of this kind. During this month alone with respect to Indochina—there are three meetings this month, in April alone . . . (Hagerty conferred with the president). Mr. Hagerty is afraid I left the inference, these three meetings in April, that I participated in them; they were by the Secretary of State."

Hagerty told Ike the names of all those funny-sounding federal agencies and international groups:

Question (Marvin L. Arrowsmith, Associated Press): "Mr. President, can you say specifically whether Russia and other Communist-nation observers will attend those [atomic] tests?"

Eisenhower: "Of course I can't tell what they will accept, but we are hopeful that the United Nations will designate the Scientific Committee for Detection, I believe it is, of Radioactivity—that's about its name . . . (confers with Hagerty). Mr. Hagerty wants me to read the full—the United Nations Committee on the Effects of Atomic Radiation, that's the name of the committee."

When Eisenhower winged it on names, without Hagerty's help, the reporters were on their own. Once, answering a question about agriculture, Ike referred to "the subsidization we give to [farm] exports through this wheat distribution pool—I forget its exact name, but you people will know it, so we won't worry about it."

When it came to relations with the news media, anything Hagerty said was fine with Ike:

Question (Anthony H. Leviero, *New York Times*): "Mr. President, your opening statement [on the Korean peace negotiations] is a pretty important one. . . . I wonder if you would consider letting us quote you directly on it. . . ."

Eisenhower: "I think you had better take the usual rule, because I don't know whether I used even grammatical language."

Leviero: "The grammar is incidental; we will be willing to forgo that."

Eisenhower: "I will say this: I don't know what the practices are, but if you find something there that you think is worthy of quoting, you bring it to Mr. Hagerty. If he says, 'Yes, that's what the general said,' it's okay by me. I don't care."

When Eisenhower was president, the reporters spent a lot of time figuring out what he had said. They had to decipher him. It was usually possible to get his drift, but they had to work at it. Nineteen fifty-seven was a tough year.

Press conference, May 15, 1957: "Yes. Well, I don't believe that. I don't believe there are three war plans, but I do believe this: that each one, trying to protect very earnestly what he believes should be his own capabilities and to get the things for him, for example, guided missiles of all kinds, every kind of bomb, I believe then that the war plans are not clear enough in fixing responsibility, possibly, and we could do it cheaper there."

Press conference, June 5, 1957: "Well, that is quite a lecture, I should think, you are asking for. He [the president] is the leader not of the, you might say, hierarchy of control in any political party. . . ."

Press conference, July 17, 1957: "Well, I said this: I said when you are talking with the Communists, you find it a little difficult, for the simple reason that you say a man can earn what he pleases, save what he pleases, buy what he pleases with that. Now I believe this, because I believe in the power for good of, you might say, the integrated forces developed by 170 million free people."

Eisenhower often appeared to be very poorly informed about things. He answered many questions at his press conferences by saying: "Well, this is the first I have heard about that," or "You are telling me something I don't know anything about." The trouble was that they were things he *should* have known about, being president and all.

Asked whether he was going to propose a new department of health, education and welfare, he said: "I certainly intend to recommend that. Now, I am not certain whether it's right in the plan, whether that's the way it will be done, but I think so."

Or "Well, I'll tell you: I have a very definite personal opinion on the question you asked me. It has not at this moment been studied by my associates who should appropriately take it up and come to advise me, because I could easily be mistaken. I will see whether I can answer that question at the next meeting."

Each reporter had his favorite. Mine was this one, on March 19, 1953, in response to a question about the St. Lawrence Seaway: "Well, we have reached some tentative conclusions for the moment, but I must admit you caught me to this one extent—I have forgotten whether we have agreed to keep these confidential until we could examine them a little bit more among ourselves. I am not certain. I will say this: I personally have held for a long time several things about this."

The classic was Ike's reply to a question about one of the major scandals of his administration—the Dixon-Yates contract. For months, the reporters had questioned Eisenhower persistently about Dixon-Yates. Finally, on July 27, 1955, Clark R. Mollenhoff of the *Des Moines Register* and *Tribune* asked him whether he knew that the name of a key figure had been deliberately removed from the government's official chronology of the Dixon-Yates negotiations.

"I don't intend to comment on it any more at all," Eisenhower replied. "I think I have given to this [press] conference, time and again, the basic elements of this whole development, and everything that I could possibly be expected to know about it. . . . Now, they [officials of the Budget Bureau] can tell the entire story, and I don't know exactly such details as that. How could I be expected to know? I never heard of it."

However, there are always two ways of looking at things, as the congressman said when they got him for buggery. Recently, a revisionist examination of Eisenhower's presidency has been under way. In the revisionist view, Ike knew exactly what he was doing. To the reporters, he seemed to be going under for the third time in a sea of syntax. But revisionists such as Fred I. Greenstein, Blanche W. Cook and William B. Ewald have concluded that the inner Eisenhower was far more complicated than his grammar. That would make him very complicated.

The revisionists believe Ike concealed what he was doing behind a smoke screen of fractured phraseology. He was protecting "his options as a decision-maker" by posing as ill informed. When he said he had never heard of something, it is argued, he often knew all about it. But he was not going to tell the reporters that he knew *anything* about it until he was ready to act. And even when he did act, the press and public might not know about it, because of what the revisionists call Eisenhower's "hidden-hand leadership."

Professor Greenstein cites a press conference of March 16, 1955, at which Eisenhower warned that in the event of a general war in Asia, the United States was prepared to use tactical nuclear weapons. This made many people nervous, showing that nothing changes over the years. Immediately after the press conference, the State Department "urgently requested" that the president not discuss this delicate subject any further.

Just before the next press conference, Hagerty relayed State's request, and Ike told him: "Don't worry, Jim, if that question comes up, I'll just confuse them [the reporters]."[4]

The question did come up, although it was in a limited form relating to the use of nuclear weapons to defend the offshore islands of Quemoy and Matsu. Eisenhower *did* scatter dust over the issue; he said it was impossible to predict what weapons a president might have to use.

So he did know what he was doing? He was not ill informed? He was deliberately spreading a fog?

Unfortunately, the sequence of events is not conclusive. Eisenhower may simply have been trying to cover up his own mistake. He may have been doing what any president does when he has said something too definite and then finds it necessary to fuzz it over. The reporters have seen this many times. Eisenhower had gone too far on the subject of nuclear weapons at the March 16 press conference; now he was pulling back.

Greenstein cites another instance. It is again interesting for the differing interpretations that can be placed on it. Talking with his staff before a press conference on July 17, 1957, Eisenhower expressed annoyance with John Foster Dulles. He said the secretary of state had commented publicly on an issue that he should not have talked about—namely, the stockpiling of American missiles in Europe. Pretty much the same kind of issue on which Ike himself had been too forthcoming two years before. More people were nervous.

Eisenhower then called Dulles to find out exactly what Dulles had said about the missile stockpiling plan. After which, Ike told his staff that if the question came up at his press conference, "I will be evasive."[5]

And he was. When he was asked about Dulles's remarks on the stockpiling plan, Eisenhower replied: *"Now, I don't know what he* [Dulles] *told you about a plan* [emphasis added]. What we have just been doing is studying means and methods of making NATO effective as a defense organization. This means they must be armed properly. Now that is all there is to that. There is no specific program laid down at this minute by which are taking place all these things that you mentioned [stockpiling nuclear weapons and fissionable materials in Western Europe]."

But Eisenhower had talked to Dulles just before the press conference. He knew what Dulles had told reporters about the stockpiling plan. As Professor Greenstein argues, Ike was certainly pretending to be ill informed when he actually was well informed ("I don't know what he told you about a plan"). And to conceal what was being done, he was denying that there was a plan to stockpile nuclear weapons in Western Europe, where they are today. Another word for it is that he was lying.

The revisionist analysis may improve Eisenhower's standing as an activist president who practiced behind-the-scenes, "hidden-hand" leadership. However, it will not enhance his reputation for truthfulness. When presidents are revised, Ophelia's warning applies: "Lord, we know what we are but know not what we may be."

About one thing there is no argument. Eisenhower had a very well developed sense of self-preservation. It had been sharply honed during those long years in the peacetime Army, when promotion was extremely slow and good assignments hard to come by. It did not desert him in the presidency. He hoarded his popularity as Silas Marner his gold. What? Get into a public fight with Joe McCarthy? Array the moral force of the presidency against the demagogue? No, no, that might hurt Ike among the voters who supported McCarthy. Once Eisenhower instructed Hagerty to tell the reporters a certain thing. The press secretary protested that if he did, he would catch hell. Ike got up, walked around his desk, put his hand on Hagerty's shoulder and said: "My boy, better you than me."[6]

Eisenhower was accustomed to dealing with reporters, more or less. More as a wartime commander, with four stars on his shoulders and authority from head to toe. Less—much less—as a candidate for elective office. He was not at all prepared for the hot-eyed reporters on the campaign trail, bursting with questions, clamoring for information and not confined by wartime censorship. He was not ready for the news media as defined later by U.S. District Judge Murray I. Gurfein in the Pentagon Papers case—"a cantankerous press, an obstinate press, an ubiquitous press [that] must be suffered by those in authority in order to preserve the even greater values of freedom of expression and the right of the people to know. . . ."

The people, it appeared, wanted to know about a fund that had been set up for Richard Nixon. And even if the people did not want to know, the press was going to tell them. During Nixon's years as a senator, a group of affluent Californians had set up an eighteen-thousand-dollar fund to provide him with the usufructs of power. Nixon was now the Republican candidate for vice-president. The reporters wanted to know what Eisenhower thought about the fund and whether it had caused any change in his attitude toward Nixon as his running mate.

However, the journalists on the 1953 campaign train had not been able to get to Eisenhower. The candidate was holding himself aloof from the press. But on a memorable day near the end of the campaign, Ike decided to wander back to the club car for the purpose of "having a beer with the boys." He did so, standing receptively at the bar. Ike thought it would be a few minutes of conviviality, but for the reporters it was the blessed rain that endeth the drought. They moved en masse toward the candidate.

They invested his flanks, cut off his line of retreat and opened a bombardment. They wanted to know what he was going to do about Nixon. They wanted to know very much. They were extremely persistent.

At first, Eisenhower was bewildered. Then he grew angry. Supreme Headquarters, Allied Expeditionary Force, had not been like this at all. He extricated himself as quickly as he could and fled the madding crowd. Later he told Hagerty he would never do anything like that again, never.[7]

It did not work out quite that way, but almost. In his eight years as president, Eisenhower held a total of 193 press conferences—a respectable average of about 2 a month. But only occasionally did he talk with reporters in any setting other than a formal news conference.

Once in a while, he invited some journalists to one of his stag dinners at the White House. When he did, it was almost always those who were considered sympathetic to the administration—friendlies, as the Washington press corps calls them. His journalistic guests were usually conservative elders—David Lawrence of *U.S. News and World Report*, Roscoe Drummond of the *New York Herald Tribune*, Richard Wilson of the Cowles publications and a handful of others. The preeminent journalist of the era, Walter Lippmann, was not invited to the White House once during the Eisenhower years.[8] Lippmann sometimes criticized the administration.

On very rare occasions, reporters who regularly covered the White House were invited to an Eisenhower stag. Marvin Arrowsmith of the Associated Press remembers just one invitation in eight years. After the dinner, Arrowsmith holed up in a downtown hotel and wrote all night.[9] It was not that Ike had said anything world-shaking; it was just that a reporter so seldom got *anything* from this president on an inside basis.

That is not to say that there were no leaks in the Eisenhower administration. The political types in the Cabinet leaked information to the press when it suited their purpose. And like political types in all administrations, their leaks went to friendly publications. Attorney General Herbert Brownell, for instance, leaked the nomination of Earl Warren as Chief Justice to reporters for the *New York Times, New York Herald Tribune, Chicago Daily News, Kansas City Star* and Scripps-Howard newspapers, all of which had supported Ike in 1952. Reporters for other newspapers protested. They pointed out that the selection of a new Chief Justice was a pretty important story. They said they had been placed at a disadvantage. Eisenhower replied: "I think that I have trusted subordinates who may occasionally leak news for purposes they consider proper. If they do so, I don't think I would interfere with them."[10] Take that.

This may have sounded like a blank check, but it was not. Despite an occasional leak, the Eisenhower administration did not qualify as an open administration. Throughout those eight years, congressional committees and professional journalism societies complained about extreme secrecy in the executive branch. Administration officials did not hold very many background briefings for reporters, and the number diminished even further after Admiral Robert B. Carney presided at a disastrous backgrounder on the Formosa situation. One of the few exceptions was Secretary of State Dulles, who had many informal sessions with reporters.

After he left office, Eisenhower wrote that an unfortunate impression had taken hold that he did not like newspapers. He said this was his fault. It resulted, he explained, from an answer he had once given when asked whether he had read an article criticizing him. He had replied that he did not read newspapers.

Actually, he said in his memoirs, he *did* read newspapers. He added, however, that he did not believe it was necessary to read everything that was printed in them.[11] He said also that he became friends with several Washington journalists during his years in the White House. And he tossed a rare presidential bouquet at the reporters. Generally speaking, Ike said, "information reaching the public from my press conferences was accurate. . . ."[12]

However, that was about as mellow as Eisenhower ever got on the subject of American journalism. He was in a different mood at the Republican national convention of 1964. This was a rather agitated assemblage that nominated Barry Goldwater for president. Ike appeared as the party's elder statesman. In his speech, he urged the delegates not to heed "sensation-seeking columnists and commentators, because, my friends, I assure you that these are people who couldn't care less about the good of our party."[13] Reporters who were there, including myself, will forget the scene that ensued about the same time they forget Adolf Hitler. The convention exploded in a pandemonium of rage against the news media. The delegates stood on their chairs, shouting, raving, shaking their fists and cursing the reporters in the press section.

When the reporters complained about Brownell's leak of the Warren nomination, Eisenhower referred them to Hagerty. He said: "Let me tell you on that, if there are any complaints, I wish you would put them down in complete detail in front of Mr. Hagerty, who will bring them to me. I didn't know there were any complaints. . . ."[14]

Hagerty again. Hagerty always. There might be occasional leaks from Cabinet members, but otherwise Hagerty was pretty much the whole show. The chief of the White House staff, Sherman Adams, had almost no contact with reporters. The rest of the staff was not totally isolated from the press, but there was a strong tendency to refer inquiring reporters to Hagerty.

When a reporter called a member of the White House staff, seeking information, the almost invariable response was "Have you checked with the press office?" Which meant Hagerty. The reporters soon learned that they might as well call Hagerty first. They would do so, requesting permission to talk to a staffer with expertise in a certain area. Oh, never mind him, Hagerty would reply affably; come on over and talk to me—I can fill you in on that. And he could, too. He was extremely well informed on most of the issues facing the administration, and its policies for dealing with them. He could, and did, supply the background information that was essential to an explanatory story. Why the president had chosen one course of action over another. What were the pros and cons that went into a decision. As a result, the quest for information usually began and ended with Hagerty.

There are only two ways in which a president can organize his relations with the news media. It apparently defies the wit of man to devise any other procedure. The president can leave press relations essentially to his press secretary, or he can try to be his own press secretary. Ike left it to Hagerty.

The press secretary was not a shrinking violet. He was willing to do the job. He attended Cabinet meetings regularly and spoke up forcefully when he judged that the subject being discussed fell within his purview. He had a strong personality.

Ike responded by taking his press secretary increasingly into his confidence on policy issues. After the 1952 election, a story circulated that when Eisenhower asked Hagerty to be his press secretary, Hagerty imposed a condition. He said he had to know everything that was going on. Eisenhower asked why. Because otherwise I won't know what to put out and what not to put out, Hagerty replied. According to the story, Eisenhower agreed that Hagerty would be in on everything except national security matters. He would be told about these only when it was deemed necessary.

But by 1960, and probably long before that, Hagerty was intimately involved in national security, too. Driving back from Gettysburg to Washington on May 8, 1960, Hagerty apparently persuaded Eisenhower to assume personal responsibility for the U-2 spy plane fiasco.

After a U-2 piloted by Francis Gary Powers was shot down over the Soviet Union, Secretary of State Christian Herter (who had succeeded Dulles) convinced Eisenhower to go with a cover story that concealed the fact that Ike had authorized the flight. Hagerty disagreed with this decision. He thought the president should take full responsibility, on the ground that it was almost certain to come out anyway. Hagerty was always realistic. He knew the press would be digging hard on a story like this.

On May 8, Hagerty was with Eisenhower in the limousine that brought Ike back from a weekend in Gettysburg. As soon as he got to the

White House, the president met with Herter to discuss the U-2 crisis. He told Herter he had changed his mind. He ordered a new statement drafted. In it, Eisenhower acknowledged that he had authorized the espionage flight.[15]

In August 1956, near the end of Eisenhower's first term, I wrote that Hagerty had become "a policymaker and top political strategist" in the Eisenhower White House. Perhaps because most of the people around Ike distrusted the press, I wrote, "Hagerty has emerged as a spokesman of extraordinary power" and "one of the most powerful figures in the Eisenhower administration."[16]

Hagerty achieved this preeminence because he did *not* distrust the press. Distrust is counterproductive. Once on that merry-go-round, never off: Hagerty knew the things to do were to be realistic about the press, accept the press—and then *use* the press. That is the kind of press secretary to have.

Hagerty defined the job of White House press secretary. Not forever, because press secretaries, like everyone else, must adjust to new circumstances and new technology. But in several major areas, he created the basic characteristics of the modern press spokesman. Eisenhower was not an innovator; Hagerty was.

Hagerty established the rule that the fundamental job of the president's press secretary—his first and foremost duty—is to make the president look good. Previous press secretaries had understood this principle, but they had applied it only in a rudimentary way. They were essentially press officers, not public relations specialists. They made announcements, distributed press releases, held briefings, answered questions and handled the 1,001 details involved in facilitating and servicing press coverage of the White House.

What Hagerty did was simple in its concept but profound in its implications. He combined the roles of press officer and public relations expert, and made them one. He *serviced* the press—no one ever did it more efficiently—but he *served* the president. All subsequent press secretaries have accepted Hagerty's order of priorities: The president's image comes first. The public relations side of the White House press operation has been uppermost ever since.

Academic studies of great seriousness have been written about the inherent difficulties that confront the press secretary in trying to serve two masters. The press secretary, it is said, must promote the interests of the president and at the same time somehow intercede with him on behalf of the news media, representing their interests as well. He must be a sort of honest broker between two parties whose objectives are almost always in conflict.

Reporters are simpler souls. The old hands in the White House pressroom merely take a newcomer aside, jerk a thumb in the direction of the press secretary's office and enlighten the freshman as follows: Remember, buddy, he works for the president, not for us.

Under Hagerty, the White House was masterful with details, arrangements and schedules—the minutiae of the press officer. Hagerty was the Mussolini of American journalism; he made the trains—and the planes and buses—run on time. Speech texts were ready when promised, baggage was not sent to Anchorage when the destination was Altoona, everyone got the right hotel key unless consenting adults had covenanted otherwise and little miracles occurred by which stories got written even if their authors had strong drink taken.

Hagerty's solicitude for the working reporters was sincere; he had been one himself. But there was no schizophrenia, none of this serving-two-masters business, and no one was under the illusion that there was. Like everything else, Hagerty's attentiveness to the conditions under which reporters labored had one overriding purpose: the greater glory of Dwight D. Eisenhower.

To this end, Hagerty gathered the publicity apparatus of the executive branch into his own hands. By virtue of his position, the president's press secretary had always been paramount among the horde of assistant secretaries for public information, directors of information, press officers and assorted other flacks who give out the news and burnish the images of the Cabinet departments and federal agencies. But Hagerty explicitly established the preeminence of the White House press secretary. He institutionalized what had been a loose and tacit understanding.

When Eisenhower was stricken with three illnesses in three successive years, Hagerty swept through the departments, agencies and bureaus, gathering up news to be announced from the president's bedside. His purpose was image-making; Eisenhower was to be perceived as functioning, come what might. From this modest beginning, a mighty rule evolved that has prevailed ever since: The White House gets the first crack at the news.

If it is important, if it is a likely candidate for this evening's electronic news and tomorrow morning's page 1 and especially, most especially, if it makes the president look good, the White House announces it. This is known as skimming the cream.

The system operates as a right of first refusal. It is not that the departments and agencies are allowed only the sweepings and leftovers; they still announce a good deal of important news. But the White House takes a look at their news first, to see whether it is *presidential*. A White House press secretary who is on top of his job—who has studied his Hagerty—makes sure that the White House gets the cream. The definition of "cream" is that which makes the president appear to be on top of his job.

The system has been formalized. The White House press secretary meets regularly with the information officers for the major departments and agencies. At these meetings, the government's information policies are formulated and reviewed. Decisions are made on how to handle specific situations that require the fine art of public relations—which is just about every situation. Tricks of the trade. What is it going to be this time: fortissimo or pianissimo? The positive accentuated, the negative soft-pedaled. The president's press secretary has the dominant voice in these strategy sessions. He sets the public relations policy for the entire executive branch. He is not just the White House's press secretary. He is the boss of all the press secretaries, the capo of the capos. Hagerty's legacy.

There were other bequests. One of them is a never-ending source of frustration for the reporters. More important, it is a device for the chronic deception of the public. It is a simple technique: According to the White House, the policy of the American government never changes. Another term for it is "executive infallibility."

The decisions of the president are ever-fixed marks that look on tempests and are never shaken. Because there are so many tempests, the reporters frequently inquire whether a policy has been altered. It is clear that circumstances have changed. It is equally apparent that the government's policy has changed, in response. But the answer is always the same: There has been no change.

The obvious is denied. It is denied blandly and shamelessly. The intelligence of everyone—the reporters in the briefing room and the reading and viewing public—is insulted. Cynicism results.

The White House will go to great lengths to prevent the American people from knowing that a policy of their government has changed. In April 1965, Lyndon Johnson decided to send an additional 20,000 marines to Vietnam and to authorize them for the first time to engage in direct combat operations. Johnson did not wish this to become generally known. The reason was that he had said during the 1964 campaign that American troops would not fight the war in Vietnam. Oh, that.

So Johnson had his national security assistant, McGeorge Bundy, draft a memorandum to the secretaries of state and defense and the CIA director. The document, known as National Security Action Memorandum 328, of April 6, 1965, gave the orders for the additional troops and the change in their mission. Then it said: ". . . The president desires that . . . premature publicity be avoided by all possible precautions. The actions themselves should be taken as rapidly as practicable, but in ways that should minimize any appearance of sudden changes in policy. . . . The president's desire is that these movements and changes should be understood as being gradual and wholly consistent with existing policy."[17]

This practice has grown hoary with repetition. Its echoes spiral backward in time: no change, no change, no change. Carried to its logical extreme, American policy has not changed since George Washington's Farewell Address.

With these techniques, the imperial presidency took shape. It was not just the fleets of presidential aircraft, the ruffles and flourishes and "Hail to the Chief" and the opéra bouffe uniforms that Richard Nixon ordered for the White House police. It was much deeper than that. It was the idea that the White House announced the most important news, so that the president dominated the national debate over events and issues. It was the idea that the president was infallible, so that his policies never needed to be changed, being perfect after all, and covering every eventuality. It was the idea that the president knew everything, anticipated everything, handled everything, did not make mistakes and never grew tired.

It had been discovered that the Russians were ten feet tall. It was therefore necessary for the Americans to match them. James C. Hagerty was a public relations genius; in his hands, the modern president became ten feet tall. Hagerty's successors have used the same techniques in the same Procrustean process, stretching their men to the required height.

In November 1953, Attorney General Brownell made a speech in Chicago. It dealt with a man named Harry Dexter White, who had been an assistant secretary of the treasury in the Truman administration. Brownell, who was still fighting the 1952 campaign, charged that White "was known to be a Communist spy by the very people who appointed him," i.e., Harry Truman.

As demagoguery goes, it was not the worst the country had heard in that era of Joseph R. McCarthy. Just ordinary, garden-variety political vilification. But the reporters considered the matter worth pursuing. At a press conference on November 11, 1953, they asked Eisenhower a total of twenty questions. Eighteen of them dealt with Brownell's speech and the case of Harry Dexter White. When the news conference ended, Eisenhower's face was suffused with rage and several reporters were still on their feet, shouting for recognition.

It was rough:

Question (Edward J. Milne, *Providence Journal*): "Mr. President, do you yourself feel that former President Truman knowingly appointed a Communist spy to high office?"

Eisenhower: "You are asking me for opinions, of course, based on nothing else except what I have told you and what I have read in the papers. No, it is inconceivable; I don't believe that—put it in this way—a man in that position knowingly damaged the United States. I think it would be inconceivable."

Question (Anthony H. Leviero, *New York Times*): "Mr. President, I think this case is at best a pretty squalid one. But if a grand jury, under our system . . . has in effect cleared the man or at least has decided it [had] insufficient evidence to convict him or prosecute him, then is it proper for the Attorney General to characterize [White] . . . as a spy, and in effect accuse a former president of harboring that man? . . ."

Eisenhower: "Look, all you are trying to get now is my personal opinion about certain things. I am not either a judge nor am I an accomplished lawyer. I have my own ideas of what is right and wrong, but I would assume this: you are asking me to answer questions where, with all of this in the public mind, the Attorney General is here to answer it himself. Let him answer it."

Question (Leviero): "He has refused to answer the questions, you see."

Another reporter, Raymond P. (Pete) Brandt of the *St. Louis Post-Dispatch*, brought with him no less than seven questions about the Brownell speech. Over Eisenhower's objections, he asked every one of them. Two of the questions give the flavor:

Question (Brandt): "Do you think the FBI report is justified in calling White a spy when a grand jury refused to believe it on the basis of FBI evidence . . . ?"

Eisenhower: "I know nothing about it; you will have to go to the record and the facts."

Question (Brandt): "Do you think the administration's action in virtually putting a label of traitor on a former president is likely to damage our foreign relations?"

Eisenhower: "I reject the premise. I would not answer such a question."

The reporters were persistent about the Brownell speech. At a press conference a week later, Robert Clark of the International News Service took up the thread:

Question (Clark): "President Truman has charged that your administration has now embraced McCarthyism. Do you have any comment on that?"

Eisenhower stepped back as if he had been struck. His face flushed with anger—reporters were becoming accustomed to the crimson that raced upward from Ike's neck when he was asked a question that he regarded as impertinent. He replied that he would leave it to the press conference to decide whether his administration had embraced McCarthyism. He said he would "take the verdict of this body on that."

Impertinence won. The *New York Times*'s most stalwart stalwart, James B. Reston, joined his colleague, Leviero, in polling eighty of the reporters who had attended the press conference. Their verdict was yes. [18]

From all this, it might be thought that the newspapers of the Eisenhower era were filled with stormy accounts of the president's clashes with the press. Vivid news stories about a beleaguered chief executive dodging and ducking as he tried to evade the questions of skeptical journalists. Like Lyndon Johnson reeling and staggering under month after month of Vietnam interrogation. Or Richard Nixon coming apart as the press peeled off the protective layers of Watergate lies.

Not at all. Very little of the atmosphere of Eisenhower's confrontations with reporters found its way into their stories. There was an occasional hint that the proceedings had been raucous, but overall the news accounts were bland. What had been a knock-down-drag-out at the press conference emerged in the news stories as a waltz-me-around-again-Willie. The press conferences were essentially in-house encounters between the president and the reporters. The news, in the Eisenhower era, was objective. The flavor was lacking. So the public was not aroused. It slept easy.

This delicacy produced an impression that Ike got a free ride from the news media. That was partly true, but not altogether. There were scandals in the Eisenhower administration—bad ones—and they were thoroughly pursued by the press. Some newspapers, although not very many, criticized his policies. But somehow the scandals and the criticism did not touch Ike or rub off on him. He was immune.

In July 1960, after Eisenhower had been in office seven and a half years, his approval rating in the Gallup poll was an astounding 61 percent. He was the luckiest president who ever lived. People did not associate him with the government. Very much like Reagan.

There were reasons for this. If there were not reasons for things, the truth would get out. Respect for the presidency was still great. And nowhere was it greater than among the proprietors and editors of the nation's newspapers. The reporters on the scene might be intensely skeptical, but the good gray men who ran the newspapers saw to it that little of this disbelief found its way into print.

It is an evasion to say that a previous time was a simpler time. The problems of a given time are as difficult for those who are living through them, with their knowledge limited to that moment, as the problems of a subsequent time are for its poor sufferers. Nevertheless, it *was* a simpler time. Americans had known sin all along—their values had always been materialistic, their politics hypocritical, their governments devious. But they had not known Vietnam. They had not known Watergate. They were as yet unaware of presidential imperialism.

So the atmosphere was different. The news media were inclined to take the word of the president and his spokesmen at face value. This was unwise, but what else is new?

The Eisenhower administration lied a lot. It lied in the U-2 spy plane affair, in the Dixon-Yates scandal, the Sherman Adams–Bernard Gold-fine scandal and in some aspects of Ike's illnesses. But when these lies were exposed, they were judged to be hasty improvisations in response to specific situations. Spur-of-the-moment stuff. They were not viewed as elements in a grand mosaic of lies. The press, in those simpler times, operated under a shaky supposition. It did not assume that the government was consistently truthful (the press had not been born yesterday), but it did assume that the government told the truth more often than it lied. The journalists of the Eisenhower era did not operate on the assumption that the government's regular policy was to lie.

In due course, the press and the public learned the consequences of imperialism. They found out that the Central Intelligence Agency had organized a coup against President Jacobo Arbenz Guzmán of Guatemala in 1954, and that Eisenhower almost certainly had known of this and approved it. They found out that the CIA had been deeply involved in an attempted revolt against President Sukarno of Indonesia in 1957, while Eisenhower was telling a press conference that "our policy [in Indonesia] is one of careful neutrality and proper deportment all the way through, so as not to be taking sides where it is none of our business." Eisenhower added, however, that "every rebellion that I have ever heard of has its soldiers of fortune." [19] In the Age of Innocence, only the sophisticated knew that the soldiers of fortune were CIA agents.

Then the people found that the Kennedy administration also had been secretly implicated in the overthrow of a foreign government; this time it was President Ngo Dinh Diem of South Vietnam. They learned, too, that Camelot had practiced news management as indefatigably as Hagerty. As time proceeded, the people found out that the Johnson administration had told gigantic lies about the Vietnam war. It was apparent that lying had become the official policy of the American government. Not an occasional, *ad hoc* response to a specific situation, but a deliberate policy. Finally, the nation learned that Richard Nixon and his henchmen had engaged in criminal conspiracies to obstruct justice and subvert the Constitution. The presidency had gone out of control.

Then began a very bad period. The public, the press, the government, everyone came shivering to the edge of the abyss, there to stand stripped of certitude and confidence. Naked. Frightened. That remains the situation.

VI

JACK AND PIERRE

The first conversation I ever had with John F. Kennedy took place in 1960 on the Staten Island ferry. You have to start somewhere. I had just been assigned to cover Kennedy's presidential campaign, and the ferry ride was my first opportunity to talk to him. It was a freeze. The moment I trotted out some introductory pleasantries, Kennedy's face closed for the day. He was extremely wary. His answers to my questions were curt. We were not communicating. Later, when I got to know Kennedy better, I realized he had not been listening to my questions that day as much as he had been *tasting* them. He had been savoring the small signs like an Indian scout. Instantly and instinctively, he had begun the process of determining whether I was a friendly or an unfriendly.

A few weeks later, the Kennedy campaign arrived in St. Louis. This was my hometown, and I knew something the candidate did not. He was scheduled for a long motorcade through the suburbs, and in one split-level neighborhood a man with an unusual name was running for the state legislature. "Senator," I told Kennedy, "you are going to see some campaign signs along the way that will interest you. Keep an eye open for them." He did so, and he roared with laughter when he spotted the first sign advocating the candidacy of . . . Peter Rabbitt. After which, Kennedy's attitude changed perceptibly. In some mysterious way, the new reporter on the campaign had passed a test.

My first interview with Robert Kennedy was a rerun. Bobby fixed a cold look upon the strange reporter. I made unsuccessful efforts to break the ice. My questions brought brief, careful answers. It was uphill work. Sprawled on the floor beside Kennedy's desk was a large, shaggy dog whose name, I believe, was Brumis. My God, I thought, if this gets any worse he may sic that damn dog on me.

The Kennedys have gone down in political folklore as happy warriors who relished the game. That was true, especially when they are compared to such blithe spirits as Richard Nixon and Lyndon Johnson. But until they knew whom they were dealing with, until they had sized up a newcomer in some occult way, probably Fenian, Jack and Bobby were very cautious Irishmen.

Folklore also says that Kennedy's three years in the presidency were an era of good will between the White House and the news media. An amiable lull before the Johnson-Nixon storm, due to Kennedy's seductive powers with the press. The reality was what reality always is—relative. Compared with the *Sturm und Drang* that came after him, Kennedy had good relations with the media, and especially with rank-and-file working reporters. Nevertheless, there were frequent confrontations between Kennedy and the press, and some of them were very bitter. The significant difference, however, was that Kennedy did not permit his exasperation to poison or immobilize his relations with the news media. Unlike Johnson and Nixon, he did not allow his angry resentment to degenerate into a siege. As a result, Kennedy's dealings with the media were normal: a mixture of seduction and hostility. It was the last "normal" situation for ten and a half years.

It helped that he liked reporters. He told Ted Sorensen, the White House aide who came closest to being his alter ego, that he considered reporters his natural friends—and newspapers his natural enemies.[1] He meant the publishers and editorial writers. Kennedy had no illusions about the difficulties and frustrations that awaited a president in dealing with the press, but journalism nevertheless fascinated him. He was interested in its behavior and caprices and its in-house gossip. He was very fond of gossip. He liked to discuss the size of women's breasts—it grieved him that most of the women he knew had small ones—and who was sleeping with whom and the foibles of prominent journalists and politicians.

Above all, he was hooked on reading newspapers and magazines. He was a news junkie. As a young man, he had had two short experiences as a reporter, including a few months with Hearst's International News Service. He had considered a career in writing or journalism, not politics. But the wartime death of his older brother—who was thought to be the natural politician in the family—left it up to Jack. Someone was to be president.

However, he never got over the feeling that he would have made a helluva newspaperman. He liked to say that when he left the White House he might buy a newspaper or become a columnist. It was print journalism, not television, that interested him. Kennedy was not afraid of TV, as Johnson and Nixon were, but he had no great affection for it. He knew what television had done for him in the 1960 campaign—he told Pierre Salinger that "we wouldn't have had a prayer without that gadget."[2] But TV was merely a political weapon to be mastered and used. A newspaper, on the other hand, was a damn good read.

Behind Kennedy's desk was a table with a large selection of newspapers. Almost every time I went into his office he was standing at this table, his back to the room, snatching a quick read between visitors. He was a fast, practiced scanner, flipping the pages rapidly until he spotted something that interested him.

Salinger says Kennedy regularly read thirteen newspapers—the *New York Times, Wall Street Journal, New York Herald Tribune, New York Post, New York Daily News, Washington Post, Washington Star, Washington Daily News, Baltimore Sun, Chicago Tribune, Chicago Sun-Times, Atlanta Constitution* and *St. Louis Post-Dispatch.* The most notable omission from this list was the *Los Angeles Times,* but Salinger says Kennedy simply felt more at ease with the eastern newspapers he had been reading for years. His magazine-reading was equally extensive: *Time, Newsweek, U.S. News and World Report, Life, Look, Harper's, New Republic, The Reporter, The Economist,* and *Saturday Review.* He also read the London *Sunday Times* and the *Manchester Guardian Weekly.*[3]

Kennedy had several close friends in the press corps: Ben Bradlee, the Jason Robards of American journalism, at that time chief of *Newsweek's* Washington bureau, later executive editor of the *Washington Post;* Hugh Sidey, a student of class distinctions who was then the White House reporter for *Time* magazine; Bill Lawrence, a veteran political reporter for the *New York Times,* who switched his wrestler's face and gravel voice to ABC after one last argument with the desk; and columnists Charles Bartlett, Joseph Alsop and Rowland Evans.

An old hand, James Reston of the *Times,* warned Salinger that these journalistic friends would have—or would be thought to have—an advantage over other reporters. He said this would be resented. Reston suggested that Kennedy cut his social ties with Bartlett, Bradlee and the rest. But Kennedy told Salinger that the presidency was not a good place to make new friends; he said he would stick with the old ones.[4] Reston was right. The media pals were souvenirs that should have been discarded.

With one exception, whom he does not identify, Salinger says none of the journalistic in-group ever violated a presidential confidence. Lawrence says he sat on several good stories that Kennedy gave him but asked him not to write, including the fact that neither Adlai Stevenson nor Chester Bowles would be named secretary of state.[5] But a magazine article by two other cronies, Bartlett and Alsop, severely damaged Kennedy among liberal Democratic voters.

As a consolation prize, Stevenson was appointed U.S. ambassador to the United Nations. In this capacity, he took part in some of the National Security Council meetings during the Cuban missile crisis. Bartlett and Alsop reported in *The Saturday Evening Post* that Stevenson had proposed that the United States offer several tradeoffs, among them withdrawal of U.S. nuclear weapons from Turkey, if Russia would remove its missiles from Cuba. Then, in a passage that hit the fan, the columnists quoted an anonymous administration source as saying: "Adlai wanted a Munich." The Stevenson–Eleanor Roosevelt Democrats had never liked or trusted Kennedy very much; their hearts remained with Adlai. But, perforce, they had begun to reconcile themselves to Kennedy's presidency. The reference to Munich infuriated them. They had had enough of that sort of thing from Nixon and Joe McCarthy.

"Everyone will suppose that it came out of the White House because of Charlie [Bartlett]," Kennedy said to historian Arthur Schlesinger, Jr., his liaison with the liberals. "Will you tell Adlai that I never talked to Charlie or any other reporter about the Cuban crisis, and that this piece [the *Saturday Evening Post* article] does not represent my views?"[6] Well, yes. You can tell him, but will he believe it? This and other denials did not convince the Stevenson Democrats or the Washington press corps. The reporters noted that a White House statement of support for Stevenson did not explicitly deny the Bartlett-Alsop version. They remembered that an earlier Bartlett column on some inside White House maneuvering had turned out to be true. The reporters decided Bartlett would not have used the Munich quote unless he was confident that it reflected Kennedy's attitude.

Kennedy knew he had a problem. He wrote a letter to Stevenson, reaffirming his undying esteem. It is always undying, esteem. The letter went into considerable detail about the difficulties connected with having a journalist as a close friend. "I did not feel I could tell him [Bartlett] or any other friend in the press what subject to write or not write about," Kennedy said. Come now. He had done exactly that with Bill Lawrence, and on at least one occasion with the big brass at the *New York Times*. He had asked them not to print a story about the Bay of Pigs invasion. Later, Kennedy's letter to Stevenson was published—with the references to Bartlett deleted.[7] National security, presumably.

Bartlett and Alsop may have got the Munich quote from Kennedy. Or they may have got it from some other official, in which case the fact that they were close friends of the president probably helped them get it. Either way, Kennedy's rapport with newspapermen had hurt him. But he liked to talk, and journalists were such interesting people to talk to. They could keep up with him.

In the interval between Kennedy's election and inauguration, the

Washington Post broke a story that he had decided on Dean Rusk for secretary of state. The president-elect was furious at the leak. He told Salinger: "Stop everything else you're doing. I want the name of the person responsible for this, and I want it today. This has got to stop."[8]

Salinger checked with the small group of Kennedy advisers who knew that Rusk had been selected. All of them denied leaking the story. In his book on the Kennedy years, Salinger says he then made a further investigation. He does not say what it was, but it was probably what every press secretary does when the president complains about a leak: He checked the log of presidential telephone calls. Secretaries learn to do that in their infancy. At any rate, Salinger reported to Kennedy that he had tracked down the leaker.

"All right, who is it?" Kennedy demanded.

"You."

"What do you mean, me?"

Well, Salinger asked, had Kennedy talked to Phil Graham about the Rusk appointment? Graham, then publisher of the *Post* and an indefatigable Warwick, was another of Kennedy's journalistic friends.

"I did talk to Graham about it last night," said the president-elect. The penny was about to drop.

"Did you tell him he couldn't use the story?" Salinger inquired.

There was, Salinger recalls, a long silence. Then Kennedy said: "No, I guess I didn't."[9]

Later, Salinger said the New Frontier was "the only ship of state that leaked from the top."[10]

The young, new, confident Kennedy administration came to Washington in a great rush of activity. Kennedy had based his campaign on the assumption that Americans were ready to wake up and smell the coffee after eight years of national torpor. It was a risky supposition, but he pulled off a narrow victory. It helped that Eisenhower could not run again. Without taking on the general directly, Kennedy had presented himself as a vigorous contrast to Ike's septuagenarian, boardroom government. He wanted his administration to offer the same contrast. It would be energetic and innovative. It would be a ferment of ideas, creativity, new approaches.

So he brought in a team of intelligent, hardworking political operatives: his brother Robert, and Kenneth O'Donnell, Lawrence F. O'Brien, Ralph Dungan, Mike Feldman, Lee White, Timothy Reardon, Pierre Salinger and others. Young-old men, experienced hardball players, intensely pragmatic but aware, too, that ideas could be important assets in politics. Then Kennedy stirred some intellectuals into the mixture—Ted Sorensen, Richard Goodwin, McGeorge Bundy—and topped it off with three of the most intelligent men in the United States: Arthur Schlesinger, Jr., John Kenneth Galbraith and Walter W. Heller.

Bliss was it in that dawn to be alive. The Kennedy administration was a reporter's dream. All those bright, articulate people willing and anxious to talk. All those ideas tumbling and frothing over the dinner tables in Georgetown and Cleveland Park. All those new programs and policies to get America moving again. In the Eisenhower years, there had been no one to talk to but Hagerty. Then the New Frontier came bursting in, and suddenly there was everyone to talk to.

It was one of the most accessible administrations in history. The leading columnists of the day—Walter Lippmann, Scotty Reston, Joseph and Stewart Alsop, Mark Childs, Joe Kraft, Doris Fleeson, Drew Pearson, Bill White, Rollie Evans and Bob Novak—were briefed frequently to make sure they knew the White House's views on major foreign and domestic problems. The briefer would be Bundy or Sorensen or some other senior policymaking official—or very often the president himself. "In any crisis situation," Salinger has said, "it was standard operating procedure to be in touch with these columnists to give them background on the government's actions."[11] Working reporters had little trouble getting to Kenny O'Donnell on a political story, Larry O'Brien on the White House's legislative strategy, Arthur Schlesinger on a wide range of issues and problems facing the nation and Walter Heller on economic policy. It was some economic policy. In the three Kennedy years, the wholesale price index never rose more than 1 percent a year. Bliss.

Salinger exercised almost no control over these appointments. The reporters simply called a presidential assistant and talked to him on the telephone or requested an in-person interview. Salinger seldom knew about it beforehand. In the Hagerty regime, telephone and personal interviews with members of the White House staff had to be arranged and cleared through the press secretary. Often, Hagerty blocked access to the staff by talking to the reporter himself. But at the outset of the Kennedy administration, Salinger rejected this role.

It was a deliberate decision that reflected Salinger's temperament—and it was also a realistic appraisal of the facts of life. The new press secretary did not have Hagerty's standing with the president and the senior staff. And it could not have been enforced. Kennedy and the men around him were strong, self-confident individuals. They liked to talk to journalists. They had a sense of history and the part they were playing in it. They wanted their thoughts and deeds recorded. Only Kennedy himself could have restrained their contacts with the news media, and he was not about to do this. His sense of history was the strongest of all. Hagerty, moreover, had worked with a White House staff that had a team mentality. Signals were called—by Hagerty and Sherman Adams—and the squad obeyed. Republicans are team players. Democrats have other faults.

Much has been said and written about Kennedy's "favorable" treatment by the news media. It is attributed to journalism's liberal bias— usually by persons with a conservative bias. Actually, Kennedy and his administration were severely criticized and roughly handled by the news media at every juncture, but memory is selective. Nevertheless, there *was* a bias; indeed there was. The reporters were favorably disposed toward an administration to which they had some degree of access. The rule is: the greater the access, the greater the favorable bias.

There is no word more important to a journalist than "access." It sums up his world. Deny him access and, like Mr. Bogart deprived of money, he grows wan, pale and has trouble with his complexion. And beyond the crucial question of access, there is something even more overriding: the *quality* of the access. All administrations provide information, but it is wariable, milord, wariable. It varies in quality and content. The Kennedy people understood the material of journalism—the stuff it lives on. So they provided explanations and insights and the reasons for policy decisions. This is the deeper information that reporters must have if they are to do more than a superficial job. Kennedy and his staff rated high on access and high on the quality of access. They liked to talk to reporters about the reasons for things. It came naturally to them.

The reasons for things. The factors that went into a presidential decision. The pros and cons that were considered. The alternatives that were rejected and why they were rejected. The political, social and economic forces and how they acted on one another. The causal connections. The way in which the solution to one problem creates another problem, which is the central dilemma of modern government.

There is a massive outflow of information from the American government every day—news releases, announcements, reports, fact sheets, speeches. This official line, however, is indomitably superficial. It seldom provides the deeper explanations and reasons that are the heart of real understanding and real communication. Much of the time, the news media simply shovel this stuff out to the public. They thereby earn a reputation for light-mindedness. But sometimes they dig and root and scrounge for the true material of journalism. Those are the good days.

It is one thing to conduct an open, accessible administration. It is another thing when the newspapers print things the administration does not want printed. Before the inaugural applause had died away, Kennedy was confronted with a paradox: How does a president give the American people a reasonably open government and at the same time retain some control over that government? "I can't believe what I'm reading!" the new president exclaimed. "Castro doesn't need agents over here. All he has to do is read our newspapers. It's all laid out for him."[12] The government's secret plans for an invasion of Cuba at the Bay of Pigs were being revealed.

All presidents are afflicted with this perpetual problem of openness versus control. Some of them, notably Richard Nixon and Ronald Reagan, solve the problem with the awesome simplicity that is so appealing. They conduct a closed government. But Kennedy was in the mainstream of the American presidency. So he tried to have it both ways. He endeavored to open his administration, and then when certain circumstances arose, he endeavored to close it.

These two processes took place simultaneously. It is not possible to comprehend government unless it is understood that mutually contradictory things happen at the same moment. This is true of human affairs generally. It makes it hard for ideologues.

In the Bay of Pigs episode, Kennedy failed to close the government. In the Cuban missile crisis eighteen months later, he was more successful. The missile secret, at least in its crucial stages, was well kept. Kennedy controlled the disclosures and the timing. Mark Childs, one of the columnists who were briefed regularly "to give them background on the government's actions," tried urgently to find out what was going on. A presidential aide hinted blandly that it was a crisis over Berlin.[13] There is nothing like experience.

In the process of having it both ways, an irony occurred. The most open administration of the postwar era was, at the same time, the administration responsible for awakening concern over three issues that have plagued the press-government relationship ever since: news management, censorship, national security. Most of the controversy over these issues has centered on Lyndon Johnson and Richard Nixon, and properly so. But it began with Kennedy. The lead-off man, before Kennedy himself got into the game, was Pierre Salinger.

Pierre Emil George Salinger, also known as Lucky Pierre, Plucky Pierre and, to the cognoscenti, as Emil Flick, was thirty-five years old when he was appointed press secretary to the president. Salinger was a quick-witted, convivial man of the rotund persuasion. He was fond of cigars and good food—one Christmas card from Nicole and Pierre Salinger consisted of recipes for Filet de Boeuf Rossini (beef with *foie gras*— very rich), Farce aux Marrons (turkey stuffed with pork belly, chestnuts and other things—very rich), and Bûche de Noël (a coffee and buttercream cake—very rich). As a child in San Francisco, Salinger had been a piano prodigy. But only Gershwin smoked cigars while playing the piano, so Salinger went into journalism. He was a reporter and night city editor for the *San Francisco Chronicle* from 1946 to 1955. For the *Chronicle*, he investigated the treatment of prisoners in California jails, posing as a vagrant under an alias, Peter Emil Flick. This was a little Salinger joke, *flic* being French slang for cop. The authorities in Stockton and Bakersfield, where Flick spent seven days in jail, were not well versed in French.

After that, Salinger became an investigative writer for *Collier's* magazine, digging into corruption in the teamsters' union. This brought him to the attention of Bobby Kennedy, then chief counsel of a Senate committee investigating labor racketeering. Salinger joined the committee staff. When Jack Kennedy, a member of the committee, decided to run for president, he asked Salinger to be his press secretary. Salinger now lives in a château outside Paris, under his own name.

Salinger did not have the power in the Kennedy administration that Hagerty had wielded under Eisenhower. "In addition to running the press shop, he [Hagerty] was one of President Eisenhower's advisers on foreign and domestic policy," Salinger has said. "My only policy duties were in the information field. While Jim had a voice in deciding *what* the administration would do, I was responsible only for presenting [policy decisions] to the public in a way and at a time that would generate the best possible reception."[14] Flick was a flack.

Salinger's biggest assets as press secretary were an irrepressible sense of humor and the fact that he had been a practicing journalist. He spoke the lingo. An administrator he was not; he did not make the mimeograph machines run on time. But he conducted most of his briefings with gusto and got along well with the reporters—with the usual reservation that all bets were off when the press suspected evasion, concealment or manipulation.

He was especially good at animal briefings. The White House reporters welcome an animal briefing. Their working days are full of international problems, complicated domestic issues and the intricacies of the federal budget. An animal story relieves the tedium. Salinger picked up quickly on things. He knew that Caroline Kennedy's various pets would make good copy. They would also ease Lucky Pierre through another briefing. He was good with hamsters. His handling of the arrival of Tom Kitten was adroit. But his masterpiece was a rabbit that played the trumpet.

Rabbits have played a part in the American presidency. There was the Rabbitt candidacy that gave John F. Kennedy a guffaw in St. Louis. There was the infuriated rabbit that menaced Jimmy Carter in Georgia. And there was Zsa Zsa, a white rabbit that was sent to Caroline as a gift. Salinger played this one with a cigar accompaniment.

Question: "When did Zsa Zsa arrive?"

Salinger: "This morning." (Gestures with cigar, indicating morning.)
Question: "What will you do with her?"
Salinger: "Zsa Zsa is going to an orphanage." (Cigar is pointed in general direction of orphanage.)
Question (from a reporter who arrived late): "Who is Zsa Zsa?"
Salinger: "A rabbit. Sent to us by a Pittsburgh, Pa., magician. Zsa Zsa is supposed to be able to play the first five bars of the Star-Spangled Banner on a toy trumpet." (Cigar is centered in Salinger's mouth, simulating trumpet.)
Question: "Have you tried this out?"
Salinger: "No." (Cigar droops forlornly; he hadn't thought of that.)
Question: "Was Zsa Zsa playing the trumpet when she came in?"
Salinger: "No, the trumpet came separately." (Cigar revives.)
Question: "Is the trumpet going to an orphanage?"
Salinger: "I don't think the rabbit should be without its trumpet." (Cigar is pointed ecstatically at ceiling.)

Very good. Salinger had his story. He had managed the rabbit news. But then he made the great mistake of stating publicly that he was going to manage the *important* news as well. He should have gone ahead and done it and kept his mouth shut.

Actually, what Salinger did was essentially what Hagerty had done. Hagerty had arranged things so that major announcements by Cabinet departments and executive agencies were cleared with him beforehand. This centered the management of important news in the White House—a significant characteristic of the imperial presidency. The system also is intended to control the timing and the flow of news, so that it will be announced at the most advantageous moment. When something goes wrong for the president, it is wondrous how often some "good" news is found, and announced at the same time. It is the short arm of coincidence.

Early in 1967, Lyndon Johnson got word that Senator Robert F. Kennedy was planning to deliver a major speech attacking his Vietnam policy. On the day of the speech, Johnson held a press conference. He announced that he had received a message from Soviet Premier Aleksei N. Kosygin, agreeing to negotiate the limitation of anti–ballistic missile systems. That made great big headlines. Then Johnson rushed off to Howard University and delivered a civil rights speech. That made big headlines. Then he dashed over to the Office of Education and spoke about the nation's education problems. That made pretty big headlines. In the morning papers, Bobby Kennedy's speech struggled for attention against an avalanche of managed news. No one ever figured out how

Johnson learned anything, since he did all the talking. Nevertheless, he was a student. He had studied, among other persons, Hagerty.

What Salinger did was to put the system on a regular, formal basis. He set up a "coordinating committee" consisting of the chief information officers of the government departments and agencies. He met with this committee on Tuesday afternoons, for the following purposes:

1. "To survey the latest executive policies, and news developments within the . . . departments." In other words, here is the official line, and what have you got that the White House can announce?

2. "To agree on the form and procedure" for releasing information. Who makes the announcement, and what is the most advantageous timing?

3. "To range generally over questions of prime interest to the reporters covering [the] departments." Let's get our story straight before they ask.[15]

On several occasions, Salinger has said, this arrangement helped avert mistakes. He recalled an incident in which the Defense Department spokesman, Arthur Sylvester, told him that the Pentagon was preparing to construct nuclear testing sites in Alaska. It occurred to Salinger that the Russians might react adversely to nuclear tests so close to their territory. He does not mention the Alaskans. Salinger told Kennedy about the plan. Kennedy had never heard of it. Kennedy called Robert McNamara, the secretary of defense. McNamara had never heard of it. The plan was dropped.[16]

In addition to averting mistakes, the arrangement was intended to assure that the government spoke with one voice on important policies. Salinger says Kennedy did not object to in-house disputes and disagreements before decisions were reached, but he insisted that everyone in the administration line up behind a policy once it had been decided on. No second-guessing, at least not in public. It was the control problem again. The coordinating committee was a control mechanism.

It was not illegal. In retrospect, it was pretty mild stuff when compared with what came along under Johnson and Nixon. But it *was* news management. And it was out in the open, where it would alarm the news media, which it did. Later, Salinger reflected ruefully that Hagerty had exercised "invisible" control over the executive branch's news operations. "My crime," Salinger said, "was to formalize the arrangement [and] to announce [it] publicly."[17] News management was not new; it was only born again. The news media had winked at the same practices under Eisenhower and Hagerty. Ike was a Republican, and very popular.

But there was more to it than just a committee of government flacks. The news management issue under Kennedy was not a one-shot deal. It was learned that Kennedy was requiring that speeches by senior government officials be cleared in advance with the White House. And all questions from reporters about the Cuban missile crisis and the administration's confrontation with the steel industry were to be referred to the White House. And there was the Bay of Pigs.

Early on the evening of April 6, 1961, the news editors of the *New York Times* "dummied in" a story that would appear in the *Times* the next morning. The story was written by Tad Szulc, a *Times* reporter. It said the Central Intelligence Agency had trained a force of insurgents for an invasion of Cuba, in an attempt to overthrow the government of Fidel Castro. The story said the invasion was imminent.

It was not the first story on the clandestine project. In October 1960, a scholarly journal—the *Hispanic American Report*—published an article that said anti-Castro guerrillas were being trained in Guatemala. In November of that year, *The Nation* carried a similar report. The magazine urged the American news media to look into the situation. The response was erratic.

On November 23, 1960, the *St. Louis Post-Dispatch* carried the first of a series of stories by reporter Richard Dudman of its Washington bureau. The stories gave details of the guerrilla training camp and suggested that the CIA was preparing an invasion of Cuba. In late 1960 and early 1961, the *Los Angeles Times*, the *Miami Herald*, the *Washington Post* and *U.S. News and World Report* carried stories on various aspects of the guerrilla training.

None of these stories forked any lightning. There was no great national debate, no outpouring of public alarm, no demands that the government stop and think it over. Some Americans probably would have felt that an invasion of Cuba was a fine idea. Others would have dissented. But the point was that the matter was not brought fully to their attention. Not in any sustained way. Not in time. It takes persistence—or prestige—to get the attention of 200 million people; there are many distractions in their lives. But most of the newspaper stories had only fragmentary information. No one tied it all together and focused it. No one persisted, except a reporter for a newspaper in St. Louis. For chrissake, St. Louis. That was not enough.

Harrison Salisbury of the *New York Times* wrote later: "With the curious compartmentalization that renders the national press blind to the reports of even such distinguished regional papers as the *St. Louis Post-Dispatch*, Dudman's [stories] produced no answering echo in the media. . . ." Salisbury added that "the flurry of individual stories [in other newspapers] made no impact on public perception or knowledge. The great television . . . networks, which served as the sources of information for so many Americans, said no word [about the invasion plans]." Probably no more than a couple of thousand Americans, Salisbury estimated, really knew what was going on. [18]

Then, on January 10, 1961, three months before the Tad Szulc story, the *New York Times* published a page-1 story by a reporter named Paul Kennedy. It had a three-column headline: U.S. HELPS TRAIN AN ANTI-CASTRO FORCE AT SECRET GUATEMALAN AIR-GROUND BASE. A sub-head said: CLASH WITH CUBA FEARED. The *New York Times*. That made a difference. Yeah it did.

The president had complained about the other stories. He had told Salinger that all Castro had to do was read the American news media to find out about the invasion plans. But the story in the *New York Times* upset him more than any of the others. The *Times's* managing editor, Turner Catledge, pointed out that other publications had carried stories about the invasion preparations. Ah, yes, said Kennedy, "but it wasn't news until it appeared in the *Times*."[19]

It is a matter of wonderment that the president complained about the January 10 story. Because the story was all wrong. Paul Kennedy had got it exactly ass-backward. His story strongly implied that the insurgents were being trained to defend Guatemala *from an invasion by Cuba*. He quoted the president of Guatemala to that effect. Kennedy's lead paragraph said: "This area [the training site] is the focal point of Guatemala's military preparation for . . . an almost inevitable clash with Cuba." *Guatemala's* preparation? That plucked the Central Intelligence Agency neatly off the hook.

"Had the story been dictated by the CIA as a cover, it could hardly have done better," Salisbury wrote later. The president had no beef. The January 10 story in the *Times*, as much as any one thing, *prevented* a public debate on the issue of whether the United States should sponsor an invasion of Cuba. Who cared whether Guatemala and Cuba had at it? The public was lulled.

That was where matters stood on April 6. On that evening, the senior news editors of the *Times*, Theodore Bernstein and Lewis Jordan, had Tad Szulc's story in front of them. This one was accurate. Szulc had pinned down the crucial facts: (1) It was to be an invasion of *Cuba* by anti-Castro Cuban insurgents, not Guatemalan patriots defending the fatherland, (2) the invasion was coming soon, and (3) it was organized and led by the CIA.

Bernstein and Jordan considered this an important story. They dummied it in as the lead story on page 1—the "turn story" (so called because it would be in the first column on the right-hand side, where the page is turned; readers are conditioned to look at the turn story first, knowing that the editors consider it the most important news of the day). And Bernstein and Jordan scheduled a four-column headline for Szulc's story. No more Mr. Nice Guy.

The *New York Times* is conscious of its importance. It does not run many headlines that stretch halfway across the front page. When it does run a big headline, it is not solely for the enlightenment of ordinary readers. It is also a message to the movers and shakers. It is to attract the attention of the establishment. The four-column head that Bernstein and Jordan ordered would have said to the television networks, the news-magazines, the *Wall Street Journal*, the *Washington Post* and the rest of journalism's big-leaguers that the *New York Times* saw something important and urgent at hand. Something they should get to work on. Something they should follow up.

However, a funny thing happened on the way to the presses. Just imagine the surprise and chagrin of the news editors when the managing editor stepped in and ordered some changes. Catledge removed Szulc's statement that the invasion was imminent. He took out all references to the CIA. Having emasculated the story, he moved it to a less prominent position on page 1; it was no longer the turn story. Then he reduced the headline from four columns to one column. The new head made no mention of an invasion, no mention of the CIA, no mention of United States involvement. It said "anti-Castro units" were being trained at bases in Florida and Central America. Period. This was not much of a message to anyone.

Catledge had received a call from the publisher of the *Times*, Orvil Dryfoos. The publisher had talked with the president. It seems the president had been disingenuous with the publisher. Kennedy implied that the invasion was not a certainty at all. He told Dryfoos he had not even authorized the release of the necessary fuel.

There is not much doubt that Kennedy tried to persuade Dryfoos not to run the story, but the *Times*'s upper echelons already had a severe case of cold feet. Catledge wanted to run the story but not all of it. He did not want to identify the CIA. He did not want to say the invasion was imminent. Except for those items, let 'er rip. The chief of the *Times*'s Washington bureau, James Reston, was for the story, but he, too, did not want to report that the invasion was coming soon. Reston said this would tip off Castro. Moreover, the *Times* would look foolish if the operation were delayed.

The publisher, Dryfoos, was even more anxious about the story; he told Catledge he was not sure it should be run at all. According to Peter Wyden's authoritative account of the Bay of Pigs, Dryfoos was worried that the *Times* might be "tampering with national security."[20] Presumably Cuba might invade the United States in retaliation. Dryfoos also wondered whether the *Times* would be held responsible "if hundreds or possibly thousands of Cubans died on the beaches and the invasion failed," Wyden wrote. Or, Dryfoos said, the invasion might be canceled and the *Times* might be blamed for *that*.

The publisher was seducing himself. Kennedy did not have to do much. But the responsibilities that Dryfoos was assuming were not the *Times*'s responsibilities. They were the government's responsibilities. It was the United States government, not the *New York Times*, that had originated, planned, organized, financed and directed the Bay of Pigs expedition. It was not the *Times*'s baby. If the invasion succeeded, it was the government, not the *Times*, that would get the credit. If it failed, it was the government, not the *Times*, that would get the blame. Except, of course, in the enduring temples of irrationality.

Certainly the *New York Times* had a responsibility. But it was a different responsibility. It was a responsibility to define its own responsibility and then stick with it. Of all human activities, this is one of the least pleasurable. The customary solution is to compromise. The *Times* compromised. It decided it must print the news. But it decided it did not have to print *all* the news.

So the story was watered down and played down. Ten days after it appeared, Kennedy and the CIA launched their effort to overthrow Fidel Castro. Then a lot of people looked foolish.

Two days after the invasion ended in failure, the State Department held a briefing. Allen Dulles, director of the CIA, was there. He told the assembled journalists that the Bay of Pigs demonstrated that the United States should have an "official secrets act," as Britain does. In consequence, Britain has never made a mistake. Dulles admitted that many lawyers believed an official secrets act would be unconstitutional. But he said he was a lawyer, too, and he knew what the country needed.

Dudman of the *Post-Dispatch*—remember him?—was at the briefing. He stood up and said, "The problem is not too much information but too little information. If there had been enough information [about the Bay of Pigs], the American people would have risen up and stopped it."[21] Well, they certainly would have if they had known it was going to fail. But if the American people had known the invasion was going to fail, Kennedy would have known it, too. And if he had known . . . That is the way these things go.

On April 27—ten days after the fiasco—Kennedy went to New York and delivered a speech to the American Newspaper Publishers Association. He said the nation's news media must recognize that they had responsibilities "in the face of a common danger: the totality of the Communist challenge to our survival and to our security. . . ."

"If the press is awaiting a declaration of war before it imposes the self-discipline of combat conditions, then I can only say that no war ever posed a greater threat to our security," Kennedy told the publishers. "If you are awaiting a finding of 'clear and present danger,' then I can only say that the danger has never been more clear. . . ."

The president acknowledged that "the very word 'secrecy' is repugnant in a free and open society." But he asked "every publisher, every editor and every newsman in the nation to re-examine his own standards, and to recognize the nature of our country's peril.

"For the facts of the matter," Kennedy said, "are that this nation's foes have openly boasted of acquiring through our newspapers information they would otherwise hire agents to acquire through theft, bribery or espionage; that details of this nation's covert preparations to counter the enemy's covert operations have been available to every newspaper reader, friend and foe alike; [and] that the size, the strength, the location and the nature of our forces and weapons, and our plans and strategy for their use, have all been pinpointed in the press . . . to a degree sufficient to satisfy any foreign power. . . ."

Then Kennedy made a suggestion: "Every newspaper now asks itself, with respect to every story: 'Is it news?' All I suggest is that you add the question: 'Is it in the interests of national security?' . . . And should the press of America consider and recommend the voluntary assumption of specific new steps or machinery [to do this], I can assure you we will cooperate whole-heartedly with those recommendations. . . ." You bet we will.

Kennedy was asking the nation's news media to censor themselves in peacetime. In a torrent of indignant editorials and columns, the media declined to do so. They said the president was blaming them for the failure of the Bay of Pigs invasion. They said he was asking them to do what he was not asking the rest of the nation to do—go on a war footing. They said they were being asked to define "national security," a profoundly elusive concept, an ignis fatuus, a will-o'-the-wisp. Or to accept the definition of an individual president. Temporary. Subject to change.

Salinger says he and Kennedy were surprised and disappointed by the "violent" reaction of the news media. "He [Kennedy] had no right, apparently, even to suggest that the press was not entirely responsible—and omniscient—in the handling of highly sensitive information," Salinger wrote later.[22]

That was not quite the point. Every president, like every citizen, has the right to believe and to state that the press is irresponsible. The real question is: Does a president have the right to do something about it? If he does, it is to be hoped that he, not the news media, is omniscient. Because in the absence of presidential perfection, one man's irresponsibility is another man's public service.

In this case, both men were Kennedy. When he made the New York speech, he was damn sore. A major enterprise early in his presidency had failed ignominiously. Kennedy was humiliated and bitterly disappointed. Being human, he sought a scapegoat. It was all the news media's fault.

And then, being human again, he cooled off. After that, still being human, he contradicted himself. What had been irresponsible became a public service. Having said the press should not have printed anything about the Bay of Pigs, on national security grounds, Kennedy proceeded to reverse his field. He informed the *New York Times* that it should have printed *more*, not less, about the invasion plans. This is the kind of thing that gives national security a bad name.

A few days after the April 27 speech, a group of editors and publishers went to the White House to talk to Kennedy about it. During the meeting, Kennedy took Turner Catledge aside and told him: "Maybe if you had printed more about the operation, you would have saved us from a colossal mistake."[23]

The might-have-beens were still on Kennedy's mind more than a year later. On September 13, 1962, Dryfoos went to the White House. He talked with Kennedy about national security. During the conversation, Kennedy said: "I wish you had run everything on Cuba. I am just sorry you didn't tell it at the time."[24]

This, of course, was hindsight. Would Kennedy have said it if the invasion had succeeded? He might have said many things, but not that. And journalism's assumption as stated by Dudman—that the American people would have stopped the invasion if they had known about it—was hindsight, too.

Everything was backward vision. Then what can be said with assurance about the Bay of Pigs and the news media? Only this: A major newspaper had forgotten that the purposes of the press and the purposes of the government are not the same, should not be the same, cannot be the same. The *Times* had permitted its purposes to come close to coinciding with the government's purposes. Its perceptions had gone awry. It had seduced itself into seeing an event in almost the same way that the government saw the event. This was not wise. It almost never is. It could lead to no good. It almost never does.

In 1852, the *Times* of London broke a story on secret negotiations between Britain and France. The prime minister, Lord Derby, was outraged. The editor of the *Times*, John Delane, replied: "We cannot admit that a newspaper's purpose is to share the labors of statesmanship, or that it is bound by the same limitations, the same duties, the same liabilities as [the government]. The purpose and duties of the two . . . are constantly separate, generally independent, sometimes diametrically opposite. . . ."[25]

The government never ceases its efforts to get the press into its bed, using the old national security dodge or whatever seduction comes to mind. The press's duty is grim. Celibacy.

Never say die. A year and a half later, Kennedy tried again. On October 24, 1962, during the Cuban missile crisis, the White House issued a memorandum to the news media. It listed twelve categories of information that the government considered "vital to our national security." The memo warned that "it is possible that such information may come into the possession of news media. During the current tense international situation, the White House feels that the publication of such information is contrary to the public interest." The twelve categories were:

1. Plans for the use of U.S. strategic or tactical forces, including the type of equipment to be used and the location of command centers or detection systems.

2. Estimates of the United States' capability to destroy targets, including the number of weapons required, the size and nature of the forces required, the ability of these forces to penetrate defenses and the accuracy or reliability of U.S. forces or weapons systems.

3. Intelligence estimates concerning targets or targeted systems, such as enemy missile and bomber forces.

4. Intelligence estimates of enemy plans or capabilities, or information that would reveal the success or failure of U.S. intelligence operations in Cuba or the Communist bloc.

5. Details on numbers or movements of U.S. forces, including naval units, ground forces, aircraft, missiles, ammunition and equipment. These activities, however, could be revealed after they had been completed.

6. The degree of alert of U.S. military forces.

7. The location of military aircraft or supporting equipment. However, the presence of aircraft could be revealed if they could be observed by the public.

8. Emergency plans for dispersing military aircraft and other units, including dispersal capabilities, times, schedules and logistical support.

9. Official estimates of the United States' vulnerability to various forms of enemy action, including sabotage of military installations.

10. New information on the number, distribution and operational readiness of U.S. missiles. Also, estimates of their strike capability and effectiveness.

11. Details of command and control systems, including new or planned command posts, estimates of their ability to survive enemy attack and security measures.

12. Details of airlift and sealift capabilities, including the size and nature of the military forces involved and the timing and supply factors.

It was a remarkable document. It was the only official censorship plan ever announced by the United States government in peacetime. There was, without question, an extremely serious crisis under way. Soviet intermediate-range ballistic missile sites had been discovered in Cuba. But there had been no declaration of war. There had been no proclamation of national emergency. Nothing had been done to enlist the nation as a whole in an effort to repel a threat. There was only an effort to censor the news media. First things first.

Censorship had been in effect in World War II and the Korean conflict. But there had been a declaration of war in the first instance, and a United Nations resolution in the second. The program announced by Salinger was "voluntary." There was a general feeling that it was necessary and justified. And it was in effect for less than a month. Nevertheless, it was censorship.

Then, in that same grim October, the State and Defense departments imposed a rule about interviews. Officials of those departments could not talk to journalists unless a third person—usually an information officer—was present or the details of the conversation were reported afterward to the department's information office. In the rally-round atmosphere of the missile crisis, this slipped by without much initial controversy, but later there was a problem. When the crisis was over, the State Department rescinded the rule, but the Defense Department did not. The rule remained in effect at the Pentagon for many months after the missile crisis had ended.

As a result, the quality of access was called into question. The reporters had grave doubts that officials would be as candid or informative with someone else in the room. They had that Big Brother feeling. The wrath of the news media descended on the man who had issued the interview rule—the assistant secretary of defense for public affairs.

His name was Arthur Sylvester. He was a controversial, outspoken individual, and he was, good grief, a former newspaperman. Before joining the Kennedy administration, he had been Washington correspondent for the *Newark News*. Sometimes these former-journalists-turned-government-officials get into no end of trouble. Sylvester became the center of a furious fight over news management, censorship and national security.

What caused the trouble, in addition to the interview rule, was something Sylvester said in New York on December 6, 1962, shortly after the missile crisis ended: "It would seem to me basic, all through history, that a government's right—and by a government I mean a people, since in our country, in my judgment, the people express, have the right to express and do express, every two and every four years, what government they want—that it's inherent in that government's right, if necessary, to lie to save itself when it's going up into a nuclear war. That seems to me basic. Basic."[26]

He was not a great orator. But after wandering around a while, Sylvester's meaning had emerged. It was a restatement of Sophocles: "Truly, to tell lies is not honorable, but when the truth entails tremendous ruin, to speak dishonorably is pardonable."

In the context of the missile crisis, this had a certain appeal. National survival was involved. Who was going to boggle at a little lying? But there were some questions. There are always questions. Kennedy's strategy in the crisis was to make it clear to the Russians that the United States was prepared to use military force as a last resort, if the missiles were not removed. It was no secret to the Soviet Union that extensive American military preparations were under way. If it had been a secret, the United States would have had no leverage. It may have been wise to conceal the details, but it would have been disastrous to conceal the broad knowledge. Suppose Khrushchev had got the impression that the United States was *not* willing to use force, that it had lost its nerve, that it would be supine in the face of whatever he might do? Then he would have done whatever he wanted to do.

So the American government was not concealing anything from the Russians or lying to them. Not in any real or important sense. It was concealing things from the American people. It was lying to *them*. First things first.

That was the way the news media saw it. Kennedy and Salinger, of course, saw it quite another way. At various times during and after the missile crisis, they cited several news stories that they said had jeopardized national security or had impeded the conduct of foreign policy:

- A story that revealed the United States' negotiating position at a forthcoming Geneva conference on a nuclear test ban treaty. Salinger, in his book on the Kennedy years, called this an "entirely irresponsible" story that "gave the Soviet negotiators a distinct advantage" before the Geneva talks began. [27]
- A story on U.S. surveillance of the Soviet space program. This article, Kennedy told a group of editors, gave complete details of intelligence methods that enabled the United States to learn of Soviet space launches in advance.
- A story that revealed details of a "secret mechanism" for tracking Russian space satellites. This story may have been the same one that Kennedy referred to in the meeting with the editors; it was not clear whether he was talking about one story or two.
- A story on a conversation between Adlai Stevenson and UN Secretary-General U Thant, in which they discussed U Thant's trip to Cuba. Stevenson's report on the conversation arrived at the State Department at eight o'clock one morning, intended for Secretary of State Dean Rusk. At 10 A.M.—before Rusk had had time to read it—a full account of the report was on the news tickers.

● A report prepared for the CIA during the Eisenhower administration. Salinger, who saw this document after he became press secretary, said the CIA had assigned two college professors to assess the United States' "entire defensive and retaliatory posture." The professors had access only to public sources—material that had been published. Their report, Salinger said, "was such an exact picture of our military capability that it was immediately classified 'top secret.'"[28] The CIA at work.

Salinger did not address himself to the absurdity. Instead, he said he found it shocking that so much information on the nation's military strength had been revealed publicly. He was expressing not only the government's view but also the attitude of many citizens: How can the United States be safe against its enemies if national security information finds its way into the news media?

That is a crucial question. To answer it, all that is necessary is to define national security.

But national security is the Schleswig-Holstein of modern government. No one knows what it is. There is no agreement as to what constitutes national security. It is a bottomless pit of legal and constitutional confusion. Lord Palmerston, when asked to explain the profoundly complicated dynastic quarrel between Denmark and Germany over Schleswig-Holstein, replied that only three persons in the world understood it: the prince consort and an obscure German professor, both of whom were dead, and Palmerston himself—"and I have forgotten everything I knew about it."

With two possible (and disputed) exceptions involving the disclosure of nuclear secrets and the identities of intelligence agents, the United States has no law dealing with national security. Nor should it have, unless it wearies of democracy. The constitutional clause defining treason has seldom if ever been invoked in the recurring national security arguments between the news media and the government. Even the Nixon administration, which drew back from very little, drew back from that; in one of the most serious "national security" confrontations between the news media and the government—the Pentagon Papers case—the government did not charge that treason had been committed.

The First Amendment's guarantees of free speech and freedom of the press have thus far stood as bulwarks against the enactment of a law defining national security. So has the doctrine that the government shall not impose prior restraints on expression of views or publication of material. In the Pentagon Papers episode, the government argued that the *New York Times* and other newspapers must be prohibited from publishing classified documents in order to prevent a breach of national security from occurring. The Supreme Court held that such prior restraint was unconstitutional. That being the case, how could a national security law be enforced before the fact? After the fact, the matter presumably would be academic. The Russians would know all.

There is another obstacle. Members of Congress and other politicians are aware that a national security law might be used against them, if they were so unfortunate as to find themselves out of power or so misguided as to criticize the administration. The same is true of the general public, which is chronically out of power and chronically fond of criticizing. In consequence of enlightened self-interest, Congress has declined to write a statutory definition of national security.

The result is that national security is what the president says it is. Any president, at any given moment. However, the president's definition lacks the force of law. It prevails only if he can convince the public, the news media, his own party, the opposition party, the federal bureaucracy and the Supreme Court that it should prevail. So it seldom does.

One reason for the lack of enthusiasm is that presidential definitions of national security are notoriously capricious. A president may say at one moment that national security is one thing and a short time later that it is something quite different. At one point, Kennedy defined the nation's security as requiring a certain course of action; a few days later, he said an exactly opposite course should have been followed. Some presidents have declassified national security information whenever it suited their purposes. They disclosed the information in a public speech or press conference or gave it to an individual reporter to do with as he pleased. After leaving office, presidents and other senior officials have used classified material in their memoirs. One moment it was secret information that could not be revealed without doing immense harm. Then, poof! The former chief executive waved his magic wand and rendered it as innocuous as a presidential memoir.

Dwight Eisenhower, a five-star general, presumably knew a national security when he saw one. But his press secretary, Jim Hagerty, said Ike had no illusions about official secrets. Hagerty told a House subcommittee in 1972 that material which was to be released at his daily press briefings would arrive from government departments "literally covered with classified stamps, including the highest [secrecy] ratings." Before he could make the announcement, Hagerty said, "I would . . . actually have to take these reports to the president and have him declassify them on the spot. And, believe me, the only thing that was 'Top Secret' about that was what he [Ike] would say when he . . . had to go through such nonsense."29

But Eisenhower's national security assistant, Robert Cutler, complained that "I am convinced that leaks to the press of matters in a discussion stage, of working papers, or [National Security] Council deliberation[s] . . . play into the enemy's hands."[30] Mr. Eisenhower, meet Mr. Cutler. And Eisenhower himself said he had been "plagued by inexplicable, undiscovered leaks in this government."[31] Ike, meet Ike.

On May 3, 1965, Lyndon Johnson held a walking press conference. It was one of the greats. A crisis had developed in the Dominican Republic, the big American military buildup had begun in Vietnam, the temperature in Washington was 91 degrees, and Johnson traipsed around the south lawn of the White House for an hour and fifty minutes. While he was walkin' and talkin' an aide hurried across the lawn and handed him a document. It was a report from the Central Intelligence Agency. It informed Johnson that 1,500 to 2,000 persons had been killed in the Dominican fighting, and gave other information. David Wise, then a reporter for the *New York Herald Tribune,* was standing near the president. Wise said later that he could clearly see the word SECRET stamped on the document in large letters. National security is all very well, but Johnson had uses for this information. He wanted to justify his decision to send the marines into the Dominican Republic. So he read the CIA report to the press corps.[32]

Johnson, like other presidents, complained bitterly about leaks in his administration. He wanted to do all the leaking himself. In 1967, he held a summit meeting with Premier Aleksei N. Kosygin of the Soviet Union. The conversations, naturally, were entirely secret. The next day, Johnson flew to his Texas ranch. There, he invited Max Frankel of the *New York Times* to join him in the swimming pool. Standing waist deep in the warm water, the Texas sky arching overhead, national security vigilantly protecting America's blessings, Johnson gave the reporter an hour-long, detailed account of his discussions with Kosygin.[33]

The list is as endless as an Ingmar Bergman summer:

- The Eisenhower administration leaked the Yalta Papers to James Reston of the *New York Times.* For generations of fearful patriots, this record of Franklin Roosevelt's negotiations with Joseph Stalin was incontrovertible evidence that all had been lost since 1945. They trembled in their Mercedeses.
- John F. Kennedy leaked parts of a highly classified presidential memorandum to reporter Ben Bradlee of *Newsweek.* It suited a Democratic president's political purposes to reveal this account of his 1961 summit talks with Nikita Khrushchev, just as it had suited a Republican administration's purpose to leak the Yalta documents. National security is politics.
- Lyndon Johnson, in his memoirs, related details of Operation Mar-

igold, an unsuccessful Vietnam peace effort. Marigold already had been disclosed in the Pentagon Papers, but as far as the government was concerned it was still officially a national security secret when Johnson wrote his book.

● Johnson's last press secretary, George Christian, also wrote a book. Christian's memoir, Max Frankel said later, contained "seventy pages of narrative on the decisions to end the bombing of North Vietnam [and] a great deal of detailed information, all still highly classified, about the secret negotiations with North Vietnam. . . ."[34]

● Presidential assistant Theodore Sorensen, in a book on the Kennedy administration, revealed "dozens upon dozens of actions, meetings, reports and documents, all still treated as 'classified' by the government," Frankel said. Former State Department official Roger Hilsman "poured his files and secrets into a quick memoir," and former ambassador John Bartlow Martin, in his book, recounted "numerous confidential messages and communications."[35] At the White House, the State Department, the Defense Department and the Central Intelligence Agency, one man's national security is another man's bestseller. Available at all bookstores.

National security's *reductio ad absurdum* took place on the night of February 6, 1970. Millions of Americans watched as Lyndon Johnson, on prime-time television, nonchalantly declassified a secret presidential memo. Walter Cronkite asked the former president whether his last secretary of defense, Clark M. Clifford, had initiated the reappraisal of Vietnam policy that led to a partial limit on the bombing of North Vietnam. Johnson did not want Clifford to get the credit. So he read a directive he had issued at the time, ordering a study of possible alternatives to bombing. To make sure everyone knew what was going on, Johnson identified it as a classified document.

In the presidency, Johnson did as he pleased with national security. In March 1967, he delivered a speech to a group of educators in Nashville, Tennessee. About 125 persons, including 50 White House reporters, were in the room as Johnson disclosed a closely held secret: Newly developed space satellite photography had given the United States precise knowledge of the number of Soviet ballistic missiles. As a result, the president said, "I know how many missiles the enemy has." It's all over town.

When it is time for another Red scare, the Pentagon leaks like a two-dollar radiator. On September 29, 1981, the Defense Department made public a previously classified, ninety-nine-page report on "Soviet Military Power." It was packed with detailed information. The Russians, it revealed, had 180 divisions, 50,000 tanks, 20,000 artillery pieces, 250 triple-warhead SS-20 missiles, 3,500 military aircraft in Eastern Europe, 180 nuclear-powered submarines and much, much more. Head for the hills.

The report was declassified at a moment when the United States was engaged in one of its chronic efforts to persuade Western Europe to deploy more U.S. missiles. Anticipating skepticism over the timing, Secretary of Defense Caspar W. Weinberger offered the ritualistic denial that there were any ulterior motives behind the release of the report. He said it was not intended to frighten the Europeans into accepting more American missiles. He said the Soviet military threat was very real.

Weinberger was undoubtedly correct that the Russians are armed to the teeth. So is the United States. It is fashionable. But what about the declassification? If the information in the report was so vital to the nation's security that it had to be classified and kept secret, why was it declassified and made public? These questions have a way of answering themselves. But what, then, is national security? Who is she, that all our swains commend her? She is what someone says she is, and then suddenly she is not. *La donna è mobile*. She is fickle.

The problem is that Washington reporters know all this. The reporters have seen too many instances in which national security was simply a *convenience* for a president, a senior official or even a junior official. Not a consistent, unchanging and reliable standard defining what is needed for the protection of the nation; just a convenience.

Sometimes the "top secret" stamp safeguards a legitimate, truly important secret. More often, it conceals from public view a piece of information that appeared months or years ago in the *New York Times* or *The Congressional Record*. Sometimes it is affixed out of conscientious concern for the nation's safety. More often, it is slapped on for momentary advantage, or to make an official feel important, or just out of habit. Especially just out of habit. Then it is discarded when circumstances change, as they will do. In Washington, intelligence expert David Wise has said, government secrets "are handed around like popcorn by presidents and lesser officials, when it suits their political purpose."[36] So the reporters are skeptical when the government cops the old national security plea.

The reporters know something else: Hypocrisy endures. The government must not be taken too seriously when it goes haring around the landscape trying to stop leaks and proclaiming that they endanger the national well-being. The reality is quite different. The government and the press actually are engaged in a close working relationship in which leaks of information play an important role. Very few leaks pose a demonstrable danger to the nation. Most of them are integral although informal instruments of government and diplomacy. They always have been, from ancient times forward. It is a shame the way leaks are maligned. The government could not conduct its business without them.

Taken as directed, leaks are very useful. The government gets fully as much from them as the news media do. It uses leaks to convey information to the American public or to foreign governments without taking responsibility for the information; there are many occasions when officials find it advantageous to be anonymous, as the congressman said to the FBI sheik. The government uses leaks to engage in discussion and argumentation with itself; it sends messages to itself in the *New York Times* and the *Washington Post*—the Miss Lonelyhearts of American journalism. Most important of all, the government uses leaks to manipulate the news media and influence public opinion.

The reporters, from their experience, know something else: There are very few *real* secrets. The government's obsession with secrecy, the millions of classified documents, the trees of rubber stamps that enable even minor officials to consign information to obscurity, the enormous apparatus of security and concealment—all this actually cloaks very little that is vital to the safety of the American people and nation.

Under a system known as derivative classification, everything in a government document is classified if one part is classified. As a result, the "top secret," "secret" or "confidential" designation often confers secrecy on a newspaper clipping, a speech or some other widely circulated information that has been public for years. The researchers in the think tanks grind out endless studies and reports for the Pentagon, the CIA and other agencies involved in national security. They support their conclusions and recommendations with facts. Many of these facts come from public sources—books, newspapers, magazines, unclassified research work and so on. All these public sources vanish under a "secret" stamp.

In the Pentagon Papers case, the Nixon administration sought to prevent publication of a "secret" history of the American role in Vietnam. One of the lawyers for the *New York Times* was James C. Goodale, a former Army intelligence officer. In the Army, Goodale said, he had worked on official histories similar to the Pentagon Papers. "I've written many just like it and taken *New York Times* articles and used them as footnotes, just as these guys did, and stamped the result classified," the lawyer said. "In effect, [I] classified the *New York Times.*"[37]

A few days before Jimmy Carter's trip to Poland, Andrew Glass of the Cox newspapers and I asked for a CIA briefing on U.S. relations with that country. The CIA's background briefings for reporters are off-and-on affairs; they depend on the mood of the administration. This time the agency agreed, and Glass and I drove out to CIA headquarters in Langley, Virginia. We were shown into a sparsely furnished room. The entire decor consisted of very large photographs of Idi Amin, Muammar Qaddafi and a third dictator whose face was not familiar to me.

For years, a standard joke in Washington has been that the CIA reads the *New York Times* each morning and then stamps it top secret. But that day in Langley, with the mighty apparatus of intelligence all around me, thousands of highly trained specialists sifting and evaluating mountains of data from spooks and satellites, I thought: Surely it is only a jest. Reassured by the surroundings, I asked the briefing officer a question about the Polish economy. He replied: "Have you read So-and-so's series in the *Times* on that? A damn good job."

Occasionally a government official, in a fit of candor, admits that the secrets business is not what it seems. Of all the officials who deal with this hidden world, none is more qualified to evaluate it than the president's national security assistant. He sees the intelligence community's "product" every day. No one is in a better position to know whether a secret is a *real* secret whose disclosure would harm the nation, or whether the secrecy stamp was merely the mindless result of bureaucratic habit.

McGeorge Bundy was national security assistant in the Kennedy and Johnson administrations. A very knowledgeable foreign affairs reporter for the *Washington Post*, Murrey Marder, once suggested to Bundy that only 5 percent of the classified information he received actually contained secrets. Bundy told Marder that his estimate was too high; it was less than 5 percent. Those damn reporters can't get anything right.

And then, according to Marder's affidavit in the Pentagon Papers case, Bundy told him something else: "The importance of actual secrets in terms of their impact on national security was limited to a relatively brief time span—usually measured in hours or a very few days, before they either became known or their secrecy significance virtually disappeared." [38]

Bundy spent six years in the national security business. He was not overly impressed. In May 1974, he told a Senate subcommittee that most of the secret information that came across his White House desk was not notable for importance or substance. Its outstanding features, he said, were "the inferior quality of its English and the parochial character of its argumentation. . . . Legitimate secrets, while important, are relatively few. . . .

"It is . . . a myth that because of access to classified documents the White House or the State Department or anyone else in the government 'knows best,'" Bundy said.

He spoke of addiction. Secrecy becomes an addiction of those who hold high office, Bundy said. "There is no virtue in secrecy for its own sake, and much danger."

"I see no need to accord the president any special primacy with respect to access to or control over secret information," Bundy told the subcommittee. "It is entirely true that he has a necessarily primary role in foreign affairs and defense, but it does not follow at all that he should have an unfettered right to decide what is and is not secret."[39] Exit Bundy.

So a reporter, after a few years in Washington, learns several things. He learns that national security is what the government says it is at any moment. This makes it too inconsistent to be a reliable guide. He learns that leaks of information are as vital to the government as they are to the news media. He learns that real secrets are to official secrets as real moralities are to mountebanks. Outnumbered. And the reporter learns one more thing: He learns about the dog in the night.

In "Silver Blaze," Holmes calls Watson's attention "to the curious incident of the dog in the night-time." But, Watson protests, "the dog did nothing in the night-time." To which Holmes replies: "That was the curious incident."

And so it is, over and over again, with "national security" secrets that are revealed in the news media. The dog does nothing in the night. Nothing happens. The government huffs and puffs and rips and snorts. It threatens dire punishment if it can find the leaker. It orders the FBI into the hunt. Lie detector tests are administered. Dark warnings issue against the offending newspaper, magazine or network. But when the outraged rhetoric dies away—outraged rhetoric is always dying away—it is seen that nothing has happened. To hear the government tell it, great injury to the Republic was inevitable, if indeed the Republic did not fall altogether. But nothing happened. Nothing happens most of the time.

Most presidents, many government officials and a substantial number of ordinary citizens do not accept this relativistic description of national security. They dismiss it as sophism that merely reflects the self-interest of the media. To them, national security is a more absolute proposition. The nation's safety must be preserved—against enemies that are real and formidable, and against the intrusive and often dangerous claims of journalism. They argue that there *is* a consistent and reliable standard for measuring national security. It consists essentially of four things:

● The collective judgment of senior foreign policy, military and intelligence officials. This judgment is based on their experience and on their knowledge of a given situation. It is necessary and proper that the information they possess must be closely held and not shared with the public or the press until it is safe to do so.

- The judgment of the president as the person ultimately responsible for the nation's security. After receiving and evaluating the judgments of senior officials, the president in effect defines national security by deciding what course of action it requires and what can and cannot be made public.
- The need for the government to maintain control of a situation, insofar as possible. This is the aspect of national security that has the greatest appeal for some persons. They have a high regard for authority. They are uneasily aware of the chaos of the human condition, but perhaps it can be made to go away. At any rate, as much control as possible must be exerted over human events and over humanity itself, due to its base instincts. When a president complains about leaks of information, he really means they threaten his control of a situation.

  However, relativity persists. Leaks that benefit a president are fine; those that do not are not. "What bugs a president," David Broder has written, "is not leaks, but leaks from people who may disagree with him. Time after time . . . [reporters] have sat in the office of some senior official who . . . has divulged the substance of, or even read from, highly classified documents. The purpose, in almost every case, was to advance the president's policy line—in Vietnam, in some international negotiation, in some domestic political fight. No, it's not . . . leaks that infuriate them. It's the leaks they don't control: the logs of private meetings with interested parties in regulatory matters, or evaluations of weapons systems that cast doubt on a multibillion-dollar boondoggle. Those leaks, they say, are dangerous."[40]
- A world view. Secrecy prospers in an absolute, good-and-evil view of the world. It thrives on fearful choices. God or devil. Orthodoxy or heresy. Barbarian or aristocrat. Have or have-not. Capitalism or communism. The secret world of national security has thrived. It has only been necessary to arrange the choices so as to scare people silly.

VII

AT HOME

Sinister forces were in motion on that obscure day early in 1969. Although it was a Sunday, Richard Nixon spent some time in his office. Then he got up from his desk, crossed the West Lobby and walked into the White House pressroom. The pressroom? Nixon in the *pressroom*? But he was curious about the place where the reporters worked. He had been president for only a few months and had never seen it. He had been told that the White House pressroom was cramped, over-crowded and messy. It certainly was. The pressroom dated back to the administration of Theodore Roosevelt and looked every year of it.

Teddy Roosevelt, needing more space for his ebullient presidency, had added a wing to the west side of the White House. The president's office, which until then had been in the White House itself, was relocated in the new West Wing. The famous Oval Office came into existence. The rest of the new wing provided offices for the growing presidential staff.

One day, Roosevelt noticed a group of reporters standing outside the northwest gate of the White House, at the end of the driveway that leads to the West Wing. In accordance with the custom of the time, they were waiting to interview presidential visitors as they came through the gate. The journalists would ask the visitors what they had discussed with the chief executive, in the hope of picking up some news. The weather on this particular day was inclement. The reporters were cold and wet. They were considering whether they would be better off working for the steel trust. Why, look at those poor chaps, Roosevelt said, in effect. They are cold and wet and are probably thinking of going to work for the steel trust. Let us set aside a room for them in the West Wing. And so it was done. The press moved into the White House.

The founding pressroom was immediately to the right of the West Wing entrance. Beyond it was a large reception room known as the West Lobby. In the middle of this lobby was an immense and somewhat battered round table on which visitors deposited their coats and hats. An usher then escorted them through a door at the far end and down a couple of short corridors to the Oval Office. The furnishings of the lobby consisted of a number of venerable couches and armchairs in cracked leather. The reporters spent much of their time sprawled on the couches, reading newspapers, chatting or drowsing. Mostly drowsing. When a visitor emerged from the president's office, they sprang to life and rushed forward to interview him. The importance of a visitor was measured by the number of journalists who left off dozing.

The pressroom itself was not large, and its decor was not lavish. Facing the door was a tall room divider made of some nondescript brown composition material. The divider made it impossible to enter the pressroom directly; it was necessary to turn to the right or left and go around the thing. The barrier gave the reporters a measure of privacy. The room divider also was used as a bulletin board on which the White House press office posted announcements and press releases.

On one side of the pressroom were three old-fashioned telephone booths with folding glass doors. These were for the exclusive use of the wire services—the Associated Press, United Press and International News Service (the UP merged with Hearst's INS in 1958, becoming United Press International). The wire service reporters used the booths when they were dictating stories or other information that they did not wish to be overheard. In front of the telephone booths was a desk for the AP reporters, with a typewriter and another telephone.

On the other side of the room were three more desks—for the UP, the *Evening Star* (then the dominant newspaper in Washington) and the National Broadcasting Company. Beyond these desks was a long table. As far as the nation's newspapers were concerned, this table was the White House pressroom. It was the White House "office" of the *New York Times*, the *Chicago Tribune* and the rest of journalism's giants. That was all: one long, battered table with several telephones on it. Except for the fortunate four, everyone used the communal table and the communal telephones.

The telephones were on a first-come-first-served basis, except for one true relic, an old-fashioned upright model with the earpiece on a hook that could be jiggled to get the operator's attention. Hello, Central. This antique was the prized possession of Edward T. (Eddie) Folliard, the veteran White House reporter for the *Washington Post*.

There were not enough telephones. There never are. A reporter who was assigned to the White House quickly located a phone somewhere else, to use when big stories broke. In the 1950's, when I began covering the White House, I found a pay phone in the basement of the West Wing, near the area now occupied by the National Security Council staff. I thought I had this one to myself until the day Dwight Eisenhower had a stroke. Every phone in the pressroom was in use; the place was a madhouse. I sprinted down the driveway to West Executive Avenue and into a side entrance to the basement. However, someone had beat me to it. The dirty dog. Up West Executive to Pennsylvania Avenue, at a fast trot. Down Pennsylvania at full speed to Seventeenth Street, where there was, in those days, a drugstore. It's a young man's game.

The reporters competed with the photographers for space on the pressroom table. Not wishing to leave their cameras and light meters on the floor to be kicked around, the photogs put them on the table. Everybody put everything on the table. The focal point of national journalism was a litter of telephones, cameras, newspapers, notebooks, empty coffee containers and oddments.

There was no other furniture. There wasn't space for any. The walls were bare except for a few group photographs of long-ago White House reporters. They wore derby hats, handlebar moustaches, spats and supercilious expressions, having covered a lot of politicians. The paint in the pressroom was cracked and peeling. The floor was scarred and pitted. It was a low-budget set for *The Front Page*. Hildy Johnson and the rest of the boys at the Chicago police station would have fit right in. The reporters had wrought the same devastation upon the White House pressroom that they wreak upon the Hotel Splendide-Plastiques of the world, and they had had years in which to do it. They liked it that way. It was home. It had not been imperialized. Nixon changed all that.

The new president regarded the mess. He regarded it distastefully. He spoke to Helen Thomas of UPI. "Is this where you have to work?" asked Nixon. "You should see it when the others are here," Thomas replied. [1] She explained that when big news was breaking at the White House, the pressroom was extremely crowded. How was she to know the president did not like crowds?

Nixon decided there would have to be a new pressroom. He discovered that the General Services Administration, the government's housekeeping agency, had developed a plan. There is always a plan. This one called for an underground pressroom. An excavation would be dug under the north lawn of the White House, and the press would be installed therein. The cost was estimated at about $1.5 million. [2]

This was considered too expensive. Even in those pre-Watergate days, the cost of the imperial presidency had begun to cause some grumbling. Shortly after Nixon took office, it was disclosed that the price of operating the White House had reached $70 million to $100 million a year. There were, at that time, 2 presidential yachts, 20 White House cars and limousines, 40 chauffeurs and a presidential staff that officially numbered 548 persons but was probably considerably larger. It had been disclosed that the Secret Service had spent $342,358 to construct a helicopter pad for Nixon at his Florida home (it was built on pilings in Biscayne Bay) and $250,000 to set up a Western White House in San Clemente, California. Things were adding up. [3]

So Nixon decided not to spend $1.5 million to bury a bunch of reporters under the north lawn. Instead, the West Terrace was chosen as the location of the new pressroom.

The West Terrace is an enclosed corridor that connects the White House and the West Wing. The north side of this structure faces Pennsylvania Avenue; the south, or inner, side looks out on the Rose Garden. Between the West Terrace and the Rose Garden is a covered walkway that the president uses to get from his living quarters in the White House to the Oval Office in the West Wing. If you look at the White House from Pennsylvania Avenue, you see a long, low structure connecting the mansion and the two-story West Wing on the right. That is the West Terrace. Inside it, nowadays, is the White House pressroom.

Before Nixon decided to rearrange things, the West Terrace was a sort of catchall for imperial odds and ends. It housed a sauna, two massage rooms (one for ladies, one for gents) and a flower room where floral decorations were prepared to brighten the White House and adorn state dinners. It also had kennels for the president's dogs. This symbolism did not escape the reporters when they moved in. Underneath the West Terrace was the White House's swimming pool.

All gone now. Swept away by the Albert Speer of American politics. Other locations were found for the sauna, the massage parlors, the flower room and the dogs. The swimming pool was covered over with two thicknesses of plywood. This gave the floor of the briefing room a hollow sound, akin to a press secretary announcing bad news. A rug took care of that, and a heated outdoor swimming pool was built for Jerry Ford and his successors. The old pressroom in the West Wing became the office of the president's national security assistant and is now much fancier. This three-way shift of dogs, reporters and Henry Kissinger was known as the triangular relationship. There is still a West Lobby; it is now much smaller but considerably more elegant. And it is off limits to journalists.

Under the new arrangement, the reporters can no longer sit in the lobby and watch the president's visitors come and go. They are separated from the reception room by a phalanx of press secretaries, deputy press secretaries, assistant press secretaries, press assistants, stenographers and other personnel of the White House's mammoth press and publicity operation. All of these functionaries have been installed in a beehive of offices between the pressroom and the lobby. Occasionally, visitors are brought to the briefing room for a press conference after seeing the president, but in most cases the reporters have to work it another way. If they want to talk to someone who has just conferred with the president, they must leave the pressroom and wait in the driveway outside the West Wing. So that is what they do.

It has a deterministic ring to it. In Teddy Roosevelt's time, the journalists stood outside the northwest gate and waited for people to come out. Eighty years later, they stand outside the West Wing and wait for people to come out. They have progressed about 100 feet up the driveway. If the weather is inclement, they get cold and wet. They consider whether they would be better off working for the oil cartel.

When Nixon decided that dig we must not for a greater pressroom, he saved the taxpayers $1.5 million. Instead, they paid $574,000. This sum created the most gorgeous pressroom in Washington, a town with a lot of pressrooms. It was so elegant that a sturdy old word like "pressroom" was not good enough. Instead, it was officially designated the West Terrace Press Center. Here the media personnel could interface with their occupational responsibilities and activate their meaningful functions. In a world where pressrooms were called West Terrace Press Centers, they could even engage in an activity defined by a professor of educational psychology as "a processing skill of symbolic reasoning, sustained by the interfacilitation of an intricate hierarchy of substrata factors. . . ."[4] They could read. They could sit around the pressroom and read. But don't mess up the place.

The new pressroom was ready for business in the spring of 1970. Nixon was proud of it. But he was concerned that it might not get any respect. A few days after the reporters moved in, Lyndon Johnson happened to be in town. Nixon gave the former president a tour of the new press center. Encountering a group of reporters, Nixon inquired anxiously: "Have you messed it up yet?"[5]

Nixon remarked to Johnson that he had been impressed by the "magnificent facilities" available to journalists in some European nations. Press secretary Ron Ziegler told me later that the president had been particularly affected by the federal press center in Bonn, West Germany. This Teutonic marvel has an immense, modernistic briefing room of the Hyatt Regency school. News conferences are conducted with great efficiency. The place is never messy.

However, tradition was too strong. Milhous could not put Bauhaus in the White House. Instead, the new briefing room was furnished in Orange County Dental. When the reporters saw it for the first time, they could scarcely credit their eyes, so great was the change. Gone was the scarred and battered equipment of the old pressroom, gone the bare floor and peeling walls, gone the familiar filth and clutter.

Opulence had arrived. The West Terrace Press Center had chesterfield sofas and high-backed Tudor chairs upholstered in red. The doctor will see you now. The walls were freshly painted in restful tones, and prints were hung upon them. There was wall-to-wall carpeting. There were coffee tables. My God, coffee tables! And what was this ultimate refinement? On the coffee tables were vases of yellow and white chrysanthemums. The flowers had been placed there by express instruction of Richard Nixon, to usher in The New Order. The White House put out a press release to describe the press center. It said the decor was based on "English and early American public houses and inns."[6] It was the only pressroom ever to have its own press release. An historic first.

There were only a few discreet reminders that this was a place where news was made and reported. And at first the Nixon administration concealed even these.

It was very genteel. At one end of the room was a heavy curtain. When Ziegler was ready to hold a briefing, the curtain was drawn aside. A podium was revealed, recessed in the wall like an old-fashioned Murphy bed. Sex reared its ugly head, they used to say, and the world turned into a Murphy bed. They did not, of course, say this about the Nixon administration. The podium was lowered, a lectern was placed on it, the press secretary mounted the podium and stood behind the lectern, and the briefing began. If the president was coming to the briefing room to announce something, a functionary hurried in ahead of him and affixed the presidential seal to the lectern—just like the Hotel Splendide-Plastique.

At the other end of the room was another curtain. This one concealed a row of cameras on a slightly higher platform. The television networks keep these cameras in the briefing room at all times, and film footage from a White House briefing is used occasionally on the evening news shows. On rare occasions the news is so important that live coverage of a briefing is allowed, breaking into the daytime soaps to the dismay and outrage of housepersons throughout the land.

It was too genteel to last. It was too much trouble to keep lowering and raising the podium. After a while, both curtains were just left open. The podium was left down, the lectern remained permanently in place and the cameras were permanently exposed.

With these developments, a general deterioration of standards began.

On opening day, the reporters had found little signs warning that "drinks and food are not permitted in the briefing lounge." The signs were ignored. A television set soon appeared in the briefing room, and reporters and photographers sprawled around in untidy attitudes, watching the soaps. The ashtrays quickly overflowed. Newspapers, notebooks, coffee cups and softdrink cans littered the dainty coffee tables. There was a chronic shortage of seats, so a miscellany of folding chairs, captain's chairs and other oddments materialized. The briefing room was acquiring that lived-in look. Nixon had hoped that decorum and order could be introduced. He probably entertained the further hope that tidiness would discourage journalistic irreverence and nasty questions. Milhous, oh Milhous, it did not work.

Ten years later, the government made another effort to impose order on chaos. Early in 1981, under the Reagan administration, the briefing room was again remodeled. Rows of permanent seats were installed, transforming it into a small auditorium. The metamorphosis was striking. The new decor was Investment Seminar Modern. The briefing area now resembled one of those motel conference rooms in which the sleek instruct the suckers in the enhancement of greed.

The briefing room is twenty feet wide and fifty feet long. However, the podium at the front is five feet deep, and the camera platform at the rear cuts off another ten feet. This leaves a twenty-by-thirty-five-foot room. Into this space, the Reagan renovation installed eight rows of auditorium seats, with six seats in each row. There was not much room left for anything else, so the Nixon furnishings had to go. The sofas and armchairs disappeared. The television set was removed. No more coffee tables. Hard times.

Forty-eight news organizations and individuals that were regularly covering the White House in 1982 had assigned seats, designated with brass nameplates. The seating order was determined by the Reagan staff. The official explanation was that it was based on the frequency with which organizations attended the daily White House briefings, but never mind the official explanation. The *New York Times* covers the press secretary's briefings as regularly as CBS. That is, every day. So the real question was: Of the regulars, who would get the front seats?

In Washington, a question often can be answered only with another question. This illuminates the realities. Since the wire services obviously would get three front-row seats, the illuminating questions were: Would the remaining three go to the *New York Times*, the *Washington Post* and another print organization? Or would they go to the TV networks?

They went to the networks. Reality. No newspaper or magazine got a front-row seat. Of course, the wire services furnish news to the print media. However, they also serve the networks, and to a greater extent than many people realize. In any event, the first-row seats went to the AP, UPI, Reuters, CBS, NBC and ABC.

Sixteen of the remaining seats were assigned to newspapers that cover the White House regularly: the *New York Times*, the *Wall Street Journal*, the *New York Daily News*, *Newsday* of Long Island, the *Washington Post*, the new *Washington Times*, the *Boston Globe*, the *Christian Science Monitor*, the *Baltimore Sun*, the *Chicago Tribune*, the *Chicago Sun-Times*, the *Detroit News*, the *St. Louis Post-Dispatch*, the *Dallas Morning News*, the *Dallas Times Herald* and the *Los Angeles Times*. The *Washington Post* was in the second row. The *New York Times* was in the third row.

Six seats went to newspaper chains: the Gannett, Knight-Ridder, Newhouse, Cox, Scripps-Howard and Hearst newspapers. Three were assigned to newsmagazines: *Time*, *Newsweek* and *U.S. News and World Report*. Other seats went to Agence France-Presse, the French wire service; the Bureau of National Affairs, a private firm that publishes materials dealing with national issues; the U.S. Information Agency; reporter Sarah McClendon, a Washington institution; and Trans Features, a news service operated by Trudi Feldman.

There are about 1,750 daily newspapers in the United States. But as of 1982, only 16 independent (nonchain) dailies were covering the White House regularly enough to rate an assigned seat in the briefing room. However, the 6 newspaper chains furnished news to an additional 199 newspapers. At the end of 1981, Gannett owned 85 dailies; Knight-Ridder, 35; Newhouse, 28; Cox, 19; Scripps-Howard, 17; and Hearst, 15. Together with the independents, this meant that 215 of the nation's daily newspapers were represented at the White House, either directly or through chains. That was about 12 percent.

The sixteen independent newspapers were located in nine metropolitan areas—four in the New York area; two each in Boston, Washington, Chicago and Dallas; and one each in Baltimore, Detroit, St. Louis and Los Angeles. The Sun Belt was not very interested. Three of the sixteen circulated throughout the nation, especially in large cities, and could be considered national newspapers or close to it: the *New York Times*, *Wall Street Journal* and *Christian Science Monitor*. Some others, notably the *Los Angeles Times*, *Chicago Tribune* and *Boston Globe*, had large regional circulations.

Even so, it was a poor showing. At the end of 1982, there were 305 metropolitan areas in the United States. A metropolitan area has many shopping malls. But only nine areas had newspapers that were sufficiently interested in national and international news to assign their own reporters to cover the presidency on a regular basis. The rest of the nation's newspapers (many of them very profitable) either were represented by chains or relied completely on the wire services.

There are more than 1,000 television stations in the United States, and more than 9,000 radio stations. As of September 30, 1982, according to the Federal Communications Commission, the nation had 802 commercial TV stations and 277 educational stations, for a total of 1,079. There were 4,668 commercial AM radio stations, 3,380 commercial FM stations and 1,112 educational FM stations, for a total of 9,160. [7] More than 600 of the commercial TV stations were affiliated with a network. At the end of 1981, NBC had 215 affiliates and CBS and ABC about 200 each.

In addition to CBS, NBC and ABC, five other television organizations were allocated seats in the White House briefing room. They were Westinghouse Broadcasting and RKO General (which own both TV and radio stations) and three newcomers—the Cable News Network, Independent Network News and the Independent Television News Association. Ted Turner's CNN hired some of Washington's ablest journalists, including Stuart Loory and Daniel Schorr, and then fought and won a battle for equal status with the older networks at the White House. Eight TV organizations, not three, were covering the White House as technology surged along. On Capitol Hill, it was not uncommon for the electronic media to request space for fifteen or twenty cameras at a newsworthy event. The congestion was the finest in the Free World.

Rounding out the picture, seven seats in the briefing room went to radio organizations: Mutual Broadcasting, AP Radio, UPI Audio, RKO Radio, Sheridan Broadcasting (a black radio network), National Public Radio and the Voice of America.

The newspaper reporters had watched electronics overtake print with the customary mixed emotions. The process had begun with a single desk, manned by Ray Scherer of NBC, in that long-ago pressroom off the West Lobby. It ended with three first-row seats for television in the new briefing room and the *New York Times* in the third row. The *third* row! Scherer was a tall man with an easygoing manner. The print reporters liked him, and as a matter of principle they believed the more coverage, the better. Who could gainsay the power of television to convey news widely and quickly? Who could complain? News, disseminated widely and quickly, is the journalist's justification. But the reporters sensed what was coming. Those who worked for afternoon newspapers in large, old cities, and then some who worked for morning papers, came to think of themselves as dinosaurs on the way to the tar pits. Journalists are for the most part professionally aggressive and privately inoffensive. But the newspapermen often raged in their hearts against this *thing*, this enormous, overwhelming *thing*. They coveted its influence and deplored its effects. They envied, except when they were feeling noble, its salaries. They entertained Luddite fantasies. They would smash the cameras that jostled them. They would shatter the lights that blinded them. They would demolish all the rest of the equipment that crowded them and made it difficult for them to do their work. However, none of this was permitted.

Nixon had spent $574,000 to build a new pressroom. But he did not get any respect. Reagan spent an additional $166,000 to install auditorium seats and repair the roof of the West Terrace. Perhaps now there would be some respect. The rows of permanent seats made the briefing room much more formal. This punctilio might discourage the reporters from lolling around and indulging in irony and wit. They would have to sit in assigned seats, like ladies and gentlemen, while the president's spokesmen made announcements and dodged questions. The journalists could no longer array themselves casually on the couches and floor. From these informal positions, and with deceptive nonchalance, they had inquired whether the president had stopped beating his wife. At Reagan's formal press conferences in the East Room, a rule had been imposed that required the reporters to remain seated and raise their hands to be recognized. Now the same decorum was sought at the daily briefings by his spokesmen, Larry Speakes and David Gergen. The Reagan administration was proceeding against irreverence on all fronts.

Would it work? What did the future hold for disrespect? The likelihood was that a TV set and miscellaneous chairs, clutter and mess would creep back into the corners and crevices of the briefing room. The reporters would find places to sprawl and loll and discourse humorously. Journalism would contrive a way. And with all this would come, again and always, irreverence.

In March 1981, Reagan was wounded in a shooting outside a Washington hotel. Deputy press secretary Larry Speakes informed the press corps that the White House had received 7,500 telegrams and other communications in the first forty-eight hours after the shooting. A reporter inquired blandly: "Pro or con?"[8]

At the rear of the briefing room, next to the camera platform, there is a short corridor that leads to another room. On the wall of this narrow passageway is a bulletin board on which the press secretary's staff posts announcements, schedules and other information. Below the bulletin board are slotted compartments containing additional copies of this material. The reporters and the staff refer to these compartments as the bins. One of the first things a reporter does when he enters a pressroom—at the White House or anywhere else—is to check the bulletin board. If there is a press release that interests him, he takes a copy from the bins.

Just past the bulletin board is the pressroom itself. The nomenclature is confusing to the laity, but it has a logic. To the reporters and the White House staff, the room where the reporters have their work spaces, type-writers and telephones is known as the pressroom. The room where the briefings are held—the room with the rows of assigned seats—is called the briefing room. At the other end of the briefing room, in the opposite direction from the pressroom, is the beehive of offices for the president's press secretary and all those deputy press secretaries, assistant press secretaries and other publicity personnel. A map would help. These offices are known collectively as the White House Press Office, or simply, the press office. In other words, the press office does not house the press; it houses the flacks. The press is housed in the pressroom. But the whole setup—pressroom, briefing room and press office—is known colloquially as the White House pressroom or just the pressroom. Or, if you like, the West Terrace Press Center. But no one calls it that anymore.

The pressroom, like the briefing room, was formed from the long, narrow West Terrace. So it, too, is twenty feet wide and about fifty feet long. Into this space, Nixon's builders crammed working facilities for twenty-five news organizations. It is very compact.

At the front of the room are glassed-in booths for the Associated Press and United Press International. Each wire service regularly assigns three reporters to the White House. They work in a booth that is seven feet wide and nine feet deep. Much of this space, moreover, is occupied by a large video display terminal, desklike counters, shelves, telephones and newspapers. The wire service reporters try to arrange things so they will not all be in their booth at the same time. And yet, these days, the cubicles are unimaginably luxurious, having been enlarged in the Reagan renovation. Under Nixon, they were about half their present size. For many years, the chief White House reporter for the Associated Press was a man named Frank Cormier. He was six feet, four inches tall. Cormier did not exactly sit down in the AP booth. He folded himself into sections.

In the center part of the pressroom are individual work spaces for news-papers and other news organizations. Each cubicle is forty-one inches wide and twenty-three inches deep. There is enough space for a type-writer or a video display terminal, a telephone and not much else. This is known as pack journalism. As of 1982, these compartments were the White House "offices" of thirteen of the sixteen newspapers that assigned their own reporters to cover the presidency—the *New York Times*, the

Washington Post, the *Los Angeles Times* and the others. Reuters, Agence France-Presse, Hearst, Scripps-Howard and some others also have work spaces in this "upstairs" pressroom. There have been changes over the years, and presumably there will be more. The *Washington Star, Philadelphia Bulletin* and *Chicago Daily News* once had work spaces. They are gone now, but as they say in the business schools, it frees up the resources. More space is needed constantly for TV organizations.

On one wall of the pressroom is a long row of telephones. Some of these are extra phones for the wire services and networks. A few are used by reporters who cover the White House occasionally. Others are for newspaper chains and other news organizations that cover frequently but do not have a cubicle. Among these, in 1982, were the Gannett and Copley chains, the Jewish Telegraph Agency (whose reporter, Joseph Polakoff, asks some of the sharpest questions at White House briefings; no press secretary has ever matched Polakoff's knowledge of the Middle East), the British Broadcasting Corporation, the Canadian Broadcasting Corporation and several Japanese and West German news organizations. These are found everywhere. One of the wall telephones belongs to Tass, the Soviet news agency. Tass has had a phone in the White House pressroom for many years. It is sometimes pointed out to visitors as an example of democracy's greater tolerance. Would the Associated Press be permitted to have a telephone in the Kremlin pressroom? If the Kremlin had a pressroom?

At the rear of the pressroom are three more glassed-in booths, similar to the AP and UPI booths. These are the network booths. Each is six feet wide and twelve feet deep. And each is subdivided down to a truly Democritean smallness. There is a front compartment with a counter-type desk, typewriter and telephone. Back of that is an infinitesimal cubicle used for radio broadcasts. Like the wire services, each TV network regularly assigns three reporters to the White House. It is from these modest cells at the back of the pressroom that the TV reporters dominate the national psyche. Here the political agenda is determined. Here the elite conspiracy is carried insidiously forward. All in six by twelve feet. A miracle of miniaturization. Finally, squeezed into a corner across from the ABC booth, and hardest of all to find, is the Mutual Broadcasting booth.

Due to crowded conditions, it was necessary to construct another pressroom downstairs. This room is directly underneath the upstairs pressroom and is approximately the same size. It has booths for several more radio networks and the radio news services of the AP and UPI. There are also cubicles for some additional newspapers, including the *Christian Science Monitor* and the Dallas newspapers, the USIA and the redoubtable Sarah McClendon.

The main activity in the White House press center is the news process. The press secretary or some other official holds a briefing, the reporters ask questions and then write or broadcast their news stories. When they are not doing these things, they spend a good deal of time telephoning news sources or talking to their offices. They also do a lot of reading— newspapers and magazines mostly but books, too—and they watch TV. But even with all this, there is a certain amount of idle time. That is when the devil finds work for reporters. That is when they converse among themselves—irreverently.

Often the disrespect is directed at their own colleagues. Nothing, for instance, calls forth greater scorn than a "soft" question at a presidential press conference. Time is precious at a press conference; most reporters hate to see it wasted on questions that challenge the chief executive to speak of motherhood and apple pie. At a Reagan press conference in November 1982, a reporter asked: "Mr. President, in two weeks the United States will celebrate Thanksgiving. Given the passing of [Soviet leader Leonid] Brezhnev, inevitably there are comparisons between the [American and Soviet] systems. Could you take just a minute to tell Americans why at this time they especially should be thankful for their blessings and give a comparison of the two systems?" Why, of course he could. Happy to.

In their idle moments, the reporters play little games. One of them mocks colleagues who ask questions like that. Sarcastic competitions are held for the softest question that could be asked at a press conference. Lou Cannon of the *Washington Post* once triumphed with this suggestion: "Mr. President, how old were you when you discovered you were a genius?"

But the chief target, inevitably, is the president. Of Dwight Eisenhower, the reporters said that the motto of his administration should be: Don't just do something, stand there. Of Lyndon Johnson, that he had written the world's shortest book. Its title was *Humility*. Of Jimmy Carter, that he would never join the sculptures of other presidents on Mount Rushmore because there wasn't room for two more faces.

Journalism's irreverence focuses on the deceptions, artifices, stratagems, posturings, lies, evasions, self-aggrandizements, self-delusions, ambitions, runaway egos, crippled psyches and fallibilities of presidents, candidates, Cabinet members, White House advisers, senators, congressmen and other politicians of the moment.

Shortly after I came to Washington, I had my first encounter with the inner Richard Nixon. I was assigned to cover a speech by the then vice-president. Nixon spoke in Constitution Hall, which is owned by the Daughters of the American Revolution. (The DAR is a haven of the Red

Scare and the Blue Rinse. Franklin Roosevelt loved to tease these ladies; he once began a speech by addressing them as "my fellow revolutionaries.") On this day, however, Nixon was speaking to some other group. His subject was not controversial, and he delivered his speech seriously and straightforwardly. It was received with enthusiasm. Afterward, Nixon came backstage, where some reporters were waiting. He was glowing with pleasure. "Did you hear that applause?" he exclaimed. "Wasn't it great? And you know something? I didn't have to demagogue it at all." Oh my, I thought, what have we got here?

Against this background, a reporter for a radio news service observed Nixon in the presidency. In his private conversation, this reporter never referred to Nixon by any name except The Trick. He would say: "The Trick says . . ." or "The Trick is going to . . ." It was the reporter's summary. These days, there is a Washington journalist who never calls Ronald Reagan anything but The Actor.

Not all journalists are irreverent. Some are humorless. Some are accepting of establishments and traditions. Some make a lot of money. Some are stuffy even when they do not. Some have impulses toward respectability. Some have sensibilities that are affronted by irreverence. Judy Woodruff, when she became White House correspondent for NBC at the beginning of the Carter administration, was appalled by her colleagues' jaundiced view of the new president. [9] And she had a point. How could they arrive at such a despairing judgment so quickly, with so little evidence? How did Carter stand a chance against such skepticism? The unfairness of it, when his presidency was only a few months old, was striking.

Woodruff may have sensed, too, the fatal temptation to proceed from irreverence to cynicism. But the problem with cynicism, delightful companion though it is over drinks and dinner, is that it is paralytic. Nothing can be done, because nothing will work. But in the White House pressroom, a distinction is drawn between irreverence and cynicism. What Woodruff did not know was that most of the journalists *wanted Carter to succeed.* This did not affect their professional responsibility to report other views, to draw attention to mistakes and misdeeds and to criticize. But the reporters, while performing these irritating duties, nevertheless want *every* new president to succeed. They consider the alternative.

When they are irreverent, the reporters are simply arming themselves against what they fear may happen, what their experience tells them probably *will* happen. The record of the recent past being what it is, the problems being as intractable as they are, human limitations being eternal. Irreverence is the scar tissue that covers disappointment. But hope is there. Cynicism lays traps for irreverence, but there is no conflict between irreverence and hope. The journalists are part of the general human situation as defined by Samuel Johnson. They live from hope to hope. They are simply less respectful about it.

And there is another reason for irreverence. There can be no free press, no free inquiry of any sort, no freedom itself, without irreverence. The connection is simple: Irreverence is an assertion of independence. Without constant, hearty doses of disrespect, there is no freedom. Irreverence is sometimes juvenile. It is sometimes petulant. It is sometimes unjustified. It is sometimes lacking altogether, when the journalists let their guard down and become lax. But irreverence is absolutely vital, because all institutions seek to capture the individual and all presidents seek to capture the press. The reporters have only two defenses against this. One was discussed in a previous chapter. It is their professionalism—the pursuit of facts and explanations that challenge the official version. The other is their independence.

At the front of the White House briefing room, next to the podium, there is a door. It leads to the press office—that maze of rooms occupied by the press secretary and lesser functionaries. Nearby are a director of communications, an Office of Media Liaison or whatever the president chooses to call it, as well as resident political and public opinion specialists and dozens of other officials who deal with the news media. With this immense apparatus, the president endlessly attempts to control the media and the public. It is the Great White House Publicity Machine. It is a huge machine, and it is very powerful. The reporters know what would happen if they treated it *reverently*.

The Great White House Publicity Machine. It had modest beginnings, and then it grew. In Eisenhower's time, it consisted essentially of two persons. There was a press secretary, Hagerty, and there was an assistant press secretary. The original assistant, Murray Snyder, later moved over to the Pentagon as its press secretary. He was succeeded by Anne Wheaton, the woman who presided over the fall of the Bastille. The White House's chief of records, Wayne Hawks, occasionally functioned as an unofficial assistant press secretary when Hagerty needed more help. A few secretaries, stenographers and clerks completed the staff.

Hagerty held his briefings in his office; there was no separate briefing room, no podium, no camera platform. The procedure was simple. Someone from the press office, usually Betty Allen or the indomitably cheerful Helen Ganss, came into the West Lobby and called, "Press." The reporters filed into Hagerty's office and stood around his desk for the announcements and questions. There were two briefings a day. The first was at 11 A.M. and was primarily for the benefit of afternoon-paper reporters. The news it produced could make their late editions. Another briefing was held at 4 P.M. At this one, Hagerty tried to give the morning-paper reporters something fresh that had not been announced at the earlier session. He split the news between the morning and evening papers.

The twice-daily briefings continued in the Kennedy and Johnson administrations, but they were cut to one a day during the Nixon era. The press secretaries began complaining that they spent an unjustified amount of time getting ready for briefings; then, they said, the reporters did not ask many of the questions they were prepared to answer. Jimmy Carter's press secretary, Jody Powell, said his briefing preparation took "three or four hours out of the day and [was] not worth the time."[10] It was another conflict in perceptions between the government and the news media. The White House viewed the reporters as shallow types. They were preoccupied with sensation and controversy. They were easily bored by substantive matters such as presidential programs. The reporters, according to a succession of press secretaries, "did not do their homework." The press was superficial. Considering those 400-word wire-service stories and one-minute-fifteen-second TV standups, the government had a point. "I spent about five hours a day gathering information in anticipation of questions," said Jerry Ford's press secretary, Ron Nessen. "I . . . was usually better prepared at my briefings than the reporters. I almost always had more information than I was asked about."[11]

Marvelous. Better prepared, was he? That was supposed to be the idea. Since he had available the resources and information of the entire executive branch of government, it was assumed that the press secretary knew more than the reporters. Why not give this information to the American people? Not being mind readers, the reporters wondered why the press secretary did not simply announce the material he had not been asked about. They took to ending briefings by asking the man on the podium whether he had anything else he wanted to tell them. Were there any questions they should have asked but had not? This did not work. The White House's spokesmen were as demure as maidens used to be; they not only had to be asked, they had to be asked at the right time. They would have sung such wondrous songs but no one asked them to. I'd give the cars away but my wife won't let me.

Oh, no, the press secretaries replied, it wasn't like that at all. If we *had* volunteered the information, you wouldn't have used it. The *New York Times*, maybe. But the *San Jose Mercury*? The *Biloxi-Gulfport Daily Herald*? The networks, with their 100-word standups? Don't shit a shitter. The conflict in perceptions was not resolved. All that happened was that the briefings were put on a once-a-day basis. This arrangement has continued.

Pierre Salinger's staff also was small by today's standards. At first, Salinger had only one assistant, Andrew Hatcher, who had the title of associate press secretary. Later, an assistant press secretary was added—first Jay Gildner and then Malcolm Kilduff. Under Salinger, the entire White House press office occupied two rooms, and its budget was about $150,000 a year. At that time, the State Department's press budget was more than $1 million a year, and the Defense Department was spending about $30 million annually on press and publicity activities. 12 The bureaucracy was way ahead of the White House, which in financial matters is bureaucracy's little trick. Salinger, like Hagerty, held briefings at 11 A.M. and 4 P.M. The procedure was the same. One of the secretaries, usually Barbara Coleman or Barbara Gamarekian, called, "Press," and the reporters filed into Salinger's office. ("Barbara Gam" later became a mainstay of the *New York Times*'s Washington bureau.) Imperialism had hit the presidency but not the White House press office. Not yet.

Nor did it under Lyndon Johnson, not exactly. As Senate Democratic leader, Johnson had been notorious for seeming to operate with a small staff while secretly emplacing hordes of loyal henchmen in other offices or on other payrolls. In the White House, he was equally intent on a frugal image; he went around turning off the lights and made sure everybody knew about it.

On official rosters, available to the public, Johnson's White House staff always looked small. This official modesty applied to the press office as well as everyone else. No assistant press secretaries, for instance, were listed in the White House section of *The Congressional Directory*. But Joe Laitin, unmentioned in the directory, was an assistant press secretary and often more than that. Johnson's last press secretary, George Christian, had an assistant press secretary, Loyd Hackler, and a "press assistant," Tom Johnson, but neither was listed in the directory. Notwithstanding these taradiddles, however, the press office under Johnson never approached the imperial proportions of later administrations.

The explosion took place in the Nixon, Ford and Carter administrations. Under Nixon, the White House press operation grew to include a press secretary (Ron Ziegler), two deputy press secretaries (Gerald Warren and Neal Ball) and then three deputy press secretaries (Warren, Ken W. Clawson and Andrew Falkiewicz), a director of communications for the executive branch (Herbert Klein) and a deputy director of communications (first Jeb S. Magruder and then, Magruder having gone on to other things, Clawson).

Under Ford, the press office blossomed into full imperialistic flower. There was a press secretary (Jerry ter Horst, briefly, and then Ron Nessen), two deputy press secretaries (Gerald Warren and John Hushen), *seven* assistant press secretaries (Paul Miltich, John Carlson, Thomas DeCair, John Roberts, Edward Savage, Larry Speakes and Louis Johnson, Jr.), an assistant to the president for public liaison (William Baroody, Jr.) and a deputy director of public liaison (Donald Webster). Later there was still another assistant press secretary, Margareta White, but perhaps she replaced someone.

One of the assistant press secretaries, Ed Savage, was the spokesman for the National Security Council. Another, John Carlson, handled domestic affairs. In effect, the NSC and the Domestic Council now had their own press secretaries. The White House, which for a long time had been a government within a government, was now a government within a government within a government. The press office had grown so large that one assistant press secretary, Louis Johnson, devoted his full time to administration. When you have an assistant press secretary for administration, you are gaining on the bureaucracy.

Under Carter, another new wrinkle was added. There was, of course, a press secretary (Jody Powell), two deputy press secretaries (Rex Granum and Walter Wurfel), four associate press secretaries (Walter Duka, Patricia Bario, William Drummond and Jerrold Schecter, who was the NSC spokesman), a deputy assistant for public liaison (Robert Nastanovich) and an associate for public liaison (S. Stephen Selig III). At a later point, there were two other associate press secretaries (Claudia Townsend and Marc Henderson). And then—the new wrinkle—there was a special assistant to the president for media and public affairs (Barry Jagoda) and a deputy assistant for same (Richard Neustadt). Later there was an assistant to the president for communications (Gerald Rafshoon).

These lists do not include the large number of other White House activities and personnel that have come under the control of the press secretary or work closely with him. These include the president's speechwriters (sometimes called the editorial office); the staff that prepares a daily news summary for the president and his senior advisers; the president's photographers (now so numerous that they are known as the Photo Office); the advance men who arrange presidential trips; the media advance men (a specialty within a specialty) who arrange media coverage of presidential trips; the White House Transportation Office, which handles travel arrangements for the press; the First Lady's press secretary; and the vice-president's press staff.

Nor do the lists include the staff members who work in the Office of Media Liaison, the Office of Public Liaison, the office of the assistant to the president for communications or whatever each president chooses to call the publicity apparatus that he sets up in addition to the regular press office. And, naturally, the heads of all these offices have personal secretaries, receptionists and other clerical personnel.

These scores of persons labor anonymously, but Connie Gerrard must be mentioned, inasmuch as she has held the press office together through five administrations. For many years, I did not understand how the government worked. Finally I decided that the whole thing—presidents, Cabinet members, senior bureaucrats—rested on some obscure minor functionary who had a tiny office in a basement. This person, like Mycroft Holmes, knew everything and had every detail at his fingertips. At night, and in great stealth, the higher-ups came to him and he told them what to do. Someone had to. I decided it was Joe Laitin, but Laitin upset the theory by leaving the government after serving since Franklin Pierce. Now I suspect it is Connie Gerrard.

When Ron Nessen became White House press secretary in September 1974, he discovered that the press office staff numbered forty-five persons. That was approximately seven times larger than it had been in 1960, and most of this increase had taken place since 1969—that is, during the Nixon administration. The entire White House staff was about 500 persons, so the press office accounted for almost 10 percent of the total. It was, Nessen said, "one of the largest offices in the White House."[13] But that was just for openers.

Michael Grossman and Martha Kumar, the political scientists who studied the White House press operation in the mid-1970's (see Chapter Three), concluded that at least 30 percent of the president's professional staff was directly engaged in publicity work. The professional staff excludes stenographic, clerical and other service personnel. Grossman and Kumar scrutinized the work of the forty-nine presidential aides who were making forty thousand dollars or more at the beginning of the Carter administration. They found that fifteen of these persons—or slightly more than 30 percent—were "clearly involved [in] media relations and policy." Later, after some additional high-paid publicity jobs were created, Grossman and Kumar said "the estimate of 30 per cent . . . is probably a low figure."[14]

Yes, it probably is. The two political scientists also talked to a "high-ranking official in the Ford administration." (Even when speaking for posterity, many former officials insist on anonymity, having got into the habit.) This official estimated that more than 60 percent of Ford's professional staff had been engaged in "promoting and publicizing the president." It did not achieve the desired result. And then, for a broader view, Grossman and Kumar consulted a congressional authority who had studied every presidential staff since the end of World War II. He estimated that 85 percent of the modern White House staff, including the service people as well as the policymakers, is "involved directly in public relations activities."[15]

It is never easy to determine the actual size of the White House staff. The true number is almost always greater than the official total. Among other devices, many presidents borrow people from elsewhere in the government, and these persons are listed on the payrolls of their original agencies. Somewhat like the CIA. However, a conservative estimate is that the modern White House staff has at least 500 persons and probably 600 or more. If the number engaged in publicity work ranges from 30 to 85 percent, this means that a president has between 150 and 500 people who devote a substantial portion of their time to glorifying the chief executive and trumpeting his marvels. The Great White House Publicity Machine.

Several factors contributed to the growth of the White House's press and publicity apparatus:

1. The Washington press corps has proliferated like corporate tax exemptions. This means that the White House press office has more work to do. Pursuant to an iron rule of the presidency, the press office has grown faster than the press corps, but nevertheless there are a great many more journalists in Washington than there used to be. In 1937, there were 504 accredited journalists in the nation's capital.[16] In 1982, the number had grown to about 4,300.[17] This was an eightfold increase in forty-five years—compared with the press office's sevenfold increase in fourteen years.

Not all Washington reporters cover the White House; in fact, many seldom set foot in the place. But the growth of the press corps has meant that the White House press office has had to deal with more journalists every year. There are more questions, more telephone calls, more requests for appointments, more transcripts to be run off. The television age has imposed huge logistical and technical burdens on the press office. And TV has created a vastly larger audience for the president; it has been necessary to add experts to the staff to take advantage of this stupendous opportunity—and to try to avert its dangers.

2. Ideologies come and ideologies go, but the presidency grows regardless. Franklin Roosevelt had no National Security Council, no Domestic Council, no Council of Economic Advisers, no special trade representative. But Jimmy Carter did, and the NSC had a staff of 64 persons; the Domestic Council, 50; the CEA, 35; the special trade representative, 116. The Office of Management and Budget has become one of the most important arms of the presidency. Under Carter, it had a staff of 558. It was only to be expected that the White House Press Office would share in

this general prosperity. There are problems and crises at home and abroad. The imperial presidency responds to these, sometimes with actions, more often with rhetoric. Either way, it means that the press office issues more and more presidential announcements and statements, more and more reports, more and more press releases.

3. There was a big spurt in the size of the White House's publicity operation in the Nixon administration, and there was a direct, specific reason for it. Nixon had decided, long before he became president, that he had met the enemy and it was the Washington press corps. He could never, as he construed it, get fair or impartial treatment from the Washington regulars. They were stubborn in their refusal to forget his smear campaigns against Jerry Voorhis and Helen Gahagan Douglas, the McCarthy-Nixon witch-hunts (the reporters often pointed out that John F. Kennedy had been most reluctant to disavow McCarthy, but this cut no ice with Nixon), the phony political committees and the you-won't-have-Nixon-to-kick-around-anymore tantrum in the 1962 California governorship contest and all the other indications of the inner Nixon. How to handle these journalistic incorrigibles once he became president?

It was simple. They would have to be bypassed. Press secretary Ziegler would deal with the White House regulars; except for routine stuff, he would tell them as little as possible. Meanwhile, a separate, brand-new apparatus would be set up to carry Nixon's message to the rest of the country without subjecting it to the news media's "liberal" filter. Nixon would communicate directly with newspaper editors, news directors of television and radio stations (Nixon loved radio; you couldn't see him on radio), civic leaders and other opinion-makers around the nation. "This was, in effect, going over the heads of the [Washington] newsmen so that what was said would not be strained through their political bias," said Nixon aide James Keogh. [18] The word would be pure. It would be undefiled.

The new operation was put in the hands of a veteran newspaper editor named Herbert G. Klein, whose title was director of communications for the executive branch. Klein had been Nixon's press adviser at various times over the years, on leave from his newspaper, the *San Diego Union*. In two important respects, he was an ideal choice for the new job. He was well known and well liked in journalistic circles from coast to coast. And in the "good angel–bad angel" struggle that supposedly was waged for mastery of Nixon's soul, Klein was perceived as one of the seraphim. Unlike the Haldemans and Colsons, he was not identified with the dirty tricks department. If anyone could restrain Nixon's impulses, perhaps it would be mild-mannered, sleepy-eyed Herb Klein. Unfortunately, when Clark Kent's outer garments were ripped off, Clark Kent was revealed.

Klein's new Office of Communications sent out thousands of pages of material to news organizations, interest groups, civic associations and individuals throughout the country. There were texts of Nixon's speeches. There were reports, fact sheets and backgrounders on his domestic and foreign programs. There were progress reports on his accomplishments, compilations of favorable editorials, and laudatory comments by leaders of other nations. Leaders are very free with laudatory comments as long as things are going well. These mailings were accompanied by a letter from Klein, of the I-just-thought-you-might-be-interested sort.

Considering Nixon's feelings about the Washington press corps, it was inevitable that some such end-run operation would be set up in his administrations. What was significant was that his successors found it so useful that they retained it. Sometimes it was called the Office of Communications, sometimes the Office of Public Liaison, or the Office of Media and Public Affairs, or the Office of Media Liaison. It did not make any difference what it was called; it meant that Nixon, Ford, Carter and Reagan each conducted a massive publicity and propaganda operation from the White House. In a four-month period in 1978, Carter's Office of Media Liaison sent out an average of 35,551 items each month. There was a mailing list of 6,500 news organizations, ethnic groups and individuals. [19]

4. This interest in informing the nation is accompanied by an interest in manipulating the nation. The political techniques of an advanced civilization—the electronic media that reach every citizen; the public opinion surveys that measure the nation's whims and moods; the experiments in which citizens can render judgments on politicians and issues by pushing a button on the television set, like the *pollice verso* (thumbs down) in the Roman Colosseum; the network computers that project the winners faster than a speeding interest rate—all these new wonders require a new breed of soothsayers. Each age has its entrails. Each age has its entrail-readers. The "political consultants," "media specialists," polltakers, direct-mail experts, film-makers and other high priests of the new political technology have become indispensable to candidates for public office.

Blue smoke and mirrors. That was the description given to it by two savvy journalists, Jack W. Germond and Jules Witcover, in a book about the 1980 presidential campaign. [20] Germond and Witcover argued that issues and events—honest-to-God real things, not incantations and entrail-readings—determined the outcome of the contest between Jimmy Carter and Ronald Reagan. But that did not discourage the oracles. They are here to stay. It was only a matter of time before a president decided he must have his political priests constantly at his side, on the White House staff. To the marriage of true minds, let us not admit impediments. The

Great White House Publicity Machine has been wedded to the New Political Technology.

How does the White House define "news"? How does it decide what information will be announced? And when and how it will be announced? Not surprisingly, this is another area in which the government and the news media often see things quite differently. It is one of the most important of the many differences in perception, and it is suffused with acrimony. The White House and the rest of the government conceal or suppress much information that the news media consider legitimate news that should be disclosed. The press devotes considerable time and effort to ferreting out as much of this information as it can. But a large amount of news—a staggering amount—is disclosed voluntarily, without prodding, prompting or investigations. What does this "voluntary" news consist of?

At the White House, it falls into four categories. The definitions are informal and fuzzy and often overlap, but they are basically as follows: minor routine news, major routine news, "good" presidential news and "bad" presidential news.

Minor routine news consists of announcements and activities of an ordinary, uncontroversial, essentially neutral nature. Major routine news consists of important developments that are also relatively neutral; that is, they do not significantly affect the president. Good presidential news can be either minor or major, although if it is minor there is usually an effort to make it appear major. Its distinguishing feature is that it makes the president look good. Press secretaries live for it. Bad presidential news is almost always major. Therefore, a reverse rule applies; the effort is to make it appear minor or, if possible, to go away altogether. Its salient feature is that it makes the president look bad. Something must be done about this. Bad presidential news is an exception to the definition of voluntary news. It may be dug up by reporters or political opponents. Or it may be an unfortunate event that simply happens. The White House then is compelled to acknowledge a reality. It is all over town.

A large amount of routine news is announced by the White House press office almost every day. December 11, 1981, was a fairly typical day in the Reagan administration. The following announcements and items were posted on the bulletin board:

● "The President today announced his intention to nominate Anthony J. Calio to be Deputy Administrator of the National Oceanic and Atmospheric Administration. He would succeed James Patrick Walsh." This press release then gave four paragraphs of biographical information about Calio.

- A pool report on a meeting between Reagan and former President Ford: "They were sitting in wing chairs in front of a crackling fire, chatting quietly and laughing." The pool report was very brief. The pool reporters had been permitted in the president's office for only a few moments. They asked Reagan and Ford a few hurried questions about a situation involving Libya, which was the most urgent news story at that moment. The pool report gave a transcript of the questions and the answers by Reagan and Ford. The answers were bland and for the most part not newsworthy. However, Reagan did say that he wanted Americans in Libya "to leave as quickly as possible." Whether this was news would depend on whether it was new. The reporters would know. If it was new, there would be major stories that said: "President Reagan today urged Americans in Libya to leave that country as quickly as possible." If it had been said before, by Reagan or the State Department, there would be fewer stories. And although the wording would be almost the same, the tone would be a little less dramatic: "President Reagan again today urged Americans in Libya . . ." If the warning had been given several times previously, there might not be any stories at all. Or the renewed warning might be included in stories that led off with newer developments in the Libyan situation. Somewhere in these stories would be that useful journalistic word "meanwhile." The eighth or tenth paragraph would begin: "Meanwhile, President Reagan again urged . . ."

  After asking their few questions, the pool reporters were ushered out of the Oval Office. Reagan and Ford then talked about whatever they really wanted to talk about.
- A "Notice to the Press" giving "print pool" assignments for the following week. This showed that if there were any pools on December 14, the *Wall Street Journal* reporter would represent the newspaper and magazine reporters. On December 15, it would be the *Washington Post* reporter, on December 16, the *Baltimore Sun* reporter and so on.
- The president's schedule for December 11. At 9 A.M., he would meet with members of the White House staff; at 10:15 with a group of congressmen; at 10:30 with the architect of the Capitol, who was going to present him with a souvenir gavel; and at 10:45 with Ford. At 11:45, Reagan would take part in the presentation of an honorary Olympic gold medal, and at 1:45 P.M. he would meet with Ambassador Philip Habib, the Middle East troubleshooter. That was the last item on Reagan's official schedule. If he followed his customary routine, he would then return to his living quarters in the White House and take a long nap. The reporters would try to talk to Habib after his meeting with the

president; it looked like the best bet for a story. They might succeed, although in Habib's case probably not.

● A statement by Reagan praising a "continuing resolution" that had just been enacted by Congress. The resolution extended the authority for federal agencies to spend money at previously authorized levels while the president and Congress tried to resolve a dispute over new funding. The approval of the resolution gave Reagan another opportunity to assert that the federal budget must be brought under control. He availed himself of the opportunity. The budget did not heed him.

Most of these items had been posted on the bulletin board early in the day. The press secretary would draw attention to some of them at his briefing later, but the reporters already had seen them. How would they handle this routine news?

Two of the releases—the president's schedule and the pool assignments—were strictly informational "housekeeping" items. The pool report on the Reagan-Ford meeting would be evaluated for its newsworthiness, as previously described. The reporters would note the Reagan-Habib meeting as a possible story or at least an insert in the almost daily Middle East wrap-up stories. The other items on Reagan's schedule probably would be "photo opportunities." The AP and UPI would move photographs of Reagan holding the gavel and the gold medal. Whether newspapers used these photos would depend on their interest in the subjects. Or they might simply decide they needed a picture of the president in the paper that day. The same principle as royalty opening a flower show.

Reagan's statement on the continuing resolution would be handled either as a separate story or an insert in the budget dispute story. Either way, the statement probably would get only a few lines. The resolution had been passed, a presidential statement on it was obligatory and the spending controversy had been postponed so that everyone could get away for Christmas. We fight a while and we rest a while.

The nomination of Anthony Calio to be deputy head of the National Oceanic and Atmospheric Administration was a quintessential example of a routine story, except of course to Calio. It matters not how intense are the efforts to reduce the size of government; the White House issues hundreds of press releases every year announcing presidential nominations and appointments. The Calio nomination would rate short wire-service stories that would be carried by . . . whom? Perhaps the *New York Times*, the *Washington Post* and a few other major newspapers, because it was a reasonably important federal job. Perhaps the newspapers in Philadelphia, because that is where Calio was born. In Pittsburgh, where he had worked for Westinghouse as a nuclear physicist? In Houston, where he had worked at the Johnson Space Center? Reporters for the St. Louis newspapers, if alert, might notice that he had an honorary degree from Washington University in that city. Did you miss that one?

Major routine news is not easy to define. Sooner or later, much of the major news involving the White House either helps or hurts the president. It then becomes good or bad presidential news. But controversy varies in intensity. Otherwise everyone would be burned out before his time. A certain amount of important news that originates at the White House—perhaps a popular Cabinet appointment that will sail through Congress or a long-overdue reform that has wide support—is not especially controversial. At least, it is not as controversial as some other important news. This is major routine news.

The reporting of minor and major routine news is the purest example of the symbiotic relationship between the news media and the government. This cooperative relationship was described by Grossman and Kumar in their study of the White House press operation (see Chapter Three). They concluded that there was as much cooperation as conflict in this relationship, because each side has such great need of the other. [21] They were talking about ordinary news.

When the White House unveils a new presidential program, for example, the initial reaction of the reporters usually is not antagonistic. They ask questions about points that are not clear to them. They seek amplification. There may be some skeptical or probing inquiries, especially if the issue already is controversial or has tendencies in that direction. But for the most part, the first announcement is a neutral, professional exercise. At this point, the new program is essentially major routine news. The procedure, therefore, is symbiotic. The reporters are seeking information and explanation, and the White House is responding. Later on, things may change. The program may falter. It may not fulfill its high expectations. It comes under attack in Congress and on the editorial pages and among the citizenry. Then the symbiotic relationship fades, frail jonquil of spring that it is. The program becomes bad presidential news. It is the time of *Sturm und Drang*. It is the testing of the president.

The president, the president, the president. He makes the news—good, bad and ordinary. He bestrides the news like a colossus. It has become fashionable to say that the news media, especially television, determine the nation's political and social agendas. The media, it is said, decide which issues will preoccupy the American people and excite their emotions, and which will be neglected or ignored. There is a measure of truth in this, but how much? Have we arrived at government by the media? Another factor intrudes insistently, as it did in St. Louis in the last century. A group of citizens approached the mayor with a progressive suggestion. Why not install gas lights on the streets of the city? The mayor was of German extraction. His English was shaky, but his character was firm. He replied: "We got a moon yet, ain't it?" When it comes to the power of the news media, we got a president yet, ain't it?

Bill Moyers, who has had careers in both the media and government, was quoted in Chapter Three. "Most of the news on television is, unfortunately, whatever the government says is news," Moyers said. [22] Many political scientists agree that the president and the rest of the government at least try to keep up with media in making the news. "The desire of presidents to dominate the news," write Grossman and Kumar, "has been so universal during recent decades that it has become an attribute of the job. . . ."[23] Even those academics who argue that the media make the news and thereby set the national agenda have a little problem with that other newsmaker and agenda-setter, the president. "Because the president is so newsworthy," write Professors David Paletz and Robert Entman of Duke University, "he can produce news of his own devising, knowing the media will cover . . . it. Especially in foreign affairs, his agenda items become the media's priorities. . . ."[24] I will tell you whether the tail is wagging the dog if you will tell me which is the tail and which is the dog.

News of his own devising. If the president of the United States decides to devise some news, boy can he devise it. The preceding chapter described the tidal wave of manufactured news with which Lyndon Johnson submerged Bobby Kennedy's anti-Vietnam speech in 1967. And in the news-devising category, little can equal and nothing can excel the events of Saturday, March 12, 1966:

On that day, a group of state governors came to the White House. They were scheduled to have a routine discussion of federal-state relations. Johnson, however, turned it into a full-scale, action-packed, razzle-dazzle. In the lead role, of course, was the president himself. As supporting players, he called in Vice-President Hubert Humphrey; Secretary of State Dean Rusk; Secretary of Defense Robert S. McNamara; General Earle G. Wheeler, the Chairman of the Joint Chiefs of Staff; General Maxwell D. Taylor, special presidential adviser on Vietnam; General Ellis Williamson, who had just returned from the war zone; Jack Valenti's curly-headed daughter, Courtenay; and four dogs.

First Johnson met with the executive committee of the National Governors' Conference. Then he held a press conference to tell about the meeting. Then he met with the governors of the Appalachian states and held another press conference to talk about *that* meeting. Then he presided at a three-hour session at which Rusk, McNamara and the generals reported to all the governors on the Vietnam situation. Then Johnson held a *third* press conference to describe *that* meeting. After that, he announced the appointment of former Governor Farris Bryant of Florida as director of the Office of Emergency Planning. Then he played for a half hour with Courtenay Valenti and his four dogs, while photographers took pictures. Three meetings, three press conferences, a major appointment and a romp. And all in time for the Sunday editions. It was a good news day for Lyndon Johnson. [25]

Not all press secretaries have the advantage of working for a president with such an acute sense of public relations. In Johnson's case, six men eagerly sought the privilege. This interpretation may not be exactly correct.

The president dominates the news in another way. At the beginning of each year, he sends a message to Congress on the state of the Union. This is followed by the federal budget and the Economic Report. These three great state papers may or may not dictate the national agenda, but they sure as hell dictate the reporters' agenda. Much of the working time of White House reporters is devoted to covering the big three and the subsequent messages that spell out the president's programs more specifically. The TV networks trot out charts and graphs for lengthy explanations of the federal budget. Their agenda-setting impulses apparently are unable to withstand the agenda-setting impulses of the president. After that, the scene shifts to Capitol Hill, where congressional reporters chronicle the ups and downs of the president's programs in committees and on the floor. Other reporters describe the impact of the programs on consumers, wage-earners, taxpayers, farmers, educators, scientists, artists, special interests, the poor, the rich, the young, the old, the lame, halt and blind. Newspaper columnists and television commentators endlessly discuss the president's policies and programs.

Unless it is overshadowed by extraordinary events, the *president's* agenda dominates the news from Washington all year round. Lyndon Johnson placed Vietnam on the national agenda, where it produced discussion and controversy. Ronald Reagan placed the repeal of the New Deal on the national agenda, where it produced discussion and controversy. What has CBS done for us lately?

In the case of good presidential news, a simple practice operates. The White House merely tries, on all possible occasions, to present the news in such a way that it will reflect favorably upon the president. "I was responsible only for presenting [a presidential decision or action] to the public in a way and at a time that would generate the best possible reception," Pierre Salinger wrote. [26]

This raises a question. Does the White House have only one definition of news? Is all news evaluated solely in terms of whether it will help or hurt the president? Or does the White House acknowledge an obligation to inform the public of its actions simply as things the public has a right to know, regardless of their effect on the chief executive? The answer is that both definitions come into play but usually at different times. Some members of a president's staff feel a responsibility to inform the public. However, the intensity of the feeling varies from individual to individual and from administration to administration. It is not usually overwhelming. And it is in a ceaseless grapple with loyalty to the president. He *must* be made to look good. The public service definition of news, therefore, is applied most regularly and comfortably to routine, uncontroversial, "neutral" news.

There are three types of good presidential news. The first consists of any event or development that benefits the president. It may be the occasional success of a presidential program, a rare improvement in the economic situation, a triumphant space venture, an international agreement or, in general, anything that makes the nation feel momentarily happy. Presidents associate themselves with these joyful interludes. Whether they had anything to do with it or not, they accentuate the occasion. No matter how vast or remote the ocean in which the early American astronauts splashed down, the president was usually there.

The second type of good news consists of news that is manipulated, managed or manufactured to publicize the president favorably. It is news that makes it appear that he is performing effectively in his job. The Great White House Publicity Machine operates untiringly to transform sows' ears into silk purses. As often as possible, routine news is metamorphosed into good news. At the most routine level is the photo opportunity. This is a stupendously ordinary or even non-news event that is raised several notches by the president's presence. At its most blatant level, it was Jimmy Carter's announcement of a potentially encouraging development in the Iranian hostage crisis on the morning of the Wisconsin primary. Or Henry Kissinger's "peace is at hand" statement on the eve of the 1972 presidential election. Or Ron Nessen's braggadocio about the Ford-Brezhnev nuclear agreement at Vladivostok. And there are many levels of exaggeration and manipulation in between.

The third type of good news consists of good news that is devised to offset or overshadow bad news. Now, at last, we are at the crunch. The White House's publicity apparatus undergoes its severest test when good news must be found and timed to distract attention from bad news. A favorite good-news technique of both Lyndon Johnson and Richard Nixon, when things turned sour, was a trip in the opposite direction. They took a journey to some place distant from the scene of their troubles. Johnson did this so often that the reporters called it the LBJ shuffle. At the height of the Watergate crisis, Nixon fled to the Middle East. Things could not be any worse there.

A great many journalistic clichés have come into use to describe the rather frequent, rather awful occasions when bad news overtakes a president. The White House is "drawing its wagons into a circle." A "siege mentality" has developed. The press secretary is "stonewalling." He is "ducking and weaving" to evade embarrassing questions from the reporters.

Bad news is a time of meetings. The White House is holding crisis conferences. The press secretary's daily briefings are delayed and the reporters fume impatiently, while behind closed doors the president and his advisers try to come up with something. They talk of "press strategies" or "damage control tactics" or "containment plans" or "limited hangout routes." The Watergate transcripts—the inner record of one of the worst disasters that ever befell a president—are full of urgent "press strategy" meetings:

Nixon: ". . . Let's go back now to the decision. First, should we make a statement today?"

Haldeman: "I would say yes."

Nixon: "I think so."

Haldeman: "Ziegler should make it."

Ehrlichman: "Well, if it is a carefully-limited statement."

Nixon: "No questions [from the reporters]."

Ehrlichman: "I think—no. I think it should be a very tight statement—very conservative—well at least you should think it through *so that you can stay away from the soft places.* [emphasis added]. But I think broadly—across the country—people are waiting to see your face on the evening news talking about the Watergate case. And making more assurances. . . ."

Nixon: "Fine. All right. I think I got the message. If you will write up a brief, brief, brief statement. You know—I can use—or do you have one you can get back to me? I have to do it at 3. How much time do I have?"

Ehrlichman: "You've got about 45 minutes."

Nixon: "I've got plenty of time."

Haldeman: "Ziegler should delay the 3 [P.M. briefing]. They've only scheduled a posting. He can make it 4. Briefing at 4."

Nixon: "Yeah, that's right."

Haldeman: "You ought to tell him now, though, that you're going to do it. . . ."

Haldeman: "Better get Ron in quickly and review this. Just tell them to send Ron in. . . ."

Nixon (to Ziegler): "I think what we do, I think I will make a brief statement today, and I was wondering how late I can make it. Don't believe I can make it at 3. What do you think?"

Ziegler: "You got to make it at 4 or 4:15 [in order to make the evening TV news programs]."

Nixon: "Fine, but I'll have to go to work on it."

Ziegler: "We'll have to call them [the reporters] in."

Nixon: "Let me ask you this, fellas, you want me on the television [rather than having Ziegler make the statement]?"

Ehrlichman: "Yes sir, that would be my preference."

Nixon: "I'll just walk out [in front of the cameras in the pressroom]."

Ziegler: "I think depending on the statement, they'll get it to the lab [in time for the film to be processed]. Don't worry, they'll get it out. . . ."

Ehrlichman: "Yes. Where's page one?" (They begin going over the statement.)[27]

It did not work. All the twistings and turnings and obstructions of justice and misprisions of felony did not work. However, hope sprang eternal. At one point in the transcripts, Nixon and Haldeman discuss the outcome if their press strategy succeeds. A prediction is made:

Haldeman: "You know where the Watergate story is in the *Washington Post* today? Page 19 . . ."

Nixon: "I know, I know. And it'll be Page 19 five months from now if we handle it right."[28]

VIII

LYNDON AND
PIERRE, GEORGE, BILL,
BOB, JOE AND GEORGE

The president thought it was a terrific idea. A question had been planted at his last press conference. The result was gratifying. He was able to say something he wanted to say, without volunteering it. To most of the reporters, and to all of the public, it seemed that the information had been elicited by the question. It did not appear that the president was trying to sell anything. He had not initiated the matter. He was merely responding to an inquiry from the news media. Democracy in action. But to the president, it was a revelation. Prearranged questions that did not appear prearranged! Self-serving answers that did not appear self-serving! How long had this been going on? Then the idea burst upon him. He directed a guileful look at his press staff. I'll tell you what we'll do, said Lyndon Johnson. Next time, we'll plant *all* the questions. [1]

The whole thing was Joe Laitin's doing, and he rued the day. Laitin was an assistant press secretary at the White House, having moved over from the Budget Bureau. He was a small, wispy man; he looked like the third gnome from the left. And he had quickness of mind, as befitted someone born in the shadow of the Brooklyn Bridge. Laitin had begun his journalistic career as a high school editor and a stringer for the *Brooklyn Eagle*; in those days, Flatbush had its own newspaper. For the *Eagle*, the teenage aspirant wrote a story about his school's football team. The story said no games were being won on Saturday afternoons because the team was holding advance celebrations on Friday nights. That was the end of Laitin's formal education; he was ready for big-time journalism. He became a reporter for the *Eagle* and later worked for United Press in Washington and for Reuters in the Pacific during World War II. Then he gravitated to Los Angeles, where he was a successful free-lance writer and broadcaster until a chance encounter led to a job as the Budget Bureau's press spokesman.

So Laitin knew a lot about journalism. Whereas Johnson's new, young press secretary, Bill Moyers, did not. Look, Laitin told Moyers, once in a while you can plant a question at a presidential news conference. "It has more credibility," Laitin said, "because you're [being] responsive rather than volunteering. When [the president] volunteers something, everybody immediately is on guard: What's he trying to sell?" Moyers took the suggestion to Johnson who liked it just fine. The president gave Moyers a question to be planted. Laitin did the planting. "I had a couple of days," he recalled later. "I got hold of a couple of guys [reporters] and said, 'You know, if somebody would only ask the president this, you would get a very interesting answer.'" [2]

What Laitin did not know a lot about was Lyndon Johnson. He was dumbfounded when Johnson suggested planting *all* the questions at the next press conference. "I thought he was kidding," Laitin said. "But came the next press conference, and about 15 minutes before . . . Moyers comes out to me with something like 10 questions. He said, 'Here, the president wants you to plant these questions.' Well, to do it in 15 [minutes]—they [the reporters] were gathering in the lobby already! In a panic, I said, 'Bill, this isn't the way it's done.' He said, 'Do it!'

"So in desperation, I went out to look for a friendly face. . . . There was a man there, John Pomfret of the *New York Times* [Pomfret later became executive vice president of the *Times*], and I had developed a very warm relationship with him . . . down in Texas he . . . and I played chess. We spent a lot of time down there after [Johnson's] gall bladder operation, and I had an arrangement with him where he could come up to the press secretary's suite. We would play chess, and if the president called me, he [Pomfret] had cotton in his ears—he did not hear anything; and if there was any story involved . . . he would wait until I could call [the other reporters] so there would be no disadvantage. He [Pomfret] always abided by that. We developed a nice, warm relationship; it was pleasant. . . .

"So I saw John Pomfret. In my desperation . . . I said, 'John, would you mind asking the president this question?' There was no time for amenities; I had to be blunt because they were waiting and it was now eight minutes away from call time. He looked at me and said, 'How dare you try to plant a question on the *New York Times*? I'm offended by this, and it's highly unethical.' And in fury—of course, my fury was not really against him, it was against LBJ but I couldn't very well vent it against LBJ—I snarled at him, 'Look, if you don't want to ask the question, don't ask it, but don't give me a lecture on ethics!'" [3]

Things pile up. It now became necessary for Laitin to tell Moyers what had happened. He said he had succeeded in planting one or two questions, but he had to confess that, on the whole, the Grand Plan had failed. To illustrate the difficulties he had encountered, he told Moyers about Pomfret's recalcitrance. These heartrending scenes take place frequently at the White House, as bad news is passed up the line. Moyers in turn relayed the sad story to Johnson. And then something interesting occurred:

Johnson "began calling Pomfret into [his office] and giving him exclusive stories," Laitin recalled. The president had decided that Pomfret's show of independence required executive attention. He responded with "the Johnson treatment"—a brief but intensive display of generosity, flattery, cajolery, inducement and whatever else he could think of. "When somebody's nipping at your ass," he told Laitin, "you throw him a piece of raw meat."[4]

Several reporters who covered the White House during the Johnson years have commented that Johnson was a good deal nicer to his critics than to his friends. This kept him busy. My own experience was similar to Pomfret's except that it did not involve any exclusive stories. The *St. Louis Post-Dispatch* did not rank as high in Johnson's order of priorities as the *New York Times*. Otherwise, it went like this:

Reporter: "Mr. President, in connection with the appointment to the Housing and Urban Affairs Department, there have been reports of a task force headed by Dr. Wood, which recommended—."

Johnson: "What reports? I want to know who reports what."

Reporter: "There have been published reports in the newspapers—."

Johnson: "Whose?"

Reporter: "There have been published reports in newspapers—."

Johnson: "Well, who published it? That's what I want to know."

Reporter: "I saw something in the *Washington Post*, for one."

Johnson: "Go ahead. The *Washington Post*. What did the *Washington Post* say?"

Reporter: "That a task force headed by Prof. Wood had recommended the transfer of the community action program and the Office of Economic Opportunity to the new [Urban Affairs] Department, and there have been subsequent reports that you have decided against this. Can you make any comments on that?"

Johnson: "I would say that, insofar as a report that I have made a decision on the matter, it is more propaganda than accurate. I have made no decision. We will, in the days ahead, consider a good many reorganization proposals, but the best authority for a presidential decision is the president or the press secretary, and you can always get guidance on that if you have the time or the disposition to obtain it."[5]

So far, so good. It was a routine intimidation. Johnson had interrupted me three times before I could ask my question. He wanted to know the source of my information before I could tell him what the information *was*. A light working-over with a baseball bat. Then he launched into a song and dance that by now was familiar to every White House reporter: If you wanted to know something, why didn't you call *me*? Why don't you go directly to the source? The horse's mouth, as they say. You just pick up that telephone and call the White House. Ask for the president, and Juanita Roberts (Johnson's secretary) will put you right through. I may be busy with Vietnam or something, but I'll drop everything and tell you all about a task force report on the Urban Affairs Department. Nothing to it. Once, at Andrews Air Force Base, Johnson noticed some reporters chatting with Jack Valenti of the White House staff. The president stormed over to the group. "Why are you talking to *him*?" Johnson asked contemptuously. "*He* doesn't know anything!" More morale-building.[6]

The reporters had encountered this kind of thing again and again. The bullying, the scorn and sarcasm, the insistence that only one person knew Lyndon Johnson's intentions (which was true enough, unless there is a God) and the profound insecurity that had to insist that no one else knew *anything*. The journalists understood that Johnson was not really serious when he said they should call him on the telephone to check things—and yet, he *was* serious, too. He didn't mean anything he said—and yet, he *did* mean it, too. The president's staff and the White House reporters and ultimately the American people would just have to figure the whole thing out for themselves, while Lyndon went his way. The public, however, does not appreciate too much confusion and too many contradictions in a president. It will tolerate some, but too many are wearying.

This was the time I got tired. Johnson finished his non-answer to my question and turned to recognize another reporter for the next one. Before he could do so, I said something. I said it harshly. I put into it all the disgust I felt, which was a lot. Johnson's last words had been: "The best authority for a presidential decision is the president or the press secretary, and you can always get guidance on that if you have the time or disposition to obtain it." So:

Reporter (with bitterness): "That's why I asked you."

Johnson (with surprise and anger): "You got it. That's why I told you."[7]

Then as it had with Pomfret, something interesting happened. For several weeks afterward, presidential solicitude was lavished upon me. When I asked questions at subsequent press conferences, Johnson addressed me courteously as Mr. Deakin and then gave a polite answer. A couple of times, he made other reporters wait: "I think Mr. Deakin has a question over there." It was Mr. Deakin this and Mr. Deakin that. He interrupted his answers to other questions to go back and amplify his answers to my questions. He told his staff to track down additional information for me. It was nice while it lasted.

He looked like a tragedy. Or at least a big sadness. His face was pendulous; it seemed to hang down mournfully, so that he resembled a costive bloodhound. His features were large and heavy. He had warts or wartlike growths on his hands; occasionally he would have these growths removed. He would hold out his hands to the reporters and urge them to touch the warts or scars. It was easier to sell shoes.

The fate of this physically unappealing man was to follow one of the most handsome presidents in history. Kennedy was lean, clean-cut and sexually magnetic. Johnson, on the other hand, had taken the world as Anthony Trollope defined it—a place of hard words and harsh judgments—and had battled his way to prominence and prosperity. His face looked like the battlefield.

Kennedy, moreover, was well educated and well read; he was unquestionably the only American president ever to quote Mme. de Staël on national television.[8] Equally unquestionably, Lyndon Johnson had never heard of Mme. de Staël, the celebrated literary salonist. One of his biographers said Johnson could not remember having read as many as six books since graduating from Southwest Texas State Teachers College in 1930.[9] Johnson became president in 1963, so it averaged out at one book every five or six years. At a briefing one day, the question of Johnson's background in foreign affairs came up. A reporter asked press secretary George Reedy for the names of some books on foreign policy that the president had read. Reedy managed to produce one: Barbara Ward's *The Rich Nations and the Poor Nations*. Other reporters took to calling Reedy and asking the same question. They asked it in the most innocent manner, as if the idea had just occurred to them. Reedy gave each caller the same short list: the Barbara Ward book. The reporters then wrote stories about this intellectual richness.

Johnson resented the affinity between Kennedy and the Washington press corps. He envied Kennedy's skill in dealing with reporters. It apparently never occurred to him that Kennedy's adroitness in handling individual journalists had not insulated him from sharp and sustained criticism by the news media. For Johnson, the grass was perpetually greener in Kennedy's yard. He had it all. He not only had been in the candy store, he had been *born* in it. The East Coast–Ivy League–inherited-wealth–old-boy-network candy store. Johnson seemingly could not accept that the profound differences between him and his predecessor made it impossible for him to have a Kennedy-type relationship with the reporters—or for that matter, with the American people. He would have to devise a different relationship, based on *his* strengths, not Kennedy's. He tried to do this; he told people repeatedly that "they say John Kennedy had style, but I'm the one that got the bills passed." But style nagged at him. And one day in April 1966, all the pent-up bitterness and frustration erupted. And this time, it really *was* the news media's fault.

Johnson attended the dedication of a housing project in San Antonio, Texas. He was introduced by San Antonio's congressman, Henry B. Gonzalez, who made the most of the opportunity. Gonzalez spoke at great length. He not only introduced the president, he introduced some thirty persons in the audience. The White House reporters covering the ceremony began to smile. Gonzalez introduced several of his relatives. The press began to chuckle. Gonzalez introduced members of the San Antonio fire department. The press began to laugh. Then Gonzalez moved on to other things. Gonzalez spoke grandiloquently. Gonzalez invoked the name of "that great Greek statesman, Pericles." But Gonzalez was not altogether familiar with Pericles. He pronounced it Paraculls. The press was rolling in the aisles. The press was whooping and hollering.

When Johnson rose to speak, he was in a fury. "First, I want to explain that the reason Henry [Gonzalez] took so much time was because I asked him to," the president said. Then he referred to his father, Sam Ealy Johnson, who had served in the Texas legislature:

"I remember what my father said to me about public service when I was a little boy walking around following him barefooted, and standing there in the hot sand of Blanco county, and squeezing the dirt up between my toes. He used to say to me, 'Son, if you are to speak for people, you must know them, and if you are to represent them, you must love them.' "

The president was warming up. The line had been drawn. How many of those eastern-elite journalists had ever squeezed the hot sand of Blanco County between their toes? Then, the preliminaries having been disposed of, Johnson directly and wrathfully addressed the trestle tables where the reporters were sitting. He said:

"Sometimes among our more sophisticated, self-styled intellectuals—I say self-styled advisedly; the real intellectual I am not sure would ever feel this way—some of them are more concerned with appearance than they are with achievement. They are more concerned with style than they are with mortar, brick and concrete. They are more concerned with the trivia and the superficial than they are with the things that have really built America."[10]

No one ever said Lyndon Johnson was uncomplicated. In those few, furious words, he had accomplished several things. Some of them were obvious. Some were subtle. Some were revealing—more revealing than he intended. He was always doing that.

- Johnson had rebuked the reporters, myself included, for unbecoming behavior. If the press corps wanted to laugh at Congressman Gonzalez, it should have done so in private. That is what pool reports are for.
- Moreover, the president had excommunicated the reporters. He had cast them out of the intelligentsia. They were not real intellectuals. They were phony, smartass intellectuals. In this, Johnson probably was doing the news media a favor. If he could convince the American Pleistocene Movement that journalists were not intellectuals, it would save a lot of trouble. However, the movement is hard to convince.
- More subtly, Johnson had redefined intellectualism. It turned out it was not ideas at all. It was mortar, brick and concrete. This came as a surprise to the intellectuals, but never mind *them*. The real consternation was among construction workers.
- The rest was easy. Johnson was certainly building things—urban renewal projects, hospitals, mass transit systems. Having redefined intellectualism materialistically, he clearly qualified as an intellectual leader. The ultimate truth about Lyndon Johnson was revealed. He was an intellectual. He had style. He was Kennedy.

It was hard. Johnson envied Kennedy to the point of despising him, but in public he had to be the keeper of the Kennedy flame. He could not disparage the murdered president and hope to govern a nation traumatized by the deed. Johnson's achievement was of a high order; in the aftermath of November 22, 1963, he took a horror-stricken people firmly in grasp and held them together. He provided the vital assurance that America's national life—its social fabric, its continuity of government, its order and progress—would not be torn asunder by a maniacal event in Dallas. He was doing it for the rapacious glory of Lyndon Johnson, of course, but he had a feeling for the occasion, too; there was no doubt about that. It was an awesome collaboration of personal ego and political skill. The period immediately after Dallas was the closest Johnson ever came to realizing his overriding ambition: to be as great a president as Franklin Roosevelt. Later, Johnson's deficiencies as a national leader became glaringly obvious. He was not a Roosevelt after all. Not even a Kennedy. Then the game was over.

However, this was not immediately apparent. The nation thought it had one thing when actually it had something quite different, which is a common experience of nations. So the presidential election of 1964 was the high-water mark of the Johnson presidency. The Republicans did him the great favor of putting up a candidate who did not have a consuming desire to be president; during the campaign, Senator Barry Goldwater told the reporters he was "just pooping around." It is not possible to poop your way to the White House. Goldwater had a firm, square jaw. But Johnson wanted the job.

Huge crowds turned out in 1964 to see what fate had dealt them. Johnson campaigned eighteen and twenty hours a day, shouting, sweating, his voice hoarse, his face red, his arms flailing. It seemed perpetually late at night. The presidential limousine in the midst of an anonymous tide. The president standing up in the open car, holding a microphone, imploring the people to come visit him at the White House. Surrealism in spotlights, television lights, the flashing red lights of the police escort. The reporters are slumped in the press bus, thinking of Scott Fitzgerald; in the dark night of the press bus, it is always three o'clock in the morning. Then a race back to Air Force One. Johnson works the crowd at the airport, then bounds up the steps to the plane and bursts into his compartment. He is undressing as he comes in. He takes off his coat and tosses it at Mrs. Johnson: "Here, Bird." He rips off his tie and tosses it at Mrs. Johnson: "Here, Bird." He tears off his sweat-soaked shirt and tosses it at Mrs. Johnson: "Here, Bird."

So he went roaring and snorting around the country, bulldozing his way to his goal: the biggest victory in the modern history of the presidency. He won with an astonishing 61.1 percent of the popular vote. He did what he wanted most to do: He beat the previous record of 60.8 percent set by Roosevelt in 1936. The only other president in this century to get more than 60 percent of the popular vote was Warren Harding, with 60.3 in 1920.[11] Harding. Roosevelt. Johnson. The lesson is elusive.

And then, very quickly, it all fell apart. Throughout the campaign, Johnson had promised that he would not send combat troops to Vietnam; Americans would not fight "a war that I think ought to be fought by the boys of Asia to help protect their own land."[12] The promises continued after he won a full term as president. Seven times between June 23, 1964, and April 25, 1965, Johnson or White House officials speaking for him stated that the United States would not widen the war.[13] In this same period, the fullscale bombing raids on North Vietnam began, and Johnson ordered 20,000 combat troops to South Vietnam. By the time he left office, he had sent in 542,588 American troops to fight the war that "ought to be fought by the boys of Asia." Other lessons are *not* elusive.

But first, before Vietnam overwhelmed him, there was the credibility gap. This began early; Johnson never wasted time. Specifically, it began at his first presidential press conference, on December 7, 1963. A reporter asked Johnson about the new federal budget. He began his reply by pointing out that Kennedy's last budget had totaled $98.8 billion. Then Johnson said about $3.5 billion would have to be added to the next budget to cover "built-in" increases such as interest on the national debt and government pensions, together with the cost of new programs. The reporters wrote stories saying that the new budget apparently would be between $102 and $103 billion. They were misinformed.

At his next news conference, Johnson seemed to back away from breaking the $100-billion mark. He said: "I am working from a budget of $98.8 billion this year. It appears we will expend about that amount, and maybe a little under or a little over, but substantially $99 billion will be the expenditures this year. That was the amount of Mr. Kennedy's budget." So it looked as if the new budget would come in under $100 billion. Or did it? In the next breath, Johnson again mentioned the $3.5 billion in new expenses. Then he noted that the population of the United States had increased by 21 percent since the Truman era. "When we have an increase in population, we are going to have an increase in the budget," the president said. The reporters could write that the budget was going to be about $99 billion, or they could stick with the $102 billion to $103 billion. They had freedom of choice. They were not grateful.

Johnson now moved the shell game to Texas. While he was at his ranch, anonymous White House "sources" told the reporters that the new budget would be $100 billion, give or take only a few million dollars either way. Then they switched the shells. They said it would be $100 billion, give or take one or two *percentage points* either way. In a total of $100 billion, one or two percentage points represent $1 billion or $2 billion, not a few million. This gave a range of $98 billion to $102 billion. The anonymous sources, of course, were Johnson himself. The reporters were summoned to the LBJ ranch, the president manipulated the shells with dazzling dexterity and the journalists came away muttering, "What the hell is going on?"

In those halcyon days, there was a mystique about the $100-billion barrier. Except in wartime, the American government had never spent $100 billion in one fiscal year (conveniently ignoring Social Security and other transfer payments). However, life was continuing to complicate itself. The budget was pushing close to the magic limit. Would Lyndon Johnson be the first president to spend $100 billion in peacetime? From the ranch, the anonymous sources portrayed a chief executive waging a valiant but probably unavailing effort to hold the line. I'm sweating and I'm straining, boys. I'm wrestling with it, but I don't think I can do it. The reporters wrote story after story preparing the taxpayers for the first peacetime $100-billion budget. The president was giving it everything he had, but that $3.5 billion in new costs was going to do him in.

But when the new budget was submitted to Congress, it was not $100 billion. It was not $102 or $103 billion, either. It was not $98 or $99 billion, or any of the figures that had been mentioned. It was $97.7 billion, and this was later reduced to $97.2 billion. Johnson had pulled it off. He had kept the budget under $100 billion. A triumph. He had even brought it in *under the last Kennedy budget*. Substance, not style. Who needed Camelot?

Johnson's three-card monte with the budget had sandbagged the reporters. This was not a high crime or misdemeanor. It is not illegal to lie to the media. But the reporters, in their stories and broadcasts, then misled the American people. The media had been used as a means of deceiving the public. It had not involved some urgent national-security crisis in which it might have been argued that deceit was necessary. The federal budget, except for the customary hanky-panky with CIA spending, has never been regarded as a state secret. It was just fancy footwork to make Johnson look good. For a while.

Johnson's credibility had been a problem for a long time, but it was like social justice. It had escaped general attention. As Senate Democratic leader, his veracity became so suspect that a veteran congressional reporter finally refused to interview him any more. The speaker of the House, Sam Rayburn, remonstrated with the reporter. Rayburn pointed out that Johnson was a major news source that the reporter could not afford to bypass. The reporter replied that he could not afford to file misleading stories, either. [14]

On a trip to Texas in his Senate days, Johnson escorted a group of reporters around his ranch. They stopped in front of a shanty bearing the unmistakable marks of a hard life. In reverent tones, the senator identified this almost log cabin as the place in which he had been reared. His mother, Rebekah Baines Johnson, had come along for the walk. She adored Lyndon, but even mother love has limits. She listened to the Abe Lincoln spiel for a few minutes and then spoke up. "Why, Lyndon," she said, "you *know* we had a nice house over on the other side of the farm."[15] A man who will lie in the presence of his own mother is a man to be reckoned with.

Later, the White House reporters grew accustomed to these endless tours of the boyhood home, the boyhood grandfather's house, the boyhood school, the boyhood store, the boyhood pond. Weekend after weekend, they drove down the narrow roads and stumbled through the fields with Johnson as he poked around in the faded memorabilia of his childhood, searching for . . . what?

What was he looking for? There is an old photograph of Johnson as a small boy. He is wearing an oversize cowboy hat and he is staring unwinkingly in the hot sun. He is like the children in Katherine Anne Porter's "Noon Wine." They are digging barefoot in the ragweed, a little grubby, more than a little unwilling to go to school, restlessly energetic, the dispossessed children at the end of the frontier. They are isolated, inbred, suspicious of strangers. In "Noon Wine," when Olaf Helton comes to work on Mr. Thompson's farm in south Texas, the Thompson kids call him Big Swede and ridicule him; in later life, Lyndon Johnson was to say that the trouble with foreigners was that "they're not like folks you were reared with."[16]

Then a gangly red-neck youth, vaguely and inarticulately discontented, a drifter until he tires of working with his hands and decides to go to college. Then a young congressman from nowhere, clawing his way up in a national capital casually dominated by eastern Brahmins (one of his biographers noted that "the American Establishment . . . excluded Lyndon Johnson for years").[17] Then a senator and Senate Democratic leader, coming into his own in the branch of government that gave rural nonestablishment types the best chance to rise to the top.

Then a three-year eclipse as vice-president. When Kennedy sends him on missions to Europe, Johnson pours out his frustrated vanity in transatlantic telephone calls to an aide, Walter Jenkins. He asks Jenkins anxiously whether the New York and Washington newspapers are playing his trip "outside" (on page 1); when they are not, he sinks into despondency.[18] Then a cosmic accident, and Lyndon Johnson is president. His ego blooms again like a giant tropical flower.

But it is not enough. He must go back. The reporters marvel at the insecurity of the man, at the complexity of the man. Then, being reporters, they grow irreverent. They invent an irreverent itinerary. The boyhood beer joint. The boyhood privy. The boyhood whorehouse. The boyhood clap-doctor's office.

In the Senate, Johnson was dealing with a small group of professional politicians. They understood his jiggery-pokery. They realized that it often went beyond the accepted limits, but they knew how to be on their guard against this. It was essentially an in-house matter. Games politicians play. But when Johnson became president, he was no longer dealing only with professional politicians. Now he had to deal with 200 million Americans who were not full-time political practitioners. They might not understand. They might become confused and then resentful, when lied to.

It was no longer in-house. Generally speaking, the day-to-day operations of a Senate wheeler-dealer are not scrutinized intensively by the news media, which is a great help. But when Johnson moved into the White House, his methods came under immediate and persistent examination. A politician with an intuition for national leadership would have realized that an obvious, flagrant sleight-of-hand style would not do. Style again. The techniques for leading a small group of politicians are not the same as the techniques for leading a large nation. A measure of trust must be established. But Johnson had no intuition for *national* leadership. He had an intuition for *legislative* leadership. These are not the same things. He had learned to do one job extremely well. So they gave him a different job. To succeed, he had to change. But he could not change. Visiting India as vice-president, he was shown the Taj Mahal. He let loose a huge Texas yell, to test the acoustics. When he became president, his greeting to the American people was in effect another great, boisterous shout: "Hello, suckers." It was, at least, in character.

- The *Washington Post* reported that Johnson would propose a reduction of $4 billion in federal excise taxes. The president spread the word that this was false. His press secretary, George Reedy, said "that figure bears no relationship to any decision that has been made." The press corps reported both versions; when burned, journalists learn quickly. But the American people were still of a disposition to believe what their president said. So they were misled. Johnson then asked Congress to cut excise taxes by $3.964 billion. [19]
- The *Washington Star* reported that Johnson would recommend a 3-percent average pay increase for federal employees. The president said the story was erroneous. A short time later, he proposed a 3-percent pay increase for federal employees. [20]
- While Johnson was touring Asia in 1966, his staff spread the word that when he returned he would campaign for Democratic candidates in the November congressional elections. It was called the Boston-to-Austin trip because the president would start in Kennedy's hometown, campaign in as many as fifteen states and wind up at his ranch for a short rest. The information was on an informal basis, for the reporters' guidance—when we get back to Washington, keep your bags packed. However, Secret Service agents and White House advance men began to fan out around the country, preparing for the trip. Concealment is difficult when presidential teams show up in cities, checking hotels and auditoriums, conferring with local police officials and planning motorcade routes. The word gets out. Local newspapers carried stories about the impending Johnson visit. They asked their Washington bureaus or the wire services for more information about the trip. The reporters who had accompanied Johnson to Asia were restricted by the off-record

rule, but other reporters were not. They quickly ferreted out the details. More stories appeared.

Johnson did not like this. He wanted the trip to be a secret until he announced it. "Fundamental to his operations," Bill Moyers once said, "is surprise, which keeps his foes off balance. He wants to retain the advantage of calling his own signals and deciding on his own timing."[21] Surprise is dandy, but in this case who were the foes? The American people? The president was going out to speak to the American people. Did he need to keep these "foes" off balance? It may have been a good tactic in the Senate, although even there he had been distrusted in greater than usual measure. But Johnson could not make the necessary distinctions once he became president. He could not switch from legislative to national leadership. The shells had to be kept moving. If someone spotted the pea, move 'em faster. So when his plans became known, he canceled his plans. He called off the trip.

When he got back to Washington, he held a press conference. He announced his travel plans. He was going to his ranch—period. Then he mentioned the stories about the Boston-to-Austin trip. It turned out the news media had made it all up. The American people, Johnson said, "ought to know that all these canceled plans primarily involve the imagination of people who phrase sentences and write columns and . . . report what they hope or what they imagine."[22] The reporters had imagined the whole thing—the information from the staff, the Secret Service agents and advance men, the dates and places, the whole megillah.

- In a speech to the United Steelworkers convention in 1964, Johnson lashed out at "a ranting, raving demagogue." The context made it clear he was referring to his Republican opponent, Senator Goldwater. A few minutes later, the president had second thoughts. He decided he had gone too far. However, he did not retract or apologize. Instead, he tried to rewrite. On the helicopter flight from Atlantic City back to Washington, he insisted to the reporters that he had not said "*a* ranting, raving demagogue." He swore up and down he had said "ranting, raving demagogues," plural. In other words, he had not singled out Goldwater. It was just some anonymous demagogues. He wanted the reporters to write it that way. The reporters looked at their notes. They showed "a." They checked the stenotypist's verbatim transcript. It showed "a." They listened to several tape recordings of the speech. It was "a." There are many uses for tapes.[23]
- On April 28, 1965, Johnson ordered U.S. marines into the Dominican Republic. He did this at the request of a right-wing military junta that was trying to suppress a rebel movement. The junta said the rebels

were Communists. Juntas only know one thing. Foreign policy officials in Washington had grave doubts that the revolt was inspired or dominated by Communists. However, the Johnson administration was disposed to intervene. It suggested that the junta revise its request. It told the Dominican generals to ask for U.S. troops to protect American citizens. Sure, said the generals, we'll take 'em anyway we can get 'em. The marines went in.

Shortly thereafter, Johnson decided he needed a stronger justification. On May 2, he told the nation that the rebel movement had come under the "increasing control" of Communist leaders, "many of them trained in Cuba." The next day, Johnson held one of his walking press conferences around the White House lawn. John Chancellor of NBC asked him at what point he had learned that the Communists had taken over the Dominican revolt. "At no point," Johnson replied. It was the only time he told the truth during the entire Dominican crisis.[24]

Then, at a press conference on June 17, Johnson gave another reason for sending in the marines: "Some 1,500 innocent people were murdered and shot, and their heads cut off, and . . . as we talked to our ambassador to confirm the horror and tragedy and the unbelievable fact that they were firing on Americans . . . he was talking to us from under a desk while bullets were going through his windows. . . ."

It sounded dreadful. However, almost none of it was true. The United States ambassador, William Tapley Bennett, said later that he was not under a desk while talking to the president. No bullets came through his windows. No one was beheaded by the Dominican insurgents. Most of the atrocities were committed not by the rebels but by the junta.[25] No Americans were harmed—except for two reporters. They were shot by American marines.[26] When Johnson made his June 17 statement, it had been six weeks since the first marines had been sent into the Dominican Republic. There had been plenty of time to check the facts.

• Philip Potter, a reporter for the *Baltimore Sun*, was one of Johnson's oldest and closest friends in the press corps. They were such good friends that once, when a group of anti-Vietnam protesters got into the White House and staged a sit-down strike, Potter sent a note to the president. The note said: "Who's running this country? You or a bunch of snot-nosed kids?" Potter was not a flaming liberal. Despite their years of camaraderie, however, Johnson was outraged when Potter dug up a scoop about something he was planning to do. The story gave extensive details of Johnson's new Food for Peace program. Johnson had intended to announce the new program in a few days. But when he read Potter's story, he canceled the announcement and ordered his staff to destroy the news releases that had been prepared. Much later, the Food for Peace program was put into effect, but it was done in a piecemeal fashion, a bit at a time. This was an effort to conceal the fact that Potter's story had been correct. Johnson did not speak to Potter for months.[27]

- One day in July 1965, Johnson presided at a ceremony in the Rose Garden. Afterward, he invited the reporters into his office. Someone asked him a question, and an impromptu press conference began. Johnson had recently persuaded Justice Arthur Goldberg to leave the Supreme Court and become U.S. ambassador to the United Nations. So one of the important issues of the moment was who would be named to replace Goldberg on the court. Specifically, would it be Johnson's longtime adviser and confidant Abe Fortas? I asked Johnson if he could give us any indication of his choice for the Supreme Court. He looked me straight in the eye. His reply was simple and direct. He said: "I have not even begun to consider that matter." The reporters wrote stories saying it did not appear that a Supreme Court nomination was imminent. It would be a while. Almost exactly twenty-four hours later, the White House announced the nomination of Fortas to the Supreme Court. Once again, dear friends, down the garden path with Lyndon.

There was a sequel. A week or so later, Johnson received the credentials of some new foreign ambassadors. After the envoys had gone, Johnson sat down in an armchair and invited the reporters to stay a while and chat. A conversation with Johnson was a Johnson conversation; he did all the conversing. In the course of things, he brought up the Fortas nomination. It had been, he said, extremely difficult to persuade Fortas to give up his lucrative law practice and go on the Supreme Court. But he, Johnson, the great persuader, had done it. Why, just look here, this will show you how hard it was. Johnson's pockets were always stuffed with memos, notes and other pieces of paper. He rummaged around and produced a letter. He handed it to the reporters. It was an impassioned plea from Fortas to Johnson not to appoint him to the court; he used the expression "Let this cup pass from me." I read it and was about to give it to the next reporter when I noticed something. The letter was dated July 19. That was eight days *before* the press conference at which Johnson had said: "I have not even begun to consider that matter."[28]

In *Twelfth Night*, Fabian says: "If this were played upon a stage now, I could condemn it as an improbable fiction." For crying out loud. Did Johnson think no one would notice the date? So what was going on? Either he had forgotten what he had said a short time before, which was not like Johnson (he read the transcripts of his press conferences regularly and carefully), or he did not care if he was caught in a thumping big lie, or he just could not help himself. He had to lie and he had to be caught. Consult your local psychiatrist.

It became necessary to take precautionary measures. The reporters adopted a policy. If Johnson or one of his spokesmen said something was *not* going to happen, the journalists assumed it probably *was* going to happen.

At the end of 1966, Johnson was at his Texas ranch. In Washington, word began to circulate that contract awards for a supersonic transport plane would be announced over the New Year weekend. The stock exchanges would be closed, preventing trading in the stock of the winning and losing companies. In Austin, where they were staying, the reporters asked deputy press secretary Robert H. Fleming whether the SST announcement would be made during the holiday.

Fleming replied that the president had not received a report on the SST from an advisory committee headed by Secretary of Defense Robert S. McNamara. "I am sure you can assume that since the president does not have the report, there would be no decision very soon," Fleming said. "I am sure the president would want the report and would want to study it after he gets it." In response to further questions, Fleming added: "I do not know firmly that there will not be [an announcement over the weekend], but I am confident that there will be a study made of the report after it comes to the president."[29]

The deputy press secretary left himself a little escape hatch. He did not absolutely rule out an announcement over the New Year weekend. But the overall tenor of his answer was that there would be "no decision very soon."

So the reporters immediately began assembling background information on the SST. Several of them called their Washington offices to have someone read them newspaper and magazine articles about the project. Just a precaution. This was on Friday, December 30. The next day, in Washington, the Federal Aviation Agency announced that the Boeing Company and the General Electric Company had been selected as the contractors for the supersonic plane.

Then, Vietnam. The impact of Vietnam is still being felt. The nation is still tormented by it. A decade after the withdrawal of the last American troops, the war was still being debated in books and articles and on television programs. An elderly, conservative president proclaims that it was a noble cause, but that is the way of old men.

The news media's role in the war was and is a matter of deep dispute. Vietnam was the first rec-room war. The villages were burned, the helicopter gunships roared down, the refugees fled—all on television, every night.

It was gruesome, but it was not new. Public opinion had turned against other wars as the atrocities, casualty lists and military mistakes slowly became known. British governments had hung on for dear life as the news trickled in from the Crimea and the Transvaal. But the news from Vietnam was different in three profoundly important ways. It was almost instantaneous. It was pervasive, entering every home. And it was *visual*. People could *see* these things happening. They did not have to *imagine* a village being napalmed. There is inevitably an element of personal detachment when something must be visualized in the mind, when a mental picture must be summoned up on the basis of a written or spoken account. If the narrator is very skillful, reality can be recreated. Homer had a large following. But it requires a conscious effort of imagination. Some people are not given to imagination, others will not take the trouble and *quandoque bonus dormitat Homerus.* Sometimes even good Homer nods. Enter television. There was no nodding in the rec room.

So a great gulf in perceptions opened up. The news media were performing a notable public service. They were reporting the horrors, casualties, lies and mistakes of the Vietnam war. They were thereby arousing public opinion to a justified attitude of anger and opposition. The war should not have been fought and could not have been won. Or the media were engaged in an ignoble enterprise. They were distorting and falsifying the news from Vietnam. They were viewing the war through an antigovernment prism and a pessimistic lens. They were thereby arousing public opinion to an unjustified attitude of despair and defeatism. The war should have been fought and could have been won.

Of course, the media were not monolithic on Vietnam, any more than Southeast Asia was solidly Communistic. Instead, the press was divided over the war. Chapter Three pointed out that the *Washington Post* and other influential newspapers supported Johnson's Vietnam policy for a long time. A widely read columnist, Joseph Alsop, accused the American reporters in Vietnam of "carrying on another of these egregious crusades."[30] Only Alsop's crusades were approved by Alsop. They were usually military in nature. Reporter Marguerite Higgins, another well known journalist, wrote in the *New York Herald Tribune* that the U.S. reporters in Nam "would like to see us lose the war to prove they're right."[31] Journalist Peter Braestrup wrote a big and influential book in which he argued that the media misrepresented the 1968 Tet offensive as a Communist victory, in part because the Johnson administration failed to present effective counterarguments to news organizations at home.[32] (Braestrup believes, however, that much of the other reporting of the war was accurate.) More recently, journalist Robert Elegant has weighed in with the contention that the news media fostered defeatism when the war actually was being won.[33]

The problem was a small group of American reporters who were covering the war. They were mostly young men—David Halberstam of the *New York Times*, Neil Sheehan of United Press International and Charles Mohr of *Time* magazine (both of whom later went to work for the *Times*), Malcolm Browne and Peter Arnett of the Associated Press, Stanley Karnow of *The Saturday Evening Post* (later with the *Washington Post*), Francois Sully of *Newsweek*, Peter Kalischer of CBS. In addition, there were a few older hands, notably Homer Bigart, a nonpareil who had moved to the *Times* from the *Herald Tribune*, and Richard Dudman of the *St. Louis Post-Dispatch*. Young or middle-aged, they were indefatigable, independent, skeptical. Bigart was fifty-five and his stomach was bothering him, but Halberstam says he "simply outworked every young reporter" on the scene.[34] Which was saying something, because Halberstam himself was a prodigious worker, as were Mohr, Arnett, Browne and the others. Neil Sheehan was one of the most intense, hard-driving reporters American journalism ever had, and Dudman never stopped working.

Month after month, the American reporters went out into the field. Month after month, they went to places like Ap Bac and Cho Gao and the Mekong delta, to see things for themselves. They counted the bodies; they talked to the village chiefs; they looked at the results of the air strikes; they interviewed lower-echelon military officers to find out what actually had happened. They badgered and prodded the American embassy in Saigon and MACV (the American Military Assistance Command, Vietnam) for more information. Then they got hold of secret reports that showed MACV and the embassy were not telling the truth. The results were cumulative and could not be ignored. The reporters could not find a war that was being won or showed any prospect of being won. That was the problem

To win the war, several things were necessary: The South Vietnamese Army had to fight, a lot of Viet Cong had to be killed, the infiltration rate had to be cut so the Viet Cong casualties could not be sufficiently replaced and the villages of South Vietnam had to be made secure from the guerrillas. This last effort was known as the pacification program. In all these areas, the reporters' observations did not agree with the official statements of the South Vietnamese and American governments. The reporters were correct.

- The fighting qualities of the South Vietnamese Army (ARVN) were such that it was ultimately necessary to send in more than 500,000 American troops. The ARVN did not like to fight in the daytime. To offset this, it absolutely refused to fight at night. John Mecklin, the press spokesman for the United States embassy, wrote later that the ARVN "developed subtle ways to avoid a fight . . . to the despair of their American advisers." Arriving in a combat area, the government troops would "fire their weapons needlessly and talk and shout to each other . . . to alert the Viet Cong to their presence."[35] The Viet Cong, if outnumbered, could then steal away. Or the ARVN troops would just sit down and eat lunch. First things first. On those occasions when ARVN troops did locate a Viet Cong concentration, Mecklin wrote, they often neglected deliberately to close off the guerrillas' escape route. A fight would thereby be avoided.[36]

  The South Vietnamese government's "body counts" of slain Viet Cong enriched the word "absurd." The American reporters disproved the body counts so often that they wearied of the exercise. Becoming irreverent, they devised "the Cao formula." This was named after ARVN Colonel Huynh Van Cao, a terror with statistics. The reporters noted the number of Viet Cong casualties claimed by the government and subtracted the number of announced government casualties. They then divided the result by 3.[37] It worked every time.

  In private, even some American officials did not believe the body counts. Mecklin wrote later: "Each month, the [South Vietnamese] government claimed a thousand or more Viet Cong killed; yet intelligence estimates showed [a] steady, relentless growth of V.C. strength."[38] The Communists were not being killed in the numbers claimed. The infiltration rate was not being reduced to the extent claimed. The American government did not disclose these things to the American people. The reporters did. Defeatism.

- Nor was the pacification program working. Halberstam related an interview with a local chief whose district included twenty-four villages. How many were under control—that is, secure from the Viet Cong? Eight, said the chief. How many did you report as being under control? Twenty-four, said the chief.[39] The Viet Cong were commuters. During the day, they left the villages. At night, they came back. The reporters wrote that the pacification program was not succeeding. Defeatism.

"To the best of my knowledge, no responsible U.S. official in Saigon ever told a newsman a really big falsehood," Mecklin wrote later. "Instead, there were endless little ones. They were morally marginal. . . ."[40] That is the way these things are done. But perhaps Mecklin sensed that the endless little lies added up to one great big lie. At any rate, he agonized over his experiences as a government spokesman in Vietnam. His book was entitled *Mission in Torment*. General Maxwell D. Taylor, who was Lyndon Johnson's special adviser on Vietnam, was less introspective. On the *CBS Morning News* in June 1971, he was asked: "Well, what do you make, General, of the principle of the people's right to know?" Taylor replied: "I don't believe in that as a general principle."[41]

The government of the United States had a very controversial war on its hands. So when it responded to criticism of the war, it waved the flag. Johnson and Secretary of State Dean Rusk took to questioning the patriotism of the reporters (see Chapter Two). That had an ominous ring. Admiral Harry D. Felt, the American commander in the Pacific, snapped at Malcolm Browne of the Associated Press: "Why don't you get on the team?"[42]

But reporters are not on the government's team. They do not consider that their job. If they are on the official team, who will do the reporting? As a result, Mecklin wrote, "the feud [between American officials and reporters] reached a degree of bitterness such as I had never before encountered in some 20 years of foreign duty." American officials in Saigon, he said, came to regard "a journalist as a natural adversary who was deliberately trying to sabotage the national interest, or as a child who would not understand and should not be asking about grown-up affairs. . . ."[43] War is very grown-up.

In Saigon, the procedure may have been only endless little lies. But in Washington, the American involvement in Vietnam was handled from beginning to end with big lies and gigantic concealments. The credibility problems that had arisen over such things as the federal budget and the Dominican crisis were child's play compared to the adult performance on Vietnam. There had been nothing like it before, and there would be nothing like it again—until Watergate. That was coming soon; there was not to be much breathing space in between. It was the war itself that brought Lyndon Johnson down—the faulty premises of the war, the futility of the war, the casualty lists of the war—but the mad tapestry of lies that was woven around the war contributed hugely.

It began soon after Johnson had been elected to a full term. In March 1965, two battalions of marines were sent to Da Nang. Secretary of State Rusk announced that the marines would be used only for "local, close-in security." That is, they were being sent only to protect American installations. They would fight only if attacked. They would not seek out the

Viet Cong for combat. Secretary of Defense McNamara added more as-surance. The marines, he said, would "not tangle with the Viet Cong." However, things were about to get tangled.

Two months later, in Saigon, an American military spokesman said the marines would "render combat support, which includes, if necessary, fighting." Reporters at the State Department read what had been said in Saigon. They sought comment from the department's chief press officer, Robert McCloskey. On June 8, McCloskey said it was true. Other State Department officials said an order authorizing combat had gone out to General William C. Westmoreland within "the past several weeks." This left the secretaries of state and defense in an anomalous position.

The White House came to their rescue—temporarily. It was furious with McCloskey. It disavowed McCloskey. It issued a denial that there had been any change in the mission of U.S. ground forces in Vietnam. It denied that the president had sent any combat authorization to West-moreland. In the next breath, however, the White House said Westmore-land had had "discretionary authority" to use his troops in combat from the beginning. Rusk and McNamara were left up the anomaly, to paddle their way back as best they could.[44]

The difficulty was that Lyndon Johnson was sending troops to South Vietnam to fight, but he did not want the American people to know this. He was moving the shells as fast as he could. No, the marines would not fight. Well, yes, they might fight. No. Yes. Perhaps.

At the start of April 1965, they made it official. The basic policy of the American government would be to lie. They made it official, but they did not make it public. You can't have everything. On April 6, Johnson's national security assistant, McGeorge Bundy, sent out National Security Action Memorandum 328. In it, Johnson ordered an additional 20,000 marines to Vietnam and authorized them to engage in combat. The rele-vant quotes from this document were given in Chapter Five. Bundy had been a dean at Harvard. He put things elegantly. He said "the president desires that . . . premature publicity be avoided by all possible precau-tions."

After that, everything fell into line. There was a policy. But the cred-ibility gap grew and grew. It was no mere spat between a bunch of report-ers and a flimflam artist. Gradually, it sank into the national fabric. The American people came to realize that the president was a chronic liar. It became clear that the government had adopted lying as a consistent, offi-cial policy:

● At a White House ceremony in January 1967, Johnson said the Air Force was "conducting the most careful and most self-limited air war in history." In 1965, the Air Force had flown 24,570 sorties over North Vietnam. In 1966, the Pentagon stopped listing the number of individual sorties. Instead, it began listing "missions." It said there had been 23,577 missions over North Vietnam in 1966. That made it sound as if there had been a little less bombing in 1966 than in 1965. But a mission normally consisted of four planes. That figured out to 94,308 sorties in 1966—almost four times *more* than in 1965. It was all done with words.[45]

● At a press conference in February 1967, Johnson said the U.S. bombing raids on North Vietnam had been effective in achieving their main objectives. He listed these as: making the war more costly for North Vietnam, making it more difficult to infiltrate men and matériel into South Vietnam and improving the morale of the South Vietnamese people. Johnson did not mention that he had on his desk at that moment a report from the Central Intelligence Agency and the Defense Intelligence Agency. It said the bombing had not broken North Vietnam's will to fight and had not reduced the infiltration rate.[46] The war was indeed very costly. It was costing the United States $3 billion a month. And nothing, but nothing, could improve the morale of the South Vietnamese people.

● The oldest established permanent floating credibility gap in Vietnam was the domino theory. This one went all the way back to Harry Truman and his National Security Council. In February 1950, the NSC decided that "the neighboring countries of Thailand and Burma could be expected to fall under Communist domination if Indochina is controlled by a Communist government. The balance of Southeast Asia would then be in grave hazard."[47] This insight into the future became the official policy of the American government.

Dwight Eisenhower, an unlikely source, supplied the catchy phrase. He told a press conference: "You have a row of dominos set up. You knock over the first one, and what will happen to the last one is the certainty that it will go over very quickly."[48]

John F. Kennedy accepted the domino theory and reaffirmed the policy. He approved a memo written by Rusk and McNamara. It warned that if South Vietnam fell to the Communists, "we would have to face the near-certainty that *the remainder of Southeast Asia and Indonesia* would move to a complete accommodation with Communism, if not formal incorporation within the Communist bloc [emphasis added]."[49]

Kennedy should have known better; he had read some books. But who was Lyndon Johnson to argue with the experts? He adopted the domino theory enthusiastically. The Communists, he said repeatedly, "want what we have, and we are not going to let them get it." Color television, patios, electric toothbrushes, the works. But the worst was still to come. In a speech to the Veterans of Foreign Wars on August 19, 1968, Johnson said: "There are some among us who appear to be searching for a formula which would somehow get us out of Vietnam and Asia, leaving the people of South Vietnam and Laos and Thailand—*and all of the others*—to an uncertain fate [emphasis added]." Not only Indochina but also Thailand, Malaysia, Singapore and Indonesia could fall to communism if the United States withdrew from Vietnam, the president warned. And then the clincher: "Pretty soon we could be back to the Philippines and even Honolulu." It looked bad. No more surfing at Waikiki. No more condos on Maui.

But the last American troops were withdrawn from Vietnam years ago. And one after another, Thailand, Malaysia, Burma, Singapore, Indonesia, the Philippines and Hawaii have not yielded up their treasures to communism. It was another of those dog-in-the-night national security sequences: dire forebodings, and then nothing happened.

However, Johnson, Rusk and McNamara could not predict the future. Nor could the other U.S. policymakers who preceded them in the Truman, Eisenhower and Kennedy administrations. It is unfair to reproach them on the basis of hindsight. Like all policymakers, they were operating with the information available at the moment. But as it happened, there *was* information available at the moment. Hindsight is not necessary.

On June 9, 1964, the Central Intelligence Agency sent Johnson a report. "With the possible exception of Cambodia," it said, "it is likely that no nation in the area would quickly succumb to Communism as the result of the fall of Laos and South Vietnam. Furthermore, a continuation of the spread of Communism in the area would not be inexorable. . . ."[50] Where did all the bushwa about Indonesia and the Philippines and Hawaii come from?

Johnson declassified secret information and made it public when it suited his purposes (see Chapter Six). This report did not suit his purposes. The CIA did not agree with the domino theory. But its dissent did not come to light until 1971, when the *New York Times* and other newspapers obtained and published the Pentagon Papers, a secret history of the U.S. involvement in Vietnam.

However, enough came out at the time to make government duplicity a major issue during Johnson's presidency. Some of the lying was so crude it was easy to expose. But suppose the American people had known that the government's own intelligence specialists did not accept the basic premise of the war? A Louis Harris poll in January 1966 showed that 61 percent of the nation favored "all-out bombing of North Vietnam" if the

Communists refused to negotiate.[51] Suppose the 61 percent had known that the CIA and the Defense Intelligence Agency had informed Johnson that the bombing had not broken North Vietnam's will to fight? The credibility gap was not just an insiders' game between the reporters and the government. It was deception on a grand, national scale.

Johnson's first press secretary was Pierre Salinger, who stayed on for a while after Kennedy's assassination. Salinger's few months in the Johnson White House were not especially notable, except for one thing. The new president went to Los Angeles in February 1964 to meet with President Adolfo López Mateos of Mexico. Salinger persuaded Johnson to include Palm Springs, California, on his itinerary. Johnson did not have much in common with Palm Springs, and he never went back. No cows. No Pearl beer. No boyhood stuff. However, the trip had two interesting features:

In Los Angeles, the two presidents and their wives attended a Mexican fiesta in the sports arena. They sat on a platform watching the dancers. Mrs. López Mateos asked for a glass of water. An attendant brought the water but handed it to Johnson, either by mistake or with the thought that he would pass it to the lady. Johnson did pass the glass to Mrs. López Mateos. But first he took a big, healthy drink.

Then Johnson went to Palm Springs, where he spent a restless day or two. The reporters did not have much to do. They relaxed at poolside during the day and occupied the remainder of the time trying to find a decent place to eat. One evening, a group of journalists, searching, searching, searching for food, drove through many blocks of Palm Springs. Although it was February, Christmas was still being celebrated. The impoverished natives, unable to afford Christmas trees, had covered their houses with lights of many colors. Not content with this, they had strung lights over the cacti, over the sagebrush, over every piece of vegetation the desert offered. Thousands of garish lights obscured nature's magnificence. Tom Wicker, a country lad from North Carolina, was covering the trip for the *New York Times*. Wicker regarded the gaudy night. He regarded it dubiously. "Good grief," he said, "they're fucking up God's desert."

Salinger resigned in March 1964. He was succeeded by George E. Reedy. Everyone had figured Reedy would get the job eventually; if ever there was a Johnson man, it was old George Reedy. He was not really so old, but association with Johnson accelerated time. Reedy, a former reporter for United Press, had gone to work for Johnson in 1951. First he analyzed military policy for a Senate subcommittee of which Johnson was chairman; then he became staff director of the Senate Democratic Policy

Committee when Johnson was elected Senate Democratic leader; and then he served on Johnson's vice-presidential staff, handling press relations among other things. When Johnson became president, Reedy was the second-oldest member of his staff in years of service. He was six feet, two inches tall, and until he went on a diet, he weighed over 250 pounds. When he took over as presidential press secretary, he was forty-six years old. His hair was white.

Reedy was an intelligent man. Later, after leaving Johnson (the reporters said, after *escaping* from Johnson), his mind got a second chance. He became a journalism professor and dean, an astute observer of the public mood and the author of a thoughtful and influential book on the presidency. But during his years with Johnson, he was extremely cautious. He spoke slowly, very slowly, in a rumbling baritone that moved carefully, looking for land mines and booby traps. Reedy was well informed on national issues; he was helpful to the reporters when the subject being discussed did not affect Lyndon Johnson. But if it did, he sent out a protective screen of pipe smoke and said almost nothing. Since virtually everything that comes to the attention of the White House affects the president, Reedy was an uncommunicative press secretary. In a two-hour conversation shortly after Johnson became president, the reporters could not even get Reedy to say what duties had been assigned to the various members of the White House staff. Johnson would announce that.[52]

When Reedy first went to work for Johnson, he told a friend: "I'm hitching my wagon to a star. Lyndon Johnson is a great man, and he's going to be president some day."[53] One out of two is not bad. His star made it to the White House, but Reedy was able to share the glory—if that is the right word—for only sixteen months. A painful foot condition compelled him to leave in July 1965. For his next press secretary, Johnson turned to a very different personality.

Bill Moyers was thirty-one years old when he became chief spokesman for the president of the United States. That made him one of the youngest men ever to hold the job. He was also an ordained Baptist minister. That was an *only*. Moyers was raised in Oklahoma and Texas, acquired first a journalism degree and then one in theology, both with honors, and did graduate work at the University of Edinburgh. He joined Johnson's senatorial staff in 1959 and then became associate director of the Peace Corps in the Kennedy administration, at the age of twenty-six. When Johnson became president, Moyers moved over to the White House staff. Twenty months later, he was press secretary. His journalistic experience was slight, but he was a very rapid learner. And the reporters quickly realized something: His relationship with Johnson was very different. At

Moyers's first briefing, he was asked a question about a change of U.S. ambassadors in South Vietnam. He did not know some of the details, so in mid-briefing he picked up the telephone, called the president and got the information. Reedy would never, but never, have done that.[54]

Faster than Einstein's light waves is the White House press corps when it comes to knowing how a press secretary stands with a president. The reporters sense the nature of the relationship immediately, and it governs their dealings with the man on the podium. They knew Johnson would never admit any member of his staff very far into his thought processes, but Moyers seemed to be getting more glimpses into the labyrinthine world than anyone else. The reporters never knew exactly why, but there it was: Moyers could speak *for* Johnson and *to* Johnson. And, wonder of wonders, the wrath did not descend upon him, and the rug was not pulled out from under him.

Many of the White House reporters were much older than Moyers, in age and in Washington experience. Nevertheless, he conducted his daily briefings imperturbably, a slim, cool young man standing behind a desk, speaking in a clear, precise voice with a trace of twang and puffing occasionally on a thin cigar. Now and then, if the going got rough, he would allude to lions and Christians. Moyers's self-possession was a sort of armor, in that it was hard to shake. But more than that, there was the ever present realization that he was close to Johnson.

The reporters deal harshly with a press secretary who does not seem to know what the president is doing. They are not kind to a press secretary who seems to be afraid to talk. They are downright carnivorous with one who appears to be covering up mistakes or misdeeds or otherwise suppressing information. But there is a different reaction if the press secretary speaks right up and conveys information and answers questions and seems confident that what he is saying reflects the president's views. Then things get very crisp. The guy has something to tell us. It seems to be legit. It is time to get down to business. An air of authority and self-confidence, based on a close relationship with the president, is a press secretary's greatest asset. This was Jim Hagerty's armor, and Moyers conveyed the same impression. The briefing room is no place for the faint of heart.

The biggest problem confronting Moyers was the administration's credibility. The new press secretary did not overcome the problem. But he tried hard, and the technique he used was instructive. As noted in Chapter Two, Moyers was more interested in policymaking than mechanics. Routine announcements and travel schedules did not fascinate him. He liked to sit down with individual reporters and reflect aloud on the problems facing the president and the options available to him. In these conversations, Moyers was candid about Johnson's shortcomings.

He avoided the pit into which so many press secretaries fall: He did not insult the reporters' intelligence by attempting to defend the indefensible. What he did was more clever, more subtle and more realistic. Instead of defending *Johnson*, he defended Johnson's *decisions* and Johnson's *reasons*. He argued the case for the policies, not the personality. Never mind what you think of Lyndon Johnson; here was the problem he had to cope with, here was the narrow range of choices open to him, here was the danger in each choice. The focus was on the limitations of policy, not the limitations of the president. You see, he *had* to do thus-and-so; there really was no alternative. It was a skillful performance.

In the end, of course, it did not work. Vietnam proved to be an indefensible policy. And the president would not stop lying.

And that was the summation. Moyers made no headway on the credibility issue. When he left the White House staff in December 1966, after seventeen months as press secretary, he admitted privately that the problem was worse than ever.[55] Only the president, he said, could do anything about it. But the president would not do anything about it. So that was that. Moyers said later that Johnson "was a complicated man who wanted the world to behave in a simple and straightforward way—*his* way. . . . He thought if he said something wasn't so, it wasn't so. He lived in the world's largest goldfish bowl, but [he] didn't want anyone to know what he was doing until he was good and ready to tell them. And even when they [the reporters] caught him in the act [of lying] . . . he denied it."[56] He did it his way. Dream world and all, he did it his way.

At this point, deputy press secretary Robert Fleming ("my press secretary") was gradually disappearing from the scene, like the Cheshire cat. As Moyers's successor, Johnson appointed a Texan named George Christian. In one of those coincidences that keep turning up, Warren Harding's secretary was also named George Christian. The coincidences usually involve Harding or Herbert Hoover.

Christian was Captain Bligh's last press secretary. After graduating from the University of Texas with a journalism degree, he was a reporter for the old International News Service from 1949 to 1956. From 1957 to 1966, he was executive assistant and press secretary for two Texas governors, Price Daniel and John B. Connally. He was a tall, somewhat fleshy, moon-faced man, thirty-nine years old when he became White House press secretary, and he was not given to saying very much:

Reporter: "How does the president feel about General De Gaulle's statement that the 'scandal of foreign intervention in Asia' must cease?"

Christian: "I don't have any comment on it."

Reporter: "Does the White House confirm the Mansfield statement that we are giving serious consideration to going back to the United Nations on the Vietnam problem?" (This referred to a statement by Senate Democratic leader Mike Mansfield.)

Christian: "I was asked that yesterday."

Reporter: "Are you denying it?"

Christian: "I didn't have a comment on it yesterday, and I don't have a comment on it today."

Reporter (not too hopefully): "George, can you tell us anything at all about what the president and Ambassador [Llewellyn E.] Thompson discussed? Failing that, even how long they talked?"

Christian: "No, I don't have any more information on it for you, other than the fact that they met."

Reporter: "Has the president read the statement [by a group of peace demonstrators]?"

Christian: "I don't know."

Reporter: "Is there going to be any response?"

Christian: "I don't know."[57]

The reporters called him Old Blabbermouth. At last, Lyndon Johnson had found a press secretary who suited him. Christian gave out information only when the president told him to. Even then, it seemed to cause him pain. He announced only what Johnson wanted him to announce, and not a syllable more. Stolidly and tirelessly, he declined to amplify the information. He explained the reasons things had been done only when Johnson wanted him to explain, which was hardly ever. And he never, never speculated on what might be done in the future. Christian announced almost no significant news at his briefings. However, symmetry was maintained. He answered almost no significant questions, either. Day after day, his meetings with the press were confined to routine business and housekeeping details. On controversial issues, and especially on Vietnam, Christian simply stonewalled. The term "stonewalling" is sometimes thought to have originated in the Watergate era, but it was used to describe Christian's briefings in the bleak and weary final two years of the Johnson presidency.[58]

Having said nothing publicly, Christian seldom if ever invited reporters into his office to tell them something privately. He held no background sessions to discuss important issues. Johnson, who had held scores of backgrounders himself, was now saying they had been impudences on the part of presumptuous subordinates. "I don't believe in backgrounders," he declared after Moyers left. "That's why I fired Moyers and [McGeorge] Bundy. They gave too many backgrounders."[59] He resented it when anyone resigned from his staff; his response was to bad-mouth the departed.

Christian almost certainly could have held backgrounders if he had wanted to. He had quickly become a member of the inner circle, he had Johnson's confidence, and he attended the president's weekly foreign-policy meetings with Rusk, McNamara and national security assistant Walt W. Rostow. God knows why Johnson had Christian sit in on these sessions; the press secretary acquired a lot of information, but it went no further. After Johnson left office, Christian wrote a book that contained material from the foreign policy meetings and other White House discussions.[60] But during his time as press secretary, he did not use the information as Moyers had used it. He did next to nothing to explain or defend Johnson's policies. He did not look for opportunities to inform the reporters and, through them, the public. He sought neither to educate public opinion nor to manipulate it.

There are those, predisposed to authority, who will find all this exactly as it should be. Why shouldn't a press secretary announce only what the president wants him to announce? Why should he be permitted to answer questions or amplify or explain or speculate or hold backgrounders if the president does not want him to? He is a member of the president's team; why should he be allowed to roam around the field, creating confusion and turbulence?

It is a tidy view. But there are difficulties. One problem is that a president harms himself if he gives his press secretary no leeway, no latitude. It does not help the president; it hurts him. The public comes to believe that information is being withheld. Things it has a right to know are being concealed. The nation's confidence in the president diminishes. So American presidents have to walk a tightrope. It is sometimes necessary for them to be secretive, although not nearly as often as they think. But while they are being secretive, it is imperative that they not appear to be *unduly* so. A president must give the nation a certain amount of information. He must offer a certain amount of explanation of his decisions and policies. He must submit himself to a certain amount of questioning about them. Or he must deputize someone to do these things. The usual arrangement is that the president does some of it himself, and the press secretary and other officials do the rest. At any rate, someone has to do it. If no one does it, the president is in trouble:

In June 1967, Israel and the Arab nations fought a six-day war. The attitude of the American government toward the war was of great importance and interest. The reporters at the State Department sought to find out what it was. The department's spokesman, Robert McCloskey, responded that the United States would be "neutral in thought, word and deed." McCloskey was still on the job.

All hell broke loose. The United States seemed to be abandoning its long-standing commitment to Israel. Nowadays, the roller-coaster, up-and-down relationship between the United States and Israel has become familiar, but back in 1967 it was rather new. At the White House, the reporters went to war with George Christian. Did the president endorse McCloskey's statement? Was it a change in U.S. policy? Or had McCloskey made a mistake? The reporters remembered that McCloskey had had trouble with Johnson over Vietnam two years before. The State Department spokesman had been so intrepid as to tell the truth.

Christian responded by reading a statement. However, it was not a new statement. It was a statement that Johnson had made on May 23. In it, he had said the United States would respect the territorial integrity of all Middle East nations. The May 23 statement did not deal with the question of U.S. neutrality.

The reporters pointed this out to Christian. They asked him to respond to the new situation created by McCloskey. Respect for territorial integrity did not tell them very much. Unless they could get an explanation from the White House, they would have to interpret the new statement in light of the old statement, and the old statement in light of the new statement. And where would that get them? Suppose Israel appeared to be losing the war and its territorial integrity therefore was threatened. Did "respect for territorial integrity" mean the United States would then assist Israel in some way? In that case, what about neutrality? Could the United States be neutral in "deed" and still assist Israel? The same questions applied to the Arabs, who ended up losing the war and a considerable amount of territory. But that was later. Right now, the reporters wanted the government's answers to these questions. They wanted the government's interpretation of the two statements.

There is much controversy these days over "news interpretation." The media, it is argued, are using the insidious device of interpretation to inject liberal bias into newspaper stories and TV news programs. (This disputatious subject was discussed in Chapter Three.) But working reporters and their editors or producers almost always want the government's interpretation first—if they can get it. They tried to get it from Anne Wheaton when Eisenhower had a stroke. They tried to get it on Vietnam and Watergate—and were lied to. They tried to get it when Nixon stopped repaying foreign debts in gold (oh, Lord, how they tried to get the government to explain what was going on that time). They tried to get it from Ron Nessen when Ford permitted the evacuation of 70,000 South Vietnamese on U.S. ships and helicopters in apparent defiance of Congress. They try to get it on almost every major issue.

The news media vastly prefer an *official* explanation of things, at least at the outset. Some presidents and press secretaries do not appreciate the depth of this desire and do not take full advantage of the opportunity it offers. Give them lots of information—*your* information. Give them lots of explanation—*your* explanation. Give them lots of stories to write—*your* stories. Love 'em to death. Fill their every hour. Keep them off the streets. They will not be fooled; they will know what you are doing and why you are doing it. But they will have to write the stories; that is their business. You will not be able to prevent them entirely from going out and stirring up trouble, but you do the best you can. You play the percentages.

Other presidents and press secretaries assume the reporters will simply take the official explanation and beat the government over the head with it. They will do this by picking it apart and finding fault with it, and by reporting criticisms and conflicting explanations. That is true. They will do exactly that. It is up to the government to defend its explanations; it has plenty of opportunities to do so, and plenty of people to do it. The journalists seek out—or are given—other interpretations that conflict with the official version. And there is never a shortage of criticism for them to report; criticism is the crabgrass of politics. But first the reporters want the government's explanation. They will not defend it, and they will afford others an opportunity to challenge it, but they want very much to report it.

And here they were again, this time trying to get the White House to explain McCloskey's statement. But Christian would not do this. He would not go beyond Johnson's statement of May 23. No amount of questioning or hectoring would induce him to do so. Apparently he lacked the latitude to endorse or disavow the neutrality declaration. And he lacked the imagination, the inclination or the native hue of resolution to toss around some words that might appear to reconcile the two statements.

Meanwhile, a great deal of damage was being done to the president and the administration. McCloskey's statement had been carried in midafternoon on the AP and UPI wires. It had made the late editions of afternoon newspapers and radio news bulletins. More important, the mindsets of network producers and editors of influential morning newspapers were being formed. The impression was rapidly taking hold that the United States was turning its back on Israel. Unless the White House moved quickly, no amount of explanation would prevent this impression from dominating that evening's TV news programs and the next morning's newspapers. But the White House could not move quickly, because the man on the firing line, the man who would have to provide a speedy explanation if there was going to be one, would not do so. This is what happens when the press secretary has no latitude, no leeway. The president is hurt.

The key to the unsatisfactory situation was Lyndon Johnson. He had issued a directive to all government officials not to discuss the Arab-Israeli war with the news media.[61] The order was aimed chiefly at preventing leaks of information to reporters. It did not contemplate the kind of crisis created by the neutrality statement. But it created an atmosphere in which officials were afraid to talk under any circumstances. Therefore, flexibility was lacking. When a firestorm broke out and talking became very necessary, everyone was struck mute. The Houdini in the White House had built another of his boxes from which there was no escape. It is not supposed to work that way.

There was nothing else to do; they took the firestorm to Johnson. He called Secretary of State Rusk and told him *he* could talk. Rusk hurried over to the White House. At a hastily summoned briefing—the salient characteristic of a crisis is the hastily summoned briefing—Rusk informed the reporters that neutrality did not imply indifference. The United States would not be indifferent to Israel's cause. *Voilà*, an explanation. It was not a paragon among explanations, not a textbook example. But as improvisations go, it was a journeyman job. The furor did not end immediately—things had gone too far for that. But it cooled down considerably. The only wonderment was why Christian could not have said the same thing at the outset—before so much damage had been done.

Finally, it all ended. One of the most turbulent presidencies in American history ran down. The sum was about to be calculated:

The antipoverty program. Compulsive lying. Medicare. Obsessive secrecy. Civil rights bills. Grossness in office. Air and water pollution controls. Intervention in the Dominican Republic. Education, health and housing programs. Razzle-dazzle with the budget. Social Security increases. Public distrust of the presidency. Wilderness preservation. Inflation. Urban mass-transit programs. A simplistic world view. Drug and pesticide controls. Ignorance of history. Manpower-retraining programs. Manipulation of reality. Holding the nation together after Kennedy's assassination. Vietnam. And Vietnam. And Vietnam. And Vietnam.

IX

DICK AND RON

The year was coming to an end, and there had been only five press conferences. It had been almost nineteen weeks since the last one. For a long period, there had been no questions. No questions at all. The world turned. The human condition continued to display discord, strife and variety of opinion. The United States was influential, wealthy, puissant. But more than four months had gone by without an opportunity to ask its leader about the many events that had occurred at home and abroad. The president had abolished questions. Answers, too.

The last press conference had been held on July 30, 1970. Then in December, the president emerged. Suddenly, and with fanfares. It was announced that he would meet with the reporters on December 10. Richard Nixon was going to hold a press conference. Fancy that.

This created two problems for the journalists. The first was a matter of procedure. How would they handle a press conference that was being held more than four months after the last one? They would have thirty minutes with the president. In thirty minutes, they could not possibly ask him about every major development since the end of July. At best, they could touch on only a few. They would have to leap, like the agile mountain goat, from subject to subject. They would not be able to do justice to any of them. The amount of accumulated material to be covered would prevent in-depth questioning on most issues. This presumably had occurred to Nixon.

What would the reporters do? Each of them would consider his question vitally important. Each would believe that his query cried out for a presidential response. But the questions would deal with a wide variety of subjects. So the reporters were faced with a dilemma that was not new: What kind of press conference would it be?

If it went the way press conferences usually go, it would be a superficial survey of many events and issues. However, there was another possibility. The reporters could sublimate their egos. Some of them could forgo their own questions—important and brilliantly insightful as these might be— and instead ask follow-up questions on issues raised by other reporters. Only if some of them were willing to do this could there be an intensive exploration of any subject; the term "follow-up question" is journalistic shorthand for in-depth inquiry. However, there was another however. If some of the precious thirty minutes were devoted to follow-up questions on a few issues, other subjects would have to be ignored. These, too, would be issues of interest and importance to the public. The president should be asked at least one question about them. His position should be elicited, even if only superficially. Something would be better than nothing.

That was the dilemma: quantity or quality? Which procedure would serve the public best? Which would cheat it least? Of course, if a president held frequent press conferences, the problem would be less acute. Because the intervals between news conferences would be shorter, there would not be as much material to cover. There would be more time for in-depth questioning. When reporters talk about the presidential press conference, the word they use most often is "frequency." They want the president to hold more of them. Frequency yields quality or at least gives it a fighting chance. Infrequency yields superficiality. However, it is entirely up to the president. There is no law that says he must have news conferences.

So there was another problem, a larger problem. The presidential press conference was disappearing. It was an endangered species. Franklin Roosevelt had met with reporters on an average of six times each month. Harry Truman had averaged more than three press conferences a month, Dwight Eisenhower and Lyndon Johnson two a month, John F. Kennedy almost two a month. The trend had been downward for quite a while— and then it reached Nixon. He was in office five and a half years. He held a total of thirty-nine press conferences. This meant that the average interval between them was more than two months. The questions piled up.

The presidential press conference strongly resembles the other institutions created by humans. It is not perfect. But, as noted in Chapter Two, it is one of the few mechanisms for *two-way* communication between the president and the public.

Nixon did not like two-way communication. He preferred the one-way type. He made many appearances on television; before he had been in office a full year, he had been on national TV at least fourteen times. Julian Goodman, then president of NBC, was asked to define his policy toward Nixon's repeated requests for network time. "Our attitude," said Goodman, "is the same as our attitude toward previous presidents: he can have any goddamn thing he wants."[1] But most of Nixon's television appearances were speeches. He was talking *at* people, not with them. Those who did not agree with him or believed he was saying something inaccurate, incomplete or misleading . . . well, what could they do? They could shout a question or a comment at the TV set, but Nixon did not hear. If, in frustration, they switched channels, there was Nixon again. He still did not hear. They could turn the darn thing off, or they could express themselves with whatever was at hand. Beer cans were favored. He still did not hear. But in press conferences, he heard the reporters. He could not avoid it.

At the end of 1970, however, it was evident that the press conference was in trouble. Nixon was doing it in. The reporters believed the problem was serious and urgent. Now it was about to be underscored by the first press conference in four months. What would the reporters do?

They held a meeting. By God, that showed how serious it was. Bureaucrats hold meetings; businessmen hold meetings; parents, teachers, doctors and dentists hold meetings. The meeting is the national solution. But reporters do not hold many meetings. Most of them are not especially fond of meetings. They have covered too many. They have grown calluses here and there from reporting other people's meetings. As a rule, journalists are sociable enough. They attend parties, they finance college educations for the children of bartenders and they hold professional conventions, where they successfully impersonate insurance agents. But when they are on the job, they tend to be lone wolves. It is rare for a group of working reporters to hold a meeting for the purpose of agreeing on some collective action. Their personalities and mindsets do not run in that direction.

After observing reporters during the Nixon-McGovern campaign of 1972, Timothy Crouse came to believe they could accomplish more if they were willing to cooperate. Specifically, Crouse wrote, they might have compelled Nixon to hold more press conferences. Or they might have forced his press secretary, Ron Ziegler, to give out more information at his briefings. A petition or a boycott "supported by the whole White House press corps," Crouse said, might have pressured the administration "to change its smug ways" and open up.[2] The sun might have risen in the west. The Nixon administration distrusted the news process too deeply. It could not open up.

And there was a practical objection to collective action. The reporters were keenly aware of Nixon's possible response if he found out that they had held a meeting to discuss some kind of common effort. He almost certainly *would* find out, and it would give him a perfect opportunity to cry news management. Several reporters drew attention to this possibility. I remember warning that the next press conference might go as follows: Nixon would be asked a question. Before answering, he might say something like this: "I understand that you ladies and gentlemen of the press held a meeting the other day to plan your questions. Now, it is perfectly all right if you want to do this, but I think the American people have a right to know that the news media are getting together to prearrange these press conferences. . . ." Wham. Pow. Zap. Nixon had set up the reporters as villains many times before ("You won't have Richard Nixon to kick around anymore") and he would do it many times in the future. Could he pass up a chance like this?

As things turned out, he made only an oblique reference to the meeting. He did not attack the press—that time. The reporters never knew why, although it may have been because they took precautions. With Nixon, precautions were a good idea. The reporters did not wait for him to find out about the get-together. They told him about it, through Ziegler. One of the organizers of the meeting, Stuart Loory, said later that "the one action we took . . . was to name John Osborne, who was acting chairman of the meeting, to go . . . to Ziegler and tell him what we [had] talked about. . . . That was mainly for the purpose of protecting ourselves against the charge of news management. . . ."[3] If Nixon had brought the matter up at his press conference, the reporters would at least have been able to reply that there had been no attempt at concealment.

Nixon said nothing direct that time, but that did not change the problem. If reporters act collectively, they lay themselves open to a suspicion that they are managing the news. The indictment would also charge aggravated hypocrisy. Because news management is precisely what journalists accuse the *government* of doing. They criticize almost every administration, persistently and vociferously, for trying to manipulate the news to its own advantage. Most presidents—not just Nixon—would find it hard to resist an opportunity to arraign the news media on a charge of doing the same thing. The elitist media conspiracy at work. The right wing would be ecstatic. It does not even need a meeting to discern a plot.

But despite all this—their aversion to meetings, their reluctance to work together, the fear that they might be playing into Nixon's hands— the reporters got together that one time. The decline of the presidential press conference—the threat to its continued existence—overcame their dislikes and reservations. So they held a meeting. At this point, the

Lysistrata Principle in American journalism came into play. Unanimity was lacking. Several major news organizations refused to participate. The reporters who did attend agreed informally that a couple of things should be done, but nothing was binding. There was no decision to take any formal, collective action. As a conspiracy, it was the Chicago Cubs.

Nevertheless, the meeting may have accomplished something. An atmosphere, a mood, was created. It was almost six months before this new mood produced any consequences, and it cannot be proved that they were a direct result of the December meeting. They may have been Nixon's own doing as much as anyone's. But the fact is that something unusual happened six months later.

The meeting took place on the morning of December 8, 1970, two days before Nixon's long-delayed press conference. It was organized by two reporters—Jules Witcover and Stu Loory, both of whom were then in the Washington bureau of the *Los Angeles Times*. They invited about forty reporters to have breakfast at the Washington Hotel. The purpose was to discuss what Richard Nixon was doing to the presidential press conference, and what could be done about it. Twenty-seven reporters and one "observer" showed up.

Some of those who decided not to attend were concerned that the meeting might be interpreted as a media conspiracy or as news management. The *Washington Post*'s national editor at that time, Ben Bagdikian, said it was "a kind of prearrangement and management of news [that] I don't approve of."[4] *Newsweek*'s Washington bureau chief, Mel Elfin, said his magazine traditionally had avoided meetings of this type.[5] Max Frankel, then chief of the *New York Times* Washington bureau, sent his White House reporter, Robert Semple, but only as an observer. Frankel said the *Times* was wary of a casual approach to "a very important topic."[6] Semple informed the other journalists that he was there to observe the proceedings. He said the *Times* would not be bound by any decisions that might be reached. He said he might take notes. Witcover and Loory wondered whether they should set up a press table for the *New York Times*. Droll.

In addition to Witcover and Loory, the reporters who attended the meeting, not casually, were Bruce Agnew of *Business Week*, Don Bacon of the Newhouse newspapers, Charles W. Bailey of the *Minneapolis Tribune*, Laurence Barrett and Simmons Fentress of *Time* magazine, Aldo Beckman of the *Chicago Tribune*, Frank Cormier of the Associated Press, James Deakin of the *St. Louis Post-Dispatch*, James Doyle and Garnett Horner of the *Washington Star*, Clifford Evans of RKO General, Jack Germond of the Gannett newspapers, Paul Healy of the *New York Daily*

News, Ted Knap of the Scripps-Howard newspapers, Erwin Knoll of *The Progressive* magazine, William McGaffin of the *Chicago Daily News*, Loye Miller of the Knight newspapers, Lawrence O'Rourke of the *Philadelphia Bulletin*, John Osborne of the *New Republic*, John Pierson of the *Wall Street Journal*, Dan Rather of CBS, Eugene Risher of United Press International, Thomas B. Ross of the *Chicago Sun-Times*, Martin Schram of *Newsday* and Matthew Storin of the *Boston Globe*.

It was only a moderately representative group. Very light on television and radio—Dan Rather was the only TV reporter who showed up, and Cliff Evans the only radio reporter. Otherwise, it was all print media— newspapers, magazines and wire services. And the print media had to struggle along without the *New York Times* and the *Washington Post*.

The first subject discussed was whether it was proper for a group of reporters to hold this sort of meeting. How would the White House react? How would the public react? What with all the media conspiracies floating around already? The public, it turned out, was not noticeably interested. However, the reporters spent several minutes worrying about the White House. This was foolish, but it always happens. The secret records of governments, when they come to light, are invariably crammed with agonized fears and speculations about what other governments may do. While Chamberlain and Daladier trembled and quaked over German intentions, Hitler and the German generals trembled and quaked over British and French intentions. The Americans contemplate Soviet military strength and are filled with dread; the Russians contemplate American military strength and are terrified. What is power? Power is what someone else has. No one knows what others may do, so everyone is frightened. The reporters were no exception, but after a while they pulled themselves together.

Then they got down to business. After much discussion, they reached agreement on three points they already agreed about: first, that the only way to revive the presidential press conference was for the president to hold more frequent press conferences. Second, that someone should ask Nixon at the upcoming news conference whether he intended to hold more of them (it was left charmingly vague who would do this). Third, that the reporters themselves should try to ask more follow-up questions at press conferences. "Everybody [at the meeting] was exhorting everybody else to ask follow-up questions," said Chuck Bailey of the *Minneapolis Tribune*. "That was all [it] was about."[7]

There was one more item on the agenda. By acclamation, John Osborne of the *New Republic* was designated to go to the White House and brief press secretary Ziegler on the meeting. At last, Ziegler was involved in a briefing. Osborne gave him a short account of what had taken place. Ziegler said, "Fine." And that was that.

No, not quite. Although Nixon referred only indirectly to the reporters' meeting, his director of communications was more explicit. A short time later, an article by Herb Klein appeared on the . . . for goodness' sake . . . the op-ed page of the *New York Times*. It was one of those they-say-it-wasn't-a-plot-but-we-know-better jobs. Klein, who last appeared as the guardian of Nixon's better nature, wrote that ". . . some of the reporters who were [at the meeting] took pains to say they were not part of a cabal or conspiracy and that in no way did they discuss the order or the subject matter of the questions that would be asked at the forthcoming [press] conference. Whether or not they did, the timing of the meeting did nothing to enhance press credibility."[8] Witcover and Loory then wrote a letter to the *Times*. They denied the cabal. They denied the conspiracy. As an old politician once said, they denied the allegation and they denied the alligator. It did no good.

The last words were left to literature, more or less. Allen Drury, in whose novels the conservative always gets the girl, wrote a book about the Nixon administration. Published in 1971, it was called *Courage and Hesitation*. In the book, Drury referred to the reporters' meeting: "A group of major correspondents . . . actually held a secret [sic] meeting, their ostensible purpose to arrange the sequence of questions [at Nixon's press conference], their real aim to get Dick Nixon."[9] Al wrote that all by himself.

A year later, there was another book. This one was written by James Keogh, a reporter and editor for Henry Luce at *Time* magazine in the 1950's and 1960's. Like a good many people in *Time*'s upper echelons, Keogh supported Nixon fervently. It was the anticommunism that appealed. When Nixon won the presidency, Keogh became chief of the White House's research and writing staff—in other words, chief speechwriter. He stayed for two years and then left to write a book entitled *President Nixon and the Press*. In it, Keogh was bitterly critical of the Washington press corps. He said its treatment of Nixon "dismayed and even appalled" him.[10]

The reporters' meeting, Keogh wrote, took place in an atmosphere of "'let's get him for sure this time.' . . . [Nixon] had not held a televised session with the newsmen for more than four months, and the vultures were circling ominously. . . . One of the organizers of the meeting was Stuart Loory of the *Los Angeles Times*, whose [stories] had placed him well up in the ranks of the Nixon-haters." Keogh knew what he knew. Never mind the letter, Stu.

On December 10, Nixon held the long-awaited press conference. He was asked twenty-seven questions. The reporters tried to cover the many issues that had piled up in four months—Vietnam, Cambodia, the Sontay raid, the firing of Secretary of the Interior Walter Hickel, economic problems, racial problems, the Middle East, the domestic political situation, U.S.-Soviet relations, textile import quotas and others. On some major subjects, more than one question was asked, but only three questions came close to being follow-ups that explored an earlier answer in greater depth. And none of them were follow-ups in another sense of the term; no question probed a weakness, contradiction or evasion in a previous answer. There was too much ground to cover.

At their meeting, the reporters had agreed that someone should ask Nixon to hold more frequent press conferences. However, no one had volunteered to do this. Nor was there a move to nominate anyone or to draw lots for the honor. The reporters were wary of doing anything that might be interpreted as a conspiracy to prearrange *even one question* at a presidential news conference.

Nevertheless, the issue came up. Herbert Kaplow of NBC asked Nixon whether he thought the public interest was served when four months went by without a press conference. Kaplow had not been at the meeting.

Nixon's reply defined his relationship with the Washington press corps. There was to be as little relationship as possible. He acknowledged an obligation to keep the American people informed, but he said there were many ways he could do this. Televised press conferences, he said, were only one method. There were also speeches to the nation and interviews with the anchormen of the television networks. But especially speeches. He told Kaplow: "I think the American people are entitled to see the president *and to hear his views directly and not to see him only through the press* [emphasis added]."

Perceptions differ. As Nixon saw it, he was going to do everything he could to ensure that his decisions and policies were communicated to the nation without passing through the distorting prism of the news media. He had already set up an office of communications under Herb Klein to bypass the Washington reporters. Keogh wrote later that this was done so that the administration's message would not be strained through the "political bias" of the press corps (see Chapter Seven). For the same reason, Nixon would hold as few press conferences as possible.

Keogh wrote that Nixon viewed press conferences "as only one form of communication—and a limited one at that. He did not see [them] as a place to develop or . . . enunciate important policy." At his first presidential press conference, Keogh pointed out, Nixon had said: "I do not believe that policy should be made by off-the-cuff responses in press conferences or any other kind of conferences. I think it should be made in an orderly way." Keogh added that "any fair judgment" would agree that "answering bent [biased] questions in a crowded press conference under hot television lights with 300 reporters clamoring for attention and 50 million viewers watching was not necessarily an ideal place for a president to try to outline delicate nuances of policy."[11] Speeches were better.

The reporters saw it another way. They saw it several other ways:

What "off-the-cuff responses"? Every president since Eisenhower has carefully prepared himself for his press conferences, and especially for the televised spectaculars. The rehearsals are usually longer than the press conferences themselves. The president's press secretary prepares a list of issues that are likely to come up, and the president decides on his answers in advance. Several former press secretaries have said they were able to anticipate almost all of the questions. The chances that a president will be caught off guard are slight.

And what was that song and dance about the press conference being a poor place to enunciate policy? Every president uses his news conferences to make policy announcements whenever he feels like it. The president has a variety of formats available for disclosing his programs and policies—the State of the Union address, the budget message and other messages to Congress, speeches to the nation or to various groups—and press conferences. As Mr. Teagarden sang, I choose the way that suits my means—here's what won a gal down in Noo Orleeens. The press conference, for instance, is often chosen as the vehicle for sending signals to foreign nations or to Congress.

The vast majority of questions at news conferences give the president an opportunity to restate existing policies or to amplify them, explain them, defend them, hint at changes or announce actual changes. And that is exactly what he does. The president is asked about some situation or development at home or abroad. He replies that his policy on this has already been stated. It is thus-and-so. Then if he chooses, he explains the policy further and defends it against criticism.

At Nixon's December 10 press conference, no less than fourteen of the twenty-seven questions dealt directly with administration policies and programs. In answering these questions, Nixon announced his policy on holiday cease-fires in the Vietnam war, reaffirmed his policy on bombing North Vietnam, restated the U.S. position at the Paris peace talks, said flatly he would never send American troops into Cambodia (now *there* was an enunciation of policy if ever there was one—he had already done it, but he would not do it again), said he would not change his economic policy and then hinted he might change his economic policy after all, discussed U.S. policy toward the Soviet Union and the People's Republic of China, sent a signal to Congress on trade policy and on and on and on. Several of his answers involved those "delicate nuances of policy" that Keogh said the press conference was not suited for.

Nixon said he did not believe the presidential news conference was a proper place to develop policy. If he had been challenged on this, he probably would have said that he meant policy should not be *formulated* in public. That is a perfectly defensible position; the reporters do not expect a president to go through the actual process of making policy at his press conferences. Under those hot TV lights, in front of clamoring journalists and all. But the impression Nixon left—the impression he *wanted* to leave—was that the press conference was no place to *discuss* policy once it had been formulated, no place to expound it, explain it, defend it. He wanted to leave that impression because he wanted to downgrade the press conference. He did not want to hold press conferences.

The reporters' overriding point, however, was that the presidential press conference is two-way communication. This is true despite the fact that persons who follow current events reasonably closely will find most of the questions and answers as predictable as a suburb. Build thee more prefabricated mansions, O my soul. The president's staff has anticipated most of the questions and the president has his answers ready. But, by God, questions *are* being put to him. He has to give at least some sort of answer or run the risk of appearing shifty and evasive. Some kind of dialogue is going on. Nixon, however, favored one-way communication. No questions. No challenges. Ready with the beer can?

And there is always a chance at a press conference. There is a chance that a perceptive question or a probing question will give the public an insight into the president's personality or character or his real motive for doing something. An insight the public otherwise would not have had. There is a chance that an acute question may elicit some information that otherwise would not have been disclosed. And above all, follow-up questions may explore an important subject in greater detail and greater depth. Then the press conference is truly informative, explanatory and *educational*. If there *are* follow-up questions. If there is *time* for follow-ups. If the president holds news conferences frequently enough so that the entire session does not have to be devoted to catch-up ball.

Occasionally, it happens. The December 10 press conference was not notable for follow-up questions. Nor were the four news conferences that Nixon held in the first five months of 1971. But on June 1, 1971—almost six months after the reporters' meeting—he had another one. This time there *were* follow-up questions.

There was a background to it. In May 1971, thousands of persons came to Washington to demonstrate against the Vietnam war. Some of their leaders announced that the goal of the protest was to "shut down the government." The demonstrators committed some illegal acts. These consisted chiefly of lying down on some main thoroughfares and on the bridges that connect northern Virginia and the District of Columbia. The idea was to prevent bureaucratic commuters from reaching their offices. As it turned out, the government was not shut down. Something else was. The Constitution was shut down.

The demonstrators having committed illegal acts, Washington's police force then committed illegal acts. However, the situation quickly became asymmetrical. The police committed more illegal acts than the protesters. They swept through the streets, indiscriminately gathering up thousands of persons and carting them off to makeshift prisons. Many of these persons had no connection with the demonstration. Ordinary people on their way to work—businessmen, sales clerks, physicians and even a judge—were hauled away. Spectators, bystanders and passersby were hauled away.

Between 12,000 and 15,000 people were arrested—except they were not really arrested. That was the problem. Arrest forms required by law were not filled out. Specific charges of criminal conduct, also required by law, were not brought—there having been, in thousands of cases, no criminal conduct. The right to bail was ignored. It had an authoritarian ring to it.

An assistant attorney general named William Rehnquist defended the mass detentions. He invoked the doctrine of "qualified martial law." Martial law had not been proclaimed. A state of emergency had not been proclaimed. However, Rehnquist asserted qualified martial law, whatever that was. He said the government had the authority "to protect itself and its citizens against actual violence or threat of violence." He said this authority outweighed "the normal right of any individual detained by the government to insist on specific charges of criminal conduct being promptly made against him, with the concomitant right to bail. . . ."[12] Later, Nixon appointed Rehnquist to the Supreme Court. Citizens can rest easy.

But the citizens did not rest easy. Some of them were held at a football practice field, behind a high wire fence. They were chilled by stiff winds and temperatures in the 40's. They scrounged for wood to build fires. The police used tear gas to drive them back from the fence. For most of a day, there was only one toilet for the 1,500 to 2,500 persons detained at the practice field.

Later, these and other citizens were transferred to the Washington Coliseum. There, some 3,000 persons were herded onto the concrete floor. They were forbidden to use the seats. Thirty-six hours went by without hot water or a hot meal. Bright overhead lights were left on all night. The building was cold. The concrete floor was cold. The authorities ignored repeated requests for blankets but finally supplied some in response to pleas from physicians.

Washington's jails were crowded with citizens. Thousands of them were held for periods of twenty-four hours to four or five days without being told the nature of the charges against them or given access to bail. In one cell, there were eighteen men; in another, seventeen women. Twelve persons were confined in one five-by-seven-foot cell with no water for twenty hours. In another jail, 200 detainees had to use one toilet. A physician testified later that he saw 700 to 850 persons in a cellblock at the U.S. Courthouse that had been built for a maximum of 150 prisoners. The detained persons, he said, "sat and stood in shifts. . . . The air was foul, and the temperature rose to nearly 90 degrees. . . . Many [persons] were brought to me hysterically crying because of the befouled air and were panicked because of the crowded conditions. The sense of fright and depression was rampant. . . ."[13] Under the Nixon administration, the United States came close.

When the citizens were finally brought into court, the judges dismissed the cases. They said there were no cases. They spoke of the Constitution and laws of the United States. They spoke of wrongful arrest. They freed the citizens.

Then, on June 1, Nixon held a press conference. He defended the police. He defended the mass detentions. He did not defend the Constitution.

The first question was asked by Herb Kaplow of NBC News, the reporter who had raised the issue of more frequent press conferences. In his deep voice, Kaplow now asked Nixon "whether you think the police handled [the May Day episode] properly" in light of "the broader Constitutional question."

Nixon replied that he believed the police had handled the situation correctly, "with the right combination of firmness and restraint." He said those demonstrators who conducted themselves peacefully had not been thrown in the slammer. He said their rights had been protected. Oh. Oh, my.

"But when people come in and slice tires," Nixon went on, "when they block traffic, when they make a trash bin out of Georgetown and other areas of the city, and when they terrorize innocent bystanders, they are not demonstrators, they are vandals and hoodlums and lawbreakers, and they should be treated as lawbreakers. . . . I approve the action of the police in what they did. . . . And in the event that others come [to Washington] not to demonstrate for peace but to break the peace, the police will be supported by the president and by the attorney general in stopping that kind of activity. . . ."

And that seemed to be that. Nixon had disposed of the May Day issue with one of his all-purpose homilies on law and order. Available for wakes, weddings and bar mitzvahs. He then turned to Bill Theis of the Hearst newspapers, who asked him a question about Vietnam. After that, there was another question—a good, sharp one by the good, sharp veteran Edward P. Morgan of ABC News—but it, too, dealt with a different subject. Nixon was sailing along.

Then he struck a rock. For the next question, Nixon recognized Forrest Boyd, then the White House reporter for the Mutual Broadcasting System. Boyd was a very soft-spoken man, even-tempered, dignified, gray at the temples. He was an ordained Wesleyan Methodist minister and at various times in his career had specialized in religious news. Definitely not a fire-eating journalist—but his question touched off a vigorous May Day follow-up.

Question: "Mr. President, regarding the mass arrests . . . you seem to have thought that [not] closing down the government—keeping it running, in other words—was so important that some methods such as suspending Constitutional rights [were] justified. Was it that important? Do you think it was?"

Nixon: "I think when you talk about suspending Constitutional rights that this is really an exaggeration of what was done. What we were talking about here, basically, was a situation where masses of individuals did attempt to block traffic, did attempt to stop the government. They said in advance that is what they were going to do. They tried it, and they had to be stopped. They were stopped without injuries of any significance. They were stopped, I think, with a minimum amount of force and with a great deal of patience. And I must say that I think the police showed a great deal more concern for their rights than they showed for the rights of the people of Washington."

Boyd said later that he asked a follow-up question on the May Day episode "because I thought the president hadn't dealt fully with the question as it was posed by Herb Kaplow."[14] Had not dealt fully with the question—it was a classic definition of the reason for follow-ups. It also illustrated the professionalism that is so often mistaken for journalistic elitism and liberal bias. By no stretch of the imagination could Forrest Boyd be considered a liberal elitist. He was not even a secular humanist. He was a reporter doing his job. He was trying to get an answer to a question.

Boyd's question further defined the relationship between Richard Nixon and the Washington press corps. Nixon and his people could not understand journalistic professionalism. They did not accept it—even a little bit of it. They viewed it as the Duke of Wellington viewed the Order of the Garter. The duke said the thing he liked about the Garter was that there was no damned nonsense about merit connected with it. Journalistic professionalism is imperfect, like all professionalism. Sometimes it functions and sometimes it does not. But to Nixon, it *never* functioned. The concept had no merit at all, not even occasional merit. When he read a critical story in a newspaper, Nixon's favorite comment was "Those liberal bastards are fucking me again."[15] It was *never* professionalism. It was *always* bias.

Nixon may have thought he was finished with May Day when he turned to another mild-mannered and inoffensive reporter for the next question. This reporter was the key. There had been one follow-up question, but that could have been an aberration. And although Boyd's question had shown persistence, it had not really added to the sum of human knowledge. Nixon had simply repeated his first answer. He was stonewalling. But if a *third* question were asked about May Day, what would Nixon do? If he continued to stonewall, the television audience might draw conclusions. They might not be helpful conclusions for Nixon. On the other hand, if the president said something additional, something different, it might add to human knowledge. Especially if *the reporter* took the May Day issue a step further—if his question examined another aspect of the situation. *That* might be educational. And that is what the reporter did.

His name was Jerald F. ter Horst. He was chief of the Washington bureau of the *Detroit News*. He had started in 1946 with the *Grand Rapids Press* as a cub reporter fresh from the University of Michigan. Later, he had a brief and not very happy time as press secretary for his old friend from Michigan, Jerry Ford. Ter Horst lived with his wife and four children in Alexandria, Virginia. He smoked a pipe, he was a quiet, private man and his colleagues thought highly of him. Like Forrest Boyd, he was not by any measurement a liberal elite journalist dedicated to discrediting or destroying Richard Nixon. But as he listened to what Nixon was saying about the May Day episode, he grew dissatisfied.

"When I stood up," ter Horst said afterward, "I had not intended to ask that [May Day] question . . . but listening to the answer to the previous question, I felt there was an obvious need for a further presidential explanation, and I tried to get one."[16]

Question: "Mr. President . . . if that is true [that the police showed concern for the rights of the demonstrators], then why are the courts [dismissing] so many of the cases and [releasing] so many of the people that have been arrested? If they were lawfully and properly arrested, why are the courts letting them out?"

That was a follow-up question. Beautiful phraseology. Neutral in thought, word and deed. It could be viewed two ways: Were the demonstrators being released because their constitutional rights had been violated, or were the courts at fault in releasing people who had been lawfully and properly arrested? Either way, ter Horst was moving things along. He was asking the president to explain something he had not explained in his previous answers. So he explained:

Nixon: "Because, of course, Mr. ter Horst, as you know . . . arrest does not mean that an individual is guilty. The whole constitutional system is one that provides that after arrest, an individual has an opportunity for a trial. And in the event that the evidence is not presented which will convict him, he is released. I think that proves the very point we have made."

Beautiful phraseology by all hands. Nixon's previous answer had implied that the demonstrators had been lawfully arrested. Therefore, the police must have had evidence against them. But the evidence was not presented in court, so the demonstrators were freed. The evidence must have been lost.

There now had been three questions about May Day. The crucial moment had come when ter Horst decided to scrap the question he had in mind and ask a May Day question instead. At that point, an atmosphere developed. Very suddenly, the reporters had hold of something. Nixon knew there would be more May Day questions—unless the Lysistrata Principle could be made to work. He had to find someone who would not go along with the pack.

His eyes swept the room swiftly, looking, looking, looking for a journalist who would ask him about something else. At least a dozen reporters were on their feet, waving their hands and shouting, "Mr. President!" The undignified clamor that so offended James Keogh and other orderly persons was in full and insistent cry. Democracy is rowdy. But democracy was not Nixon's problem at the moment; he had to guess which one of the rowdies might ask a non–May Day question. He missed.

He got me. When his eyes reached my side of the room, I did not wait for a go-ahead sign. He was looking at me, there was no doubt about that, but he did not nod or give any other signal. I did not wait for one. The important thing was to keep the follow-up going. If I let his eyes slide away, he might call on a reporter who would change the subject. The next question might deal with, let us say, telephone poles in Vietnam. So I dispensed with the niceties.

Question: "Mr. President . . . they are not being released on the grounds that guilt hasn't been proved. They are being released on the grounds that they weren't properly arrested."

Nixon: "It seems to me that . . . we have to look at it in terms of what the police were confronted with when those who contended they were demonstrators, but actually were lawbreakers, came into Washington.

They were confronted with what could have been a very difficult crisis. They dealt with it, it seems to me, with very great restraint and with necessary firmness. I approve of what they did, and in the event that we have similar situations in the future, I hope that we can handle those situations as well as this was handled. . . ."

In there somewhere may have been an answer to the question, which was about improper arrests. You find it.

And that was the end of *that* news process. Nixon's eyes went roving again, and this time they found a non-pack journalist. They found Sarah McClendon. His sigh of relief was almost audible. McClendon had a mindset of her very own:

Question: "Mr. President, sir, I wonder what you are going to do about the oversupply of goods in Vietnam. I understand we have enough telephone poles over there for 125 years. . . ."

The June 1 press conference will go down as a difference in perceptions. And in most cases, the difference will be due to political attitudes. The behavior of the reporters will be judged not in and of itself but in an ideological framework. It is the way of the world.

Those who agree with Nixon's view of the demonstrators and the actions of the police will perceive the May Day questions as harassment. Liberal, biased journalists were trying to hector and embarrass a conservative president. They were trying to make him look bad on national television. There was no merit in the questions and no merit in the motives. It was malign. It was destructive.

Those who disagree with Nixon's view of the demonstrators and the actions of the police will perceive the May Day questions as valuable. Independent, skeptical journalists were trying to delineate and reveal an authoritarian president. They were trying to sound an alarm on national television. There was merit in the questions and in the motives. It was a service. It was constructive.

However, the June 1 press conference can be perceived another way. The reporters were acting *professionally*. This meant they were challenging the president to explain and justify his position. They were telling him also that there was another view of the May Day situation and that this view conflicted with his view and that a substantial number of Americans held this conflicting view. The reporters were stating this other side and asking the president to respond to it. In the unlikely event that Nixon had said the mass detentions were *illegal*, if he had disavowed them, there would have been reporters who would have stated the view that they were *legal*—and would have asked him about *that* view. Ter Horst's follow-up question stated both positions; it was the critical process in capsule form.

Journalists engage in this process with *all* presidents, regardless of what political philosophy occupies the White House. It is a news process in that it seeks to elicit the president's views. And it is a critical relationship, not an adversary relationship. Some of the reporters who asked the May Day questions were liberals; others were conservatives or middle-of-the-roaders. But all of them were examining Nixon's position critically or analytically, in the light of other views, other positions, other facts, other explanations. It was not an adversarial effort to discredit or punish a president. It was professionalism. The critical relationship is an integral component of journalistic professionalism. That is the way it works.

But it does not work often enough. One introductory question, three follow-up questions—and then a question about telephone poles. The reporters did their job for a while—and then they stopped. This is a prominent characteristic of American journalism. There were more follow-up questions that cried out to be asked: Why weren't arrest forms filled out? Whatever happened to bail? Why wasn't evidence presented? Did it get lost? Was it suppressed? Or wasn't there any evidence after all? Who issued the orders to the police? What was the extent of the White House's involvement? Was there ever any real danger that the government would be shut down? What was the evidence for *that*? And as long as we are on the subject, one more question: What in the world is qualified martial law?

These questions might have shed additional light on the May Day episode. But they were not asked. However, the questions that *were* asked did produce a certain amount of information and a considerable number of insights. It was a partial thing. Journalism is a partial thing.

Under Nixon, there were two administrations in Washington. One consisted of a group of normal people led by a man who appeared to be normal. The other consisted of a group of thugs led by a man who was abnormal. It was, unhappily, the same person. Henry Kissinger resolved the contradiction. "We've got," he was quoted as saying, "a madman on our hands." [17]

There was a precedent. Lyndon Johnson was so apprehensive about what he was doing in Vietnam that he decided the Holy Ghost was visiting him in the White House at two or three in the morning to tell him it was all right. [18] Then came Richard Nixon, who told David Frost: "When the president does it, that means it is not illegal. The president's decision in that instance is one that enables [his subordinates] to carry it out without violating a law. . . ." [19] He was the only president or former president who ever publicly expressed the view that the president was above the law.

William Safire, who worked for Nixon, has spoken of the "deep, dark rage" within him. Bob Haldeman and John Ehrlichman have described Nixon's wild tantrums; Ehrlichman says they were like the "dark side of the moon." Psychiatrist David Abrahamsen evaluated Nixon as a psychopathic personality suffering from a severe character disorder. Senator Barry Goldwater said he "came as close to destroying America as any man in that office has ever done." Nixon's own doctor said he had "a death wish." Historian Henry Steele Commager called Nixon "the first dangerous and wicked president." Evangelist Billy Graham said it was demons: "I think there was definitely demon power involved."[20]

These quotes and assessments are taken from historian Fawn Brodie's monumental study of the thirty-seventh president, *Richard Nixon: The Shaping of His Character*. Brodie concluded that Nixon was "an identity failure" who had a "grandiose fantasy life." He was also a compulsive liar. Brodie describes him as a man whose lying was so frequent, so unnecessary and so obsessive that it suggested a pathological origin.

He enjoyed lying. He got his jollies that way. A conversation recounted by Ken Clawson after the resignation made it clear that Nixon had some knowledge of his condition. He understood some of the reasons. "What starts the process," he told Clawson, "are [the] laughs and slights and snubs when you are a kid. . . ." But "you can change those attitudes" if "your anger is deep enough and strong enough."

And then: "It's a piece of cake until you get to the top. You find you can't stop playing the game the way you've always played it, because it is part of you and you need it as much as an arm or a leg. So you are lean and mean and resourceful and you continue to walk on the edge of the precipice because over the years you have become fascinated by how close to the edge you can walk without losing your balance."[21] Don't forget to vote.

So, like Johnson, he was often self-revelatory. The I-didn't-have-to-demagogue-it-at-all incident was recounted in Chapter Seven. The I-am-not-a-crook episode became famous; the ultimate expression of a tormented soul that had found its way into the White House and out again.

The reporters knew about Nixon. John Osborne, one of Washington's most respected journalists, wrote near the end that his fellow reporters had the feeling that Nixon "might go bats in front of them at any time."[22] But that was when it was almost over. Did they know earlier? Yes, they did.

They did not know everything. Very few of them, for instance, knew Nixon drank heavily; that was a well-kept secret until the final days. But they knew a lot. They knew he was utterly without principle, a complete opportunist and a man with an unlimited capacity for hatred. They knew he was a demagogue, a character assassin, a defamer. They knew his war record was mostly lies. They knew his smear campaigns against Jerry Voorhis and Helen Gahagan Douglas were lies from beginning to end. ("Of course I knew Jerry Voorhis wasn't a Communist," Nixon said later. "The important thing was to win. . . ."[23]) The reporters had seen Nixon, his face contorted with rage, issue storm-trooper orders to throw hecklers out of his rallies. They had seen him, in a fury, shove his press secretary down a ramp. They knew of the 1960 incident in which he became incensed with Don Hughes, a member of his staff. Nixon was sitting in the back seat of a car, Hughes in the front. Nixon drew up both feet and began kicking the front seat furiously and repeatedly—thump, thump, thump, thump; he would not stop. The reporters knew that the Checkers speech in 1952 and the you-won't-have-Nixon-to-kick-around-anymore press conference ten years later were signs of a deeply flawed personality. They knew all these things.

And so did the American people—if they wanted to. All the information was there, in newspaper stories, magazine articles and books. But it had to be looked for. It was not widely available. It was not in *every* newspaper and *every* magazine. The early alerts about Nixon were in small magazines that were read by relatively few Americans—the *New Republic, The Progressive, Commonweal, The New Leader* and some others. There were a few early books—notably William Costello's prescient *The Facts About Nixon.* And the *New York Post* (pre-Murdoch), the *St. Louis Post-Dispatch* and Herblock in the *Washington Post* were on to Nixon almost from the beginning.

But it was hardly a national call to arms. The giant organs of American journalism did not sound deep, sonorous chords of warning about Richard Nixon. A few reporters and authors dug and probed, but the results did not achieve wide circulation in the years when Nixon was first fastening himself on the body politic. On the contrary, two well-known reporters— Kyle Palmer and Bert Andrews—were of immense assistance to Nixon in the early stages of his career. So were the influential newspapers they worked for—the *Los Angeles Times* and the *New York Herald Tribune.* In the early days, *Time* magazine and *The Saturday Evening Post* were indefatigable in Nixon's behalf. And when the "secret fund" scandal broke in 1952, imperiling Nixon's place on the Republican ticket, most of the nation's large newspapers initially tried to bury it. William Costello studied seventy-five major dailies; most of them played the story on an inside page as long as they could, five suppressed it altogether and the *Los Angeles Times* published a denial (NIXON ANSWERS

CRITICS) before printing the original disclosures.[24] But Nixon told John Dean later: "Nobody is a friend of ours; let's face it."[25] It was strange, his hatred for the press. It had done such nice things for him. However, if you hate, you hate.

And now, at last, he was president. Now the reporters would have to deal with Nixon not as Tricky Dicky but as president. And Nixon would have to deal with the press and the public not as Tricky Dicky but as president. But the presidency changes nothing. There was a feeling, long ago, that men often grew larger in the White House. George Reedy did a service in pointing out that the presidency merely intensifies the qualities a man already has—good or bad. If reality is a service.

On December 12, 1968, President-elect Nixon held his first meeting with the members of his Cabinet and their wives. Among the subjects he discussed was the news media and what to expect from them. He anticipated the worst:

> Always remember, the men and women of the news media approach this as an adversary relationship. The time will come when they will run lies about you, when the columnists and editorial writers will make you seem to be scoundrels or fools or both, and the cartoonists will depict you as ogres. Some of you wives will get up in the morning and look at the papers and start to cry. Now, don't let this get you down—don't let it defeat you. And don't try to adjust your actions to what you think will please them. Do what you believe is the right thing to do, and let the criticism roll off your back. Don't think the criticism you see or hear in one or two places is all that is getting through to the public. . . . [26]

He had the news media on his mind. But not all the media. Just "the criticism you see or hear in one or two places." So he was not talking about the 80 percent of the nation's newspapers that had supported him in the campaign. He was not talking about the *Los Angeles Times* or the *New York Herald Tribune*. When his speechwriter, James Keogh, wrote a book about the Nixon administration's relations with the media, he praised some additional publications and individuals: the *New York Daily News*, the *Chicago Tribune*, the *Christian Science Monitor*, the *Washington Star*, *Fortune* magazine, *U.S. News and World Report*, Howard K. Smith of ABC, C. L. Sulzberger of the *New York Times*, Richard L. Wilson of the Cowles publications and columnists William F. Buckley and Joseph Alsop.

So not everyone in the media was against him. Then who was it? Keogh supplied the answer. It was the *New York Times* (C. L. Sulzberger excepted), the *Washington Post,* the *Boston Globe,* the *St. Louis Post-Dispatch, Time, Newsweek,* CBS, NBC and columnists Tom Wicker, Marquis W. Childs and Jack Anderson. Let's not always see the same old faces.

Time magazine was a disappointment to its former editor. "In an earlier period," Keogh wrote, *Time* had offered "a counterpoint to . . . doctrinaire journalism." But now that Nixon was president, *Time* was displaying the same "political orthodoxy" as the others. Keogh defined these terms. Doctrinaire journalism and political orthodoxy meant that "what was deemed to be liberal [was] good and what was considered non-liberal was not good."[27] Doctrinaire journalists almost always had elite eastern backgrounds and were out of touch with Middle America. It was not Mark Childs who had graduated from the University of Iowa; it must have been Bill Buckley. The Yale thing was a cover. It was not Tom Wicker who had gone to the University of North Carolina; it was probably Joe Alsop. Groton and Harvard had the wrong alumnus.

Doctrinaire journalists practiced "slanting . . . misconception, distortion and outright error." It kept them busy. Keogh's book, based essentially on the first two years of Nixon's presidency, listed instance after instance in which he discerned anti-Nixon doctrinism in the *New York Times,* CBS and the other orthodoxians. His fundamental premise was that if a newspaper, magazine or network criticized Richard Nixon, it was biased, slanted, distorted or erroneous. Things were off to a bad start.

But on the surface it seemed things were off to a good start. Nixon's relations with the news media in the early months of his presidency were better than anyone had expected. He held his first press conference nine days after taking office, and six in his first five months. This was not the promised land—Kennedy had held twice that number and Johnson three times as many—but it was better than the reporters had anticipated. It was generally agreed that Nixon handled himself very well in these early news conferences. He was crisp, firm, by turns serious and affable—all the adjectives that journalists use when they are being given only the information the president wants to give them but at least are being given some information.

If Nixon wanted a honeymoon, the press was willing. For years, Herblock of the *Washington Post* had drawn Nixon with a heavy, ominous five o'clock shadow. Nixon was extremely sensitive about these caricatures; he said they made his daughters cry. Now Herblock drew a cartoon depicting a barbershop in which he was offering the new president a shave. It reflected a feeling on the part of many Washington journalists that they were willing to make a fresh start with Nixon. They were intensely wary. Nixon had been around a long time. So had they. But he was president now. They were willing to meet him halfway—and see what would happen.

So there was a honeymoon. Even James Keogh, the antidoctrinarian, admitted Nixon had one. In the early months of the administration, Keogh wrote, "the tone in the news media . . . was generally mild."[28] But the honeymoon varied in duration, depending on perspective. To the working reporters in the White House pressroom, and to Nixon himself, it was short. To the American people, it seemed longer. Nixon arranged this—but the media helped him. They told the public little about the news process. They still do not.

The reporters' view: Nixon held six press conferences in his first five months, but after that there was a gap of more than three months before he held another one. During this time—from June 19 to September 26, 1969—the reporters first encountered a situation that was to become extremely familiar: There was no news. Except for routine announcements and housekeeping details, there was no information—and of course, no explanations. The reporters badgered and hectored press secretary Ziegler, but it did no good. They ran into a stone wall of no-comments on Vietnam, inflation, the controversy over the nomination of Clement Haynsworth to the Supreme Court, the administration's policy on school desegregation and virtually every other issue of the day. Ziegler, as one reporter commented later, was not programmed to give out information.

The daily encounter sessions became heated. The frustration level began to rise. It reached a pre-Watergate height over developments in Southeast Asia.

On February 8, 1971, South Vietnamese troops invaded Laos, with the assistance of American air and artillery forces. The military buildup for the "incursion" into Laos was under way when Ziegler held his daily briefings on February 2 and 3. The reporters tried to find out what was going on:

Question: "Can you say whether the president [has] had any contact with Souvanna Phouma [the prime minister of Laos] in the past several days?"

Ziegler: "No, I wouldn't take that question. . . ."

Question: "Why won't you take Helen's question, Ron?"

Ziegler: "I just am not prepared to do that."

Question: "When do you expect the news blackout in Southeast Asia to be lifted . . . ?"

Ziegler: "I have no comment on that."

Question: "Ron, when the American and South Vietnamese troops entered Cambodia last April, the administration said [it] was not an invasion because it was done with the assent of the government of Cambodia. Would that definition apply also to Laos, [where] the head of the government says they have not approved any entry of foreign troops?"

Ziegler: "I am not prepared to take hypothetical questions such as you put forth, and will have no comment on it. . . ."

Question: "Ron, there is an AFP [Agence France-Presse] report . . . datelined Quang Tri which says 'Thousands of military trucks moved bumper to bumper along two highways. Along the sides of the roads, troops with full field packs and arms were also moving in uninterrupted columns. Hundreds of helicopters passed overhead. . . .' Is that story true?"

Ziegler: "As you know, Dan, we don't address that from the White House, and it would be inappropriate for us to talk about details of movements of forces. So I can't answer your question."

Question: "Could you explain to us why we have to learn from the French . . . what American soldiers are doing?"

Ziegler: "You have read a portion of a report to me, Dan. It related to movement of forces. I assume you were referring to—what forces? You didn't say, the portion that you read [didn't say]."

Question: "I don't know whose forces. If they aren't ours, I would be interested in [knowing] that as well."

Ziegler: "That goes to the thrust of my point. Anything regarding movement of [U.S.] forces within South Vietnam . . . would, of course, come from MACV [the Military Assistance Command, Vietnam]. . . ."

Question: "Ron, do you mean to say that if there is an entry into Laos, that this would be merely details of movements of forces that the White House would not address?"

Ziegler: "I don't think he raised that point in his question. You raised Laos. . . ."

Question: "That is right, but you [have been] asked several times in the last couple of days for information about possible entry into Laos. . . ."

Ziegler: "I have no information to give you from here this morning. . . ."

The next day:

Question: "Ron, this is a question that you were asked yesterday. I would like to ask it again. Has President Nixon been in touch with Prince Souvanna Phouma?"

Ziegler: "Gentlemen, I am just not prepared to get into any discussion regarding Indochina with you at this time. . . . Let me just go on deep background with you for a moment. In the questions that have come from several of you this morning, you have drawn certain assumptions. . . I obviously can't address those. But I would caution you as to some of those assumptions. . . ."

Question: ". . . Are you referring to the assumptions based on foreign press reports that there have been entries of South Vietnamese troops into Laos?"

Ziegler: "You will have to determine, without my assistance, what assumptions I was referring to."

Question: ". . . It seems a little silly to me that you won't define the assumptions we are supposed to have made. Why won't you do that? It seems nonsense."

Ziegler: "I didn't meant it to be, as you say, nonsensical. I was referring to the premises put forth in some of the questions which were remembered from previous stories, Pete. I wasn't relating it to a question that some here asked on their own."

Question: "Would you consider this question, Ron: Because of the confusion and the [news] embargo and silence and everything, which is a very distorted ball of wax, is there anything on a positive note that you can tell us . . . ?"

Ziegler: "I could probably give you some positive answers to some questions, but I can't bring one to mind yet."

Question: "I am asking you whether you can tell us . . ."

Ziegler: "I really have no information to provide you."

The public's view: The American people usually know very little about these exercises in democracy. Very little of the stonewalling and frustration in the briefing room gets through to the public. Over the years, I took many groups of college students to White House briefings. The reaction of these young people was always the same: Why, he (the press secretary) is not telling the reporters *anything*! Why doesn't he answer their questions? Why is he so evasive? They had wandered into a nontextbook world. Culture shock.

There is a stenographic transcript of the daily briefings, but it is almost never printed in newspapers. The atmosphere in the briefing room remains an in-house matter. Occasionally, when things get really bitter, a little of the flavor is reported in a few large newspapers and in the media sections of *Time* and *Newsweek*. But this type of story seldom appears in the *Muncie* (Indiana) *Star* or the *Monterey* (California) *Peninsula-Herald*. More important, the evening television news programs seldom show reporters trying by every device of cajolery, guile or insult to extract some information from the American government. In twenty-one and a half precious minutes, Rather and the other anchormen have enough difficulty covering the news itself; they cannot cover the *process* of gathering the news. So the process by which the reporters try to obtain information for the public remains largely unknown to the public, even in a media age.

I go to the White House one afternoon for a little postgraduate session with some former press secretaries, and of course I drop in to the pressroom. Nostalgia gets us all. In the *Washington Post's* cubicle, Lou Cannon is talking on the telephone. He is a medium-size man with a quizzical expression and a straggly mustache; he looks like a Welsh schoolmaster. When I leave an hour and a half later, Cannon is still on the phone. I do not hear what he is saying, but I know exactly what he is *doing*. I did the same thing for twenty-five years and you develop a feel. Ronald Reagan's press spokesman, Larry Speakes, had not been informative that day on the great budget stalemate between the president and Congress. Larry speaks, but he don't say much. So Cannon is on the phone, talking to sources at the White House and on Capitol Hill. What are the chances for a compromise? What form might it take? Any chance that Reagan will yield on tax increases, Social Security, defense spending? Have you guys started writing your own budget? What happened at today's meeting? What does Tip O'Neill say? Do you think . . . ? How about . . . ? What if . . . ?

That is the *process*. But the public, the academics who study the news media and the students who crowd the journalism schools are not greatly interested in the process. They are interested in other things: How much power do the media have? Don't they have too much? Aren't they making candidates one week and unmaking them the next? Aren't they hyping up some things and ignoring other things? Aren't the journalists overeducated snobs? Aren't they trying to foist socialism on the country? How do I get to be Bob Woodward? If I can't be Woodward, can I be Bernstein? Dan Rather's salary? Dan Rather's sweater?

And perhaps the process is not important. It is the news itself that is important, isn't it? Who cares how the reporters get it? Who cares what difficulties they encounter? So they have frustrations—so what? Every job has frustrations; let me tell you what happened at the office today. What difference does it make that the government gives out only the information it wants to give out? What difference does it make that things are concealed from the people? What difference does it make that the reporters cannot find out things that may affect the public greatly? Ah. Everything depends on how the propositions are worded. And there is one more proposition: When the American people do not know very much about the news process, it is of enormous advantage to the president.

The president's view: If there was a honeymoon with the news media, it would be short. Nixon simply did not believe it could last. And given his personality and outlook, he was correct. Only a complete psychological transformation and a rewriting of twenty years of American political history could have produced a new relationship between Nixon and the press. Divine intervention, perhaps, but the presidency itself changes nothing. There were some little gestures in the early days, but that was all they were—gestures. The fundamental faith endured, rocklike and somehow necessary and *reassuring* to Nixon: The press hated him, hated him implacably and unrelentingly, hated him as in the anathema pronounced against Spinoza—from the sole of thy foot unto the top of thy head, when thou comest in and thou goest out, in the city and in the field—had hated him from the beginning and would hate him to the end. Thanks. He needed that.

On March 30, 1971, Nixon talked with the conservative writer Allen Drury in San Clemente. They discussed many things, among them the press. Here are Nixon's words, as recorded by Drury:

> The press? . . . I probably follow the press more closely and am less affected by it than any other president. I have a very cool detachment about it. I read it basically to find out what other people are reading, so that I'll know what is being given the country and what I have to deal with when I talk to the country and try to influence people [to support] my programs. . . .
>
> I'm not like Lyndon [Johnson]. . . . The press was like a magnet to him. He'd read every single thing that was critical, he'd watch the news on TV all the time, and then he'd get mad. I never get mad. I expect I have one of the most hostile and unfair presses that any president has ever had, but I've developed a philosophical attitude about it. I developed it early. I have won all my political battles with 80 to 90 percent of the press against me. How have I done it? I ignored the press and went to the people.
>
> I have never called a publisher, never called an editor, never called a reporter, on the carpet. I don't care. And you know? . . . that's what makes 'em mad. That's what infuriates 'em. I just don't care. I just don't raise the roof with 'em. And that gets 'em. . . .

In the 1968 political battle, 80 percent of the nation's newspapers had *supported* Nixon. At least he got the percentage right. Then the original I-don't-care president continued:

> I respect the individual members of the press—some of them, particularly the older ones—who have some standards of objectivity and fairness. And the individual competence of many of the younger

ones, I respect that too, though nowadays they don't care about fairness, it's the in thing to forget objectivity and let your prejudices show. You can see it in my press conferences all the time. You read the Kennedy press conference[s] and see how soft and gentle they were with him, and then you read mine. I never get any easy questions—and I don't want any. I am quite aware that ideologically the Washington press corps doesn't agree with me. I expect it. I think the people can judge for themselves when they watch one of my press conferences. It's all there. I can tell you this . . . as long as I am in this office, the press will never irritate me, never affect me. . . . [29]

With this stoic credo, it is difficult to see how a honeymoon with the reporters was avoided. But the thing was managed somehow.

A honeymoon with the *voters*, however, was something else. Nixon wanted that. He wanted to prolong it. All modern presidents seek to circumvent the news media and pitch their message directly to the public. But more than most presidents, Nixon had a well-developed, carefully drawn plan for doing this. The basic idea was to divert the nation's attention from the news process, with its revealing insights into governmental evasion, manipulation, concealment and deception. The public's attention was to be concentrated on the president, not the process. Starting with the least important aspect—the daily briefings—the plan would work this way:

1. The press secretary's briefings. Nixon did not care what went on in the briefing room as long as the American people did not know about it, and he could be confident they would not know much. So he sent Ziegler out to the podium every day as a human punching bag, not a communicator. A nice young man with a winning smile; let the reporters beat up on him as much as they wanted to. It would not get them anywhere. He would tell them next to nothing.

For this assignment, Ronald Louis Ziegler was ideally suited. He had never held any journalistic job whatever. No primeval memories of city editors and rewrite men lurked in the inner Ziegler. And none of that damned nonsense about the public's right to know, either. He came from a different—you should pardon the expression—culture. He had been a protégé of Bob Haldeman in the Los Angeles office of the J. Walter Thompson Company. After graduating from the University of California in 1961, Ziegler worked briefly as a soap salesman. Then, in an awesomely logical progression, he went into advertising. There had also been, in his youth, a short stint as a tour guide at Disneyland. The qualifications were complete.

Ziegler was thirty years old when he became press secretary to the president. From the beginning, the reporters had no illusions about his role in the news process. They knew he was not in Nixon's inner circle (until the final days, after Haldeman and Ehrlichman resigned). They knew he took his orders from Haldeman and reported to him, not to Nixon. They knew he was a member of the "beaver patrol" (a play on "eager beaver") of young smoothies that Haldeman had brought into the White House. They knew Ziegler's subordinate status was a deliberate symbol of Nixon's disdain for journalists. They knew they would get no real information or explanations from this press secretary because he was not permitted to engage in that activity.

And yet . . . the reporters liked Ziegler personally. He was a very pleasant individual. He had a hard side ("Contrition is bullshit," the Watergate transcripts show him saying), but in the daily briefings he was usually amiably bland and blandly amiable. And he was almost the only game in town. Ehrlichman would talk to reporters, but Haldeman almost never and Nixon only on rare occasions that had all the hilarity of a root canal job. So the reporters showed up every day and Ziegler showed up every day. And every day they had a little waltz. Round and round.

2. The Office of Communications. Herb Klein's operation has already been described. He would go over the heads of the Washington reporters to get the True Word to editors and other opinion-makers around the country. This would tell *them* next to nothing also, but it would be the *administration's* next to nothing.

3. The president's press conferences. Like the press secretary's briefings, these also reveal the news process. So Nixon would hold as few of them as possible. That did not mean he would not be on television. He would be on television a lot, but it would be speeches, dramatic announcements and other one-way communication. When it came to the two-way struggle over information, the public would be spared. It would be kept as far away from the process as possible. This would help prolong the honeymoon with the voters. Ignorance is the enormous advantage. The farther they are, the harder they fall.

4. The big surprise. In this area, Nixon improved on his predecessors. Many presidents have relished the dramatic announcement. They have realized its value in focusing the nation's attention on them and their leadership. The new wrinkle in the Nixon plan was the long silence followed by the big surprise. The reporters grew accustomed to long periods in which Nixon virtually disappeared from view. There would be occasional glimpses, a quick appearance for a perfunctory speech or ceremony, and then he would vanish into his "hideaway" office. This was located in the Old Executive Office Building next to the White House. A

Nixon aide said: "He comes in in the morning and sits down in that chair [in the EOB office] and that's where he stays all during his working day."[30]

Now and then, Nixon had a televised interview with a network biggie. Now and then, conservative journalists were invited in for a chat. But except for his infrequent news conferences, the White House regulars and the press corps as a whole saw him only on rare occasions. Lyndon Johnson had sought endlessly to seduce the press, but Nixon was having none of that. He held no marathon talking-and-bragging-and-lying sessions with reporters, which was smart. But his loathing for journalists was always evident, which was dumb. He avoided his predecessor's mistakes and then made his own. This is a characteristic of presidents.

Once in a long time, Nixon would have a social get-together with the regulars. He was awkward and ill at ease in large groups—not just groups of reporters but anybody. As a result, his social encounters with the press had a certain atmosphere: I hate what I'm doing, I absolutely despise it, but I have to do it, so I'm going to grit my teeth and get it over with. Nixon was an anomaly: an introverted politician. As a conversationalist, he was unfortunate. Something usually went wrong.

During a vacation in California, the president and his wife decided to visit San Juan Capistrano, which has a mission and swallows that return to it. In a burst of conviviality, possibly because he and Pat were fond of San Juan Capistrano, Nixon invited the reporters to have lunch with them at a Mexican restaurant. At lunch, he cast around for some small talk. The restaurant was filled with plants. That would do. Nixon began to discourse enthusiastically on the beauties of nature. How refreshing it is, he said, to see real plants. How rare in an age of artificiality. You don't often find this kind of thing these days. Pat Nixon began plucking at his sleeve, trying to get his attention. Nixon paused in mid-flow. She whispered to him, audibly. Dick, she said, they're *plastic*.

During the long periods of intense privacy and presidential silence, there is no news above the routine level. Day after day, the reporters try in vain to find out what the chief executive is thinking or doing about important foreign and domestic problems. They employ every device. They resort to sarcasm. A reporter asks Ziegler: "It has been three and a half months since the president held a general news conference. I was wondering whether he planned to put these affairs on an annual basis . . . ?"[31] The press secretary replies: "We have no press conference date set." He has been saying that for weeks.

Then, suddenly, Ziegler announces that the president has requested time on the TV networks. Seldom-seen Smith emerges. He announces that he has ordered American troops into Cambodia. He announces a freeze on wages, prices and rents. He announces that his national security assistant has made a secret trip to Peking. He announces that he will intervene in the controversial case of Lieutenant William Calley. He announces his position on the controversial issue of federal aid to parochial schools. He announces that he himself will visit China. Big surprises. One-way communication. Tune in next month.

5. Attacking the media. It was not enough to bypass the reporters. They would persist in writing and broadcasting anyway. The Nixon administration also was determined to draw attention to mistakes and distortions in the news whenever they occurred. By itself, this was an entirely legitimate activity. But the Nixon people were not satisfied with merely correcting the record. They set out to convince the American people that the media were distorting the news *deliberately*. It was a conspiracy. Not just the derelictions but *the conspiracy behind them* must be exposed.

They employed a familiar device. It was the small-little-known-group-operating-in-secret device. It has been applied to plots, cabals and conspiracies, real or fancied, throughout history. It frightens people.

- They called it "a small band of network commentators and self-appointed analysts."
- They called it a "little group of men who . . . enjoy a right of instant rebuttal to every presidential [speech]."
- They called it a "small group of men, numbering perhaps no more than a dozen anchormen, commentators and executive producers."
- They called it "a tiny and closed fraternity of privileged men, elected by no one. . . ."
- They called it "a small and un-elected elite."
- They said these persons "live and work in the geographical and intellectual confines of Washington, D.C. or New York City." Sinister.
- They said these persons "read the same newspapers and draw their political and social views from the same sources." Very sinister.
- They said "the views of this fraternity do not represent the views of America." Even more sinister.
- They said the average American "knows practically nothing" about these persons. Most sinister of all.[32]

Who were the "they" who said all these things? It is often difficult to know who the "they" are who say things. But in this case it was not a mystery. The nominal "they" was the vice-president of the United States, Spiro T. Agnew. Behind Agnew was a presidential speechwriter, Patrick J. Buchanan. And behind Buchanan was Richard Nixon. A small group of men, living in Washington, D.C., drawing their political and social views from the same sources . . . But that way lies madness.

Madness aside, it was an old-fashioned power play. It went like this:

Nixon was following a certain policy in Vietnam. Some Americans agreed with this policy. Others did not. Both points of view had a right to be expressed. On November 3, 1969, Nixon delivered a nationally televised speech on Vietnam. He spoke for thirty-two minutes. The president had thirty-two minutes in which to express his point of view. After he finished, the three TV networks presented "instant analyses." For ABC, the reporters and commentators were Frank Reynolds, Tom Jarriel, John Scali, Bill Lawrence, Bob Clark, Bill Downs, Howard K. Smith and a guest commentator, elder statesman W. Averell Harriman. For NBC, they were John Chancellor, Herb Kaplow and public opinion expert Richard Scammon. For CBS, they were Dan Rather, Eric Sevareid and Marvin Kalb. Only ABC's commentary was almost as long as Nixon's speech; it ran about thirty minutes. NBC's analysis lasted about ten minutes and CBS's about eight.

In each case, the network commentators first reviewed the highlights of Nixon's speech. By proxy, this gave his point of view several additional minutes. Then the journalists analyzed the speech. They discussed the events at home and abroad that had led up to it. They reviewed the political and diplomatic backgrounds. They speculated on the possible outcome of Nixon's Vietnam policy and how the public might react to it. And then they summarized the alternative point of view on Vietnam. They stated the case for the opponents of the war. It was this that caused all the trouble.

It was freedom of speech, but never mind that. There was something worse. It was journalistic professionalism: the pursuit of facts and explanations. *Many* facts and *many* explanations. Nixon had given *his* facts and explanations. The journalists repeated those, and then they reported the facts and explanations that *differed* from his. But Nixon denied the existence of journalistic professionalism. It was not professionalism. It was bias.

And there was another thing. Freedom of choice was being offered. Some people might prefer the alternative facts and explanations relayed by the network commentators. Some of the TV journalists (although not all of them) undoubtedly hoped for this. Some of them were opposed to the war. They hoped other policies would be adopted. However, they offered a choice. The networks gave Nixon prime time in which to make his case, and then they repeated his case, before presenting a few minutes of alternatives.

But Nixon was not big on freedom of choice. Few presidents are. He wanted his version to prevail. That was in the finest tradition of the office. All presidents wish their explanations to prevail. Few of them, however, actually try to *suppress* the alternatives. Nixon tried. To do this, a power play was necessary. The objectives were simple: "Instant analysis" must be stopped. Criticism must be stopped. The critics would be stilled by being discredited. The derogatory label of elitist would be fastened upon them. The sinister aura of conspiracy would be woven around them. Agnew was sent out to do the job.

On November 13, 1969—ten days after Nixon's Vietnam speech—the vice-president addressed a regional Republican meeting in Des Moines, Iowa. His speech was the harshest attack on the news media ever expressed publicly by an American president. The fact that Agnew was the delivery vehicle was immaterial; there was no doubt who was actually speaking. Nixon's speechwriter, Pat Buchanan, had written the speech, and the president had gone over it "line by line." He added material "toughening it up" and then told Buchanan: "That really flicks the scab off, doesn't it?"[33] He talked that way.

It is amazing how words are treated in this country. The TV networks had given Nixon thirty-two minutes of prime time in which to speak *directly* to the American people on the subject of Vietnam. And they would do this many more times on many other subjects. But the people, Agnew said in Des Moines, "have the right to make up their own minds and form their own opinions . . . *without having the president's words and thoughts characterized through the prejudices of hostile critics . . .* [emphasis added]."[34]

And prejudice was what they called it when they were feeling good. On February 7, 1972, Nixon's chief of staff, Bob Haldeman, made a rare appearance on television. In an interview on NBC's *Today* show, Haldeman said: "The only conclusion you can draw is that the critics [of Nixon's Vietnam policy] are consciously aiding and abetting the enemy of the United States. . . ."[35] The Constitution defines treason as, among other things, "giving . . . aid and comfort" to an enemy of the United States.

This was a state of mind that led directly and inevitably to Watergate. However, the Watergate saga has been told so many times that it will not be repeated in this book. There were things that happened before Watergate, and they will be recounted instead. Some were public; others were behind the scenes. They were forecast in the 1968 presidential campaign, in the form of a fantasy. The truly alarming thing about the Nixon administration was that it acted out its fantasies. It made them come true.

During the 1968 campaign, a reporter named Joe McGinniss was permitted to observe Nixon's television operation from the inside. Later he wrote a book about it, with the title *The Selling of the President 1968.*

McGinniss talked to Frank Shakespeare, one of Nixon's television advisers, and Shakespeare related a fantasy:

"'Now listen to this,'" he said. "'Here's what I thought I'd do. I thought I'd go to Walter Scott [board chairman of NBC]—this would be in private, of course, just the two of us in his office—and say, here are the instances. Here are the instances where we feel you've been guilty of bias in your coverage of Nixon.

"'We are going to monitor every minute of your broadcast news, and if this kind of bias continues, and if we are elected, then you just might find yourself in Washington next year answering a few questions. And you just might find yourself having a little trouble getting some of your licenses renewed.'"

Then, McGinniss wrote, Shakespeare paused and smiled and said: "'I'm not going to do it because I'm afraid of the reaction. The press would band together and clobber us. But goddammit, I'd love to.'"[36]

However, the fantasy *was* acted out. Not precisely in that form but close enough so as to make no difference. Two days after Nixon's Vietnam speech, the chairman of the Federal Communications Commission, Dean Burch, got in touch with the networks. According to a report by the American Civil Liberties Union, Burch asked them for transcripts of their "instant analyses" of the speech.[37] Eight days later, Agnew went to Des Moines. Things were moving right along.

In Des Moines, Agnew noted pointedly that the TV networks were "a monopoly sanctioned and licensed by the government."[38] The reference to a monopoly was not true, as the growth of cable television has shown. But that was not the part that was meant to chill the blood. It was the licenses. The individual TV stations that make up a television network—the so-called affiliates—are licensed by the federal government. The FCC is the licensing agency. A license can be revoked—and there goes all that money. If a network broadcasts things that offend the government, the affiliates may grow very nervous about their licenses. It was widely believed in the television industry that pressure from the affiliates caused CBS to remove Dan Rather from the White House beat. This was denied, of course. Unfortunately, no one kept track of how many times it was denied. In Washington, Professor Galbraith has observed, nothing is true until it has been denied three times.

In any event, there is nothing in the known world that makes a network executive more jittery than menacing noises from the government about licenses. As Nixon stepped up his campaign against the media, the network generals rushed platoons, then battalions, then divisions of lawyers to the front. Broadcasts, specials and documentaries were scrutinized for anything that might offend anyone. This kind of sanitizing is a hopeless task—something always offends someone—but the lawyers do not mind. A time sheet is a time sheet. "We have," mourned CBS's Richard Salant during the crisis, "more lawyers than reporters."[39]

The fantasy-for-real continued. Shakespeare had dreamed a dream. He dreamed of monitoring network news programs for anti-Nixon bias. So they did that, too.

At the Republican National Committee in the early 1970's, an official named Craig Maurer spent much of his time watching videotapes of television news programs. He gave a plus rating to those he considered favorable to the Nixon administration. If he decided that a broadcast contained criticism or even "suggested criticism" of the administration, he gave it a minus. It was hard to please Maurer. He watched, for instance, 107 network news broadcasts dealing with the invasion of Laos by U.S. and South Vietnamese forces in February 1971. He gave ninety-one of them a minus rating. Only five got a plus. Eleven were in neither category.

Maurer's standards were rigorous. He applied eleven criteria to each broadcast, and just one of them was enough to give a program a minus. All a broadcast had to do was to state or imply that:

1. U.S. civilian or military leaders were not telling the truth about something.

2. The South Vietnamese government, army or people were weak.

3. The North Vietnamese government, army or people were strong.

4. U.S. or South Vietnamese military morale was low.

5. The invasion of Laos threatened to widen the Vietnam war.

6. The invasion of Laos was a mistaken or futile operation.

7. U.S. or South Vietnamese authorities were trying to control the news about the Laos invasion.

8. U.S. or South Vietnamese authorities were displaying poor leadership.

9. American troops in Vietnam had drug problems.

10. American troops in Vietnam had race problems.

11. Combat exposed American troops to danger, and/or war in general was dangerous or horrible. [40]

Since most of these things were true some of the time and some of them were true all of the time, it was hard for a news broadcast to escape a failing grade.

Where did the Republican National Committee get the videotapes? That is an interesting story.

In 1968, a man named Paul C. Simpson made videotapes of television coverage of that year's national conventions. Simpson, a district manager for the Metropolitan Life Insurance Company, set up an archive of TV news broadcasts in Nashville, Tennessee. It was a personal project, at his own expense. Later, the Joint University Libraries serving Vanderbilt University and two other educational institutions became interested. With Simpson's collection of videotapes as the nucleus, the nation's first permanent library of television news programs came into existence at Vanderbilt. It has been financed mostly by grants from foundations. One of the early grants—for $100,000—came from the Carthage Foundation.[41] This foundation is one of several endowed by Richard Mellon Scaife and other members of the Mellon family. The American news media have no more dedicated foe than Richard Mellon Scaife.

He is a very wealthy man. He is a descendant of Andrew Mellon, a plutocrat. The Mellon family fortune is one of the largest in the United States, resting on Gulf Oil, Alcoa, the Mellon Bank, the First Boston Corporation and other holdings past and present. Scaife's personal fortune is estimated at more than $150 million. He gave $1 million to Nixon's reelection campaign in 1972.[42] His foundations contribute about $10 million a year to conservative groups and organizations.[43] Many of the right-wing projects he supports are devoted to proving there is "liberal elitism" or "liberal bias" in the news media. Scaife holds journalists (to use the congressional phrase) in minimum high regard. Karen Rothmyer, a free-lance writer who also teaches at the Columbia University School of Journalism, once tried to interview him about his philanthropy. Rothmyer says Scaife told her: "You fucking Communist cunt, get out of here."[44] Feelings run strong.

Officials of the videotape library at Vanderbilt emphasize that it is non-partisan. Their policy is that the tapes can be viewed by anyone with a legitimate interest. Nevertheless, right-wing organizations and neoconservative political scientists have flocked to the TV archive like Moonies to Madison Square Garden. In the videotapes, they have found proof of their preconceptions, which is what we all want.

Richard Nixon's preconceptions were like that sonnet by the other Shakespeare. They were ever-fixed marks. They looked on reality and were never shaken. It was a simple matter. The news media were criticizing him. They must be stopped.

On October 17, 1969, Jeb Stuart Magruder of the White House staff wrote a memo to Bob Haldeman. The campaign against the media did not seem to be going well, and Haldeman had instructed Magruder to find out why. The problem as Magruder saw it was that the White House was complaining about specific news stories and TV broadcasts as they occurred. Magruder did not believe this individual approach was effective. He thought something broader and more comprehensive was needed.

Why, Magruder told Haldeman, in the last thirty days Nixon had sent about twenty memos to staff member Kenneth R. Cole "requesting specific action relating to . . . unfair news coverage." And that was only part of the sad story. In the same period, Magruder said, the president had sent between forty and sixty memos to other White House staffers, also asking that steps be taken against offenders in the media. Nixon, in other words, had dictated between sixty and eighty complaints against the news media in one month.[45] It was running at least two a day.

Later Nixon told Allen Drury: "I probably follow the press more closely *and am less affected by it than any other president. I have a very cool detachment about it* [emphasis added]."[46] Keep cool with Nixon.

Magruder cited memos in which Nixon had complained about broadcasts by Dan Rather of CBS, John Chancellor of NBC, Howard K. Smith of ABC and other journalists. He had asked that a letter be written to *Newsweek*, protesting its coverage of a speech he had delivered at the United Nations. In another memo, he wanted *Newsweek's* attention drawn to "the president's tremendous reception in Mississippi and last Saturday['s] Miami Dolphon [sic] football game." Pat Buchanan and other White House aides were to get in touch with various editors about various offensive stories.[47] These last instructions may have been hard to carry out. In an earlier memo, on May 19, 1969, Nixon had forbidden his staff to have any dealings with reporters and editors of the *New York Times, Washington Post* and *St. Louis Post-Dispatch*. All contacts with these newspapers, the memo said, were to be "terminated immediately."[48] The Nixon administration was very fond of the verb "terminate."

However, Magruder said all this "shotgunning" was not an effective way to "get to the media." What was needed, he said, was a systematic, across-the-board campaign that would utilize the Internal Revenue Service, the Federal Communications Commission, and the Justice Department's antitrust division. Never mind the individual complaints; go after the media as a whole.

Magruder suggested that the FCC set up an "official monitoring system" to review TV news broadcasts. He said this should be done "as soon as Dean Burch is officially on board as [FCC] chairman." Burch was a former chairman of the Republican National Committee. If the monitoring proved that the networks were biased against Nixon, there would be a legal basis for "going to the networks and make [sic] official complaints from the FCC," Magruder said. The Republican National Committee already had or soon would have a monitoring system. What it did not have was the power to revoke licenses.

The juices were flowing now. Magruder proposed that the Justice Department "investigate various media relating to antitrust violations." The Internal Revenue Service, he said, could do its well-known number on the tax returns of impertinent journalists and news organizations. The mere threat of tax audits or antitrust investigations, our Jeb concluded, "would be effective" in changing the media's views.[49] It was to be the Vietnam tactic: Get 'em by the balls, and the hearts and minds will follow.

Several months later, Magruder came up with another idea. In addition to intimidating the press, the White House should try to destroy its credibility with the public. On July 17, 1970, Magruder wrote another memo to Haldeman, with a copy to communications director Herb Klein. This one was a four-page plan for undermining public confidence in the news media. It is a wonder why they bothered, since opinion polls regularly indicate that the public does not have much confidence in the media anyway, except for brief periods after they have helped save the public from people like Nixon.

Among Magruder's new proposals were:

- The White House should "arrange for an 'expose' [of anti-Nixon bias in the media] to be written by an author such as Earl Mazo or Victor Lasky." Neither of these writers ever wrote such a book, although Lasky later produced a work arguing that Nixon was not the only president who had committed crimes. The courts are familiar with this line of defense.
- The White House should "produce a prime-time [TV] special, sponsored by private funds, that would examine the question of [media] objectivity and show how TV newsmen can structure the news by innuendo."
- The White House should "have a Senator or Representative write a public letter to the FCC suggesting the 'licensing' of individual newsmen." Not just television stations but individual journalists would be subject to licensing and therefore to the threat of license revocation.
- The White House should arrange for FCC Chairman Burch to "express concern" about the media's lack of objectivity. The White House should have the "dean of a leading graduate school of journalism . . . publicly acknowledge that press objectivity is a serious problem." The White House should arrange for articles on this subject to be planted in various publications. And so on and so forth.[50]

All of this would have been harmless, serving only as a psychological insight, if it had been confined to the writing of inventive White House memos. And, indeed, some of the antimedia proposals were quietly sidetracked by Nixon's own staff or circumvented by the federal bureaucracy.

Nevertheless, many of the fantasies came true. When they did, everyone involved denied that they were part of a White House plan. Some of them were attributed to the normal workings of government, with no antimedia motive. Others were ascribed to the activities of private citizens, again with no antimedia motive. But most of them affected news organizations that had criticized Richard Nixon.

On April 14, 1972, the Justice Department filed antitrust suits against CBS, NBC and ABC. Our Jeb had suggested this tactic in his 1969 memo, but the department said there was no White House connection. It said it had been considering an antitrust action against the networks ever since the 1950's but had held its investigation in abeyance while the FCC conducted a study. The FCC's study had been going on for eleven years, which sounded like the normal workings of government. Sometime in 1970, it was said, Justice got tired of waiting for the FCC and decided to proceed against the networks. However, nothing happened for another year and a half, which also sounded normal. But when Justice finally did move in April 1972, the networks suspected something abnormal. It looked as if the antitrust investigation had been hastily revived, without any updating. The suits used network financial data from 1967 and 1969 and cited network practices that had long since been discontinued.[51]

In its reply to the suit, CBS said: "From at least as early as October 1969 [the date of the first Magruder memo], agents of the plaintiff prepared and carried out an unlawful plan to use the power and machinery of the federal government to restrain, intimidate and inhibit criticism of the President of the United States and his appointees, in violation of the First Amendment to the Constitution. This action [the antitrust suit] was commenced in furtherance of that unlawful plan."[52]

On September 15, 1972, Nixon, Haldeman and White House counsel John Dean discussed the *Washington Post*. They were always discussing the *Washington Post*. According to the White House transcripts, this conversation went as follows:

Nixon: "That's right, the main, main thing is the *Post* is going to have damnable, damnable problems out of this one. They have a television station."

Dean: "That's right, they do."

Nixon: "And they're going to have to get it [the license] renewed."

Haldeman: "They've got a radio station, too."

Nixon: "Does that come up [for renewal] too? The point is, when does it come up?"

Dean: "I don't know. But the practice of non-licensees filing [in opposition to] licensees has certainly gotten more . . ."

Nixon: "That's right."

Dean: "More active in . . . this area."

Nixon: "And it's going to be goddamned active here."

Early in 1973, a group of Florida businessmen challenged the license renewal of Station WPLG-TV in Miami. They sought to take the station away from Post-Newsweek Stations Florida, Incorporated, a subsidiary of the Washington Post Company. At the same time, three license challenges were filed against the *Post*'s station in Jacksonville, Florida, WJXT-TV. Several of the persons involved in these efforts were friends or political allies of Nixon. Others were business associates of Nixon's Florida companion, Bebe Rebozo.

In the initial stages, some of the Jacksonville businessmen were assisted by Glenn K. Sedam, Jr., general counsel of the Committee for the Re-election of the President.[53] This committee was known acronymously as CREEP. Sedam said there was no connection between CREEP and the effort to wrest the Jacksonville station away from the *Post*. In 1973, there were thirty-four commercial TV stations in Florida. The stations owned by the *Washington Post* were the only ones whose license renewals were opposed that year.

Beginning in December 1973, the Justice Department asked the FCC to deny license renewals for television and radio stations owned by the *Milwaukee Journal*, the *St. Louis Post-Dispatch*, the *St. Louis Globe-Democrat* and the *Des Moines Register* and *Tribune*. With the exception of the *Globe-Democrat*, all of these newspapers had frequently criticized Nixon.

Justice Department officials strongly denied that the moves against these newspapers were politically motivated. They pointed out, correctly, that the department had been concerned for a long time that newspaper ownership of TV and radio stations in the same city might violate the antitrust laws. But the situation also had been quiet for a long time. The FCC noted, for instance, that the Justice Department had been aware of the media ownership arrangement in Milwaukee for eleven years and had done nothing about it. "There has been no attempt to explain your inability to tender your protest within the prescribed period . . . ," the FCC told Justice. "We have repeatedly stated that such last-minute requests . . . will be denied."[54]

The FCC, which also had done nothing for eleven years, was blaming the Justice Department for slowness. If the missiles are entrusted to the bureaucracies, there will be absolutely nothing to worry about.

But now, under Nixon, there was a sudden burst of activity. So there was a question that was much more important than red tape and official recriminations. The question was: What kind of atmosphere was being created? The Agnew speeches, the monitoring of TV news programs, the license challenges, the antitrust suits—what effect was all this having?

The networks "are damned nervous and scared," wrote Nixon aide

Charles W. Colson after a meeting with executives of NBC, CBS and ABC. "They are . . . apprehensive about us. Although they tried to disguise this, it was obvious. The harder I pressed them, the more accommodating, cordial and apologetic they became."[55]

The American Civil Liberties Union, concerned about Nixon's real-life fantasies, assigned writer Fred Powledge to look into the situation. Powledge concluded that the Nixon administration was engaged in an attack of unprecedented dimensions on the news media. It was, he said, "a massive . . . attempt to subvert the letter and the spirit of the First Amendment." Under this assault, Powledge wrote, the media had grown timid and fearful. The press, he said, was trying to "play it safe and avoid being singled out for criticism." It was censoring itself—holding back on stories that might be controversial.[56]

It seemed Nixon was winning.

But he did not win. Not exactly. It will be seen later that time is a measure of accomplishment.

X

JERRY AND RON; JIMMY AND JODY; AND RONALD, DAVID AND LARRY

Ford and Carter. The afterthought presidents, Ronnie Dugger called them.[1] Neither had a notable presidency. Neither is likely to loom large in the American chronicle. It was not entirely their fault. They inherited a traumatized nation. Their press secretaries—Ron Nessen and Jody Powell—complained bitterly that the news media seemed unable to shake off Vietnam and Watergate, and give Ford and Carter a fair chance. It was an understandable view, but the imprint of catastrophe is slow to fade. When a full realization of disaster sinks into the fabric of 200 million people, it is hard to dislodge. It was a long time before Americans forgot the Depression of the 1930's. It was the same with Vietnam and Watergate. The public had been badly burned and was wary. The reporters, intensely so.

But the Depression had been under way for three terrible years before Franklin Roosevelt took office. And yet Roosevelt, unlike Ford and Carter, was a successful president. This was primarily because he was able to practice the politics of hope. The problems of large nations are never really solved; they are only supplanted in urgency by newer problems. The modern politician does not solve problems; he may claim that he can, but each time the dilemmas defy him. So the successful president does something else. He creates an impression. It is done with mirrors. It is an impression that despite the miseries of the age, hope remains. Roosevelt did not solve or end the Depression. But he kept alive the hope that things might get better in the future. It takes a helluva politician to do this.

Ford and Carter were not. They were just politicians. Neither was forceful or inspirational. Each was handicapped by his speaking style.

The handicap was that they had no speaking style. They did little to restore the optimism and fortitude that Vietnam and Watergate had taken from the nation.

When Ford traveled around the country, the reporters noticed a pattern. The response almost always followed the same sequence. When Ford was introduced, the audience reacted enthusiastically. People were obviously curious about the new, unelected president. They wanted to see what he looked like and to hear what he had to say. Then he began to speak. The crowd quickly grew restless. People started to talk to each other. They stared into the middle distance. They shuffled their feet. At a Republican dinner in Cleveland, the reporters watched raptly as a woman at the head table gradually fell asleep during a Ford speech. That is not supposed to happen at the head table. The woman tried to stay awake. She struggled hard. She lost.

The news media were criticized severely at the time for portraying Ford as bumbling and clumsy. Somehow there was always a camera trained on him when he bumped his head on a helicopter door or stumbled as he came down the ramp of Air Force One. He was placed in the tradition of Herman A. (Germany) Schaefer, a long-ago player with the Detroit Tigers. Germany stole first base by running thereto from second, which he was occupying at the time.

On one level, it was unfair. Ford was physically well coordinated. He was a good skier and golfer. Moreover, the cameramen of Roosevelt's time had obeyed a White House order that photographs of FDR were never to show his wheelchair, and the paralysis of his legs was seldom mentioned in news stories. Kennedy's back pain and adrenal insufficiency were not concealed by the media, but they were not given great emphasis. These conditions were more serious than a tumble on a ski slope. Why the double standard for Ford?

However, there were other levels. The presidency had become imperial, and so had the media. Virtually everything a president said and did was to be written down, tape-recorded and photographed. Every offhand remark and gesture, every burp and blooper. The nation had become fixated on the presidency. The news media were responsible for much of this—but not all of it. There are always many players in the game.

The Depression and World War II had made the American presidency a colossus. Then Eisenhower, John Foster Dulles, Kennedy, Johnson, Nixon, the Cold War, brinkmanship, counterinsurgency, Guatemala, the Bay of Pigs, the Cuban missile crisis, the Dominican Republic, Vietnam, Cambodia, Chile, the CIA, nuclear arsenals, confrontations without number, summit conferences ditto—all roads led to imperialism. The president had become warmaker, peacemaker, scourge, savior, prophet and high priest to the nation.

The news media were fascinated by these Caesars. Fascinated by them personally—and later by their excesses. In consequence, the journalists grew ever more inquisitive. No more gentlemanly agreements not to write this or photograph that. It was—and is—a good thing. Imperialism was not to operate unobserved. Madness in great ones must not unwatch'd go. Frequently, however, the curiosity was trivialized. That is an invariable tendency of curiosity. Then along came Jerry Ford, an unlikely Caesar. When he tried to act imperialistically, as in the *Mayaguez* incident, it fell short of accustomed standards. But the media gave him the full imperial scrutiny anyway.

There was another level. This one had to do with Ford's qualifications to be president. From 1969 to 1973, Ford was at the White House almost every week for the regular meeting between Richard Nixon and the Republican leaders of Congress. Afterward, Senate Republican leader Everett McKinley Dirksen and House Republican leader Ford briefed the reporters. It was called the Ev and Jerry Show. But it was really the Ev Show. Dirksen was one of the juiciest hams ever set before the American public. His voice was an astounding instrument. His mind was quick, shrewd and cynical. The performance was Richard Burton in *The Maiden's Revenge*. The old stager fenced delightedly with the reporters, bathing them in a ceaseless warm flow of orotundity.

And Ford just stood there. He said nothing at all. Occasionally, a reporter would ask him a question. Out of pity, actually. If the question dealt with the day-to-day operations of the House of Representatives, the answer would be well informed. Ford knew the House. He knew every clause of every bill. But that was all he knew. If he was asked a broader question, the response evoked the French officer who had been trained only to draw up his troops in parade formation. So when the enemy attacked, he arranged his men as for a parade. Not knowing what to do, Marshal de Saxe commented, he did what he knew.

For four years, then, the reporters observed a man who was only sketchily acquainted with the nation's larger affairs—its foreign policy, its economic problems, its social conflicts, its culture. Their memory of those years had an influence when Ford became president. The reporters liked Jerry Ford. It was impossible not to. But they had known him a long time. They were patient with him, but they did not expect much of him. That is the way it turned out.

At a press conference in the Rose Garden on October 9, 1974, I asked Ford a question about the economic situation. The question involved the two basic types of inflation. One is known as demand (or demand-pull) inflation, in which demand for goods pulls up prices. The other is a wage-price spiral, in which price and wage increases chase each other. The remedies for each type are quite different. In a demand inflation, a government usually raises taxes and tries to cut government spending, to reduce purchasing power. A wage-price spiral calls for an incomes policy—jawboning appeals for voluntary wage and price restraint, wage-price guidelines or price and wage controls.

Ford's economic program was based on attacking a demand inflation. So:

Question: "Mr. President, two of your main anti-inflation proposals, the tax surcharge and cutting government spending, are intended to curb inflation by reducing demand. But many economists do not believe this is a demand inflation. They believe it is a wage-price spiral. . . . In view of that, how can the tax surcharge and the cut in government spending reduce inflation if they are directed at a kind of inflation that we don't have?"

Ford: "Let me answer that question in two parts if I might. If the federal government reduces its expenditures, and we are going to do [that] by roughly $5 billion, it makes money more easily available in the money markets of the United States so that home purchasers will have more money at a better rate of interest to borrow so they can build homes. This will stimulate the homebuilding industry and, I think, provide jobs. Now, the 5 percent surtax is only on 28 percent of the total personal income-tax payers in the United States, the people who are better able to pay these minimal amounts extra. I don't think taking away from a family who is earning $20,000 the sum of $42 a year is going to have any serious adverse impact on the purchasing power of that family."

All right. Ford may have sidestepped my question in order to plug his tax surcharge proposal. He obviously wanted to get *his* message across to the television audience—namely that the surcharge would not hurt very much and would confer benefits. That is a standard tactic, much favored by presidents. Do not answer what the *reporters* ask. Answer what *you* want to say. But it was necessary to find something out, if possible. Was it the standard tactic? Or didn't he know there were two types of inflation? So:

Question: "I am not sure we are talking about the same thing, Mr. President. I am talking about the fact that these are proposals directed at reducing demand and many economists don't think we have that kind of inflation. You are talking about stimulating homebuilding, and I am forced to repeat my question: Why are we attacking the wrong kind of inflation?"

Ford: "I respectfully disagree with you. I think, if we stimulate home-building because we are reducing federal expenditures and providing more money in the marketplace, I think we are stimulating production. And I think the people who are being taxed, or I hope will be taxed, aren't going to lose sufficiently of their earned income that they are going to cut down significantly in what they buy in the marketplace."

They had told him about the surcharge. That was what he knew. De Saxe. And being a politician, he wanted to describe the remedy as painless. Even if it was the wrong remedy. Of course, if demand remained high ("they are [not] going to cut down significantly in what they buy"), that would not cure a demand inflation. But so what? It wasn't a demand inflation anyway. Presidential press conferences are only as enlightening as the president wants them to be. Or is able to make them.

Ford was even foggier about the world outside the government. In May 1974, I presided at the annual dinner of the White House Correspondents' Association, a mass meeting. Ford, then vice-president, was the guest of honor. Nixon had arranged to be elsewhere. During the dinner, an elderly man was brought to the head table and introduced to Ford. They chatted for several minutes. After the guest moved away, Ford said something typical of his great good nature. "I always give older people more time," he told me, "because they appreciate it the most."

But the way he said it made it clear to me that he had no idea who the man was. "Well, Mr. Vice-President," I said, "that man has had a very distinguished career." I was trying to indicate that the guest fully deserved the attention Ford had given him.

"Really?" Ford said. "The name didn't mean anything to me."

There is no law that says the top officers of government must know anything about the arts and sciences of the nation. Nevertheless, Ford was then sixty years old and had been in public life twenty-five years. So I was a little surprised. "Mr. Vice-President," I said, "let me tell you a little about Bucky Fuller."

The guest was the late Buckminster Fuller, an internationally known architect, designer, author and educator. Fuller's accomplishments, writings, professorships and honors filled two thirds of a column in Who's Who. He had received forty-seven honorary doctorates. Innumerable articles about him had appeared in newspapers and magazines. He was famous as the designer of the geodesic dome and the Dymaxion House. So I tried to tell Ford something about the geodesic dome. "You know, Mr. Vice-President, the geodesic dome. You see them at international exhibitions and world fairs. Companies use them. Sports stadiums. Theaters." I was waving my hands in the air, shaping a geodesic dome. Strange behavior at the head table.

"Nope," said Ford. "Don't think I've ever heard of them."

Expectations being realistic, and Ford being amiable, his personal relations with the reporters were fairly good. When he was defeated by Jimmy Carter in 1976, the films and photographs of bumps and tumbles had relatively little to do with it. Ford was beaten by other things. The Nixon pardon cost him dearly among independent voters and even more among outraged Republicans who had felt profoundly betrayed by the conspirator. And Ford, overruling some of his advisers, refused to do anything much to attract black voters; if he had cut just a little into Carter's big majorities among blacks, he might have won. Lastly, there was the Poland-is-not-dominated-by-the-Soviet-Union blunder in his debate with Carter. That was Germany Schaefer all right. And it was on national television. But it was Ford, not the media, who stole first base.

Things were less amiable when it came to Ford's press secretary, Ronald Harold Nessen. No presidential press secretary achieves a benign relationship with the White House reporters. If he did, neither side would be doing its job. However, Nessen's dealings with the journalists were unusually difficult. There were personality conflicts. There were credibility problems. Respect was lacking. Nessen accused the reporters of "blind, mindless, irrational suspicion and cynicism and distrust." He said in effect that they were still operating as if Nixon were president. He threatened to discontinue his daily briefings unless the press shaped up. "This president [Ford] is an honest man, and he's a man of integrity," Nessen said. "And as press secretary, I have kept the promise I made on the first day I took this job [a promise not to lie to the reporters]."[2]

By this time, however, the reporters had decided that the essence of Nessence was Ziegler. The White House press operation under Nessen remained blandly secretive and deceptive. Nessen was responsible for more of the journalistic "suspicion and cynicism and distrust" than Ford.

In the fall of 1976, Ford was running for a full term. On September 13, he signed a bill at a public ceremony in the Rose Garden. The ceremony was arranged so as to attract maximum news coverage. Television cameras were emplaced. Reporters were welcomed. Dozens of legislators and other spectators were assembled, to emphasize the power and prestige of the incumbent.

The bill, as it happened, was known as the Government in the Sunshine Act. It was intended to open the proceedings of federal regulatory agencies to the public. This gave the president an opportunity to speak about democracy. A contrast with Nixon was implied. "In a democracy," Ford declared, "the public has a right to know not only what the government decides but why and by what process." That was nice.

The day before, however, Ford had signed another bill. This signing took place in private. It was not on the president's public schedule. Nessen mentioned it in his briefing, but he was very casual about it. He tossed it off. The president, he said, "had staff meetings. He appeared on the 'Today' show. He signed this bill removing the emergency."

But a reporter had encountered Senator Frank Church of Idaho after the bill-signing. Church told him it was one of the most important pieces of legislation he had worked on in his twenty years in the Senate. Another reporter obtained the provisions of the bill. He found that it repealed four declarations of national emergency dating back to 1933. It revoked about 470 laws conferring emergency powers on the president. Among them were authority to declare martial law, seize property, seize all means of transportation, restrict travel and control industrial production.

To sign this bill in public, with the reporters and television cameras recording the event, might have made the presidency seem a little less powerful, a little less impressive. The following exchange then took place between the reporters and the press secretary:

Reporter: "On that bill-signing, why was that not on the [public] schedule?"

Nessen: "It was a private bill-signing. . . ."

Reporter (after reciting the provisions of the bill): "And did you not think that was a major bill-signing?"

Nessen: "It was decided to sign the bill privately."

Reporter: "The other day, the president signed with considerable fanfare . . . a bill affecting one relatively small river in North Carolina. . . . This bill today, by any common-sense definition, is a good deal more important to the nation than that. Will you tell us what the factors were in the decision . . . to have this signed privately?"

Nessen: "I can't. I really can't."

Reporter: "What we would like to know is what were the considerations that led to this bill being signed on a private basis?"

Nessen: "I think this is an internal White House matter that probably ought to stay an internal White House matter."

In the Johnson and Nixon administrations, this kind of stonewalling had gone on day after day. Nessen complained that the reporters were still nursing a Vietnam-Watergate hangover. Oh, Bloody Mary, it was worse than that. The reporters now had *two* hangovers. There was second-generation stonewalling:

Negotiations between the Ford Motor Company and the United Automobile Workers broke down. Union officials said a strike against the nation's second-largest automobile company appeared certain. That in turn raised the possibility of a nationwide auto strike.

Reporter: "Is the president concerned that it [a Ford strike] could hurt the economy?"

Nessen: "I think since negotiations are still going on . . . I don't think it is proper to talk about what would happen if there were a strike."

Reporter: "Do you know how the White House views this [possible] strike and what it thinks the impact will be?"

Nessen: "I said I would check to see if the Economic Policy Board has done any work on the possible impact. . . ."

Reporter: "In other words, you don't know what the White House position, the White House view, the White House preparation, the White House finding, the White House study, the White House conclusion is on the possibility of a nationwide automobile strike?"

Nessen: "I said I did not know whether the Economic Policy Board has done any work in this area."

The reporters had concluded, moreover, that Nessen's press-agentry on behalf of Jerry Ford was abnormally blatant. The journalists expect the press secretary to be a salesman for his boss; they are accustomed to it. But there are ways and ways. Nessen's stuff was egregious. Transparent, too. In a book that he wrote later, he said he told Ford at the outset that he would not be "a huckster for his programs." Nessen said he believed that "the press secretary's job . . . was to announce the president's decisions, and why and how he had reached them. But I didn't think I could be a salesman."[3]

High instincts, before which our mortal nature did tremble like a guilty thing surprised. Nessen had been a reporter for NBC. After a few days as press secretary, he wrote later, "I was surprised by how quickly I was shifting my loyalties and my attitudes."[4] His briefings were notably short on why and how and notably long on salesmanship. He wanted Jerry Ford elected to a full term. He was not subtle about it. His masterpiece— the Vladivostok commercial—was recounted in Chapter Two.

However, the curtain rose on sincerity. On the day he became press secretary, Nessen told the reporters: "I will never knowingly lie to the White House press corps. I will never knowingly mislead the White House press corps, and I think if I ever do, you would be justified in questioning my continued usefulness in this job."[5] This surprised the reporters, especially the older hands. They thought Nessen was naïve to make this promise, since he was certain to break it and certain to be caught. John Herbers of the *New York Times* observed that an experienced government press officer would never have made such a statement, "because they know there are times they are required to mislead the press."[6]

But Nessen wanted to present a quick, sharp contrast to the Nixon era. So a few days later, he again surprised the reporters. He spoke on the record about the technique that government spokesmen use to confirm a news story without appearing to do so. "You know the code," Nessen said. "I say I am not able to confirm or deny [the story]. . . . I am not going to lie to you. You know the code."[7] Then on April 23, 1976,

Nessen took part in a symposium at the University of Texas. During the discussion, he stated: "I have not ever been asked to lie since I have been the press secretary."[8]

Curtains go up. And then they go down. After Ford was defeated, Nessen wrote a book. In it, he told of encountering several reporters just after he had agreed to become press secretary. Nessen said the reporters had "put two and two together and asked me if I was going to be the new press secretary. 'Not that I know of,' I lied." A few pages later, he admitted that he had lied to the press about how much time Ford had spent with Nixon when he visited the former president in the hospital.[9]

However, this was small stuff. There were grounds more relevant. There was the seven-day coverup of Ford's meeting with former Secretary of the Treasury John B. Connally. Nessen said the meeting had slipped his mind. There were several days of fancy footwork over a reported change in U.S. policy on the use of nuclear weapons. There was more heel-and-toe on the delay in releasing the Rockefeller report on the CIA and on the related question of how much information the White House would furnish to the Senate committee investigating American intelligence operations.

And then there was the secret war with Henry Kissinger. Intrigues and dangers with skillful Lone Rangers. Press secretaries should not do this. The reporters find out about it. Then the White House spokesman is seen as a conspirator. No one expects a conspirator to tell the truth about anything.

For a time after Ford became president, Kissinger continued to serve as both secretary of state and presidential national security assistant. But on April 9, 1975, Bob Schieffer of CBS reported that a backstage effort was under way to take the national security post away from Kissinger. White House sources told other reporters, including myself, that presidential aides Donald Rumsfeld, Robert Hartmann and Nessen were trying to put "a little open space" between Ford and Kissinger.

Schieffer's story created a flap. The reporters were told that Nessen had sent a memo to Kissinger in which he denied that he was the source of the CBS story. He said also that he had located the source. It was a person in his office. Nessen said he had taken "appropriate action" against this person. At the same time, it was announced that Nessen had dismissed an assistant press secretary named Louis Thompson. However, Nessen denied that Thompson had been fired to appease Kissinger, who in those days required a lot of appeasing. Nessen said Thompson had completed the administrative duties for which he had been hired.

How did Thompson get into this? Sir, I don't even *know* your wife. Both Thompson and Schieffer flatly denied that Thompson had been the

source of the CBS story. Nessen said, lastly, that the story had "no relationship to anything that is going on in the White House."

It did not make all that much difference whether Nessen had been the
source of the story. Or Thompson. Or someone else. It was that last
sentence that tore it. No relationship to anything that was going on at the
White House? Too many reporters had been told by too many people that
it *was* going on. Nessen was blandly denying what the reporters had every
reason to believe was true. Their intelligence was being insulted. They
were supposed to be so dumb they would *believe* the denial. It happens all
the time. It is one of the least appetizing aspects of the job. But it has
consequences. Nessen's credibility with many White House reporters
vanished at that briefing.

A few days later, the press secretary was so incautious as to begin a reply
to a question by saying: "To tell you the truth . . ." The reporters burst
into applause. Reporters know how to applaud sarcastically.

Jimmy Carter. The many sides of Jimmy Carter. There is not enough
space here to discuss them in detail. He was ambitious, tireless, shifty,
self-righteous, self-controlled, intelligent and a great many other things.
Bill Pope, an early Carter strategist, once said: "He is a most complicated
man." [10] James Wooten of the *New York Times*, one of the reporters who
knew him best and studied him most closely, wrote finally of Carter: "It
was so damned hard to bracket the man. . . . He was a quicksilver bubble,
a living, breathing, grinning paradox, maddening for those who tried to
define him." [11]

At the outset, there was one certainty. The Jimmy Carter who wrested
the 1976 Democratic nomination from the party establishment was an
extremely skillful politician. He had decided, Wooten wrote, that "the
best candidate is the candidate who adapts himself to the instincts of the
voters within the specific context of the campaign moment." [12] Opportunism has never been described more delicately.

Emotionally, there was only one issue in 1976: Watergate. Carter
grasped this issue more surely than any other candidate. Not the details;
everyone knew those. The *psychology*. The betrayal. The shock of the
betrayal. So "the essence of his candidacy was the projection of an honest, straight-forward, candid man," Wooten wrote. "He cornered the
trust market, and he cornered it early, and once he had, [the election] was
never really in doubt, so deep was the country's thirst for someone—
anyone—it could trust." [13]

"I will never lie to you or make a misleading statement," Carter told
the voters. He said it again and again. "If I ever lie to you, if I ever
mislead you . . . then don't vote for me, because I won't be worthy of

your vote if I'm not worthy of your trust."[14] This kind of promise is even more dangerous for presidential candidates than for press secretaries. However, there was the specific context of the campaign moment.

Nor is there enough space to examine why Carter's presidency was not successful. There were many reasons. He believed one of the most unstable and unreliable governments in the world when it said it could guarantee the safety of U.S. embassy personnel in Iran. He considered Congress a basket case, so he and his staff never learned how to work with the legislators. That was not sensible. Congress may *be* a basket case, but the president has to put his case in that basket. And on and on. But one reason was basic. There is a difference between the political process and the governmental process. One consists of getting nominated and elected. The other consists of governing the nation. "Jimmy Carter," wrote reporters Jack Germond and Jules Witcover, "never managed to convey the image of optimism and confidence that Americans seem to want in a president."[15]

Carter was an engineer by training. A technocrat. The central feature of the technological temperament is the belief that problems can be solved. Define them, study them, solve them. Progress ensues. Carter came into office believing that the immense, adamantine problems of a large nation could be solved. He worked very hard, and he achieved some successes, notably the Middle East peace agreement. But the economic problem, the energy problem, the Iranian hostage problem and others defied him. When these difficulties would not yield, his temperament prevented him from employing the alternative: the politics of hope. He had to instill a communal spirit in the face of adversity. He had to encourage people and make them feel that things could get better. He had to foment inspiration. He could not do this.

Charles Kirbo, an Atlanta attorney who knew Carter very well and was one of his most trusted advisers, once said: "There are two things that Jimmy Carter hates. He hates making a mistake, and he hates admitting it."[16] But there was this other thing called the news process. During the 1976 campaign, and later in the White House, the reporters sometimes wrote about Carter's mistakes and failures. That was very bad.

The problem was compounded by Carter's self-righteousness. Those who disagreed with him or criticized him were benighted. Those who caught him in mistakes, evasions or contradictions were forsaken by God. Wooten quoted one of Carter's political opponents in Georgia: "He was always so right about everything. Always so goddamned right, and righteous. . . . If you happened to agree with him, he thought you were one of God's chosen tribe—but if you didn't, you were automatically in league with the devil himself, and probably a whoremonger and a child molester to boot. I tried to like him and tried to work with him for a while until I figured out that I'd never be able to disagree with him without him taking out after me like an avenging angel. He was righteous all right. Too goddamned righteous." [17] Wooten wrote that, to Carter, "the very suggestion" that he occasionally engaged in political equivocation "was blasphemy." [18]

Carter was not a limousine liberal. As a matter of fact, those were the people he had defeated to win the nomination. He was something different. Although he portrayed himself as a homespun farmer, he belonged to a new class that has risen in the South and Southwest: the formerly poor now become affluent but retaining a religious fundamentalism of the utmost rigidity and militancy. They are the Cadillac Calvinists.

In 1979, after the Tokyo economic summit conference, Carter went to South Korea for a brief meeting with its dictator, Park Chung Hee. White House spokesmen said the two leaders discussed Southeast Asian problems and other weighty matters. A short time after his return, Carter flew to Louisville, Kentucky, to inspect new developments in the coal industry. On the flight back to Washington, he told a group of legislators and coal industry officials what he and Park had really talked about. The president said he had spent much of the time attempting to convert Park to Christianity. "I almost had him," Carter said proudly. "He was down on his knees praying with me." Asked whether he thought Park would be born again, Carter replied: "It's in the hands of God." Oxenstierna was right. After a lifetime in European statecraft, Count Axel Gustafsson Oxenstierna wrote a letter to his son. "My son, my son," he said, "if you only knew with what little wisdom the world is governed."

Dost thou think, because thou art virtuous, there shall be no more cakes and ale? During the New Hampshire primary campaign, Carter and a reporter were having lunch. The reporter questioned something Carter told him. "That's hard to believe," he said.

"Carter stared at the reporter. . . ." Wooten wrote. "His voice was almost a whisper. 'Listen,' he hissed. 'I'm not a liar. You get that into your head. I'm not a liar.' He stalked away from the table and out of the restaurant, still hungry and mad as hell." [19] No cakes. No ale.

Virtue was further outraged when a sequence of statements indicated that Carter had said contradictory things for political purposes. "If some Iowans thought they had heard him say that he opposed a Constitutional amendment banning abortion, and others thought they heard him support such a move, it was only because he was misunderstood . . . ," Wooten wrote. "If hundreds of voters thought they heard him say he would [eliminate] the home mortgage interest deduction . . . that was another misunderstanding."[20]

Reporters are very good at keeping track of earlier statements that are contradicted by later statements. They believe this adds to the public's knowledge of candidates and issues in a campaign. They believe it is equally valuable to recognize the unfulfilled promises and altered positions of politicians once they are in office.

Is this fair? Does it serve any useful purpose? If the problems are so hard to solve, what good does it do to recall the pledges that they *would* be solved? Does this not make it more difficult for leaders to govern? Of course they made promises that could not be kept. Of course they said different things in different places. They had to do these things in order to get elected. But now they must govern. They must try to cope with obstinate problems and irreconcilable realities. They need all the help they can get. Does it help when the journalists rake up the blemishes of the past? The journalists have only one answer. They offer it in this instance and in many others: Would you prefer *not* to know? Would it be better if you did not? Would it be better to have *no* discussion? But if it is better to have a discussion, then the unfulfilled pledges and altered positions are part of that discussion.

Carter, however, saw it another way. Differing perceptions again. "The problem," he said, "is that reporters like to take little snippets of what I say, and then compare them to little snippets of what I've said before, and [then] make something of it."[21] Exactly. Reporters do this frequently. But Carter then raised an important point: "We're discussing large, complex, complicated issues in this campaign, and it isn't fair to me or to the voters to treat them in little snippets like that."[22]

It was a legitimate point, and it comes up often. Were the reporters emphasizing the personal and the trivial? Even worse, were they quoting words out of context to prove contradictions? And worst of all, were they neglecting the broad, significant issues of the campaign, in favor of snippets?

The coverage of issues is subject to perpetual argument between politicians and journalists. Carter stated the view of almost all candidates for office. They wish to have their positions on the issues reported. But they also wish to have their views reported in *their* context, which is the context of a given moment. They want the voters in Detroit to accept the position they state in Detroit today, just as they wanted the voters in Dallas to accept the contradictory position they stated in Dallas yesterday. They have an election to win, and it is a large country, with many differing opinions. Therefore, the candidate wishes to have his positions reported *uncritically*. He wishes to have them reported without reference to the past and without reference to conflicting views. When the journalists report his positions *critically*—that is, in the context of other things he has said in other places at other times, or in the context of opposing views or contradictory facts—the candidate complains that the news media are not covering the issues. It is true. The media are not covering the issues *as the candidate defines them.* His definition customarily resembles Barabas's reply to the charge of fornication: "But that was in another country; and besides, the wench is dead."

Some politicians are quite serious about the issues in a campaign. They are called issue-oriented candidates and usually lose. Adlai Stevenson in 1952 and 1956 and George McGovern in 1972 were contemporary examples. To most candidates, however, media coverage of "issues" actually means constant, uncritical coverage of themselves and their campaigns. The candidate's basic speech, mentioned in Chapter Four, has been carefully crafted for maximum appeal and minimum offense. It has been designed to fuzz over controversial issues. So the candidate would not object if the news media reported the basic speech again and again, in every shopping center and at every rally, *ad verbum, ad summum, ad infinitum, ad nauseam*—but never *ad meliora vertamur* (let us turn to better things). He would be happy if the media reported every handshake, every endorsement, every immense turnout, every poll favorable to him and every discomfiture suffered by his opponent. He does not demur if the media actually report the issues—*as long as the issues are going his way.* What he does find objectionable is coverage of the issues when they are *not* going his way. This pattern continues in the presidency.

Nevertheless, no aspect of a presidential campaign troubles news organizations more than the question of whether they are covering the issues adequately and responsibly. They begin with a high resolve. This time, by God, no one is going to say we are neglecting the issues. All hands are exhorted to focus on the issues. Long articles are printed, examining the major issues in depth. Some newspapers have begun running the full texts of the basic speeches at various times during the campaign, as refresher courses. This does not add much to the sum of human knowledge. However, it is the candidates' sum. Now let 'em complain.

But all these efforts notwithstanding, the problem of covering the issues continues to bedevil the news media. How could it be otherwise? Those 120-word TV standups. Those 22-minute prime-time newscasts. Those 400-word wire-service stories. That small number of quality newspapers. Considering their resources of money and personnel, there is no doubt that the news media could do a much better job of reporting and explaining national and international issues. The sin of incompleteness was discussed in Chapter Three. It has now reached Chapter Ten and has not improved.

Nor is there any doubt that American journalism, with a few prominent exceptions, is incorrigibly superficial. The media focus lovingly on the momentary, the transitory and the gossipy. They deal in instant celebrities, puerile personalities and honest-to-God nuts. They are obsessed with fads and fripperies. And they have an irresistible impulse to treat everything as a fight. The issues *are* reported, and often they are reported extensively. Chapter Three recounted TV's coverage of the Iranian hostage issue, Chapter Eight the coverage of Vietnam. The unemployment issue, the inflation issue, the nuclear arms race—all these and many more are reported and examined. However, there is a strong tendency to portray the problems more as fights than as problems.

Of course, that is what they are. A presidential campaign is a *fight*. The candidates are not strolling about in olive groves debating the nature of the infinite. They are brawling. It becomes necessary to cover the battle. The administration and Congress and the political parties and special-interest groups *fight* over the proposed solutions to problems. It is necessary to cover the quarrels. But the news media so relish a fight that they often fail to make it clear what the fight is about. The substance of the problem is frequently under-covered, and instead a running score of victors and vanquished is offered. It is mostly Lear: "So we'll . . . hear poor rogues talk of court news . . . Who loses and who wins, who's in, who's out."

Another factor intrudes. When they are unemployed in large numbers or face some other grave emergency, the American people become very aware of that specific issue. In the absence of clear disaster, however, the majority of Americans have only a faint interest in national and international affairs. At least, this appears to be the case when their knowledge of the participants and details is measured. After Franklin Roosevelt died and Harry Truman became president, the United States was without a vice-president for more than three years. It might have been thought that interest in the subject would have developed among the general populace. In 1948, Truman and his running mate were elected to a full term. But public opinion polls showed that only one third of adult Americans could identify the new vice-president. The envelope, please.

The situation does not seem to have changed. In 1981, the *Washington Post*–ABC News poll showed that only 25 percent of adult Americans knew that the Republicans had a majority in the Senate and the Democrats were in the majority in the House. The Reagan administration was devoting considerable attention to the small nation of El Salvador. But only 25 percent of adult Americans knew where El Salvador was. One person said it was "in Louisiana, near Baton Rouge." Fifty percent of adult citizens did not know that the United States and Russia were the nations involved in negotiations to limit nuclear weapons. Simply did not know it. Another 13 percent gave a wrong answer. Fifty-three percent did not know whether the United States or Russia was a member of the NATO alliance. Only 30 percent of the respondents answered both questions correctly. Ah, recalling Bismarck, but that 30 percent rules the United States. Barry Sussman, director of polling for the *Washington Post*, wrote an article about the results of the surveys. "Few Americans," he said, "seem to know anything at all."[23] He sounded sad.

Two other points need to be made about the media's coverage of "issues." One concerns timing. In a presidential campaign, the journalists often are accused of neglecting an issue that they have been writing about for months or years before the campaign begins. Information about the issue has been widely disseminated long before the campaign gets under way. The background, the facts, figures, details and latest developments have been extensively reported, together with the proposed solutions and the differences of opinion over them. Barring unexpected events, the fact that many millions of Americans were out of work in 1982 and 1983 will be a major issue in the 1984 presidential contest. Newspapers, newsmagazines and TV networks will have been covering the unemployment issue for at least three years *before* the campaign. But in one way or another, their coverage of this issue is almost certain to be criticized *during* the campaign. That is the nature of things. It has little to do with the news media. It has to do with *politics*. The media's presumed neglect of issues in a campaign is a political tactic. It is used by a candidate if it is to his advantage. There often is political benefit in attacking the news media. It distracts attention from other things. And there is publicity in it, because the media report attacks upon themselves. They have to. It is news, too. *Quelle politesse.*

The other point is semantic. What are "issues"? They are not confined to political, economic and social problems. People are accustomed to thinking of issues in those terms, and that is fine as far as it goes. But human beings lead nations. Humans deal with the problems and disputes, well or badly, for good or ill. So the character and behavior of a candidate for the presidency—his personality and the way he conducts his campaign—also can be issues. Sometimes they are the most important issues. They should be observed closely and reported thoroughly. The candidate may be ignorant. He may be intellectually ill equipped. He may be irresponsible or unprincipled. He may be a chronic liar, equivocator, demagogue or egomaniac. Some candidates achieve combinations of these qualities. Therefore, the reporters are correct when they treat the candidate's character and conduct as issues. They are derelict when they fail to do so. This was the basic flaw in Carter's "snippets" argument. In Richard Nixon's many campaigns, the central issue never should have been anything but Nixon. Instead, the press let him get away with calling other things issues.

However, none of these considerations—the fact that issues are also fights, the fact that many issues receive continuing coverage, the fact that many people refuse to pay attention and therefore remain steadfastly ignorant of the issues and the fact that the persona of the candidate is often an issue—none of these things absolve the news media. They are under an inescapable obligation to cover the issues. And to cover them *as issues*. They cover the substance as well as the fights. They must examine problems continuously and comprehensively. Most especially, they cannot invoke the public's indifference as an excuse for neglecting issues or reporting them sketchily. Drop it down the well, boys. It may splash sometime.

Nonsense. All nonsense. And special pleading, too. The news media perform no such heroics. Oh, there are some exceptions, but most journalists and news organizations are superficial and sensationalist. Give 'em a good fight, a juicy scandal or a colorful personality—and preferably one who gets into trouble. Those are what they *really* crave. That is the view of most presidents and politicians, many professors and legions of ordinary citizens.

It was Jimmy Carter's view. It determined his attitude toward the reporters. It determined his attitude toward the news process. If there was one theme that dominated his press relations, it was Carter's belief that the news media were not interested in serious discussion of the issues—*as he defined the issues.*

Carter was not Nixon. He did not abominate the news process so intensely that he tried to destroy it. But he disliked it deeply. "He detested the process," wrote James Wooten. He "positively loathed it—all those questions about his motives and his positions. . . . The vein in his right temple began to throb at every press conference. . . ."[24] So there was the self-righteousness problem as well. There was the Calvinist problem. "The souls of the righteous are in the hand of God," saith the Apocrypha, "and there shall no torment touch them." But here were tormentors! All those questions! Who gave them the *right?*

Nevertheless, there was a honeymoon. Carter was reviving the presidential press conference—at least to the extent of two a month. He was reasonably accessible to journalists. Not a good old buddy; it was clear that Jimmy Carter was never really going to be at ease with scribblers. But it was a vast improvement over Nixon. Howard Hughes would have been a vast improvement over Nixon.

During the honeymoon, Carter's press relations generally got good marks from students of the media and from the reporters themselves. Lewis Wolfson, director of the graduate journalism program at American University, wrote that Carter had "built up as solid a relationship with reporters as any recent president has had."[25] Lawrence O'Rourke, then president of the White House Correspondents' Association, said Carter was "making news, holding press conferences and keeping the press busy." O'Rourke praised Carter's press secretary, Jody Powell. He said Powell had been "more impressive than I had anticipated."[26] Ann Compton, covering the White House for ABC, said: "We have a normal marriage going on now. Jody Powell has what Ron Nessen didn't have—our respect."[27]

Carter's press secretary, in those early days, was a distinct asset. Joseph Lester Powell, Jr.—he was known as Jody because he had "two or three dozen relatives named Joseph"—was thirty-three years old when he became White House spokesman. He was born in Cordele, Georgia, which is about thirty-five miles from Plains and has more frills. After graduating from Georgia State University, he worked for a while for an insurance company, but he did not like that at all. So he enrolled in Emory University, aiming for a Ph.D. in political science. While researching the 1966 Georgia Democratic primary, Powell read about Jimmy Carter. Impressed by Carter's nonracist campaign that year, he volunteered to work in his 1970 drive for the governorship. When Carter won, Powell became his press secretary.

He was a fast draw up there on the podium. Very quick, very snappy with the repartee, very bright. Stonewalling has become a fixed institution of the American government, but when Powell stonewalled he at least put a little something extra into it:

Reporter: "Will President Carter meet with Prime Minister Begin when Begin is in the country about 10 days from now?"

Powell: "I don't know of any plans for a meeting. . . ."

Reporter: "Would you think it unlikely?"

Powell: "All I can say is I don't know of any plans. . . ."

Reporter: "How about Sadat?"

Powell: "The same is true."

Reporter: "Have you heard anything in the weeks that have passed—?"

Powell: "If something does develop, I will let you know."

Reporter: "Wouldn't [it] be strange for the president not to see these two?"

Powell: "Not necessarily. They are not [coming] here on official visits. . . ."

Reporter: "Doesn't he [Carter] want to pursue efforts for peace in the Middle East?"

Powell: "No, we decided we are for war. . . ."

Powell's greatest strength with the reporters was that they knew he was very close to Carter. They could be reasonably sure that when the press secretary *did* say something, it would be a reliable reflection of the president's views or intentions. The journalists then would be less likely to mislead the public. Not since Hagerty had a press secretary been as securely in a president's inner circle as Powell was. Bill Moyers came close, and probably George Christian, but Powell was positively cocky about it. When a reporter asked him to describe Carter's reaction to one of his fireside speeches, Powell responded: "I generally avoid asking him things like that. It gives him an opportunity to explain to me what a great job he did."[28]

Then the troubles came. The Bert Lance affair. The misadventures of Hamilton Jordan and Billy Carter. The energy crisis. The inflation crisis. The Soviet invasion of Afghanistan. The mass firing of five Cabinet members. The "national malaise" speech. The seizure of American hostages in Iran. The failure of the rescue mission. And credibility problems. Of course, Carter could not equal Lyndon Johnson in creativity; Salieri was not Mozart. But there were some solid performances:

- When the American hostages were seized in Iran, Carter said he would do no out-of-town campaigning until they were released. As the election grew near, however, the hostages still had not been freed. On April 30, 1980, Carter addressed a group of community leaders at the White House. He listed a number of foreign and domestic problems that confronted him. He specifically included the hostage crisis. Then he said: "None of these challenges [has been] completely removed, but I believe they are manageable enough now for me to leave the White House for a limited travel schedule, including some campaigning. . . ."

  Then on May 9, at a "town meeting" in Philadelphia, a young man asked Carter about his statement that the hostage problem was one of the situations that had become more manageable. Carter replied: "I don't think it is accurate to say—*and neither have I said*—that the hostage situation in Iran is more manageable . . . [emphasis added]" A snippet.

- On April 1, 1980, the day of the Wisconsin primary, Carter held a televised press conference at seven o'clock in the morning. He announced a "positive step" in the Iranian crisis. The positive step was a message that the militants holding the American hostages would turn them over to the Iranian government of then President Bani-Sadr.

It was widely assumed that Carter went on national television at that early hour so there would be plenty of time for the news to reach the voters in Wisconsin. Reporters Jack Germond and Jules Witcover wrote later that Carter "did not wait for the apparent good news to be confirmed . . . [he] simply called a press conference."[29]

After the president finished reading his statement, a reporter asked him: "Do you know when they [the hostages] will be actually released and be brought home?" At that moment, a credibility chasm opened for Jimmy Carter. He could halt at the edge, or he could plunge in. He plunged in.

Carter: "I presume that we will know more about that as the circumstances develop. We do not know *the exact time scheduled* at this moment [emphasis added]." The clear implication was that the hostages were going to be released. Expectations were raised, not just in Wisconsin but throughout the nation. But expectations disappointed are credibility impaired. The ayatollah had not been heard from.

It is generally agreed that Carter's relations with the news media went from honeymoon to divorce when the reporters began writing about Bert Lance's finances and Ham Jordan's social life. These stories were just too close to the bone and sinew. They involved two men whom Carter considered indispensable. The White House was outraged. It fought furiously to save Lance. It retained Clark Clifford to defend him before a congressional committee. When Clifford was called in, General Pickett was being ordered to advance, the last squadron was being thrown into the air over Britain and Leonidas was leading the Spartans to Thermopylae.

Then, one evening, Ham Jordan was drinking with some friends in a bar. He was drinking Amaretto and cream. Amaretto is an almond liqueur. It is sometimes called the drink of love. This is starting to get interesting. The *Washington Post* carried a gossip story about what allegedly happened next. According to the story, Jordan became both amorous and literary. Right there on the spot, he composed a limerick. The *Post* story said it was a dirty limerick. With this poem, the *Post* said, Jordan attempted to attract the attention of a young woman. When this failed, it was alleged, he spat a mouthful of Amaretto and cream over the woman's blouse. Drink of love or no drink of love, she slapped him. Or she allegedly slapped him. It was hard to say who did what. It was happy time.

When the *Post* story appeared, the White House reacted massively. It assigned a senior presidential lawyer to the case. The $45,000-a-year White House official interviewed the bartender. The White House then put out a *twenty-four page* statement by the bartender. He said he had not seen Jordan do anything impolite:

"It was getting crowded, and there were other girls coming up to Hamilton and woo, woo, you know what I mean? Three or four of them just kind of basically hanging around and just hoping that he would turn around and say something to them or whatever. . . . If he did spit all over the girl, it had to be an Amaretto and cream, which would have been quite a mess, and she certainly wasn't wet. . . . I didn't see it and there was no indication of it happening. . . . [On the other hand] she very well could have slapped him, but John [John Golden, one of Jordan's companions] blocked my view. . . . John turned to me and said these girls just slapped Hamilton or did something . . . you ought to get these girls out of here."[30] No one, but no one, ever sorts out the truth in a barroom squabble. Ask any bartender.

Then the White House put out nine additional pages of statements by various other persons. They denied that Jordan had misbehaved. That made *thirty-three pages* of statements totaling about 7,000 words. This was more than twice as long as Carter's State of the Union message.

Then Powell called me up and berated me for forty-five minutes for a question I had asked at the Amaretto-and-cream briefing. My question was whether it was a good idea for the chief assistant to the president of the United States to hang around in bars. Powell was infuriated. "You know damn well that nearly everyone in Washington who has access to classified information goes to bars," he said. "You're going to raise the Ham-Jordan-is-a-security-risk issue as your contribution. I really expected better of you. You've been around for a long time. . . . It's time we take a good hard look at this kind of journalism. . . . You can never win [a dispute over the accuracy of a news story], and that's where Ham is. . . . Those things aren't true. They're not fair. If people are free to write things that aren't true, then what can you do?"[31]

When I could get a word in, I protested that I had not written a story alleging that Jordan had done anything impolite. As a matter of fact, I hadn't written a story at all. Although I certainly intended to do so now that Powell had given me all these fine quotes. The fact that I had not written anything made no difference, Powell replied. He said my question and other questions at the briefing amounted to harassment.

Then Powell called Don Irwin of the *Los Angeles Times* and berated *him* for thirty minutes because Powell had somehow got the idea that Irwin planned to write a story based on my question. Irwin protested that he had no intention of doing so. When he could get a word in.

A few weeks later, Jordan met my son at a tennis tournament. "Your father is trying to kill me," Ham said sadly.

The Lance and Jordan episodes confirmed Carter's belief that the news media were sensationalist, superficial and far more interested in personalities than in serious issues. There was no point in trying to deal with these people on a thoughtful level. In the aftermath of the Lance and Jordan stories, and as the administration's other problems increased, Carter's relationship with the reporters became embittered. He announced that he was abandoning his commitment to hold two press conferences a month. In his last four months in office, he held none at all. That brought back memories. He said there were other ways to reach the public that did not "rely so heavily . . . on the White House press corps." That had a familiar sound. And he lectured the reporters: "I think it is time for you all, if you don't mind my being blunt, to look at the substance of what I have done . . . [to] take a look at the substantive questions that I have to face as president and quit dealing almost exclusively with personalities. . . ."[32]

The substantive questions. They were the problem, no doubt about that. The news stories about Bert Lance and Ham Jordan and other "personalities" did not defeat Jimmy Carter. They certainly made his life harder, but they did not significantly impair his ability to govern. Other things did that. So the problem was not quite as Carter described it. The problem was that the news media *were* taking a look at the substantive issues. They were reporting the Iranian crisis, the inflation and energy issues and the rest of Carter's *substantive* difficulties. They were even reporting his accomplishments—the Camp David accord on the Middle East, the Panama Canal treaties, his worldwide human rights campaign. Carter was getting the issue coverage he always said he wanted.

However, not all the coverage was going his way. Because not all the events and issues were going his way. The news media did not originate the unfavorable developments to embarrass or discredit Jimmy Carter. They did not originate them at all. They covered them, certainly. It is often argued that they overcovered some of them, especially the hostage crisis (see Chapter Three). But they did not initiate them. As Chapter Three pointed out, the events *happened*, regardless of the news media.

Many politicians, political scientists and citizens have begun using a new phrase to describe some of the things that happen in the world. They call them media events. Sometimes this simply means that an event receives a great deal of publicity. It is arranged by an individual or a group—or the White House—in such a way as to attract maximum news coverage. There is a lot of competition for media attention. Good clean fun. And as old as the hills. Saul of Tarsus—Saint Paul—was a master at it. But there are two other points about media events, and these points are much more controversial:

1. It is argued that the modern news media are so powerful that they

can actually *create* events. Do they? There is much confusion about this. But, like so many things, the confusion can be clarified by asking questions. The quality of a human mind is measured by its willingness to ask questions. Thus:

Did Roger Mudd or Teddy Kennedy drive off the bridge at Chappaquiddick? Kennedy drove off the bridge. Some years later, Mudd asked Kennedy about the episode. Some persons considered Mudd's questions unfair. Some considered them fair. Some believed it was unfair for Mudd to raise the issue so many years later. Others believed it was fair for him to raise the issue so many years later. Some believed Mudd devoted too much attention to Chappaquiddick in the interview—in other words, that it was "media hype." Others did not believe he devoted too much attention to it. These, however, are points of view. They are opinions and judgments, to which everyone is entitled. But for the central issue—do the media create events—the clarifying question is: Who drove off the bridge?

Another example: Did the news media *create* John B. Anderson as a presidential candidate in 1980? The clarifying questions are: Did Anderson make the decision to run? Or did the news media make the decision? Having been one of the reporters to whom Anderson first revealed his intention, I can testify that it was his decision. One day he asked to meet with the Washington staff of the *St. Louis Post-Dispatch*. He walked in, sat down and told us he was going to run for president. No media kingmakers went to John Anderson and suggested that he become a candidate. I'll bet he wished they had.

After he announced, the news media may have given him too much attention—or too little. Some journalists, familiar with Anderson's record, probably decided he might make a better president than Jimmy Carter or Ronald Reagan. Some probably decided that a candidate of Anderson's stature deserved serious coverage, regardless of his chances. Some probably thought a third-party candidate would be a good thing. Some citizens agreed with one or more of these judgments, and some disagreed. On the other hand, some journalists and news organizations dismissed his chances as negligible and gave him scant coverage. Some citizens agreed with this judgment, and some disagreed. All these, again, were opinions and points of view. From the standpoint of whether the news media create events, the clarifying question was: Who decided John Anderson would run for president?

2. Many persons, however, believe clarifying questions of this sort beg the question. The issue, they argue, is not whether the news media actually *create* the event, all by themselves. The issue is whether they exaggerate its importance by focusing excessive and undue attention on it. There

is no question that the media frequently cover things with great intensity, and that they sometimes exaggerate. Do these things enlarge an event or issue beyond its real importance?

Despite the distaste for clarifying questions, there is one, and it is very simple: Was the matter important in the first place? Was it something the American people wanted to know about or needed to know about?

If an event or issue *is* important, then the amount of media coverage becomes, again, a matter of individual opinion. Many environmentalists believe environmental issues receive insufficient attention in the news media. Many other persons believe these issues get too much coverage. And so on, down the long list of issues. The matter may not be important to *you*. You may be indifferent to it. But is it important to other people? How many other people? How deeply do they feel about it? How much impact is it having on the lives or well-being of how many persons? Those are the measurements of importance.

If something is genuinely *unimportant* and the news media nevertheless play it up, then the charge of media hype is justified. But there are not many issues like that. The news media are superficial in their preoccupation with personalities and, sometimes, disputes. But it is seldom that they take a truly insignificant matter and treat it as a full-scale, sustained national issue.

There are two other points about media events. For presidents and other politicians, these events tend to balance out. The Camp David media event helped Carter. The Iranian hostage media event hurt him. He smiled as the evening TV news programs showed him shaking hands with Menachem Begin and Anwar Sadat. He groaned as the same programs counted the days of American captivity in Iran. Politicians can survive media events. It is the events *themselves* they often cannot survive.

For the nation as a whole, the deeper point is that there are two words in the phrase "media event." One is "media." The other is "event." The first is the messenger. The second is the message he brings. In distress of spirit and anxiety of mind, there is a very human, very understandable reaction: The messenger is blamed. That is easier than coping with the message itself. And the worse the message—that is, the more grievous the trouble—the more the messenger is reproached, the more fault found with him.

If the messenger has invented the whole thing, why, off with his head. If there are mistakes in his account, chide him and weigh his next tale skeptically. However, in almost all cases the event *has happened*. And most of the time it happened pretty much the way he says it did. Nor all your piety nor wit shall lure it back to cancel half a line, nor all your tears wash out a word of it.

Of course, there is no solace in this. None for individual citizens. And none for presidents. So the relationship between Jimmy Carter and the news media ended in the usual way.

In May 1978, press secretary Powell addressed the annual dinner of the White House Correspondents' Association. He was still reflecting his boss's views reliably.

"President Carter wanted very much to be here tonight," Powell said. "After all, he seldom has the occasion to dine with an institution [that is] held in lower esteem. . . . He, of course, wanted me to express his regrets. Unfortunately, time does not permit me to say all that is regrettable about the White House correspondents."[33]

Things were back to normal.

He was called the Great Communicator, and in one sense he was. His voice was relaxed and easy and *confidential*. He was almost never strident or oratorical. When he made a speech, he just spoke to people, as if he were simply carrying on a pleasant, informal conversation with them. Unlike Jerry Ford and Jimmy Carter, he had a speaking style. It was a very good style, for a basic and important reason: *He did not sound like a politician.* He was Ronald Wilson Reagan, the fortieth president of the United States. He was the first president who had been trained in Hollywood.

But casual or not, it was one-way communication again. Reagan addressed the nation on television and radio, to which his audience could make no reply. Two-way communication was something else. Then he could be asked questions or challenged to explain or justify his actions. There was not to be much of that. In his first eight months in office, he held three press conferences. It was the fewest in that period of any president in fifty years. Even Richard Nixon had held seven news conferences in his first eight months. Franklin Roosevelt had held sixty-seven.[34] Reagan held thirteen press conferences in his first twenty months as president. This was an average of 0.6 a month.

Because there were so few opportunities for sustained questioning, the White House reporters resorted to various expedients. When they were admitted to photo sessions, where traditionally they were not supposed to ask questions, they threw a few quickies at Reagan anyway. When he walked across the White House's south lawn to board a helicopter, the reporters shouted questions at him. It was unsatisfactory. Reagan would look back over his shoulder, smile, wave and say something like "Wait and see." There were no substantive answers, no follow-up questions.

Later, Reagan began holding "mini–press conferences." These lasted ten or fifteen minutes. They usually opened with a statement by the president on some subject, after which there might be time for five or six questions. These abbreviated sessions were only a slight improvement over the hurried shouting on the south lawn. They were superficial. They were a mockery of the news process.

However, they were the only game in town. So the reporters covered them. The journalists knew they were being used mostly as accomplices in a fraud on the public, but there was always an outside chance they might get some news. And if they did not get any news, let them eat cake.

On the morning of February 4, 1983, communications director David Gergen notified the TV networks that Reagan would hold a mini–press conference. The nets decided to cover it live, preempting the daytime soaps. But after Reagan had answered one or two questions, Mrs. Reagan and deputy press secretary Larry Speakes entered the briefing room. They were bearing a birthday cake. The president would be seventy-two years old in two days. A birthday party began. Nancy Reagan handed out slices of cake to the reporters. The president and Sam Donaldson of ABC engaged in their customary light banter laced with cyanide. When Donaldson persisted in trying to ask questions, Mrs. Reagan tried to hush him up by offering him some cake. National television recorded the festivities. The networks had been had. Gradually they caught on. ABC was the first to resume regular programming. CBS was next. NBC was the last to leave the party. Some of the reporters joined Mrs. Reagan and the White House staff in singing "Happy Birthday" to the president. Others remained silent, in disapproval. Soreheads. They had thought it was to be a *news* session.

In August 1981, Reagan was vacationing in California. During a photo opportunity, the reporters tried to question him about the MX missile, a major issue in the nuclear arms race. Presidential counselor Edwin Meese broke in quickly. "Mr. President," he said, "you're not obliged to answer any questions." That was true. It was legally true, and Meese was a lawyer. In addition, he had his own concept of public service. Reagan laughed. A couple of congressmen who were with him laughed also. But Judy Woodruff of NBC suggested that the president might *want* to answer some questions. These definitions of public service differ. Reagan laughed again. Meese laughed. The congressmen laughed. Everyone was merry.[35]

That same month, there was another photo session. This one involved Reagan and then-President Sadat of Egypt. The Reagan-Sadat meeting was important, but something else important was happening at the same time. The nation's air traffic controllers had gone on strike. There was monumental confusion, with potential hazards for thousands of travelers. The photo opportunity was at 10:45 A.M. Reagan had given the controllers until 11 A.M. to resume work or be fired. With fifteen minutes to go, the reporters wanted to know whether the president was going to enforce the deadline.

The questioner this time was the indomitable and invaluable Helen Thomas of United Press International. "I asked about the deadline," Thomas said later. "He answered the question, but his [staff] people had a fit. The word was passed that writers would be barred from photo opportunities if that ever happened again." Later, Thomas recalled, the staff "had second thoughts about the Constitution and [the] First Amendment, and relented somewhat."[36] Nevertheless, a notice was posted on the pressroom bulletin board. It warned the reporters not to ask questions during photo sessions with foreign heads of state. It strongly discouraged questions during *any* photo opportunity.[37] No press conferences, no photo session questions, nothing. The reporters would have to do it by divination.

In the autumn of 1982, Reagan campaigned for Republican candidates for Congress. One appearance was in Roswell, New Mexico. Just before leaving Roswell, he decided to work the crowd at the airport, shaking hands with people behind a rope. When a president does this, tradition permits the pool reporters to move along the rope with him, keeping him in view. The wire service reporters in the pool tried to ask Reagan some questions. They wanted to know how he thought the campaign was going. This was a routine inquiry. The president campaigns; the reporters ask him periodically how he rates his party's chances, and other questions. It is a standard part of the news process. This time, however, a flying wedge of Secret Service agents instantly moved between Reagan and the pool, blocking off the journalists. In the memories of the most venerable reporters, it was unprecedented. The Secret Service is always a little nervous about reporters, especially those it does not know. But something like this was obviously the result of an order: no questions from the pool. Nearby were several members of Reagan's staff. They smiled as the reporters were pushed away. Everyone was merry.[38]

What were these people afraid of? They were afraid of the news process. They were worried about what Reagan might say if there were frequent opportunities for the reporters to ask him questions. He had said enough already.

He said "fascism was really the basis for the New Deal." He said the Soviet Union, under communism, was about to collapse. He said the Russian people were "on a starvation diet of sawdust." He said tactical nuclear weapons could be used in Europe without bringing on a general nuclear war. He said three-month fetuses had been born and had lived and grown up to be "normal human beings." He said Japan had attacked Pearl Harbor because the United States did not have an effective deterrent in the Pacific. But it was that very deterrent—the U.S. Pacific fleet—that Japan had sought to destroy in the attack on Pearl Harbor.

He said it was a surprise to find out that the nations of Latin America were "all individual countries." He referred to Lenin's "Ten Commandments" for revolution when there were no such commandments. Perhaps he was thinking of the revolutionary rules set forth by Vladimir Ilyich Tse-tung. He referred to Paul Nitze, the chief U.S. arms negotiator, as Ed Nitze. Having served in almost every administration since 1941, Nitze was one of the best-known men in the American government. However, the Bible was even older and better known. Reagan invoked it. He said: "And Samson slew the Philippines."

Millions of Americans subscribe to the *Reader's Digest*. It was only a matter of time until one of them got elected president.

On the rare occasions when he did hold a formal press conference, his answers were often Eisenhowerish:

Reporter: "That wasn't my question. You answered a question I didn't ask."

Reagan: "I'm answering the question because the question you asked— the answer is so obvious. That obviously, after these years of out-of-control, and built up to the level they have, there's no one that pretended that you could—this would then have to go to the states for ratification. There would be a period of time before it was actually put in place. And in that period of time, you have an opportunity to work out a budget which would not have to penalize people who are dependent now, because, on the government for help." [39]

His director of communications, David Gergen, said he did not think Reagan's communications made much difference to most Americans. "People are much more interested in his performance as president, and the performance of the economy," Gergen said. [40] Considering the impact of Eisenhower's syntax on his popularity, that was very likely true— if things took a turn for the better. At the midpoint of Reagan's term, the American economy looked like the Pacific fleet after Pearl Harbor. But if there was a solid economic recovery before the 1984 election, and if most other things were going reasonably well, it probably would not matter whether the president knew who *George Washington* was, much less that fellow Nitze.

However, just to be on the safe side, the president would be kept away from the news process as much as possible. Television cameras? Yes. At Reagan's carefully staged White House appearances, the TV cameras were given the dominant position. He was accustomed to cameras. He memorized his lines or used a script or cue cards. But the *actual* news process? Two-way communication between the president and the reporters? No.

There were other types of communication that did not interest the Great Communicator. Soon after taking office, the Reagan administration began a sustained effort to limit the public's access to government documents under the Freedom of Information Act. In a democracy, when you come to think about it, a Freedom of Information Act should be wholly unnecessary. It is outrageous that one is needed at all. However, all large nations behave alike. It had become so difficult for American citizens to find out what their government was doing that Congress, in 1966, enacted a law that was supposed to assist them. The Reagan people saw no point in this. Space does not permit a detailed account of their campaign to emasculate the Freedom of Information Act, but it was congenial work. They went at it vigorously.

If it was to be more difficult for the public to get information *from* the government, it was also to be more difficult for the government to give information *to* the public. Reagan became increasingly irate over the fact that some White House staff members and other officials were leaking information to journalists. He said he had had it "up to my keister" with leaks.

So the lie detectors were brought out again. Reagan signed an executive order requiring additional thousands of government employees to take polygraph tests when asked to, or face "adverse consequences." The federal gumshoes were given more latitude to pry, the telephone logs at the White House were scrutinized minutely and government agencies were ordered to adopt "appropriate policies" regulating interviews and other contacts between officials and reporters. Under Reagan, the government was once again chasing around the landscape, trying to find leakers. The results were as usual. And the key omission was also as usual. The dog did nothing in the night. Reagan spoke indignantly of his keister, but his keister was unscathed. What harm had the leaks done? What damage had they caused the nation? The president presented no details. He offered no evidence. He was uncommunicative about it.

The old, familiar things are the best. To complete the well-known sequence, it was all the news media's fault. After Reagan's first year, during which he basked in favorable publicity, the inevitable deterioration began. When it did, the president blamed the press. He spoke of "misery merchants in the media." He said the journalists were hyping the unemployment problem in South Succotash. He said they had exaggerated his statement favoring the elimination of corporate income taxes. When scandals came to light in the Environmental Protection Agency, Reagan said: "The only [scandal] brewing is in the media that's talking about it." When disarray came to light in the arms control negotiations, Reagan said: "There has been such disarray, approaching chaos, in the press corps with regard to the subject of arms control that I thought, before you [reporters] unraveled into complete disorder, that maybe we should straighten out the entire subject."

The president did not straighten out the disarray, wherever it was, but the White House's policy toward the news media was tidier. It was hostile. Reagan and his subordinates criticized the press with growing intensity and frequency. Deputy press secretary Larry Speakes's daily briefings became increasingly acrimonious. Charges of lying and retorts of "Screw you" were traded back and forth. Finally, as will be seen in the next chapter, Speakes delivered the ultimate verdict. The journalists, he said, were making it impossible for the president to govern.

All this antagonism did not mean that the Reagan White House made no effort to manage the news. It did not abolish the traditional practice of manipulating the media. Reagan had certain notions regarding the enfeeblement of some governmental activities, but that was not one of them. The Great White House Publicity Machine continued to function with unabated vigor and undiminished resources. At the end of Reagan's first year in office, the White House issued a 128-page "progress report." At the end of the second year, it put out a 118-page compilation of Reagan's accomplishments. A publicity machine that can grind out 118 pages of presidential self-praise when 12 million people are out of work is a fully functioning publicity machine.

There was a press office, of course, with the usual staff. There were, in addition, an Office of Communications, an Office of Public Affairs, a director of media relations and planning—all the publicity and news management machinery that had become familiar under Nixon, Ford and Carter.

There were even some familiar faces. Deputy press secretary Speakes had served in the waning days of the Nixon administration as press spokesman for Nixon's lawyer, James St. Clair, and then in the Ford administration as an assistant press secretary. After Reagan's press secretary, James Brady, was gravely wounded in an attempted assassination of the president, Speakes became head of the press office. He was a southerner with journalistic experience, having owned some small weekly newspapers in his home state of Mississippi. However, he was not in the inner circle of Reagan advisers and did not have the determining voice in news policy.

A more powerful voice was David R. Gergen, the director of communications. Gergen was closer to the inner circle, and especially to James A. Baker, the White House chief of staff. And Gergen, like Speakes, was a familiar face. He had been a speechwriter for Nixon and later director of communications in the Ford administration. He was from North Carolina and had graduated from Yale and then from Harvard Law School. Gergen was very tall—six feet, five inches—and very hardworking. And again like Speakes, he was a former Democrat. As a result, some members of Reagan's staff suspected Gergen of latent liberalism. This could be overlooked, however, because he was an idea man. That was his chief asset. It was Gergen who suggested that Reagan use one of his campaign slogans as his crushing final line in the 1980 debate with Jimmy Carter. The Republican candidate looked straight into those millions of American eyes and asked: "Are you better off now than you were four years ago?"

The Reagan press operation was faithful to Nixonian classicism. The press office under Speakes dealt with the reporters who covered the White House regularly. Gergen's office of communications dealt with newspaper editors, TV and radio station managers, civic leaders and other opinion-makers outside Washington. This was the Nixon end run around the Washington press corps. So Speakes was Ziegler, and Gergen was Herb Klein—except that Gergen had much more power than Klein. In addition to his own turf, Gergen had authority over Speakes, over the president's speechwriters and over the Office of Media Liaison, the Office of Public Affairs or whatever the publicity apparatus was called on the latest reorganization chart. Speakes did most of the daily briefings, but Gergen took over the podium occasionally. In effect, there were two press secretaries.

On Speakes's desk, there was a sign. It was for the edification of the reporters. It said: "You don't tell us how to stage the news, and we don't tell you how to cover it." That was not subtle. Some things in Washington are handled subtly, but manipulating the news media is not one of them. A black reporter named Gerald Boyd found that out. He played an unwilling supporting role in a White House television production. Reagan for president. Jerry Boyd for best friend.

Early in 1982, Boyd was covering the White House for the *St. Louis Post-Dispatch*. At that time, Reagan was under sharp criticism for supporting tax exemptions for segregated private schools. A nonsubtlety was about to occur.

Boyd had recently completed a series of stories on the Reagan presidency. In preparing the stories, he had interviewed several senior members of the White House staff. So they knew Jerry Boyd and knew he was black. However, Reagan did not know him from Ed Nitze. But the president could be briefed. At his formal press conferences, moreover, he had a seating chart with the name of each reporter.

On the morning of January 19, 1982, Boyd got a call from the White House press office. Was he planning to attend the president's press conference? He was. When Boyd walked into the East Room for the news conference, he found he had been assigned a front-row seat. That was unusual. Normally, the *St. Louis Post-Dispatch* did not rate that well.

Reagan entered the East Room. The television cameras were on him. The tax-breaks-for-racially-segregated-schools issue was certain to come up at the press conference. Reagan's eyes sought out Boyd. "Hi, Jerry," he called out affably as he strode to the lectern. My old friend Jerry Boyd.

The press conference began. As is customary, the first questions were asked by wire service and television reporters. Then a few more questions were asked. Boyd had his hand up, seeking presidential recognition. So did a reporter seated behind him. Reagan pointed in their direction. The other reporter thought Reagan was pointing at him. He started to ask a question, but Reagan waved him off. No, said the president, Jerry first— again addressing Boyd by name—"then I'll get to you." The television audience was to understand that my old friend Jerry was a favored person.

There was a sequel. The sequels are usually the best part. Four months later, in May 1982, Boyd was invited to a state dinner at the White House, in honor of the president of Brazil. As he shook hands with Reagan in the receiving line, Boyd mentioned the January press conference. He said it would be nice if the president recognized him for another question at the next news conference. "Sure," said Reagan. But by the time the next press conference took place, the segregated-schools issue had diminished in importance. Old friend Jerry found that the *Post-Dispatch* had been assigned a seat in the fifth row. Nevertheless, he raised his hand several times, trying to ask a question. Reagan did not recognize him.[41] The heat, it comes on. Then it goes off.

XI

THE REPORTERS

What is a reporter? A reporter is a person who tells other people what has happened. A reporter is a spectator. He observes something and then informs other persons. He tells them what was said or done and, if possible, why. Everyone, methinks, is a spectator. Everyone sees and hears things and likes to tell others about them. We are very talkative. In that sense, everyone is a reporter.

However, everyone cannot be physically present at every event. Many things that are of interest to us take place at a distance from us. Moreover, we are busy. There are lives to be led, incomes to be earned, children to be raised, responsibilities, schedules, obligations, recreations. So we deputize certain persons to tell or show us what happened elsewhere. More accurately, these persons assume this function. Being interested and curious but busy and distracted, we let them be our eyes and ears. We accept their accounts of events and issues, more or less. We depend on journalists for information we cannot get ourselves.

This dependency carries a built-in irritation. Bob Woodward of the *Washington Post* has reflected on the resultant love-hate, trust-distrust relationship between the public and the news media. He points out that when people read in a newspaper that an airplane has crashed, they do not automatically assume that the crash did *not* happen. They assume it *did*. They accept the existence of a great many things that are reported. But Woodward notes that they may have a deep, *generalized* distrust of the newspaper (or TV network) itself.[1] They don't believe anything they read in that dirty rag. But if they don't believe anything they read in that dirty rag, why do they believe many things they read in that dirty rag? They must, because they base many of their opinions and actions on what they have read or seen. Dependency is one underlying reason for this contradiction. And people often resent those on whom they are dependent—employers, parents, utility companies, hospitals, creditors. Also, journalists. This, of course, is not the only reason for the love-hate phenomenon in journalism.

Why do some persons assume the function of informing others? Why do they take on this self-appointed role? The first and foremost reason is that a journalist is a person with a high degree of curiosity. He or she is simply the type of person who wants very much to know what is going on. Journalists are innately inquisitive. As a corollary, they like to know what is happening before others know it.

Beyond curiosity are other traits. Journalists are fascinated by important events and issues. They are greatly interested in powerful persons and in those who seek power. They want to find out about these things and these people and to understand them. They want to know what is going on in the inside. There is usually less to the inside than anticipated, and disillusion is therefore chronic. But that does not diminish the endless allure of the inside. Finally, journalists consider it worthwhile to provide information and explanations to other people. It is a public service.

In keeping with hoary tradition, most journalists do not like to talk about this public-service motive. They are hard-boiled, realistic, worldly. It does not fit their self-image. In some strange way, they think it makes them vulnerable. Reporters tend to regard their idealism as sex was formerly regarded. It is embarrassing. The subject comes up only rarely. When it does, someone usually introduces a distraction. Another drink is suggested. Paul Healy of the *New York Daily News*, a print reporter and therefore not wealthy and with no prospect of ever being wealthy, was once asked why he had gone into journalism. The question seemed likely to raise the forbidden subject. "I'm only in it for the money," Healy quickly replied. Others will say they became journalists because they were too nervous to steal. Or the editor was indebted to their father. Nevertheless, public service is in the mixture of motives whose end product is the journalist.

The relationship between journalists and power is a complicated question. It is difficult to generalize about it, although people are fearless generalizers. Most reporters are simply intrigued by the human activity known as power; they like to observe it and describe its interesting effects. Others, as noted in Chapter Three, have a strong streak of reformer in them; they hope to remedy ills through the power of information. However, all journalists know that knowledge is power. They know that those who communicate information are wielding power. In a recent survey, a group of prominent journalists rated the leaders of large corporations as the most powerful nongovernmental force in the nation. But the journalists rated the news media second.[2] The question of media power will be discussed one last time in this chapter. There will be no agreement.

It is the motivation that is important—because it determines the results. For the majority of journalists, the prime motivations remain sheer curiosity and the belief that communicating information and explanations is a public service. For others, the chief spur is reform. And for some, it is fame, power and $1 million a year. It is permitted to be in more than one category.

The high salaries and celebrity status of many television journalists have made the question of motivation more controversial. Whether TV has changed the chief reason for going into journalism is presently being debated. Its possible effects on the news process were discussed in Chapter Three. But although it is a more intense debate, it is not altogether a *new* debate. When newspapers and magazines were alone in the field, the leading print journalists were powerful and controversial figures. Walter Lippmann, Arthur Krock, James Reston, Mark Childs, Drew Pearson and other print panjandrums were consulted and cosseted by high officials of government. They moved in exalted circles. Their views were heeded attentively by large audiences. But they were frequently criticized. Their motives were questioned. It was said that they were biased and were attempting to impose their biases on the public. It was said they were making it difficult for the president to govern. Arthur Krock made yesterday's liberals as angry as Mike Wallace makes today's conservatives. And Pearson made everybody mad.

But when Walter Lippmann walked down the street, he was not instantly and universally recognized. He was not subjected to The Stare. And the ordinary print reporter was even more anonymous.

As a young reporter, I was sent to Denver to cover Dwight Eisenhower's heart attack. For seven weeks, I wrote my fool head off. The president then spent five more weeks convalescing at his farm near Gettysburg, Pennsylvania. I continued to write my fool head off. Every day for twelve weeks, I had a story on the front page of the *St. Louis Post-Dispatch*. The stories dealt with a major event—a presidential heart attack—and every story carried my byline. At the end of those three months of bylined, page-1 stories, I got a few days off. I went back to St. Louis for some rest. There I encountered a young woman with whom I had gone to school. She lived in St. Louis and she subscribed to the *Post-Dispatch*. We exchanged greetings and then she inquired: "What have you been doing with yourself lately?"

For a moment, my career intentions faltered. Perhaps I should have been an obstetrician, as my mother had wanted me to be. She said the money was good and most of the customers would be satisfied. But I had an itch. I *had* to be a reporter. If certain personality traits are strongly present, it is likely that the world will have another damn reporter.

How many of them are there in Washington? A great many. Thousands. They outnumber the members of Congress by a wide margin. However, they do not come close to equaling the lawyers, lobbyists, military personnel, intelligence agents or bureaucrats. Nothing could do that. Nevertheless, news coverage of the nation's capital is a growth industry. Roughly speaking, the lifetime of the Republic has seen more than a 1,000-fold increase in the number of news persons assigned to the free center of the nerve world. In 1813, there were four Washington correspondents.[3] James Madison was not troubled by the media hype. In 1982, the Washington press corps had some 4,300 accredited members.[4] In addition, there are many free-lance journalists and writers in Washington who do not qualify for accreditation by the congressional press galleries or do not need it. If these are added, it has been estimated, there are about 10,000 Washington journalists.[5] Ten thousand scribblers. Grrr.

In the beginning, a Washington correspondent was defined as a reporter who was assigned to cover the nation's capital by a daily newspaper or a wire service. To avoid conflicts of interest, the reporter had to work full-time for the news organization, deriving no major income from any other source. This is still one of the basic requirements for accreditation by the press galleries. Later, the definition was expanded to include reporters for magazines, TV and radio networks and stations, photographers, cameramen and some other news personnel. The credential showing membership in a congressional press gallery is still the basic "press card" for Washington journalists.

Throughout the nineteenth century and into the early twentieth, the growth of the press corps was slow and dignified. The Senate and House press galleries—which are for newspaper and wire service reporters—were established in 1823, although not in their present location. They had 12 members.[6] In 1868, there were 58 Washington correspondents. By 1900, the number had increased to 171. In 1920, there were 209. In 1930, the figure was 251.[7] Washington had not yet become the nation's news center.

New York was the news capital. It was the mecca to which young journalists of spirit and ambition aspired. The legendary Gene Fowler, then with the *Denver Post*, was offered a job on a Chicago newspaper on the basis of the lead paragraph on one story. The lead was "She laid her wanton red head against her lover's breast, then plugged him through the heart." They wrote 'em that way then. But Fowler held out for New York. He wanted the biggest of big-time journalism. He especially wanted the tutelage of a New York newspaperman named Damon Runyon. "As regards the human race," Runyon had written, "it's 9 to 5 against." Fowler figured he still had much to learn.

The Depression, the New Deal, World War II and the imperial presidency shifted the news focus to Washington. From 1933 to 1945, there was a substantial increase in the press contingent. In 1937, after five years of the New Deal, a young political scientist named Leo C. Rosten put together the first comprehensive profile of the Washington press corps. He found that 504 journalists were accredited to the press galleries in that year.[8] In the seven years since 1930, the press corps had more than doubled.

Rosten's book on the press corps did not make him famous. So, at virtually the same time, he wrote another book. This one did. It was one of the funniest books ever published: *The Education of Hyman Kaplan*. It is a wonder that Rosten bothered with a bunch of reporters when he had Mr. Kaplan in mind.

After World War II, the Washington press corps grew like nuclear arsenals. Much of the growth was due to television, but by no means all of it. There was, for instance, a vast increase in the number of reporters assigned to Washington by specialized publications dealing with specific industries, professions, political and social issues, recreations and scores of other activities. There are reporters for *Sports Afield, Aviation Week, Housing Affairs Letter, Alcoholism Report, Coal Outlook, Rice Journal, Dental Survey, Chain Store Age, Food Chemical News, Energy Conservation Digest, Medical Economics, Air Transport World, Automotive News, Farm Journal, Science News, Travel Agent, Oil and Gas Journal, Publishers Weekly, Public Utilities Fortnightly, Washington Insurance Newsletter* and hordes of others.

To accommodate the electronic media, the newsmagazines and specialty publications and the rest of the growth, there are now seven press galleries: the original Senate and House press galleries for newspaper and wire service reporters, the Senate and House radio-TV galleries, the Senate and House periodical press galleries and the Senate press photographers' gallery.

You find your way around somehow. Several years ago, on Capitol Hill, I encountered a family—husband, wife and two children—from Webster Groves, Missouri, an affluent suburb of St. Louis. They wanted to see the Senate and House, but they were not sure how to get there. I ended up giving them the blue-plate special tour. They watched the Senate debate something. Then I took them through the Capitol, pointing out the rotunda and other sights, and over to the House side. They watched a House debate. At the end, they thanked me profusely but said they had one more question. Sure, anything, I said. Well, said the wife, where does *Congress* meet? We wanted to see *Congress*, too. Finding the way. That is the problem.

As of 1982, about 1,475 newspaper and wire service reporters were accredited to the Senate and House press galleries. Qualified print journalists are accredited to both. Thus, in the forty-five years since Rosten's 1937 study, membership in the original galleries had increased not quite threefold.

A much more rapid increase has taken place in the Senate and House radio-TV galleries. In 1962, these galleries had 242 members. In 1979, they had about 750. In 1982, about 1,500 TV and radio journalists were accredited. The electronic-media galleries had increased more than sixfold in twenty years and had doubled between 1979 and 1982. Their membership now exceeds that of the newspaper-wire service galleries, but what else is new? Max Barber, superintendent of the Senate radio-TV gallery, has estimated that accreditation to the electronic galleries will reach 2,000 by 1985.[9]

The Senate and House periodical press galleries are for newsmagazine and specialty-publication journalists. As of 1982, about 1,100 persons were accredited to these galleries. The Senate press photographers' gallery, which serves both houses of Congress, had 230 members. All these added up to about 4,300 persons accredited to the congressional press galleries in 1982.

In the same year, about 1,700 journalists had press passes admitting them to the White House. This, however, was not an additional number because almost all reporters and cameramen who cover the White House are also accredited to the congressional press galleries. From time to time, the president's staff tries to pare down the number of White House press passes. Newspaper and network bureaus are asked whether they really need so many. They insist they do. Although only a fraction of those who are accredited to the White House actually cover the president regularly, many more need to get in when big news breaks. And many journalists want the prestige of a White House press pass. A slight decrease is sometimes achieved, but it does not last.

Who are the reporters? What kind of people are they? The personality traits that produce a journalist have been described, but what about their backgrounds, their educations, their political views, their salaries?

Nothing to it. All that is required is to make fearless generalizations about a group of several thousand people. Very dissimilar people, too.

Their incomes range from $10,000 or $15,000 to more than $1 million a year. Their ages are from the early twenties to the fifties and sixties and older. One reporter still active in 1982, the awesome Richard L. Strout of the *Christian Science Monitor*, began his Washington career in 1925, when Calvin Coolidge was president. That may be the current record, but there are many twenty-year and thirty-year veterans. They began with Dwight Eisenhower or John F. Kennedy, before the world turned upside down. Others arrived later, after it had. There are reporters whose fathers were surgeons (a correspondent for a midwestern newspaper), factory workers (a leading radio reporter), baby carriage importers (a newspaper bureau chief), nightclub owners (a prominent TV reporter) and ditchdiggers (another prominent TV reporter).

It is a group whose work varies so widely that many have only a vague idea of what their colleagues do and how they do it. A group whose employers range from small, obscure news organizations to giant news organizations of national and international reputation. A group that includes an ever-increasing number of foreign journalists. A group that includes swingers and straights, city-dwellers and suburbanites. A group many of whom are married and many of whom are single, separated, divorced or widowed. A group that includes drinkers and nondrinkers, smokers and nonsmokers. A group that includes liberals, moderates and conservatives. Nothing to it.

Nevertheless, a considerable amount of statistical information has been obtained. Data are available. Else what would data processors do? Three studies are particularly significant: Leo Rosten's 1937 book; a 1977–1978 examination of the Washington press corps, by Stephen Hess of the Brookings Institution; and a 1979–1980 study of the "national media elite," by Professors S. Robert Lichter of George Washington University and Stanley Rothman of Smith College. Rosten's older survey is interesting because it can be compared with the newer ones. When this is done, it is seen that some generalizations about the press corps are questionable. This happens all the time. For instance, there is a widespread impression that today's national journalists are intensely liberal. But a comparison of the Lichter-Rothman study with Rosten's data shows that they are considerably *less* liberal than they were two generations ago.

The Hess and Lichter-Rothman studies gave a statistical profile of the Washington press corps in the late 1970's. (Some of the "media elite" interviewed by Lichter and Rothman are based in New York, but since they deal with national and international news they are often lumped together with their Washington colleagues.) The surveys indicated that the majority of Washington journalists were white males in their thirties and forties. Of those who answered Hess's questionnaire, 96.4 percent were white, 79.4 percent were male and 62.8 percent were 30 to 49 years old.[10] Almost all of them had college degrees (92.8 percent), with a strong preference for liberal arts.[11] This rendered them happily unfit for many contemporary occupations. Almost two thirds of the journalists were from the northeastern and north-central states. And most of them came from educated, upper-income families. The Lichter-Rothman survey found that 80 percent of the fathers of media-elite journalists were professionals or businessmen.[12]

Hess's survey indicates that about 20 percent of the contemporary Washington press corps is female. This is not equality, but it is the familiar grudging improvement. Leo Rosten's 1937 study did not include a male-female ratio at all. It apparently was not considered necessary, since there were so few females. However, Rosten gave the names of 127 journalists who answered one of his questionnaires. Five of them were women.[13] That was almost a thumping 4 percent.

Then, as now, the problem for women was not just equality of numbers but equality of assignments. Most of the women in the Washington press corps in the 1930's were barred from the big-ticket assignments: the presidency, national politics, economics, foreign policy. With only occasional exceptions, their fate was the feature story, the "human interest" story, the garden party and the East Wing of the White House—covering the First Lady. When UPI first sent Helen Thomas to the White House, it was to cover the East Wing. The formidable Merriman Smith covered *the* White House for UPI. It took Helen Thomas years of the hardest kind of work to move to the West Wing. And equality of assignments is still a problem. Women "get the lower-prestige assignments," Hess found. "Three highly desirable beats—diplomacy, politics and the presidency—have the lowest percentage of women (although all three television networks have had female reporters at the White House in recent years). The three beats with the highest percentage of women are [the] regulatory agencies, domestic agencies, and law. . . ."[14]

The Hess survey found that only 3.6 percent of the Washington press corps was black.[15] The television networks and individual stations have put some blacks—and women—in highly visible assignments. Newspapers are employing an increasing number of blacks—and women—on their local staffs. But only a few black journalists have been sent to their Washington bureaus. Hess's survey was conducted in 1977 and 1978, and the percentage of blacks in the Washington press corps probably has risen a little since then. It may be 4 or 5 percent now. That means that black journalists are approximately where female journalists were in 1937.

The geographical origin of Washington journalists greatly alarms the editors of *Human Events* and other conservative theologians. "Some 40 percent of the media elite come from just three states: New York, New Jersey and Pennsylvania," *Human Events* noted in 1982. Citing the Lichter-Rothman study, the magazine added: "By contrast, only 3 percent are drawn from the entire Pacific Coast, including California, the nation's most populous state."[16]

One reason is that the newspapers of the Sun Belt do not provide many jobs in Washington. In Chapter Seven, it was pointed out that only three newspapers in the Southwest—the *Los Angeles Times*, the *Dallas Morning News* and the *Dallas Times Herald*—regularly assign their own reporters to the White House. That is no way to build an old-boy network.

Proximity is another reason. *Human Events* undoubtedly would be pleased if a larger number of influential journalists and news executives hailed from Orange County and other strongholds. However, it is a free country. Millions of Americans have gone to the Sun Belt, but few have returned. If the young aspirants in the Southwest do not wish to come east in greater numbers to compete for the journalistic jobs in Washington and New York, no one can make them. Of course, there is a way that the media elite could be drawn more equitably from the various regions of the nation. Quotas could be imposed. A new conservatism could be devised, favoring quotas.

There is similar anxiety about the educational background of the national journalists. Many of them are Ivy League. They are not only well educated; they went to prestigious schools, where it is assumed they fell under the influence of liberal professors and alien thoughts. This is a proposition with several layers that can be peeled off.

The first layer shows that the most influential news organizations are indeed taking the cream. Their hiring is focused increasingly on graduates of superior schools. Of course, an Ivy League education is not a guarantee of individual ability; the great thing about Abraham Lincoln was that he put Harvard into perspective. Nevertheless, news executives are like all white-collar employers. They assume an above-average education is a better bet than an average education. They want to hire the best prospects, and they use the standard form sheet—educational, cultural and economic background. So the leading news organizations are hiring an ever-larger number of prestige-school graduates. The statistical message seems clear: Go to a top-flight school—Ivy League, Little Ivy or something with greenery on the walls—or forget about the *New York Times*. Kiss the *Washington Post* good-bye. Trouble not deaf CBS with your bootless cries.

The second layer reveals that there is nothing especially new about this. Almost fifty years ago, Leo Rosten's study dissected a stereotype—the poorly educated, poorly paid reporter from the wrong side of the tracks. A seedy fellow of no breeding—but the stereotype did not fit the Washington press corps. Rosten's survey showed that 51.1 percent of Washington journalists had graduated from college and another 28.3 percent had attended without receiving a degree (there was a depression). Almost 80 percent of the New Deal press corps, in other words, had been to college.[17] My first boss in Washington, Raymond P. Brandt, had covered the national scene since the Coolidge administration. Pete Brandt was a wise, tough newspaperman of the old school. He had also been a Rhodes scholar at Oxford. The point is that some newspapers have always tried to assign well-qualified, well-educated reporters to Washington. This practice merely has grown more widespread as the issues to be covered have grown more complicated.

The next layer concerns the political attitudes of these educated journalists. This will be discussed later. It will be seen that stereotypes are stereotypes.

The last layer either reveals an elite or it does not. The clarifying question is whether a prestige education is *required* in order to rise to the top in the news media. That *would* be an elite, because it would be closed and self-perpetuating. It may come to this some day, if news executives are not willing to look beyond the form sheet, but at present the media's top ranks are filled with individual exceptions to the theory of educational elitism. The exceptions mostly involve ability, ambition and drive. The form sheet does not measure those.

A. M. Rosenthal is executive editor of the *New York Times* and therefore one of the news media's most powerful persons. However, Rosenthal graduated not from Harvard but from City College of New York. Hedrick (Rick) Smith has one of the most prestigious reportorial jobs in the nation's capital. He is the *Times*'s chief Washington correspondent. Smith's background is impeccably eastern establishment. His prep school was the exclusive Choate. He graduated from Williams College in Massachusetts, a highly esteemed Little Ivy. But although Smith writes many of the most important stories, the *Times*'s Washington bureau actually is directed by Bill Kovach, the Washington editor. Kovach's background is also eastern. Eastern Europe and eastern Tennessee. He is Albanian. One of the few Albanians in American journalism. And he graduated from East Tennessee State University. Among the *Times*'s columnists, there is similar diversity. Anthony Lewis graduated from Harvard. But Tom Wicker graduated from the University of North Carolina and James Reston from the University of Illinois. Columnist William Safire attended Syracuse University.

At the *Washington Post*, executive editor Benjamin Bradlee graduated from Harvard. But managing editor Howard Simons graduated from Union College in Schenectady, New York, with a master's degree from Columbia. Deputy managing editor Richard Harwood graduated from Vanderbilt. Herblock, the *Post's* renowned cartoonist, attended Lake Forest College in Illinois. Columnist Mary McGrory graduated from Emmanuel College in Boston. Columnist Haynes Johnson graduated from the University of Missouri and has a master's degree from the University of Wisconsin. The *Post's* top political reporter, David Broder, has a B.A. and M.A. from the University of Chicago. The chief economics writer, Hobart Rowen, graduated from City College of New York.

The top of television is not unduly Ivy. Dan Rather graduated from Sam Houston State College in Huntsville, Texas. Tom Brokaw graduated from the University of South Dakota. Roger Mudd is a graduate of Washington and Lee University, with an M.A. from the University of North Carolina. Bill Moyers graduated from the University of Texas and Southwestern Baptist Theological Seminary. Barbara Walters is a graduate of Sarah Lawrence. Bernard Kalb graduated from City College of New York. Marvin Kalb graduated from City College and has an M.A. from Harvard. Lesley Stahl graduated from Wheaton College in Massachusetts, Mike Wallace from the University of Michigan, Bob Schieffer from Texas Christian, Judy Woodruff from Duke, Bob Pierpoint from the University of Redlands in California, Richard Valeriani from Yale, Ed Bradley from Cheyney State College in Pennsylvania, Sander Vanocur from Northwestern University, Sam Donaldson from the University of Texas, Ted Koppel from Syracuse with an M.A. from Stanford and Steve Bell from Central College in Pella, Iowa, with a master's degree from Northwestern University. Walter Cronkite attended the University of Texas, and John Chancellor attended the University of Illinois.

NBC's 200-person Washington bureau was headed in 1983 by Robert McFarland, an alumnus of the University of Texas. His predecessor was Sid Davis, a graduate of Ohio University, who has one of the best "news senses" in TV and radio. The CBS bureau of about 120 persons (CBS and NBC split their news staffs between Washington and New York) was headed by Jack Smith, a graduate of Loyola University of Chicago. ABC's 450-person bureau was directed by Ed Fouhy, a graduate of the University of Massachusetts with a master's degree from Boston University. His predecessor, Bill Knowles, graduated from San Jose State College in California. And Knowles's predecessor, Carl Bernstein of Watergate fame, attended the University of Maryland.

The educational background of newspaper columnists is likewise diverse. William F. Buckley graduated from Yale, as is well known to all.

Joseph Kraft graduated from Columbia. James J. Kilpatrick is an alumnus of the University of Missouri. Hugh Sidey graduated from Iowa State University. Rowland Evans attended Yale and has an associate degree from George Washington University in Washington. His partner, Robert Novak, known to friend and foe as "the Prince of Darkness," attended the University of Illinois. Carl Rowan graduated from Oberlin and has an M.A. from the University of Minnesota. Jack Anderson attended the University of Utah, Georgetown University and George Washington.

Walter Mears, chief of the Associated Press's Washington bureau, is an alumnus of Middlebury College, a Little Ivy. Grant Dillman, who heads UPI's bureau, attended Franklin University in Columbus, Ohio. Jack Nelson, chief of the thirty-member Washington bureau of the *Los Angeles Times*, is one of Dave Broder's rivals in the "best newspaperman" competition. He attended Georgia State College. Norman (Mike) Miller, chief of the *Wall Street Journal*'s thirty-six person Washington staff, graduated from Penn State.

Things get somewhat more Ivy among the bureau chiefs of newsmagazines and newspaper chains, but there is still much diversity. Mel Elfin, chief of *Newsweek*'s twenty-three-person Washington bureau, graduated from Syracuse and has an M.A. from Harvard. *Time* magazine's Washington staff, which also had twenty-three persons at this writing, is headed by a Harvard graduate, Robert Ajemian. Another Harvard grad, Robert S. Boyd, is chief of the Knight-Ridder newspapers' twenty-five-member Washington bureau. The Cox newspapers' Washington staff of about eighteen persons is led by an able Yale grad, Andrew Glass. The Gannett newspapers have a Washington staff of about forty persons. It is co-directed by James Geehan, a graduate of Brown, and Robert Dubill, who graduated from St. Bonaventure University and has a law degree from Seton Hall. The Newhouse newspapers' thirty-three-member bureau is headed by Robert G. Fichenberg, a Syracuse graduate. Scripps-Howard's thirty-two-person staff is headed by Dan K. Thomasson, and Hearst's seven-member bureau by Robert E. Thompson. Both are graduates of Indiana University.

From Harvard to Central College in Pella, Iowa. From Yale to Sam Houston State. And a horde of state universities and ordinary colleges in the East, Midwest, South, Southwest and Far West. What is the message? It is that an Ivy League education does not hurt. When has it ever—for business executives, lawyers, journalists and professors? But in the news media, as in all occupations, ability and drive can do just as much. Usually more.

There is much interest in money. As a whole, the Washington press corps is well paid. But there is diversity. There are young journalists working in or near the nation's capital for ten thousand dollars a year or some other "entry-level" pittance. They land a job at a little shoestring news bureau or a suburban newspaper for two hundred dollars a week. Assistance from home may be necessary. But they are learning the ropes and hoping for better things. They bring their stereos and rock records and double up at the Lonely Arms and work like crazy and have a marvelous time. It is not the money. It is the incredible high of being in Washington. A graduate of a fourth-rate law school would sneer at their salary, but let him. They are in the *Washington press corps* or near it.

It is a very wide spectrum. At the other end are the megabuck network anchors and superstars. In the middle are the journalists most often thought of as the Washington press corps. These are men and women from the twenties to the sixties, with at least five or ten years of journalistic experience, and usually more. They work in the Washington bureaus of wire services, large newspapers or newspaper chains, newsmagazines and TV and radio networks. The salary range for these reporters is, generally speaking, $25,000 to $125,000 a year.

In mid-1982, the average "reporter top minimum" at 147 newspapers with Newspaper Guild contracts was $465 a week. This was the minimum amount that these newspapers had to pay a reporter who had two to six years' experience, depending on the contract. It meant that, on a national average, a so-called journeyman reporter (no longer a cub) earned at least $24,000 a year. In 1981, according to the Census Bureau, the median income of American families was $22,388 a year. Half the nation's families earned more than that, half less. Print reporters were in the better half. But it was close.

However, the guild minimums at large newspapers were substantially above the national average. In mid-1982, the *New York Times*'s minimum salary for reporters with two years' experience was just under $722 a week, or $37,544 a year. The *Washington Post*'s minimum after four years was $557 a week, or $28,964 annually. The minimum at the *Chicago Sun-Times* was $31,252; at the *Philadelphia Inquirer*, $27,296; at the *Baltimore Sun*, $27,144; at the *St. Louis Post-Dispatch*, $29,420, all after five years' experience. The *Los Angeles Times*, the *Chicago Tribune* and some other large newspapers are nonguild, but their salaries in most cases are comparable and sometimes a little higher.

There are two other points about salaries. One is that a major newspaper almost always pays its most valued, older reporters substantially more than the guild minimum. The other is that when large newspapers and newspaper chains assign a reporter to their Washington bureau, they usually (although not always) give him a raise above what he was making on the local staff. The Washington area is expensive. Its housing costs are maniacal. Its electric and gas companies are merely rapacious.

In 1982, Dom Bonafede of the *National Journal* studied the Washington press corps. In the Washington bureaus of the *New York Times,* the *Los Angeles Times, Newsweek* and *Time* and on the national staff of the *Washington Post,* Bonafede found that "valued, well-established reporters . . . earn $55,000 to $60,000 a year."[18] It should not be thought that David Broder, Lou Cannon, Haynes Johnson, Murray Marder, Morton Mintz, Don Oberdorfer, Walter Pincus, Hobart Rowen, Martin Schram and the other big byliners and old pros at the *Washington Post* were scraping along on $28,964 in 1982. At the *Post,* deputy managing editor Richard Harwood told Bonafede, "virtually everyone" is above the guild minimum.[19]

Outside the charmed circle of the most influential newspapers and newsmagazines, a rule of age applies. In the early 1980's, and in a very general way, a Washington reporter for a sizable newspaper or newspaper chain was earning his age—up to a cutoff point. If he was in his twenties, his salary usually was in the twenties. In his thirties, it was in the thirties. It often stuck there for quite a while; $30,000 to $35,000 a year was the most frequent salary range for experienced, rank-and-file newspaper reporters in Washington. When the reporter reached his forties, his salary often rose to the low or mid-forties. After $40,000 or $45,000 was achieved, however, the accumulation of wealth became more difficult. Wire service reporters, as is traditional, cling loyally to the bottom rung. In 1982, the guild minimum at the Associated Press's Washington bureau was $29,302 a year. At the UPI bureau, it was $26,148. It is hard to get more money out of a wire service.

At the top are the television reporters. They fear not creditors but slothful agents. In mid-1982, the AFTRA (American Federation of Television and Radio Artists) guarantee for network correspondents was $61,500 a year. A network executive knowledgeable about salaries told me in 1982 that the majority of TV network reporters in Washington were earning between $60,000 and $125,000 a year. Those who made more than $125,000, he said, had three characteristics: (1) They had achieved a high degree of prominence and recognition, (2) their networks wished to dissuade them from the seductions of other networks, and (3) although almost all TV journalists in Washington have agents, a truly energetic and persuasive agent is a jewel in the crown of affluence.

The American Dream is imperishable. Only the flickering images change. Over the years, newspapers and magazines have written breathlessly about the incomes of entrepreneurs and entertainers: John D. Rockefeller, Andrew Mellon, the Hunts of Texas, Clark Gable, John

Wayne, Elizabeth Taylor. Now it is the anchorpersons and superstars of television news. Barbara Walters's $1 million a year started it. Dan Rather is generally believed to be on top, at $1.6 million to $2 million annually. Diane Sawyer reportedly began at $250,000 when she became co-anchor of CBS's *Morning News* in 1981, beating out Susan Spencer and Connie Chung. But Chung bounced back to more than $500,000 as anchor of the CBS station in Los Angeles.[20] Tom Brokaw was making $400,000 anchoring the *Today* show. Now he and Peter Jennings of ABC are flirting with $1 million.

No issue involving the American news media is more disputatious than the political and social attitudes of the journalists. The controversy focuses with special intensity on the so-called media elite in Washington and New York, since these persons are responsible for the content and approach of the TV network news programs, the nationally circulated newsmagazines and all but one or two of the most influential newspapers.

Lichter and Rothman asked 240 leading journalists whether they considered themselves liberals or conservatives. Fifty-four percent listed themselves as liberals. Nineteen percent said they were conservatives.[21] That did it. A group of prominent and influential media figures had admitted liberalism. Out of the closet.

It was not an overwhelming margin. Although the Lichter-Rothman article did not say so specifically, 27 percent must have classed themselves as middle of the road or disavowed any political leanings, since 54 percent and 19 percent make only 73 percent. If the conservatives are added to these moderates or apoliticals, there is a 46 percent nonliberal group.

Still, 54 percent was a liberal majority, and a majority is a majority. The right wing grabbed the Lichter-Rothman findings like Ronald Reagan clutching a cue card. The far right's publications and advertisements trumpeted the gladsome news to every village and shire: The media's liberalism had been demonstrated. Nixon lives.

On many specific issues, however, the influential journalists did not come across as anything much in the extremist line. They emerged as firm believers in the system. Eighty-eight percent said they did not believe in government ownership of industry. Eighty-six percent said people with more ability should earn more money. Seventy-three percent did not believe the nation's political, economic or social institutions needed to be overhauled. Seventy-two percent disagreed with the statement that all political systems are repressive. Seventy percent said they believed private enterprise is fair to workers. Sixty-three percent said less government regulation of business would be good for the country.[22]

Lichter and Rothman concluded from these responses that "few of [the media elite] are outright socialists. . . . A substantial portion . . . accept the current economic order."[23] Outright socialists? I should think not. Haven't seen an outright socialist in years.

Nevertheless, there were ominous signs. Lichter and Rothman found that "today's divisive 'social issues'" brought the media elite's liberalism "to the fore." As though liberalism had been lurking, waiting to show its true colors. When a big, fat social issue comes along, the brave banner of conservatism is quickly lowered and the piratical flag of liberalism is run up.

Eighty-one percent of the prominent journalists said they believed today's environmental problems are serious. That left 19 percent who should be ashamed of themselves. Eighty percent believed in strong affirmative-action programs for blacks. Ninety-seven percent said the government should not regulate sexual behavior. Ninety percent said women should have the right to decide whether to have abortions. Seventy-six percent said they did not believe homosexuality was wrong. The division on adultery was closer; 54 percent said it was all right; the rest said it was not.[24] Fornication sometimes wins narrowly, but it always wins.

In the growth industry known as media studies, it seems to be taken for granted that the "liberalism" of the press corps is a recent development. As their educational level and income have risen, it is assumed, the journalists have become more liberal. This is such an article of faith that it is presumptuous to introduce more data. However, the data indicate that the contemporary Washington press corps actually is *less* liberal than it was two generations ago.

When Leo Rosten studied the press corps in 1936–1937, he included a number of questions on political and economic attitudes. Eighty percent of the reporters said they believed government regulation of big business had become imperative (today, 63 percent of the "media elite" favor *less* regulation). Sixty-seven percent favored higher taxes on wealthy individuals and large corporations. Sixty-six percent did not believe that "rugged individualism" was the best economic philosophy (today, 86 percent believe people with more ability should earn more money). Almost 64 percent indicated support of Franklin Roosevelt's National Recovery Act, which conservatives denounced as socialism. And although 54 percent were opposed to government ownership of utilities, railroads and mines, there was a substantial 38 percent in favor[25] (today, 88 percent of the "media elite" do not believe in government ownership of industry).

These reporters, of course, were living and working during the Depression. Their attitudes were affected by the economic catastrophe. Like millions of Americans, they were bitterly disillusioned with the business and financial system that had helped bring it about. They were creatures of their times—just as today's journalists are creatures of *their* times.

After World War II, the United States entered a long period of prosperity. As a result, things that had fallen into disrepute became respectable again. Affluence rehabilitated laissez faire economics and political conservatism. Cycles never being complete, this one probably will make another turn. But that will affect *tomorrow's* journalists. Today's journalists are the products of prosperity. Most of them have had no personal or common experience of privation. As a result, many have become *less* liberal, not more. Many identify more with the establishment, not less.

On these foundations—regional origin, family background, education, political attitudes and income—an imposing structure has been erected. Conclusions have been drawn, as follows:

The leading television and print journalists in Washington and New York are an elite. They are overeducated, oversophisticated products of the upper middle class and the Ivy League. They are out of touch with Middle America. They are scornful of many of the nation's traditional values and verities. They are arrogant. They are biased. Their avowals of professionalism can be disregarded, for they are imbued with a liberal ideology. The media elite.

And these people are the all-powerful "national press." They exercise tremendous influence over the political and governmental processes. They mold the public's attitudes and opinions on political, social, economic and governmental issues. The public being unable to evaluate or resist the media's subliminal propaganda, the journalistic elite determine the national agenda. They decide which issues shall be at the forefront and which shall be ignored. Media power.

The national journalists make and unmake candidates for the presidency. The contest for the White House is viewed as primarily a contest between politicians and the media. Not candidates versus candidates, except as the media create the candidates. Not candidates seeking convention delegates, except as media coverage dominates and determines the preconvention caucuses and primaries. Not candidates debating issues, except as the issues are programmed by the media. Not even candidates wooing voters, except as the voters are anonymous data bases manipulated by software. Media politics.

After a president is elected, the journalists render it well-nigh impossible for him to govern. The presidency, once achieved, is viewed as a four-year mortal encounter with media bias. The critical relationship—the press as the permanent, resident *critic* of government, regardless of which party is in power—has been renamed. It has opened under new management as the *adversary* relationship. The national media are the implacable *adversaries* of the president. They are determined to embarrass, harass and discredit him. Media government.

These descriptions and theories did not originate with Spiro T. Agnew's Nixon-inspired speeches in Des Moines, Iowa, and Montgomery, Alabama, in 1969. When Agnew spoke, it was widely remarked that he had merely brought into the open what many people had been thinking for a long time. But the speeches were immensely important as crystallizers. They helped bring some very controversial phrases into the American political discourse: the media elite. Media politics. Media government. Media power.

The next contributor was Daniel Patrick Moynihan, a former professor of government at Harvard. At various times, Moynihan held posts in the Kennedy, Johnson and Nixon administrations. He is now a Democratic senator from New York. While serving in the Nixon White House, he once recommended that the nation's racial problems be treated with "benign neglect." At another point, he gave it as his opinion that Richard Nixon was in the Adlai Stevenson tradition of "civility" in American politics.[26]

Moynihan was a member of Nixon's staff in 1969 and 1970. Then in 1971, while serving as a consultant to Nixon, he wrote an article for *Commentary* magazine. In it, Moynihan said: "One's impression is that 20 years . . . ago, the preponderance of 'the working press' (as it liked to call itself) was surprisingly close in origins and attitudes to working people generally. They were no Ivy Leaguers. They now are or soon will be. Journalism has become, if not an elite profession, a profession attractive to elites. . . ." The news media, Moynihan wrote, were recruiting "more and more persons from middle- and upper-class backgrounds" who were educated at "the universities associated with such groups." And then he added: "The political consequence of the rising social status of journalism is that the press [has been] more and more influenced by attitudes genuinely hostile to American society and American government."[27]

It was a good thing Moynihan began by saying this was only an impression. It would have been imprudent to call it a fact. He was arguing that prior to about 1950, a "preponderance" of the Washington press corps was close to the working class in origins and attitudes. But Leo Rosten's 1936–1937 study showed that 67.7 percent of the New Deal press corps came from families in which the father's occupation was professional or managerial.[28] Moreover, as noted earlier, almost 80 percent of the "working class" press corps had been to college. It is correct to call the Washington press corps an elite. It *is* an elite, if for no other reason than it is in Washington. A lot of things about Washington are elite. Out of all the cities in the United States, it is the only one that is the national capital. Out of a population of about 220 million people, there is only one president at a time and only 535 members of Congress. But it is incorrect to believe there is anything *new* about the press corps's elitism.

It has been an elite for a long time. It was an elite when Moynihan was in graduate school, preparing to join an elite himself.

Ten years later, columnist Joseph Kraft took up the theme. Writing in 1981 in the same magazine, *Commentary*, Kraft argued that the news media "increasingly . . . are staffed by an unrepresentative group—a group that is better-educated, more highly paid . . . *and more hostile to the system* than the average [American]. Indeed, far from reflecting the population as a whole, those of us in the media replicate the set of deep splits that make up the American class system. . . ." As a result, Kraft said, "we no longer represent a wide diversity of views. We have ceased to be neutral in reporting events [emphasis added]."[29]

Is it hostility or is it criticism? The journalists, when they are doing their job, expose and criticize the shortcomings, mistakes and abuses of democracy and capitalism. So does Congress, in its frequent investigations of political misdeeds and corporate chicanery. So do citizens' groups, as they try to protect themselves from these things. So do professors, in their writings on the system's travails and contradictions. So, even, do presidents, when they propose improvements in the system. A proposed reform acknowledges a fault in the status quo. Are all these persons hostile to the system? All Bolshies? There is glorious confusion over this question of the baby and the bathwater. A critic scrutinizes the bathwater and attempts to cleanse it. But he does not propose to throw out the baby. Nevertheless, the confusion persists. It is deliberate. Those who wish to prevent the bathwater from being cleansed seek constantly to persuade the public that the journalists want to toss out baby.

Then the greatly respected David Broder of the *Washington Post* weighed in. "The fact is that reporters are by no means any kind of cross-section," Broder said. "We are over-educated, we are overpaid in terms of the median, and we have a higher socio-economic stratification than the people for whom we are writing. . . . There is clearly a danger of elitism creeping in."[30]

Consider how much there is to *know*. Consider how important knowledge is. Consider the complexity of the issues that journalists must try to report and explain. Consider the terrible dead weight of ignorance that oppresses humanity. How is it possible for a journalist to be *over*educated?

Then Broder's highly esteemed colleague on the *Post*, Lou Cannon, wrote about the out-of-touch-with-ordinary-Americans problem: "As reporters climb up the income scale, their social values change. Reporters who a few years ago were preoccupied by the basic economic issues of life are now more likely to be aroused by energy or environmental issues or, for a long decade, by the Vietnam war. . . . The gulf is growing between reporters and working-class Americans."[31]

That was written in 1977, in a time of relative prosperity. But circumstances jump around. That is as hard on journalists as it is on everyone else. In 1981 and 1982, the news media were covering long lines of people seeking work, people eating at soup kitchens, people sleeping in cars, people living in tent cities. The reporters, regardless of their income scale, were very preoccupied with "the basic economic issues of life."

However, this is hindsight. No one knew in 1977 that the whole economy was going to do a Chrysler in 1982. Future circumstances will jump all over *this* book, too. But other, more legitimate questions can be asked. They deal with the news judgments that were made by journalists at the time. Was there something *wrong* about covering energy and environmental issues? Was it *wrong* to cover Vietnam? Should these things *not* have been covered? They were there, weren't they? Millions of Americans were greatly concerned about them. Never mind the income scale and the social values of the reporters. Those factors are irrelevant if the journalists do their work *professionally*. Were they acting professionally when they decided to cover what they covered? Were those events and issues important? Were the reporters *covering the right things*?

Another question: What is this Middle America? It is not easy to define. If it were, perhaps there could be more of that neutral reporting that Kraft worried about. And then again, perhaps not. If the average American could somehow be defined, and if the news media could somehow report every event and every issue exclusively from his point of view, would that be neutral? What about the very diverse remainder of the population? The below average? The above average? Hath not Joe Sixpack eyes? Hath not Joe College, likewise?

The journalists will have to stick to the original script. They will have to report *everyone's* point of view, as best they can and as often as they can. When they fail to do this, the criticism is valid and the journalistic soul-searching is anguished. But if their performance is judged in its *entirety*, a mixed picture emerges. Damn these mixed pictures. They have to be explained and explained. The mixed picture is that the journalists fail sometimes and succeed somewhat more often. Refer, in Chapter Three, to the Robinson-Sheehan study of CBS and UPI. Refer to the world according to Karp. But maintain symmetry. Refer, also, to the superficiality that often prevents a full presentation of views.

Some journalists worry about the so-called adversary relationship. They have accepted the renaming of the critical relationship as an adversary attitude. But political scientists Michael Grossman and Martha Kumar, after studying the dealings between the reporters and the White House, concluded that "the co-operative elements . . . are at least as strong as those that are antagonistic." Grossman and Kumar added that "many observers whose only view of the relationship is . . . the [press secretary's] briefing or . . . similar events mistakenly label the two sides as adversaries. They are not. They do not always share the same interests, but that is another matter." [32]

Nevertheless, Michael J. O'Neill, a former Washington reporter for the *New York Daily News* and now editor of that paper, believes the news media "treat government as an enemy." O'Neill says: "The adversarial method, as often as not, misses the truth and distorts reality. . . . Our assignment is to report and explain issues. We are supposed to be the observers, not the participants—the neutral party, not the permanent political opposition. We should rid ourselves of our adversarial mindset." [33]

The permanent political opposition? To whom? To Republicans Nixon, Ford and Reagan, all of whom were criticized by the news media? Or to Democrats Kennedy, Johnson and Carter, all of whom *also* were criticized by the media? The adversary dog won't hunt. It has been a *critical* relationship all along. Accept no substitutes. Among New Yorkers of modest means in the old days, a favorite lunch was baloney on a bun. Mike, I have a bun. Let's have lunch sometime.

So the journalists are being lured into a trap. It is hoped they will feel guilty about their presumed estrangement from Middle America, about their expensive educations, their political views and their relationship with the government. But these guilt trips are valid only if elitism affects *performance*. Sometimes it does, as when the press fell in love with Henry Kissinger. Much more often, it does not.

The journalists need not apologize for not representing some heroic Middle America; no group or occupation personifies this abstraction, this beau idéal. They need not apologize for being educated citizens. They need not apologize for drawing conclusions from facts—if the conflicting conclusions also are presented. As long as they act professionally, they need not apologize for doing their job. And they need not apologize for being persons of conscience. What they *should* worry about are other things entirely. They should be concerned with the *adequacy* of their performance. They should be concerned about the restrictions that are placed on their ability to do a good job: the inexcusably limited amount of news and explanation in most American newspapers and on most television news programs, the lack of space or time in which to analyze complex issues and to trace their connexity. They should anguish over the superficiality. They should protest the obstacles that are erected *by their own news organizations* against their professionalism. They should insist that their networks and newspapers encourage, not discourage, the fullest presentation of information and analysis. A name is needed for this struggle. It could be called the adversary relationship.

Much has already been said about media power. The question of who sets the national agenda has been discussed, and it was noted that we got a president yet, ain't it? The difference between the contemporary reality and the human reality has been described, and so has the frightful mien of journalistic bias. The semantic problem also has been examined; it is intractable and will not go away:

Early in 1983, the Environmental Protection Agency came under fire. It was charged that the EPA had shown great leniency toward the industries and companies it was supposed to regulate. The investigation involved important questions of national policy.

But many persons saw the EPA stories as simply a power struggle between the news media and the Reagan administration. Tom Tancredo, a federal official in Denver, summed up this belief. The *Washington Post* quoted him as saying: "It's a confrontation between two philosophies of government, one represented by Ronald Reagan, and the other represented by the media in Washington."[34]

This semantic difficulty was discussed in Chapter Two. And here it was again, in the EPA controversy. What is meant by the term "media power"? Is it agreement with the *media's* views? Or is it agreement with the views of other persons or groups, as *relayed* by the media? The clarifying questions were overlooked in the EPA dispute, as they so often are: Were the charges *news*? Were they of valid interest to the public? Did they involve matters that affected the nation? Did a large number of people have strong opinions on both sides of this issue? The answer to all these questions was yes. So the news media reported the story—including the views of both sides.

Power is the ability to create situations that affect people. Taxes are raised or lowered. Prices go up or down. The economic outlook improves or worsens. The poor, the old and the sick are assisted or ignored. Education is nurtured or neglected. Business enterprises are helped or hindered. The danger of war increases or lessens. The ability to create these conditions is power. By this measurement, the news media have much less power than government.

Nevertheless, the conviction persists among many persons that the news media have plenary power. Books, articles and dissertations pour out to satisfy the national obsession with the media. A high point of sorts may have been reached with the publication of a book by Tony Schwartz entitled *Media: The Second God* (New York: Anchor Books, 1983). Makes you quietly proud.

It is assumed that the media's power is based on their ability to take the great formless lump known as public opinion, and mold and sculpt it. It then becomes a thing of biased beauty and a liberal joy forever. Using the public opinion measurement, the news media do have much power. But even here, they are far from being the only players in the game. There was a time when political science and government courses taught that *many* factors contributed to the political and social opinions and attitudes of the American people. One of them, of course, was the information people received through the news media. That was important then, and it is important now. But there were also many other things: age, sex, race, occupation, income, educational level, the degree of political knowledge and sophistication, the region in which people were born or lived, their religion, their family and ethnic and cultural background, peer pressures, the interest groups and organizations and clubs they belonged to and even their hobbies and recreations. All gone now? Done to death by the great electronic homogenizer and the clever Ivy League propagandists?

Then why do so many differences of opinion persist? The news media present articles and broadcasts in which the control of handguns is advocated. Do these change the opinion of gun-owners and hobbyists? The young and the older often view things very differently; it is so pronounced that a phrase has been invented for it—the generation gap. The attitudes of the poor and the unemployed are not the same as the attitudes of the affluent and employed. Whites and blacks and males and females and corporation executives and welfare mothers differ in outlook and opinion. Television is a homogenizer; no doubt about it. But has it wiped out these distinctions?

If it has, why don't people just do what Bill Moyers and Mike Wallace tell them to do? Obstinacy? Or perhaps Moyers and Wallace lack plenary power. They convey information, and they try to explain it. They may state or imply that they have reached a conclusion about the information. They may hope that their judgment is persuasive and is accepted. Of course they do. But there are always those differences of opinion, those obstinacies of income or education or background or the National Rifle Association. This leaves information as just one of many factors in the formation of public opinion. There are still many players in the game.

The politicians know this. They use the media—oh, how they use it— but they use it in two different ways. Their "media strategies" are directed partly at creating a favorable "media image." Take off twenty pounds before you run; the camera makes everyone look fat. The hair will never do; it has to look like Jack Kennedy's. Do not shout and rant on the tube; that will make you look old-fashioned, like Lyndon Johnson. But the media strategies also use the media to appeal to the immense diversity of American public opinion. They are directed at different racial and religious and economic factions, at special-interest groups, at the deterioration problems of the old cities in the East and Midwest, and at the growth problems in the Sun Belt. The politicians woo the news media, assiduously, but chiefly as a conduit to the many elements that make up public opinion.

And yet many political scientists—and especially many young ones—

teach public opinion as *all* media. The second god. But can we assume its divinity? Can we be confident of its omnipotence? Public opinion is still divided on the subject of the *first* God.

It is further assumed that the modern news media are so powerful that they are making it virtually impossible for American presidents to govern. Ronald Reagan's deputy press secretary, Larry Speakes, had some thoughts about this early in 1983. "My question to you is, can the modern presidency survive the modern media?" Speakes asked in a speech to a government group. "Can any man in public office stand up to the daily drumbeat of morning newspapers and the flashing symbols of evening news television shows?" Speakes added that "the steady denigration of the president has gone on for two decades. It has been directed not only at the president but at his use of presidential powers. . . ."[35]

But why the modesty? Why stop at two decades of "steady denigration" of presidents by the press? George Washington complained bitterly about the "gazettes." Abraham Lincoln said he did not read newspapers; he "skirmished" with them. In the twenty-four years between the end of Andrew Jackson's second term and the start of Lincoln's first term, eight men served as president. Not one of them was reelected. There were newspapers then. Did they make it impossible for presidents to govern?

If so, how was it that Jackson and Lincoln won second terms? So did Grant, McKinley, Wilson, Franklin Roosevelt and Eisenhower. Grover Cleveland served two terms, although not in succession. Theodore Roosevelt served almost two full terms and is considered to have had a successful presidency. There were newspapers then. They criticized all *these* presidents, too. They kept up a "daily drumbeat."

Or was it that the *events* that bedeviled Van Buren, Tyler, Polk, Fillmore, Pierce and Buchanan were beyond their capacities? (William Henry Harrison and Zachary Taylor are not included here, because Harrison died after a month in office and Taylor after sixteen months). Did Van Buren and the other five fall victim to the press? Or were they *inadequate* presidents? Are the modern news media making it impossible for the modern president to govern? Or is the nation in another era of inadequate presidents? The possibility is worth considering. But it is a hard thing to consider, because it places a responsibility upon the American people. If it is true, then they must pay more attention. They must concentrate harder on identifying and electing better candidates. It is easier to blame the news media.

Speakes made his comments at the end of Reagan's second year in office. He did not mention the adulation that Reagan had received from the news media in his first year. Reagan the Great Communicator. Reagan wins big victories in Congress. Reagan pushes through mammoth tax cut. Reagan has Democrats on the run. As mentioned in an earlier chapter, the news media should be judged *as a whole*. But, as also mentioned earlier, the White House always argues *selectively*.

When people talk about the news media making it difficult or impossible for a president to govern, they usually have a presumed journalistic bias in mind. They watch a TV newscast. The president, let us say, is speaking about unemployment. He is saying his policies will solve the problem. His face is on the screen for a few moments. Then the camera cuts away to show long lines of people applying for jobs or eating in soup kitchens. The president's remarks become a "voice-over" while the camera shows economic hardship. Do some biased journalists wish the audience to conclude that the president's policies have failed? Or is it news coverage of a legitimate story: unemployment? Before answering, consider one other question: How many times has the president been on national television, *all by himself,* arguing the advantages of his programs and making the case for them? Has he been denied a fair and full opportunity? "Our attitude," said Julian Goodman of NBC, "[is that] he can have any goddamn thing he wants."[36] The news media should be judged as a whole.

One other phenomenon is worth noting. From George Washington to Larry Speakes, people have been saying that the press makes it hard for presidents to govern. The journalists render the president's life an endless misery. They carp and criticize. They slant and distort. They hinder and impede. What person of sound mind would freely subject himself to these outrageous mistreatments and indignities? Why, many persons. Candidates for the presidency are not like Social Security. There is no shortage. They start early, making speeches, shaking hands, lining up supporters, raising money, enduring motel rooms from coast to coast, talking to small groups in Iowa living rooms, slogging through the snow in New Hampshire, freezing outside factories in Wisconsin. They work their keisters off, trying, trying, trying to become president of the United States. Why? So they can be battered bloody by the news media? No.

Now it is late at night in the pressroom. The reporters are tired, but there is not much more to write. Just a few paragraphs leading up to the kicker.

Sometimes reporters put a kicker at the end of a story. It is a summary. H. L. Mencken covered the 1932 Democratic national convention for the *Baltimore Sun*. According to a tale that may be fact or legend, he wrote a story listing the disqualifications and political liabilities of Franklin D. Roosevelt. Then the kicker: For the above reasons, Mencken wrote, Roosevelt will not be nominated. When the votes had been counted and FDR had won the nomination, the sage threw down his tally sheet and growled: I hope those dumb bastards on the copy desk take off the kicker.

Here is the kicker on *this* story:

Why is there a preoccupation with the news media? There are some obvious reasons. The media are powerful, and power fascinates. Moreover, power invites scrutiny, in self-defense. The news media scrutinize government because it is powerful; they must expect the same treatment. In addition, the media are pervasive in the highest degree; therefore their potential for doing good or evil is immense.

And there is one more reason. There are people in the United States who very much want the public to believe the worst about the nation's journalists. And especially about the Washington press corps, the national press, the media elite or whatever you want to call them. These persons wish to convince the American people that the journalists are dangerous. They want to affix the sinister label of elitist upon them. They want the journalists to be perceived as a group whose politics are ultra-liberal, whose objectives are radical and whose reporting is therefore biased and untrustworthy. To accomplish this, the news process must be disparaged. Journalistic professionalism must be denied. The critical relationship must be discredited.

The far right is spending large amounts of money in an effort to do what Richard Nixon almost succeeded in doing. It is supporting a multitude of organizations, publications and other activities aimed at creating the gravest possible distrust of the news media. Why? Because the extreme right hopes to take the American nation as deeply as it can into authoritarian regions and absolutist doctrines. In the present condition of the nation, it senses its moment. *But the news media are standing in the way.* How could it be otherwise? For all its faults, journalism is one of the institutions that preserve free inquiry and therefore freedom itself. Liberals and conservatives alike can welcome free inquiry and give it nourishment. Extremists cannot. Authoritarians cannot.

Time is a measure of accomplishment. Richard Nixon operated not only in his present but in the past and the future. There are ancient dreads in every national psyche. Tribal fears. They can be reduced but never eliminated. Fear of strangers and their treacheries. Fear of far-off cities and their educated slickers. Fear of bad tidings and the messengers who bring the woeful news. Fear of knowledge and those who seek knowledge. Fear of the intellectual quests that so painfully and precariously create civilizations, cultures, sciences, reforms, equalities and freedoms. And fear of reality. Terrified by the realities of the present. Aching for past simplicities and distant virtues that never were. In the nineteenth century, thousands of Americans enrolled in a political movement that proudly called itself the Know-Nothings. It was all too much for them, late and soon. Rousseau proclaimed that civilization had corrupted the natural goodness of natural man. To which Voltaire replied: "I have received your new book against the human race." As Rousseau, Spiro Agnew was a scream. But you use what you have.

The ancient spirits can be summoned from the vasty deep, *and they will come.* Nixon summoned the old ignorances, suspicions and dreads. And they came. *And they have stayed.*

The dead, wrote Aeschylus, are come to slay the living.

If we let them.

NOTES

I

1. Dwight D. Eisenhower, press conference, Aug. 1, 1956.
2. Dwight D. Eisenhower, *The White House Years* (New York: Doubleday, 1963–1965).
3. Harry C. Butcher, *My Three Years with Eisenhower* (New York: Simon and Schuster, 1946) and Eisenhower, *The White House Years*.
4. Dwight D. Eisenhower, press conference, Feb. 25, 1953.
5. Fawn M. Brodie, *Richard Nixon: The Shaping of His Character* (New York: W. W. Norton, 1981).
6. Ibid.
7. Ibid. and Richard M. Nixon, *Six Crises* (New York: Doubleday, 1962).
8. Eisenhower, *The White House Years*.
9. Sherman Adams, *Firsthand Report: The Story of the Eisenhower Administration* (New York: Harper and Brothers, 1961).
10. Marvin Arrowsmith, conversation with the author.
11. Douglass Cater, "News and the Nation's Security," *The Reporter*, July 6, 1961.
12. Tom Wicker, *On Press* (New York: Viking Press, 1978).
13. James C. Hagerty, press briefing, Lowry Air Force Base, Denver, Colo., Sept. 28, 1955. (The transcript was made available to author by Marvin Arrowsmith.)
14. Robert J. Donovan, *Eisenhower: The Inside Story* (New York: Harper and Brothers, 1956).

15. James Deakin, "P-D Reporter Views Illness and Recovery of President," *The P-D Reporter*, Jan. 1956. (Information on the number of words filed from Denver was supplied at the time by Carroll Linkins, then White House representative for Western Union.)
16. Arrowsmith, op. cit.
17. James Deakin, "President Has Eye on Floods, Considers Aid," *St. Louis Post-Dispatch*, Oct. 17, 1955.
18. Wicker, op. cit.
19. James Deakin, "President Sees Wilson, Defense Budget Put at 34.5 Billion," *St. Louis Post-Dispatch*, Oct. 17, 1955.
20. Donovan, op. cit.
21. Ibid.
22. James Deakin, "President Talks with Adenauer, Asks for Action on German Unity," *St. Louis Post-Dispatch*, June 14, 1956.
23. Eisenhower, *The White House Years*.
24. James Deakin, "President Better, Works Half-hour," *St. Louis Post-Dispatch*, Nov. 28, 1957.
25. Ibid.
26. Adams, op. cit.
27. Ibid.
28. Ibid.

II

1. Lyndon Johnson, press conference, July 13, 1967.
2. Richard Dudman, "White House Circle Exuding Fresh Optimism About War," *St. Louis Post-Dispatch*, Feb. 15, 1968. (Several persons confirmed to the author that Rusk was the background source at the briefing.)
3. James Pollard, *The Presidents and the Press* (New York: Macmillan, 1947).
4. Ibid.
5. Jimmy Carter, "town meeting," Temple University, Philadelphia, May 9, 1980.
6. Associated Press, "Could Have Been More Effective, Carter Admits," *Washington Post*, Mar. 19, 1981.
7. James M. Perry, "Washington PR Staffs Dream Up Ways to Get Agencies' Stories Out," *Wall Street Journal*, May 23, 1979, and Rich Jaroslovsky, "Of All the Makers of Movies, Who Is the Biggest of All?," *Wall Street Journal*, May 26, 1977.
8. J. F. ter Horst and Col. Ralph Albertazzie, *The Flying White House: The Story of Air Force One* (New York: Coward, McCann and Geoghegan, 1979).
9. Pierre Salinger, *With Kennedy* (New York: Doubleday, 1966).

10. George Christian, *The President Steps Down* (New York: Macmillan, 1970).
11. Lyndon Johnson, press conference, Feb. 11, 1966.
12. Leo C. Rosten, *The Washington Correspondents* (New York: Harcourt, Brace, 1937).
13. Ibid.
14. Ibid.
15. Ibid.
16. Raymond P. Brandt, "Newspapermen Dubious of Plan to Televise Ike's Press Sessions," *St. Louis Post-Dispatch*, Jan. 22, 1953.
17. James Deakin, "Eisenhower Wins Press Card; Go Easy on Me Now, He Jokes," *St. Louis Post-Dispatch*, Jan. 14, 1959.
18. James Deakin, "Airborne Command Post: All the President's Phones," *St. Louis Post-Dispatch*, Feb. 12, 1977.
19. James Deakin, "CAA Not As Glamorous As FBI So Chief Fires Press Officers," *St. Louis Post-Dispatch*, Dec. 20, 1957.
20. Michael J. Weiss, "Coffee and Grilled Politicians," *The American Way*, Oct. 1981.
21. Rosten, op. cit.
22. Richard Valeriani, *Travels with Henry* (Boston: Houghton Mifflin, 1979).
23. Ibid.
24. Ibid.
25. Joseph Laitin, conversation with the author.
26. Ibid.
27. I. F. Stone, quoted in Phillip Knightly, *The First Casualty* (New York: Harcourt Brace Jovanovich, 1975).
28. Michael B. Grossman and Martha J. Kumar, *Portraying the President: The White House and the News Media* (Baltimore: Johns Hopkins University Press, 1981).
29. Ron Nessen, *It Sure Looks Different from the Inside* (New York: Playboy Press, 1978).
30. Ibid.

III

1. Robert Burton, *The Anatomy of Melancholy* (New York: Vintage Books, 1977).
2. Ibid.
3. Philip Graham, in a talk to his staff, quoted in *Newsweek*, Aug. 12, 1963. (A somewhat more complete version of the quote is ". . . our inescapably impossible task of providing . . . a first rough draft of history that will never be completed about a world we can never understand.")

4. Edward Gibbon, *The Decline and Fall of the Roman Empire,* vol. 1 (New York: Modern Library).

5. Grossman and Kumar, op cit.

6. The endorsement figures for the 1968 election are from a special report by *Editor and Publisher,* cited in *Congressional Quarterly Weekly,* Oct. 25, 1968. At that time, Nixon had been endorsed by 483 daily newspapers; subsequently he was endorsed by the Scripps-Howard chain of 16 newspapers, for a total of 499. The figures for the 1980 campaign are from *Editor and Publisher,* Oct. 16, 1980.

7. Michael J. Robinson, conversation with the author. The Robinson-Sheehan study was published as *Over the Wire and on TV: CBS and UPI in Campaign '80* (New York: Basic Books, 1983).

8. Walter Karp, "Subliminal Politics in the Evening News," *Channels,* Apr.–May 1982.

9. Theodore C. Sorensen, *Kennedy* (New York: Harper and Row, 1965).

10. Salinger, op. cit.

11. Harrison E. Salisbury, *Without Fear or Favor: "The New York Times" and Its Times* (New York: Times Books, 1980).

12. Howard Bray, *The Pillars of the "Post": The Making of a News Empire in Washington* (New York: W. W. Norton, 1980).

13. Ibid.

14. "TV's Controversial Role in Iran Crisis," *U.S. News and World Report,* Dec. 24, 1979.

15. Ibid.

16. Ibid.

17. Arlie Schardt, "TV Held Hostage?," *Newsweek,* Dec. 24, 1979.

18. Malcolm Browne, *The New Face of War* (Indianapolis: Bobbs-Merrill, 1968).

19. Jimmy Carter, press conference, Nov. 28, 1979.

20. Frederic B. Hill, "Media Diplomacy," *Washington Journalism Review,* May 1981.

21. Tom Shales, "Terrorvision," *Washington Post,* Dec. 11, 1979.

22. Edward W. Said, "Inside Islam," *Harper's,* January 1981.

23. Bob Woodward, conversation with the author and a group of students.

24. Jacob Bronowski, *The Ascent of Man* (Boston: Little, Brown, 1973).

25. Hoyt Purvis, ed., *The Presidency and the Press* (Austin, Tex.: University of Texas Press, 1976).

26. Chris French (administrative assistant for technology, Associated Press), conversation with the author.

27. Bronowski, op. cit.

28. Leon V. Sigal, *Reporters and Officials: The Organization and Poli-*

tics of News Making (Lexington, Mass.: D. C. Heath, 1973), cited in Lou Cannon, *Reporting: An Inside View* (Sacramento, Calif.: California Journal Press, 1977).

29. Cannon, op. cit.
30. Ibid.
31. Tom Shales, "The New Look at CBS News," *Washington Post*, Dec. 23, 1981.
32. Jean Heller, conversation with the author.
33. "The New Face of TV News," *Time*, Feb. 25, 1980.
34. Ibid.
35. Ibid.
36. Judy Woodruff, conversation with the author.
37. Osborn Elliott, "And That's the Way It Is" (interview with Walter Cronkite), *Columbia Journalism Review*, May–June 1980.
38. Ibid.
39. Walter Cronkite, Third Annual Frank E. Gannett Lecture, Washington Journalism Center, Washington, D.C., Dec. 9, 1980.
40. Tom Shales, "After the War of Ascension, Feeling No Guilt and Eager to Weigh Anchor," *Washington Post*, Mar. 12, 1980.
41. Shales, "The New Look at CBS News."

IV

1. Stephen Hess, *The Washington Reporters* (Washington, D.C.: Brookings Institution, 1981).
2. Nora Ephron, "Ken Clawson Is No Joke," *New York*, June 3, 1974.
3. Robert Trautman, unpublished manuscript (quoted with the permission of the author).
4. Art Buchwald column quoted with the permission of the author.
5. James Deakin, "It's in the Book," *St. Louis Post-Dispatch*, Jan. 13, 1978.
6. James Deakin, "It Takes a Lot of Gas to Run Summit Meeting," *St. Louis Post-Dispatch*, June 28, 1979.
7. Timothy Crouse, *The Boys on the Bus* (New York: Random House, 1973).
8. Laurence Burd, unpublished song (quoted with the permission of the author).
9. James M. Naughton, conversation with the author.
10. Ibid.
11. Thomas M. DeFrank, conversation with the author.

V

1. George H. Hall, "Post Mortems on Landslide: Why Didn't Any of Politicians or Pollsters Read Signs Right?," *St. Louis Post-Dispatch*, Nov. 7, 1952.

2. Donovan, op. cit.
3. Ibid.
4. Fred I. Greenstein, "Eisenhower as an Activist President: A Look at New Evidence," *Political Science Quarterly*, Winter 1979–1980.
5. Ibid.
6. Ibid.
7. George H. Hall, "That Eisenhower Personality," *St. Louis Post-Dispatch*, Dec. 20, 1952.
8. Ronald Steel, *Walter Lippmann and the Twentieth Century* (Boston: Atlantic Monthly Press–Little, Brown, 1980).
9. Marvin Arrowsmith, conversation with the author.
10. Raymond P. Brandt, "President Names Warren Chief Justice," *St. Louis Post-Dispatch*, Sept. 30, 1953. (Eisenhower's reply to the reporters' complaints was given at a press conference the same day.)
11. Eisenhower, *The White House Years*.
12. Ibid.
13. Wicker, op. cit.
14. Dwight D. Eisenhower, press conference, Sept. 30, 1953.
15. David Wise and Thomas B. Ross, *The U-2 Affair* (New York: Random House, 1962).
16. James Deakin, "Hagerty Has Become a Policymaker as Result of Eisenhower's Illnesses," *St. Louis Post-Dispatch*, Aug. 5, 1956.
17. McGeorge Bundy, National Security Action Memorandum 328, Apr. 6, 1965, quoted in *The Pentagon Papers*, as published by the *New York Times* (New York: Bantam Books, 1971).
18. Edward R. Harris, "Administration for McCarthyism, White House Reporters Believe," *St. Louis Post-Dispatch*, Nov. 18, 1953.
19. David Wise, *The Politics of Lying* (New York: Random House, 1973).

VI

1. Sorensen, op. cit.
2. Salinger, op. cit.
3. Ibid.
4. Ibid.
5. William Lawrence, *Six Presidents, Too Many Wars* (New York: Saturday Review Press, 1972).
6. Arthur M. Schlesinger, Jr., *A Thousand Days* (Boston: Houghton Mifflin, 1965).
7. Ibid.
8. Salinger, op. cit.
9. Ibid.

10. Lawrence, op. cit.
11. Salinger, op. cit.
12. Ibid.
13. Marquis W. Childs, conversation with the author.
14. Salinger, op. cit.
15. Ibid.
16. Ibid.
17. Ibid.
18. Salisbury, op. cit.
19. Ibid.
20. Peter Wyden, *Bay of Pigs* (New York: Simon and Schuster, 1979).
21. Salisbury, op. cit.
22. Salinger, op. cit.
23. Salisbury, op. cit., and Wyden, op. cit.
24. Ibid.
25. Arthur M. Schlesinger, Jr., *The Imperial Presidency* (Boston: Houghton Mifflin, 1973).
26. Richard Dudman, "Managed News Condemned by Reporters at House Hearing," *St. Louis Post-Dispatch*, Mar. 20, 1963.
27. Salinger, op. cit.
28. Ibid.
29. James C. Hagerty, testimony before the Government Information Subcommittee of the House Committee on Government Operations, Mar. 6, 1972.
30. Cater, op. cit.
31. Ibid.
32. David Wise, testimony before the Government Information Subcommittee of the House Committee on Government Operations, June 28, 1971.
33. Max Frankel, "The 'State Secrets' Myth," *Columbia Journalism Review*, Sept.–Oct. 1971.
34. Ibid.
35. Ibid.
36. Wise, testimony.
37. Sanford J. Ungar, *The Papers and the Papers* (New York: E. P. Dutton, 1972).
38. Ibid.
39. Curt Matthews, "Bundy Calls Secrecy in Government 'Evil,'" *St. Louis Post-Dispatch*, May 22, 1974.
40. David Broder, "Only Some Leaks Bug Presidents," *Washington Post*, Mar. 16, 1983.

VII

1. James Deakin, "Tudor Opulence for White House Press Corps," *St. Louis Post-Dispatch*, Apr. 16, 1970.
2. Ibid.
3. Ibid.
4. Theodore M. Bernstein, *The Careful Writer* (New York: Atheneum, 1965).
5. Richard M. Nixon, conversation with the author and other reporters.
6. Deakin, "Tudor Opulence . . ."
7. FCC tabulations as of Sept. 30, 1982, in *Broadcasting*, Dec. 20, 1982.
8. James P. Herzog, *The Press*, June–July 1981.
9. Judy Woodruff, conversation with the author.
10. Grossman and Kumar, op. cit.
11. Nessen, op. cit.
12. Salinger, op. cit.
13. Nessen, op. cit.
14. Grossman and Kumar, op. cit.
15. Ibid.
16. Rosten, op. cit.
17. Figures on 1982 membership in the congressional press galleries were supplied by officials of the galleries.
18. James Keogh, *President Nixon and the Press* (New York: Funk and Wagnalls, 1972).
19. Grossman and Kumar, op. cit.
20. Jack W. Germond and Jules Witcover, *Blue Smoke and Mirrors* (New York: Viking Press, 1981).
21. Grossman and Kumar, op. cit.
22. Shales, "The New Look at CBS News."
23. Grossman and Kumar, op. cit.
24. David L. Paletz and Robert M. Entman, *Media Power Politics* (New York: Free Press–Macmillan, 1981).
25. James Deakin, "The Dark Side of LBJ," *Esquire*, Aug. 1967.
26. Salinger, op. cit.
27. R. W. Apple, Jr., and the staff of the *New York Times*, *The White House Transcripts* (New York: Bantam Books, 1974).
28. Ibid.

VIII

1. Joseph Laitin, Oral History, Lyndon B. Johnson Library, Austin, Tex.

2. Ibid.
3. Ibid.
4. Ibid.
5. Deakin, "The Dark Side of LBJ."
6. Ibid.
7. Ibid.
8. James David Barber, *The Pulse of Politics* (New York: W. W. Norton, 1980).
9. Philip Geyelin, *Lyndon B. Johnson and the World* (New York: Praeger, 1966).
10. James Deakin, "Johnson Assails 'Self-Styled Intellectuals,'" *St. Louis Post-Dispatch*, Apr. 9, 1966.
11. Richard M. Scammon and Ben J. Wattenberg, *The Real Majority* (New York: Coward-McCann, 1970).
12. James Deakin, "The U.S. Presidency: War's Worst Casualty," *St. Louis Post-Dispatch*, Apr. 30, 1975.
13. Ibid.
14. James Deakin, "The Presidency and the Truth," Founder's Week address, Washington University, St. Louis, Feb. 22, 1967.
15. Deakin, "The Dark Side of LBJ."
16. Ibid.
17. Leonard Baker, *The Johnson Eclipse: A President's Vice Presidency* (New York: Macmillan, 1966).
18. Deakin, "The Dark Side of LBJ."
19. James Deakin, "LBJ's Credibility or What Happened to 'No Comment,'" *New Republic*, Jan. 29, 1966.
20. Ibid.
21. Deakin, "The Presidency and the Truth."
22. Ibid.
23. James Deakin, *Lyndon Johnson's Credibility Gap* (Washington, D.C.: Public Affairs Press, 1968).
24. Wise, *The Politics of Lying.*
25. William McGaffin and Erwin Knoll, *Anything but the Truth* (New York: G. P. Putnam's Sons, 1968).
26. Deakin, "The Dark Side of LBJ."
27. Ibid.
28. The original of the Fortas letter is in the Lyndon B. Johnson Library, Austin, Tex.
29. James Deakin, "Johnson's Statement on Plans for Supersonic Plane Adds to Controversy on Credibility," *St. Louis Post-Dispatch*, Jan. 3, 1967.
30. John Mecklin, *Mission in Torment* (New York: Doubleday, 1965).

31. Ibid.
32. Peter Braestrup, *Big Story* (Boulder, Colo.: Westview Press, 1977).
33. Robert Elegant, "How to Lose a War," *Encounter*, Aug. 1981.
34. David Halberstam, *The Making of a Quagmire* (New York: Random House, 1964).
35. Mecklin, op. cit.
36. Ibid.
37. Halberstam, op. cit.
38. Mecklin, op. cit.
39. Halberstam, op. cit.
40. Mecklin, op. cit.
41. Wise, *The Politics Of Lying.*
42. Browne, op. cit.
43. Mecklin, op. cit.
44. Deakin, "LBJ's Credibility . . ."
45. Deakin, "The Presidency and the Truth."
46. Ibid.
47. Deakin, "The U.S. Presidency . . ."
48. Ibid.
49. Ibid.
50. Ibid.
51. James Deakin, "Johnson's Advisers Opposed Putting Vietnam Situation Before U.N. Security Council," *St. Louis Post-Dispatch*, Feb. 1, 1966.
52. Thomas W. Ottenad, "'Hitching My Wagon to a Star,' Said Johnson's Press Aide," *St. Louis Post-Dispatch*, Mar. 22, 1964.
53. Ibid.
54. James Deakin, "Press Shakeup Indicates Move by Johnson to Improve Image," *St. Louis Post-Dispatch*, July 10, 1965.
55. James Deakin, "The Credibility Gap Is at Critical Stage As Moyers Resigns," *St. Louis Post-Dispatch*, Dec. 19, 1966.
56. Bill Moyers, *The Johnson Years*, Public Broadcasting Service, Nov. 3, 1971.
57. James Deakin, "Press Aide Christian Carries Out Johnson's Passion for Secrecy," *St. Louis Post-Dispatch*, June 17, 1967.
58. Ibid.
59. Ibid.
60. Christian, op. cit.
61. McGaffin and Knoll, op. cit.

IX

1. Wise, *The Politics Of Lying.*
2. Crouse, op. cit.

3. Andrew J. Glass, "Media Report," *National Journal*, June 5, 1971.
4. *Straus Editor's Report*, Dec. 14, 1970.
5. Ibid.
6. Ibid.
7. Glass, op. cit.
8. Crouse, op. cit.
9. Allen Drury, *Courage and Hesitation* (New York: Doubleday, 1971).
10. Keogh, op. cit.
11. Ibid.
12. James C. Millstone, "Protests Arising over Treatment of Prisoners," *St. Louis Post-Dispatch*, May 9, 1971.
13. Ibid.
14. Glass, op. cit.
15. John Osborne, *The Third Year of the Nixon Watch* (New York: Liveright, 1972).
16. Glass, op. cit.
17. Seymour M. Hersh, "Kissinger and Nixon in the White House," *The Atlantic Monthly*, May 1982.
18. Ronnie Dugger, *The Politician: The Life and Times of Lyndon Johnson* (New York: W. W. Norton, 1982).
19. Richard M. Nixon, interview with David Frost, May 19, 1977.
20. Brodie, op. cit.
21. Kenneth P. Clawson, "A Loyalist's Memoir," *Washington Post*, Aug. 9, 1979.
22. John Osborne, *The Last Nixon Watch* (Washington, D.C.: New Republic Books, 1975).
23. Paul Bullock, "Rabbits and Radicals: Richard Nixon's 1946 Campaign Against Jerry Voorhis," *Southern California Quarterly*, Fall 1973, quoted in Brodie, op. cit.
24. William Costello, *The Facts About Nixon* (New York: Viking Press, 1960).
25. Richard M. Nixon, conversation with John Dean, Mar. 18, 1973, in *The White House Transcripts*.
26. Keogh, op. cit.
27. Ibid.
28. Ibid.
29. Drury, op. cit.
30. Ibid.
31. James Deakin, "Nixon's Relations with Press Worsening," *St. Louis Post-Dispatch*, Nov. 21, 1970.
32. Spiro T. Agnew, speech in Des Moines, Ia., Nov. 13, 1969.

33. William Safire, *Before the Fall* (New York: Doubleday, 1975).
34. Agnew, op. cit.
35. H. R. Haldeman, interview on the *Today* show, NBC, Feb. 7, 1972.
36. Joe McGinniss, *The Selling of the President 1968* (New York: Trident Press, 1969).
37. Fred Powledge, *The Engineering of Restraint: The Nixon Administration and the Press*, a report of the American Civil Liberties Union (Washington, D.C.: Public Affairs Press, 1971).
38. Agnew, op. cit.
39. Powledge, op. cit.
40. Richard Dudman, "Administration News Control," *St. Louis Post-Dispatch*, Apr. 5, 1971.
41. Ibid.
42. Karen Rothmyer, "Citizen Scaife," *Columbia Journalism Review*, July–Aug. 1981.
43. Ibid.
44. Ibid.
45. Thomas W. Ottenad, "Nixon Role in Punish-Press Plan" and "Nixon's Fight on Media," *St. Louis Post-Dispatch*, Nov. 1 and 2, 1973.
46. Drury, op. cit.
47. Ottenad, "Nixon Role . . ." and "Nixon's Fight .   ."
48. Safire, op. cit.
49. Richard Dudman, "Opinions Differ on Motive for Moves Against Media," *St. Louis Post-Dispatch*, Jan. 7, 1974.
50. Ottenad, "Nixon Role . . ." and "Nixon's Fight . . ."
51. Richard Dudman, "TV Executives View Suits as Official Intimidation," *St. Louis Post-Dispatch*, Jan. 12, 1974.
52. Ibid.
53. Richard Dudman, "Nixon's Friends Harass Newspaper," *St. Louis Post-Dispatch*, Jan. 13, 1973.
54. Dudman, "Opinions Differ . . ."
55. Dudman, "TV Executives . . ."
56. Powledge, op. cit.

X

1. Dugger, op. cit.
2. James Deakin, "Nessen Assails White House Reporters," *St. Louis Post-Dispatch*, June 26, 1975.
3. Ron Nessen, *It Sure Looks Different from the Inside* (New York: Playboy Press, 1978).
4. Ibid.

5. Ibid.
6. John Herbers, *No Thank You, Mr. President* (New York: W. W. Norton, 1976).
7. James Deakin, "Nessen Says He Is Trying to Cure Credibility Hangover from Nixon," *St. Louis Post-Dispatch*, Oct. 5, 1974.
8. Purvis, op. cit.
9. Nessen, op. cit.
10. Thomas W. Ottenad, "Jimmy Carter: A Smile and a Shoestring," *The Progressive*, May 1976.
11. James Wooten, *Dasher: The Roots and Rising of Jimmy Carter* (New York: Summit Books, 1978).
12. Ibid.
13. Ibid.
14. Ibid.
15. Germond and Witcover, op. cit.
16. Wooten, op. cit.
17. Ibid.
18. Ibid.
19. Ibid.
20. Ibid.
21. Ibid.
22. Ibid.
23. Barry Sussman, "El Salvador Is Not in Louisiana," *Washington Post*, Jan. 2, 1983.
24. Wooten, op. cit.
25. Lewis W. Wolfson, "The President and the Press: The First Report Card," *The Quill*, Oct. 1977.
26. James Deakin, "Carter's Secretary Getting Good Reviews from Press Corps," *St. Louis Post-Dispatch*, Mar. 3, 1977.
27. Ibid.
28. Ibid.
29. Germond and Witcover, op. cit.
30. James Deakin, "Washington Mixology and Games People Play," *St. Louis Post-Dispatch*, Feb. 26, 1978.
31. James Deakin, "Ham in a Jam Again: Powell to the Rescue," *St. Louis Post-Dispatch*, Feb. 22, 1978.
32. Germond and Witcover, op. cit.
33. Thomas. W. Ottenad, "Administration's Barbs Stinging Press," *St. Louis Post-Dispatch*, May 8, 1978.
34. Lynne Olson, "The Reticence of Ronald Reagan," *Washington Journalism Review*, Nov. 1981.
35. Lee Lescaze, "Meese a Powerful, Visible Buffer Between Reagan

and Reporters," Washington Post News Service, in the *Charlotte Observer*, Aug. 23, 1981.

36. Olson, op. cit.
37. Ibid.
38. Lou Cannon and David Hoffman, "Visibility: Reagan's Aides Fear President Is Too Isolated," *Washington Post*, Nov. 7, 1982.
39. Ronald Reagan, press conference, Oct. 1, 1982.
40. Michael Barone and Jodie T. Allen, "The 'Great Communicator' or the 'Great Prevaricator'?," *Washington Post*, Oct. 10, 1982.
41. Gerald Boyd, conversation with the author.

XI

1. Bob Woodward, conversation with the author.
2. S. Robert Lichter and Stanley Rothman, "Media and Business Elites," *Public Opinion*, Oct.–Nov. 1981.
3. Silas Bent, *Ballyhoo: The Voice of the Press* (New York: Boni and Liveright, 1927).
4. Figures on 1982 accreditation to the congressional press galleries were supplied by officials of the galleries.
5. Dom Bonafede, "The Washington Press—Competing for Power with the Federal Government," *National Journal*, Apr. 17, 1982.
6. Bent, op. cit.
7. Rosten, op. cit.
8. Ibid.
9. Max Barber, conversation with the author.
10. Hess, op. cit.
11. Ibid.
12. Lichter and Rothman, op. cit.
13. Rosten, op. cit.
14. Hess, op. cit.
15. Ibid.
16. "Media Elite out of Step with the American Public," mail advertisement by *Human Events*, 1982.
17. Rosten, op. cit.
18. Bonafede, op. cit.
19. Ibid.
20. Ibid.
21. Lichter and Rothman, op. cit.
22. Ibid.
23. Ibid.
24. Ibid.
25. Rosten, op. cit.

26. Daniel P. Moynihan, "How the President Sees His Second Term," *Life*, Sept. 1, 1972.
27. Daniel P. Moynihan, "The Presidency and the Press," *Commentary*, Mar. 1971.
28. Rosten, op. cit.
29. Joseph Kraft, "The Imperial Media," *Commentary*, May 1981.
30. Cannon, op. cit.
31. Ibid.
32. Grossman and Kumar, op. cit.
33. Robert J. McCloskey, "Is the Press Too Kind to Reagan?," *Washington Post*, Dec. 15, 1982.
34. David Hoffman and Cass Peterson, "Burford Quits as EPA Administrator," *Washington Post*, Mar. 10, 1983.
35. Juan Williams, "Presidents Denigrated by Media, Speakes Says," *Washington Post*, Jan. 29, 1983.
36. Wise, *The Politics of Lying*.

INDEX